Evolution and Learning

An Annotated Handbook of Classic and Contemporary Readings

Mike Knight and Christina Almstrom

University of Central Oklahoma

Cover design by Candice Swanson

Books may be purchased for educational purposes.

For information, please call or write:

1-800-586-0330

Fountainhead Press
100 W. Southlake Blvd. Suite 142, #350
Southlake, TX. 76092

Web site: www.fountainheadpress.com
Email: customerservice@fountainheadpress.com

First Edition

ISBN 1-932274-08-1

Printed in the United States of America

Evolution and Learning

An Annotated Handbook of Classic and Contemporary Readings

Mike Knight and Christina Almstrom
University of Central Oklahoma

Table of Contents

EVOLUTION AND LEARNING

An Annotated Handbook of Classic and Contemporary Readings

Introduction

The investigation of learning, memory, and cognition has the longest experimental history of any psychological endeavor. Perhaps this is because it readily lends itself to empirical scrutiny. It is the study of what organisms "do" and "how they change"-- what they do as a consequence of experiencing the environment around them (Skinner, 1989).

There is a saying often attributed to Skinner that, "If I cannot see it I do not want to talk about it". However, it was actually E. L. Thorndike, and what he really said was, "If I cannot measure it I cannot talk about it". The quote attributed to Skinner is emotionally laden and confrontational, while Thorndike's quote is a simple declaration of the demand characteristics of the scientific method. In order to do experiments we must be able to quantify our operational definitions of variables and descriptions of observered outcomes. Why? Because at the heart of science is the necessity for replication. Science is a method and procedure designed to correct errors through empirical verification. We write the recipes for phenomenon and invite skeptics to see for themselves. If we cannot communicate with precision our ability to operationally define independent and dependent variables and the hypothesized relationship between them is compromised. Can you imagine trying to follow a recipe for cooking that did not use numbers? Thus Thorndike's axiom simply restated says: In order to do science we must be able to observe and compare, to accomplish this we must be able to measure or we are out of business.

No where have we been better able to achieve precision of measurement and concomitant efficacy of experimentation than with learning and memory phenomena. From Pavlov's slobbering dogs to Thorndike's cats in a puzzle-box, experiments in learning historically fuelled psychology's quest for legitimization as a science. With John Watson as a vanguard, experimental psychologist dawned their white lab coats and proclaimed themselves behaviorists, and scientists. And it worked. We learned how to do science, in the laboratory, with a premium on internal validity. We became adept at measuring observable behavior in every conceivable manner; latency, duration, frequency, and intensity, were all made accessible as dependent measures with greater and greater precision. It was a science of muscle movements and glandular secretions and it was great fun for psychology in its adolescence ardor to play scientist and do well controlled reproducible experiments just like the grown-ups did in physics and chemistry.

The behaviorists taught us how to do good research with an emphasis on precision of measurement and the control of extraneous confounds. Valuable skills which have served us well, but ultimately dissatisfying in and of themselves. All too often the truthful answer to the question of why the research was being done was simply because it was doable. We were scientists and we needed to do experiments, but what experiments to do? Behaviorism was avowedly atheoretical, and while it is true that, "a house devoid of facts is haunted by theory", what of facts without theory. As Martin Fisher has said, "Facts are not science - as the dictionary is not literature".

Theory in science weaves facts together to create a meaningful story. And if this story is assumed true then certain logical consequences must also follow. In this way theory guides research by telling us where to look to find new facts. That is, "It is theory that decides what we can observe" – A. Einstein. Or as Darwin put it, "Without expectancy there will be no observation". Good theories do more that tell an aesthetically pleasing story, they provide us with expectations regarding the outcome of experiments designed to test theoretical deductions. In this manner their ultimate worth to science lies in their falsifiablity.

This is why the atheoretical position of the behaviorists was so dissatisfying. Without theory you are left with little more than an indiscriminate search for facts, and perhaps more significantly, simplistic after the fact explanations which are so lousily formulate and vague that they are not readily amenable to disconfirmation. Enter neo-behaviorism with its emphasis on hypothetico-deductive theory construction in the grand tradition of Isaac Newton. This was the great age of global theories. In the hypothetico-deductive method postulates, i.e., hypotheses, are deduced from theory in the form of if-then logical consequences, empirical tests are devised to evaluate these hypotheses, and inductive inferences are made back to the theory that generated the postulates. The overriding consideration in hypothetico-deductive theory construction is prediction and disconfirmation. The neo-behaviorist, particularly Hull, Spence, and Miller taught us the worth of theories and how to build them.

Someone once said that the goal of science is theory and the goal of theory is to destroy itself. With their emphasis on disconfirmation the global theories became more and more circumscribed, the questions they generated became more widely dispersed, and new theories became more molecular and constrained.

With the neo-behaviorist, like the behaviorist before them, and the cognitivists who followed, the overriding emphasis in experimentation was on internal validity. So much so that external validity, the ability to generalize outcomes from the laboratory to the natural environment, became a major concern as more and more anomalous results began to emerge. Phenomenon like auto-shaping, and taste aversion made us take a second look at exactly what was going on in the laboratory. What we thought of as controlled often turned out to be contrived and could not be generalized. It is perplexing to realize that you have been studying artificial behavior in an artificial situation and that you have been doing a very good job of it. Many of the articles in this book are seminal works because they document the anomalies manifest during this volatile historical period. They are important because they changed forever the way we think about learning and shaped the way contemporary theories are formulated.

By definition an anomaly is a violated expectancy. It gets your attention, as if to say, "Look this way something wonderful is about to be learned". Two excellent examples of this are Robert Rescorla's research showing that, "Classical conditioning is not what you think it is"; and David Premack's formulation of a theory of reinforcement relativity. The anomalies identified in classical and operant conditioning respectively had immediate and far-reaching ramifications. They functioned as well-springs for subsequent research; for good research, like good theory, asks more questions that it answers. This is its generative nature and what makes science different from any other way of knowing the world around us.

For everything there is a price, however, and the price we pay for more knowledge through more questions is that the world becomes a more complex and chaotic place. The more we know the more complex our scientific reconstructions of reality become and the more necessary it is that we have coherent and integrative theories to glue everything together. By the mid 1980s behaviorism, neo-behaviorism, and cognitive psychology had created a fragmented field of miniature systems each focused on phenomena that were becoming evermore esoteric. The general feeling was one of discouragement. With cognitivism in particular each new experiment seemed to give rise to a new "model". The emphasis was clearly shifting away from prediction toward explanation. With many ways to explain the same results cognitivism was quickly degenerating into a new kind of mentalism. The problem, of course was that there was no theory to generate *a priori* predictions so the necessary evil was a greater reliance on *ad hoc* explanations. But this necessary evil was becoming, to borrow a phrase from Ben Franklin, more and more necessary and less and less evil. It was not good science.

Interestingly enough the way out of this self-destructive quagmire had been right in front of us ever since Darwin wrote:

> In the distant future I see open fields for far more important researches. Psychology will be based on a new foundation, that of the necessary acquirement of each mental power and capacity by graduation.
>
> --Charles Darwin, *The Origin of Species,* 1859.

Had we recognized our field as a part of the natural sciences from the beginning we would have had evolutionary theory and the Darwinian algorithm as an infrastructure for hypothetico-deductive experimentation. Why this did not happen is a matter of conjecture, but certainly the heroic efforts of Wundt to create a separated discipline, and the zeal and charisma of Watson in defining its content contributed greatly. We in the social and behavioral sciences came to think of ourselves as independent entities, islands unto ourselves. In hindsight this is perplexing. It seems perfectly obvious that the chemist would not presume to disdain a working knowledge of physics, nor would the biologist disdain chemistry, but this is exactly what psychology, with its implicit adherence to a doctrine of equal-potentiality (the blank slate) did.

A mature psychology with a natural science identity began to emerge in the 1990s. Through the work of Leda Cosmides and John Tooby, Steven Pinker, David Buss, and others, evolutionary psychology, with its emphasis on a modular brain designed through natural selection, is revolutionizing the way we conceptualize learning and behavior. The central premise of evolutionary psychology is that behavior is a verb not a noun. It is a doing not a something. As such, "doing" could not have evolved, it is brain structures that evolved, and behavior is the consequence; in the same sense that the eye evolved and seeing is what it does. Evolutionary psychology is explicitly hypothetico-deductive in method in that knowledge from evolutionary biology, paleoanthropology, and psychology are used to define adaptive problems the brain must have evolved to solve in the ancestral past given the demand characteristics of ecological constraint. It is assumed that the modules of brain structure, called psychological mechanisms, are complementary reflections of these characteristics. Given these constraints one can deduce the algorithm (the recipe) for the functioning of these information processing machines. The hypothesized algorithm for the psychological mechanism is an answer to the question, "what must happen if a particular function is to be accomplished." Then experimental tests are devised to determine if there is evidence supporting the deduced hypotheses.

This is a very powerful scientific approach to experimentation for many reasons, not the least of which is the quest for objective truth. E. O. Wilson has suggested that understanding the operations of the human mind is crucial to assessing the validity of our scientific "stories" about reality. His argument goes something like this; there exists an objective reality apart from our subjective representations of it. Subjectively we reconstruct reality from sensory input and the self-assembly of concepts and the congruence of objective reality with its inner representation is distorted by selective perception resulting from the unique species-specific idiosyncrasies of human evolution. The brain was not built for understanding itself but for survival in day to day moment to moment existence. Because of this there will necessarily be misalignments and incongruencies between external reality and the models we build of it and "the proper task of scientists is to diagnose and correct these misalignments". From this perspective then understanding cognitive functioning is integral not only for psychology but for the scientific enterprise in general.

It is our opinion that this can only be accomplished if psychology is conceptualized as a natural science, and our theories reflect our conceptualization of the brain as evolved machine, and the mind as what it does. The articles in this book were selected to represent how we arrived at this crucible in time and hint at some of the things we think the future might have in store as these mysteries are unraveled. We hope you enjoy the journey!

EDWARD L. THORNDIKE: THE SELECTIONIST CONNECTIONIST

John W. Donahoe (1999). *Journal of the Experimental Analysis of Behavior, 3,* 451 - 454.

As Louis Menand points out in The Metaphysical Club, his excellent book describing the intellectual ferment of the last half of the nineteenth century, "The purpose of On the Origin of Species was not to introduce the concept of evolution; it was to debunk the concept of supernatural intelligence – the idea that the universe is the result of an idea". In much the same way that Thorndike's Animal Intelligence debunked the idea of purposefulness in animal learning. Thorndike was tremendously influenced by Darwin, not only for liberating us from the shackles of the "the romantic fallacy" (the belief that humans are not animals), but because the Darwinian algorithm of successive change through a process of variation and selection provided an analog for understanding learning as a process resulting from behavioral variation and the survival of the effective. This is the subject of Donahoe's article. It is particularly valuable because in addition to showing that Thorndike was as much a selectionsit as a connectionist he provides numerous quotations from Thorndike in support of his thesis.

From the very outset of his work, Thorndike allied himself with the Darwinian proposition that complex phenomena can arise as the cumulative effects of a selection process, here the process envisioned by the law of effect. Thorndike's selectionist approach, when combined with his connectionism, laid the foundation for a synthesis of behavior analysis and neuroscience.

Key words: E. L. Thorndike, selectionism, connectionism, response-outcome association

Edward L Thorndike believed that complex behavior could be understood as an emergent product of the cumulative action of relatively simple processes, notably those summarized by what he came to call the law of effect. "Complex as human life is, it is at bottom explainable by a few principles" (1905, p. 316). More pointedly, "it has been shown that in great measure the intellects and characters of men are explainable by a single law [the law of effect]" (1905, p. 318). Thus, he endorsed a selectionist approach to behavior from his earliest work (cf. Galef, 1998). Thorndike was also a connectionist. That is, he believed that the strengths of connections—what we now call synaptic efficacies—changed as the result of the biological mechanisms that implemented the law of effect. The importance that he ascribed to these mechanisms led him to a neural restatement of the law of effect as the "law of acquired brain connections" (1905, p. 165). With his commitment to selectionism and connectionism, Thorndike allied himself with the resurgent Darwinism of his time and, in so doing, foreshadowed the biobehavioral approach of our time. After documenting Thorndike's selectionist views, I close by noting his prescient comments on a topic of central interest in current associationist accounts of animal learning—the nature of the associations inferred to underlie instrumental learning (i.e., operant conditioning). Thorndike was an associationist as well as a selectionist and connectionist, but his associationism differed from contemporary versions.

Selectionism

A selection process (see Figure 1) consists of three interrelated steps—variation, selection, and retention (see Dennett, 1995; D. L. Hull, 1973; Mayr, 1988; Sober, 1984). Variation provides the raw material upon which selection operates. It is the source of whatever novelty arises from repeated iterations of the three-step process. Variation is undirected (Campbell, 1974) in the sense that the factors that affect variation are not correlated with those that affect selection. Selection by the environment favors (or disfavors) some variations over others, and confers whatever direction is apparent in the process. Of course, selection is not truly directed because its trajectory is utterly dependent on the environment. When the environment changes, the direction of selection changes. Only the relative constancy of the environment permits the illusion of direction or purpose. Finally, the third step—retention—enables favored variations to endure long enough to contribute to the variation upon which future selection operates. Without retention, the effects of selection could not accumulate and the possibility of complexity would not exist (see Donahoe & Palmer, 1994; Palmer & Donahoe, 1992).

Variation. Thorndike was explicit that whatever creativity or novelty emerged from the process of selection was dependent on the pool of variation upon which the selecting environment acted. "The first necessity of mental progress is fertility in response. Unless the baby does something, it can learn nothing' (1905, p. 209). He recognized that the initial variants upon which selection acted were largely the reflexive relations provided by natural selection (i.e., respondents). "The starting point for the formation of any association … is

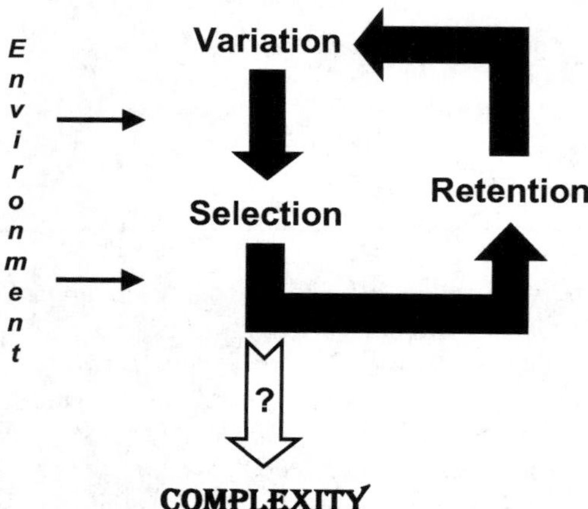

Fig. 1 The three-step process through which the repeated action of relatively simple processes has the potential to produce complex outcomes, as in the emergence of complex behavior through the cumulative effect of reinforcement.

relations provided by natural selection (i.e., respondents). "The starting point for the formation of any association … is the set of instinctive activities" (1898, p. 13). Thorndike also acknowledged the contribution to variation made by nonelicited behavior: "Progress was not by seeing through things, but by accidentally hitting upon them" (1898, p. 106). A fuller appreciation of the role of nonelicited behavior awaited Skinner's (1938) conception of the operant. Thorndike understood that variation was undirected with respect to the selecting factor. "The one impulse, out of many accidental ones, which leads to pleasure, becomes strengthened" (1898, p. 45). His designation of the selecting factor as "pleasure" or, at other times, as "satisfaction" sounds quaint to modern ears, but his conception of undirected variation has a contemporary ring.

Selection. The parallels between selection by "pleasure" (i.e., by reinforcement) and natural selection were apparent to Thorndike:

The development of human mental life may be likened to that of the animal kingdom as a whole. The present animal kingdom is the result of the extinction of those which did not fit the environment… Any man's intellect and character are the results of the existence in his past of many connections, the elimination of those which did not fit their environment so as to bring satisfaction. (1905, p. 317).

Most important, the population of variants on which selection operated was the behavior of an *individual* organism. The focus upon the behavior of the individual was an enduring characteristic of Thorndike's thinking, both his early animal research and his later educational research. It is one of the chief characteristics that differentiates Thorndike and Skinner from their fellows. Even those who otherwise embraced Darwinian thinking, such as Clark Hull (1943), sometimes inadvertently acted as if selection operated on variations in the behavior of *different* organisms. How else to explain the use of group experimental designs that Fisher had correctly devised to measure the effects of natural selection (cf. Sidman, 1960)? An analysis of variation produced by individual differences is appropriate in the study of natural selection but not of selection by reinforcement. Thorndike's focus on the single organism was apparent in the graphs of the behavior of individual animals that he used to communicate his findings (see Change, 1999) and is explicit in his writings. "The process is … simply the selection of the … movement from amongst the many sorts made because of its relatively greater amount of resulting satisfaction" (1905, p. 204). The foregoing suggests that the focus of selection was a "movement" (i.e., behavior). However, other more complete statements indicate that Thorndike considered the unit of selection to be an environment-behavior relation, not behavior alone (cf. Donahoe, Burgos, & Palmer, 1993; Donahoe, Palmer, & Burgos, 1997). To wit, "The one impulse, out of many accidental ones, which leads to pleasure, becomes strengthened … and more firmly associated with the sense-impression of that box's interior" (1898, p. 45). And, "any act which in a given situation produces satisfaction becomes associated with that situation, so that when the situation recurs the act is more likely than before to recur also" (1905, p. 203). Finally, Thorndike was sensitive to the fact that selection produces complexity only by dint of variation. "Purposive thinking equals spontaneous thinking plus selection" (1905, p. 264).

Retention. Thorndike also appreciated the essential contribution of retention of the emergence of complexity from a selection process. The behavioral repertoire initially included only "instinctive activities" and other "movements," "but this is the starting point only in the case of the first box experienced" (1898, p. 14). In subsequent boxes in which his subjects were tested, the behavioral repertoire included the environment-behavior relations that had been selected in prior chambers. The critical role of the accumulation of prior selections was especially apparent in complex human behavior: "Selection and survival of the fit thoughts … are the essentials of purposive thinking" (1905, p. 265).
Like Darwin before him, Thorndike did not know the biological mechanisms that enabled retention and upon which selection acted. Nevertheless, Thorndike believed that the full development of his approach would require the discovery of these mechanisms.

How the satisfaction following upon a connection strengthens it…must be left [an] unanswered question. Neither psychology nor physiology has yet anything much better than a guess to offer this, the most fundamental question of the mental life of man and the animal kingdom as a whole. All that can be said is that the original satisfiers are as a rule events useful for the survival of the species…; consequently any means by which the[y] …could reinforce the connections causing them…would, when evolved, be maintained by natural selection. (1905, p. 316).

(Note the use of the term *reinforce* in this statement.) "Everywhere we have to seek for the physiological basis of mental facts and connections" (1905, p. 323). The developing modern synthesis behavior analysis with neuroscience—a biobehavioral approach—would be welcomed by Thorndike as it would by Skinner. "The experimental analysis of behavior is a rigorous, extensive, and rapidly advancing branch of biology" (Skinner, 1974, p. 255).

The physiologist of the future will tell us all that can be known about what is happening inside the behaving organism. His account will be an important advance over a behavioral analysis, because the latter is necessarily "historical"—that is to say, it is confined to functional relations showing temporal gaps…It will make the picture of human action more nearly complete. (Skinner, 1974, pp. 236-237).

Skinner's earlier reservations about forays into physiology stemmed from pragmatic considerations—the absence of the requisite neuroscience—not from principled objections to such a synthesis. Behavior analysts such as Jack Michael recognize that the present situation is quite different: "I would strongly urge anyone starting a research career in behavior analysis in the late 1900s to include extensive training in the neurosciences. And I would also urge extensive training in computer science sufficient to understand computer modeling" (Michael, 1998, p. 160).

The Nature of the Selected "Association"

Consistent with Michael's admonitions, Thorndike's "most fundamental question" is currently being pursued by integrating the experimental analysis of behavior and neuroscience using neural networks (e.g., Donahoe & Palmer, 1989, 1994). The interconnected ensemble of units that constitutes a neural network may be regarded as a much-mutated descendant of Thorndike's connectionism. It is ironic that simulation via neural networks has recently been brought to bear on a matter contention between Thorndike's early views of the law of effect and current statements of associationism, that other branch of the Thorndikian tree. The issue is the nature of the association inferred to underlie operant—or instrumental—conditioning. Present-day associationism generally takes the position that an instrumental response occurs because "the reinforcer is encoded as a consequence of the response" (Rescorla & Colwill, 1989, p. 291) or, stated in other terms, "instrumental learning leads to the development of response-outcome associations" (Colwill, 1994, p. 31; see also Colwill & Rescorla, 1990). Concerning this view, Thorndike asked: "Do they [animals] ever conclude from inference that a certain act will produce a certain desired result, and so do it? ... Although it is in a way superfluous to give the *coup de grace* to the despised theory that animals reason, I think it is worthwhile to settle this question once for all" (1898, p. 39). "The commonly accepted view…is that the sight of the inside of the box reminds the animal of his *previous pleasant experience after escape and of the movements* which he made which were immediately followed by and so associated with that escape" [i.e., a response-outcome association] (1898, p. 65). Thorndike disagreed: "This view has stood unchallenged, but its implication is false. It implies that an animal, whenever it thinks of an act, can supply an *impulse to do* the act" (1898, p. 66). "The groundwork of animal associations is not the association of *ideas*, but the association of … sense-impression with *impulse*" (1898, p. 71). In short, Thorndike rejected the notion that is implicit in the concept of response-outcome association—that of a response initiated by an autonomous organism, Consideration of the discriminative effects of conditioned respondents provides an interpretation that is more congenial to Thorndike's views. The behavior that fostered inferences about response-outcome associations can be interpreted as the joint control of operants and respondents by the environment, with feedback from the respondent modulating the strength of the operant (Donahoe & Palmer, pp. 108-109; cf. Trapold & Overmeir, 1972). The law of effect, when implemented by the neural mechanisms sought in the law of acquired brain connections, supports Thorndike's views (and Skinner's as well; see Palmer, 1998) that selection by reinforcement changes the environmental guidance of behavior, a conclusion that is not well characterized as the formation of response-outcome associations.

References

Campbell. D. T. (1974). Evolutionary epistemology. In P. A. Schlipp (Ed.), *The philosophy of Karl Popper. The library of living philosophers* (Vol. 14-1, pp. 413-463). LaSalle, IL: Open Court Publishing.

Chance, P. (1999). Thorndike's puzzle boxes and the origins of the experimental analysis of behavior. *Journal of the Experimental Analysis of Behavior, 72*, 433-440.

Colwill, R. M. (1994). Associative representations of instrumental contingencies. In D. L. Medin (Ed.), *The psychology of learning and motivation: Advances in research and theory* (Vol. 31, pp. 1-72). San Diego, CA: Academic Press.

Colwill, R. M., & Rescorla, R. A. (1990). Evidence for the hierarchical structure of instrumental learning. *Animal Learning & Behavior, 18*, 71-82.

Dennett, D. C. (1995). *Darwin's dangerous idea: Evolution and the meanings of life.* New York: Simon & Schuster.

Donahoe, J. W., Burgos, J. E., & Palmer, D. C. (1993). A selectionist approach to reinforcement. *Journal of the Experimental Analysis of Behavior, 60*, 17-40.

Donahoe, J. W., & Palmer, D. C. (1989). The interpretation of complex human behavior: Some reactions to *Parallel Distributed Processing*, edited by J. L. McClelland, D. E. Rumelhart, and the PDP Research Group. *Journal of the Experimental Analysis of Behavior, 51*, 399-416.

Donahoe, J. W., & Palmer, D. C. (1994). *Learning and complex behavior.* Boston: Allyn & Bacon.

Donahoe, J. W., Palmer, D. C., & Burgos, J. E. (1997). The S-R issue in behavior analysis and in Donahoe and Palmer's *Learning and Complex Behavior. Journal of the Experimental Analysis of Behavior, 67*, 193-211.

Galef, B. G., Jr. (1998). Edward Thorndike: Revolutionary psychologist, ambiguous biologist. *American Psychologist, 53*, 1128-1134.

Hull, C. L. (1943). *Principles of behavior, an introduction to behavior theory.* New York: Appleton-Century.

Hull, D. L. (1973). *Darwin and his critics.* Cambridge, MA: Harvard University Press.

Mayr, E. (1988). *The growth of biological thought: Diversity, evolution, and inheritance.* Cambridge, MA: Harvard University Press.

Michael, J. (1998). The current status and future directions of the analysis of verbal behavior: Comments on the comments. *The Analysis of Verbal Behavior, 15*, 157-161.

Palmer, D. C. (1998). On Skinner's rejection of S-R psychology. *The Behavior Analyst*, 21, 93-96.

Palmer, D. C., & Donahoe, J. W. (1992). Essentialism and selectionism in cognitive science and behavior analysis. *American Psychologist, 47*, 1344-1358.

Rescorla, R. A., & Colwill, R. M. (1989). Associations with anticipated and obtained outcomes in instrumental learning. *Animal Learning & Behavior, 17*, 291-303.

Sidman, M. (1960). *Tactics of scientific research: Evaluating experimental data in psychology.* New York: Basic Books.

Skinner, B. F. (1938). *The behavior of organisms: An experimental analysis.* New York: Appleton-Century.

Skinner, B. F. (1974). *About behaviorism.* New York: Knopf.

Sober, E. (1984). *The nature of selection: Evolutionary theory in philosophical focus.* Cambridge, MA: MIT Press.

Thorndike, E. L. (1898). Animal intelligence: An experimental study of the associative processes in animals. *Psychological Review Monograph Supplement, 2* (4, Whole No. 8).

Thorndike, E. L. (1905). *Elements of psychology.* New York: A. G. Seiler. Trapold, M. A., & Overmier, J. B. (1972). The second learning process in instrumental learning. In A. H. Black & W. F. Prokasy (Eds.), *Classical conditioning: Vol 2, Current research and theory.* (pp. 427-452). New York: Appleton-Century-Crofts.

REVIEW OF VERBAL BEHAVIOR BY B. F. SKINNER

(The Century Psychology Series.) Pp. viii, 478. New York: Appleton-Century-Crofts, Inc., 1957.

Noam Chomsky (1959). *Language, 35,* 26-58.

This review article ushered in what has come to be called the Chomskyan revolution. In it Chomsky does a masterful job of deconstructing the behaviorist doctrine of equal-potentiality, the view that phenomenal effects can be generalized equally to all organisms. Chomsky introduced the notion of a universal grammar, and anticipating the major premise of the evolutionary psychology paradigm, argues that the term learning itself is inaccurate; rather he says we should think of the child growing language. The Chomskyan revolution in linguistics prepared psychology for a conceptualization of the brain as a collection of evolved mental modules. Some 40 odd years later we can assuredly say that he was right. "The evidence that language is a biologically determined, species-specific, genetically transmitted capacity is simply overwhelming" Calvin & Bickerton, (2001). Lingua ex Machina: Reconciling Darwin and Chomsky with the Human Brain.

1. A great many linguists and philosophers concerned with language have expressed the hope that their studies might ultimately be embedded in a framework provided by behaviorist psychology, and that refractory areas of investigation, particularly those in which meaning is involved, will in this way be opened up to fruitful exploration. Since this volume is the first large-scale attempt to incorporate the major aspects of linguistic behavior within a behaviorist framework, it merits and will undoubtedly receive careful attention. Skinner is noted for his contributions to the study of animal behavior. The book under review is the product of study of linguistic behavior extending over more than twenty years. Earlier versions of it have been fairly widely circulated, and there are quite a few references in the psychological literature to its major ideas.

The problem to which this book is addressed is that of giving a 'functional analysis' of verbal behavior. By functional analysis, Skinner means identification of the variables that control this behavior and specification of how they interact to determine a particular verbal response. Furthermore, the controlling variables are to be described completely in terms of such notions as stimulus, reinforcement, deprivation, which have been given a reasonably clear meaning in animal experimentation. In other words, the goal of the book is to provide a way to predict and control verbal behavior by observing and manipulating the physical environment of the speaker.

Skinner feels that recent advances in the laboratory study of animal behavior permit us to approach this problem with a certain optimism, since 'the basic processes and relations which give verbal behavior its special characteristics are now fairly well understood ... the results [of this experimental work] have been surprisingly free of species restrictions. Recent work has shown that the methods can be extended to human behavior without serious modification' (3).[1]

It is important to see clearly just what it is in Skinner's program and claims that makes them appear so bold and remarkable. It is not primarily the fact that he has set functional analysis as his problem, or that he limits himself to study of 'observables', i.e. input-output relations. What is so surprising is the particular limitations he has imposed on the way in which the observables of behavior are to be studied, and, above all, the particularly simple nature of the 'function' which, he claims, describes the causation of behavior. One would naturally expect that prediction of the behavior of a complex organism (or machine) would require, in addition to information about external stimulation, knowledge of the internal structure of the organism, the ways in which it processes input information and organizes its own behavior.

These characteristics of the organism are in general a complicated product of inborn structure, the genetically determined course of maturation, and past experience. Insofar as independent neurophysiological evidence is not available, it is obvious that inferences concerning the structure of the organism are based on observation of behavior and outside events. Nevertheless, one's estimate of the relative importance of external factors and internal structure in the determination of behavior will have an important effect on the direction of research on linguistic (or any other) behavior, and on the kinds of analogies from animal behavior studies that will be considered relevant or suggestive.

Putting it differently, anyone who sets himself the problem of analyzing the causation of behavior will (in the absence of independent neurophysiological evidence) concern himself with the only data available, namely the record of inputs to the organism and the organism's present response, and will try to describe the function specifying the response in terms of the history of inputs. This is nothing more than the definition of his problem. There are no possible grounds for argument here, if one accepts the problem as legitimate, though Skinner has often advanced and defended this definition of a problem as if it were a thesis which other investigators reject. The differences that arise between those who affirm and those who deny the importance of the specific 'contribution of the organism' to learning and performance concern the particular character and complexity of this function, and the kinds of observations and research necessary for arriving at a precise specification of it. If the contribution of the organism is complex, the only hope of predicting behavior even in a gross way will be through a very indirect program of research that begins by studying the detailed character of the behavior itself and the particular capacities of the organism involved.

Skinner's thesis is that external factors consisting of present stimulation and the history of reinforcement (in particular the frequency, arrangement, and withholding of reinforcing stimuli) are of overwhelming importance, and that the general principles revealed in laboratory studies of these phenomena provide the basis for understanding the complexities of verbal behavior. He confidently and repeatedly voices his claim to have demonstrated that the contribution of the speaker is quite trivial and elementary, and that precise prediction of verbal behavior involves only specification of the few external factors that he has isolated experimentally with lower organisms.

Careful study of this book (and of the research on which it draws) reveals, however, that these astonishing claims are far from justified. It indicates, furthermore, that the insights that have been achieved in the laboratories of the reinforcement theorist, though quite genuine, can be applied to complex human behavior only in the most gross and superficial way, and that speculative attempts to discuss linguistic behavior in these terms alone omit from consideration factors of fundamental importance that are, no doubt, amenable to scientific study, although their specific character cannot at present be precisely formulated. Since Skinner's work is the most extensive attempt to accommodate human behavior involving higher mental faculties within a strict behaviorist schema of the type that has attracted many linguists and philosophers, as well as psychologists, a detailed documentation is of independent interest. The magnitude of the failure of this attempt to account for verbal behavior serves as a kind of measure of the importance of the factors omitted from consideration, and an indication of how little is really known about this remarkably complex phenomenon.

The force of Skinner's argument lies in the enormous wealth and range of examples for which he proposes a functional analysis. The only way to evaluate the success of his program and the correctness of his basic assumptions about verbal behavior is to review these examples in detail and to determine the precise character of the concepts in terms of which the functional analysis is presented. Section 2 of this review describes the experimental context with respect to which these concepts are originally defined. Sections 3-4 deal with the basic concepts 'stimulus', 'response', and 'reinforcement', Sections 6-10 with the new descriptive machinery developed specifically for the description of verbal behavior. In Section 5 we consider the status of the fundamental claim, drawn from the laboratory, which serves as the basis for the analogic guesses about human behavior that have been proposed by many psychologists. The final section (11) will consider some ways in which further linguistic work may play a part in clarifying some of these problems.

2. Although this book makes no direct reference to experimental work, it can be understood only in terms of the general framework that Skinner has developed for the description of behavior. Skinner divides the responses of the animal into two main categories. *Respondents* are purely reflex responses elicited by particular stimuli. *Operants* are emitted responses, for which no obvious stimulus can be discovered. Skinner has been concerned primarily with operant behavior. The experimental arrangement that he introduced consists basically of a box with a bar attached to one wall in such a way that when the bar is pressed, a food pellet is dropped into a tray (and the bar press is recorded). A rat placed in the box will soon press the bar, releasing a pellet into the tray. This state of affairs, resulting from the bar press, increases the *strength* of the bar-pressing operant. The food pellet is called a *reinforcer*; the event, a reinforcing event. The strength of an operant is defined by Skinner in terms of the rate of response during extinction (i.e. after the last reinforcement and before return to the preconditioning rate).

Suppose that release of the pellet is conditional on the flashing of a light. Then the rat will come to press the bar only when the light flashes. This is called *stimulus discrimination*. The response is called a *discriminated operant* and the light is called the *occasion* for its emission; this is to be distinguished from elicitation of a response by a stimulus in the case of the respondent.[2] Suppose that the apparatus is so arranged that bar-pressing of only a certain character (e.g. duration) will release the pellet. The rat will then come to press the bar in the required way. This process is called *response differentiation*. By successive slight changes in the conditions under which the response will be reinforced it is possible to shape the response of a rat or a pigeon in very surprising ways in a very short time, so that rather complex behavior can be produced by a process of successive approximation.

A stimulus can become reinforcing by repeated association with an already reinforcing stimulus. Such a stimulus is called a *secondary reinforcer*. Like many contemporary behaviorists, Skinner considers money, approval, and the like to be secondary reinforcers which have become reinforcing because of their association with food etc.[3] Secondary reinforcers can be *generalized* by associating them with a variety of different primary reinforcers.

Another variable that can affect the rate of the bar-pressing operant is drive, which Skinner defines operationally in terms of hours of deprivation. His major scientific book, *Behavior of organisms*, is a study of the effects of food-deprivation and conditioning on the strength of the bar-pressing response of healthy mature rats. Probably Skinner's most original contribution to animal behavior studies has been his investigation of the effects of intermittent reinforcement, arranged in various different ways, presented in *Behavior of organisms* and extended (with pecking of pigeons as the operant under investigation) in the recent *Schedules of reinforcement* by Ferster and Skinner (1957). It is apparently these studies that Skinner has in mind when he refers to the recent advances in the study of animal behavior.[4]

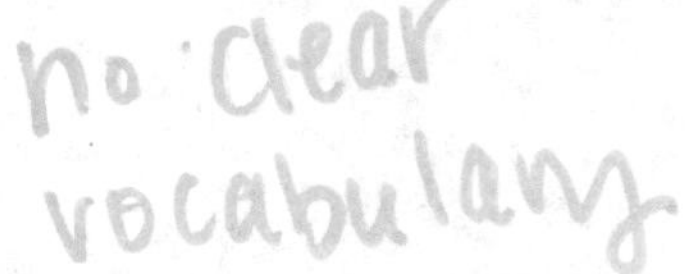

The notions 'stimulus', 'response', 'reinforcement' are relatively well defined with respect to the bar-pressing experiments and others similarly restricted. Before we can extend them to real-life behavior, however, certain difficulties must be faced. We must decide, first of all, whether any physical event to which the organism is capable of reacting is to be called a stimulus on a given occasion, or only one to which the organism in fact reacts; and correspondingly, we must decide whether any part of behavior is to be called a response, or only one connected with stimuli in lawful ways. Questions of this sort pose something of a dilemma for the experimental psychologist. If he accepts the broad definitions, characterizing any physical event impinging on the organism as a stimulus and any part of the organism's behavior as a response, he must conclude that behavior has not been demonstrated to be lawful. In the present state of our knowledge, we must attribute an overwhelming influence on actual behavior to ill-defined factors of attention, set, volition, and caprice. If we accept the narrower definitions, then behavior is lawful by definition (if it consists of responses); but this fact is of limited significance, since most of what the animal does will simply not be considered behavior. Hence the psychologist either must admit that behavior is not lawful (or that he cannot at present show that it is—not at all a damaging admission for a developing science), or must restrict his attention to those highly limited areas in which it is lawful (e.g. with adequate controls, bar-pressing in rats; lawfulness of the observed behavior provides, for Skinner, an implicit definition of a good experiment).

Skinner does not consistently adopt either course. He utilizes the experimental results as evidence for the scientific character of his system of behavior, and analogic guesses (formulated in terms of a metaphoric extension of the technical vocabulary of the laboratory) as evidence for its scope. This creates the illusion of a rigorous scientific theory with a very broad scope, although in fact the terms used in the description of real-life and of laboratory behavior may be mere homonyms, with at most a vague similarity of meaning. To substantiate this evaluation, a critical account of his book must show that with a literal reading (where the terms of the descriptive system have something like the technical meanings given in Skinner's definitions) the book covers almost no aspect of linguistic behavior, and that with a metaphoric reading, it is no more scientific than the traditional approaches to this subject matter, and rarely as clear and careful.[5]

3. Consider first Skinner's use of the notions 'stimulus' and 'response'. In *Behavior of organisms* (9) he commits himself to the narrow definitions for these terms. A part of the environment and a part of behavior are called stimulus (eliciting, discriminated, or reinforcing) and response, respectively, only if they are lawfully related; that is, if the 'dynamic laws' relating them show smooth and reproducible curves. Evidently stimuli and responses, so defined, have not been shown to figure very widely in ordinary human behavior.[6] We can, in the face of presently available evidence, continue to maintain the lawfulness of the relation between stimulus and response only by depriving them of their objective character. A typical example of 'stimulus control' for Skinner would be the response to a piece of music with the utterance *Mozart* or to a painting with the response *Dutch*. These responses are asserted to be 'under the control of extremely subtle properties' of the physical object or event (108). Suppose instead of saying *Dutch* we had said *Clashes with the wallpaper*, *I thought you liked abstract work*, *Never saw it before*, *Tilted*, *Hanging too low*, *Beautiful*, *Hideous*, *Remember our camping trip last summer*?, or whatever else might come into our minds when looking at a picture (in Skinnerian translation, whatever other responses exist in sufficient strength). Skinner could only say that each of these responses is under the control of some other stimulus property of the physical object. If we look at a red chair and say *red*, the response is under the control of the stimulus 'redness'; if we say *chair*, it is under the control of the collection of properties (for Skinner, the object) 'chairness' (110), and similarly for any other response. This device is as simple as it is empty. Since properties are free for the asking (we have as many of them as we have nonsynonymous descriptive expressions in our language, whatever this means exactly), we can account for a wide class of responses in terms of Skinnerian functional analysis by identifying the 'controlling stimuli'. But the word 'stimulus' has lost all objectivity in this usage. Stimuli are no longer part of the outside physical world; they are driven back into the organism. We identify the stimulus when we hear the response. It is clear from such examples, which abound, that the talk of 'stimulus control' simply disguises a complete retreat to mentalistic psychology. We cannot predict verbal behavior in terms of the stimuli in the speaker's environment, since we do not know what the current stimuli are until he responds. Furthermore, since we cannot control the property of a physical object to which an individual will respond, except in highly artificial cases, Skinner's claim that his system, as opposed to the traditional one, permits the practical control of verbal behavior[7] is quite false.

Other examples of 'stimulus control' merely add to the general mystification. Thus a proper noun is held to be a response 'under the control of a specific person or thing' (as controlling stimulus, 113). I have often used the words *Eisenhower* and *Moscow*, which I presume are proper nouns if anything is, but have never been 'stimulated' by the corresponding objects. How can this fact be made compatible with this definition? Suppose that I use the name of a friend who is not present. Is this an instance of a proper noun under the control of the friend as stimulus? Elsewhere it is asserted that a stimulus controls a response in the sense that presence of the stimulus increases the probability of the response. But it is obviously untrue that the probability that a speaker will produce a full name is increased when its bearer faces the speaker. Furthermore, how can one's own name be a proper noun in this sense? A multitude of similar questions arise immediately. It appears that the word 'control' here is merely a misleading paraphrase for the traditional 'denote' or 'refer'. The assertion (115) that so far as the speaker is concerned, the relation of reference is 'simply the probability that the speaker will emit a response of a given form in the presence of a stimulus having specified properties' is surely incorrect if we take the words 'presence', 'stimulus', and 'probability' in their literal sense. That they are not intended to be taken literally is indicated by many examples, as when a response is said to be 'controlled' by a situation or state of affairs as 'stimulus'. Thus, the expression a *needle in a haystack* 'may be controlled as a unit by a particular type of situation' (116); the words in a single part of speech, e.g. all adjectives, are under the control of a single set of subtle properties of stimuli (121); 'the sentence *The boy runs a store* is under the control of an extremely complex stimulus situation' (335); '*He is not at all well* may function as a standard response under the control of a state of affairs which might also control. *He is ailing*' (325); when an envoy observes events in a foreign country and reports upon his return, his report is under 'remote stimulus control' (416); the statement *This is war* may be a response to a 'confusing international situation' (441); the suffix –ed is controlled by that 'subtle property of stimuli which we speak of as action-in-the-past' (121) just as the *–s* in *The boy runs* is under the control of such specific features of the situation as its 'currency' (332). No characterization of the notion 'stimulus control' that is remotely related to the bar-pressing experiment (or that preserves the faintest objectivity) can be made to cover a set of examples like these, in which, for example, the 'controlling stimulus' need not even impinge on the responding organism.

Consider now Skinner's use of the notion 'response'. The problem of identifying units in verbal behavior has of course been a primary concern of linguists, and it seems very likely that experimental psychologists should be able to provide much-needed assistance in clearing up the many remaining difficulties in systematic identification. Skinner recognizes (20) the fundamental character of the problem of identification of a unit of verbal behavior, but is satisfied with an answer so vague and subjective that it does not really contribute to its solution. The unit of verbal behavior—the verbal operant—is defined as a class of responses of identifiable form functionally related to one or more controlling variables. No method is suggested for determining in a particular instance what are the controlling variables, how many such units have occurred, or where their boundaries are in the total response. Nor is any attempt made to specify how much or what kind of similarity in form or 'control' is required for two physical events to be considered instances of the same operant. In short, no answers are suggested for the most elementary questions that must be asked of anyone proposing a method for description of behavior. Skinner is content with what he calls an 'extrapolation' of the concept of operant developed in the laboratory to the verbal field. In the typical Skinnerian experiment, the problem of identifying the unit of behavior is not too crucial. It is defined, by fiat, as a recorded peck or bar-press, and systematic variations in the rate of this operant and its resistance to extinction are studied as a function of deprivation and scheduling of reinforcement (pellets). The operant is thus defined with respect to a particular experimental procedure. This is perfectly reasonable, and has led to many interesting results. It is, however, completely meaningless to speak of extrapolating this concept of operant to ordinary verbal behavior. Such 'extrapolation' leaves us with no way of justifying one or another decision about the units in the 'verbal repertoire'.

Skinner specifies 'response strength' as the basic datum, the basic dependent variable in his functional analysis. In the bar-pressing experiment, response strength is defined in terms of rate of emission during extinction. Skinner has argued[8] that this is 'the only datum that varies significantly and in the expected direction under conditions which are relevant to the "learning process".' In the book under review, response strength is defined as 'probability of emission' (22). This definition provides a comforting impression of objectivity, which, however, is quickly dispelled when we look into the matter more closely. The term 'probability' has some rather obscure meaning for Skinner in this book.[9] We are told, on the one hand, that 'our evidence for the contribution of each variable [to response strength] is based on observation of frequencies alone' (28). At the same time, it appears that frequency is a very misleading measure of strength, since, for example, the frequency of a response may be 'primarily attributable to the frequency of occurrence of controlling variables' (27). It is not clear how the frequency of a response can be attributable to anything BUT the frequency of occurrence of its controlling variables if we accept Skinner's view that the behavior occurring in a given situation is 'fully determined' by the relevant controlling variables (175, 228). Furthermore, although the evidence for the contribution of each variable to response strength is based on observation of frequencies alone, it turns out that 'we base the notion of strength upon several kinds of evidence' (22), in particular (22-8): emission of the response (particularly in unusual circumstances), energy level (stress), pitch level, speed and delay of emission, size of letters etc. in writing, immediate repetition, and—a final factor, relevant but misleading—over-all frequency.

Of course, Skinner recognizes that these measures do not co-vary, because (among other reasons) pitch, stress, quantity, and reduplication may have internal linguistic functions.[10] However, he does not hold these conflicts to be very important, since the proposed factors indicative of strength are 'fully understood by everyone' in the culture (27). For example, 'if we are shown a prized work of art and exclaim *Beautiful!*, the speed and energy of the response will not be lost on the owner.' It does not appear totally obvious that that in this case the way to impress the owner is to shriek *Beautiful* in a loud, high-pitched voice, repeatedly, and with no delay (high response strength). It may be equally effective to look at the picture silently (long delay), and then to murmur *Beautiful* in a soft, low-pitched voice (by definition, very low response strength).

It is not unfair, I believe, to conclude from Skinner's discussion of response strength, the 'basic datum' in functional analysis, that his 'extrapolation' of the notion of probability can best be interpreted as, in effect, nothing more than a decision to use the word 'probability', with its favorable connotations of objectivity, as a cover term to paraphrase such low-status words as 'interest', 'intention', belief', and the like. This interpretation is fully justified by the way in which Skinner uses the terms 'probability' and 'strength'. To cite just one example, Skinner defines the process of confirming an assertion in science as one of 'generating additional variables to increase its probability' (425), and more generally, its strength (425-9). If we take this suggestion quite literally, the degree of confirmation of a scientific assertion can be measured as a simple function of the loudness, pitch, and frequency with which it is proclaimed, and a general procedure for increasing its degree of confirmation would be, for instance, to train machine guns on large crowds of people who have been instructed to shout it. A better indication of what Skinner probably has in mind here is given by his description of how the theory of evolution, as an example, is confirmed. This 'single set of verbal responses ... is made more plausible—is strengthened—by several types of construction based upon verbal responses in geology, paleontology, genetics, and so on' (427). We are no doubt to interpret the terms 'strength' and 'probability' in this context as paraphrases of more familiar locutions such as 'justified belief' or 'warranted assertability', or something of the sort. Similar latitude of interpretation is presumably expected when we read that 'frequency of effective action accounts in turn for what we may call the listener's "belief"' (88) or that 'our belief in what someone tells us is similarly a function of, or identical with, our tendency to act upon the verbal stimuli which he provides' (160).[11]

I think it is evident, then, that Skinner's use of the terms 'stimulus', 'control', 'response', and 'strength' justify the general conclusion stated in the last paragraph of Section 2 above. The way in which these terms are brought to bear on the actual data indicates that we must interpret them as mere paraphrases for the popular vocabulary commonly used to describe behavior, and as having no particular connection with the homonymous expressions used in the description of laboratory experiments. Naturally, this terminological revision adds no objectivity to the familiar 'mentalistic' mode of description.

4. The other fundamental notion borrowed from the description of bar-pressing experiments is 'reinforcement'. It raises problems which are similar, and even more serious. In *Behavior of organisms*, 'the operation of reinforcement is defined as the presentation of a certain kind of stimulus in a temporal relation with either a stimulus or response. A reinforcing stimulus is defined as such by its power to produce the resulting change [in strength].There is no circularity about this: some stimuli are found to produce the change, others not, and they are classified as reinforcing and non-reinforcing accordingly' (62). This is a perfectly appropriate definition[12] for the study of schedules of reinforcement. It is perfectly useless, however, in the discussion of real-life behavior, unless we can somehow characterize the stimuli which are reinforcing (and the situations and conditions under which they are reinforcing). Consider first of all the status of the basic principle that Skinner calls the 'law of conditioning' (law of effect). It reads: 'if the occurrence of an operant is followed by presence of a reinforcing stimulus, the strength is increased' (*Behavior of organisms* 21). As 'reinforcement' was defined, this law becomes a tautology.[13] For Skinner, learning is just change in response strength.[14] Although the statement that presence of reinforcement is a sufficient condition for learning and maintenance of behavior is vacuous, the claim that it is a necessary condition may have some content, depending on how the class of reinforcers (and appropriate situations) is characterized. Skinner does make it very clear that in his view reinforcement is a necessary condition for language learning and for the continued availability of linguistic responses in the adult.[15] However, the looseness of the term 'reinforcement' as Skinner uses it in the book under review makes it entirely pointless to inquire into the truth or falsity of this claim. Examining the instances of what Skinner calls 'reinforcement', we find that not even the requirement that a reinforcer be an identifiable stimulus is taken seriously. In fact, the term is used in such a way that the assertion that reinforcement is necessary for learning and continued availability of behavior is likewise empty.

To show this, we consider some example of 'reinforcement'. First of all, we find a heavy appeal to automatic self-reinforcement. Thus, 'a man talks to himself...because of the reinforcement he receives' (163); 'the child is reinforced automatically when he duplicates the sounds of airplanes, streetcars ...' (164); 'the young child alone in the nursery may automatically reinforce his own exploratory verbal behavior when he produces sounds which he has heard in the speech of others' (58); 'the speaker who is also an accomplished listener "knows when he has correctly echoed a response" and is reinforced thereby' (68); thinking is 'behaving which automatically affects the behaver and is reinforcing because it does so' (438; cutting one's finger should thus be reinforcing, and an example of thinking) 'the verbal fantasy, whether overt or covert, is automatically reinforcing to the speaker as listener. Just as the musician plays or composes what he is reinforced by hearing, or as the artist paints what reinforces him visually, so the speaker engaged in verbal fantasy says what he is reinforced by hearing or writes what he is reinforced by reading' (439); similarly, care in problem solving, and rationalization, are automatically self-reinforcing (442-3). We can also reinforce someone by emitting verbal behavior as such (since this rules out a class of aversive stimulations, 167), by not emitting verbal behavior (keeping silent and paying attention, 199), or by acting appropriately on some future occasion (152: 'the strength of [the speaker's] behavior is determined mainly by the behavior which the listener will exhibit with respect to a given state of affairs'; this Skinner considers the general case of 'communication' or 'letting the listener know'). In most such cases, of course, the speaker is not present at the time when the reinforcement takes place, as when 'the artist ... is reinforced by the effects his works have upon ... others' (224), or when the writer is reinforced by the fact that his 'verbal behavior may reach over centuries or to thousands of listeners or readers at the same time. The writer may not be reinforced often or immediately, but his net reinforcement may be great' (206; this accounts for the great 'strength' of his behavior). An individual may also find it reinforcing to injure someone by criticism or by bringing bad news, or to publish an experimental result which upsets the theory of a rival (154), to describe circumstances which would be reinforcing if they were to occur (165), to avoid repetition (222), to 'hear' his own name though in fact it was not mentioned or to hear nonexistent words in his child's babbling (259), to clarify or otherwise intensify the effect of a stimulus which serves an important discriminative function (416), etc.

From this sample, it can be seen that the notion of reinforcement has totally lost whatever objective meaning it may ever have had. Running through these examples, we see that a person can be reinforced though he emits no response at all, and that the reinforcing 'stimulus' need not impinge on the 'reinforced person' or need not even exist (it is sufficient that it be imagined or hoped for). When we read that a person plays what music he likes (165), says what he likes (165), thinks what he likes (438-9), reads what books he likes (163), etc., BECAUSE he finds it reinforcing to do so, or that we write books or inform others of facts BECAUSE we are reinforced by what we hope will be the ultimate behavior of reader or listener, we can only conclude that the term "reinforcement' has a purely ritual function. The phrase 'X is reinforced by Y (stimulus, state of affairs, event, etc.)' is being used as a cover term for 'X wants Y', 'X likes Y', 'X wishes that Y were the case', etc. Invoking the term 'reinforcement' has no explanatory force, and any idea that this paraphrase introduces any new clarity or objectivity into the description of wishing, liking, etc., is a serious delusion. The only effect is to obscure the important differences among the notions being paraphrased. Once we recognize the latitude with which the term 'reinforcement' is being used, many rather startling comments lose their initial effect—for instance, that the behavior of the creative artist is 'controlled entirely by the contingencies of reinforcement' (150). What has been hoped for from the psychologist is some indication how the casual and informal description of everyday behavior in the popular vocabulary can be explained or clarified in terms of the notions developed in careful experiment and observation, or perhaps replaced in terms of a better scheme. A mere terminological revision, in which a term borrowed from the laboratory is used with the full vagueness of the ordinary vocabulary, is of no conceivable interest.

It seems that Skinner's claim that all verbal behavior is acquired and maintained in 'strength' through reinforcement is quite empty, because his notion of reinforcement has no clear content, functioning only as a cover term for any factor, detectable or not, related to acquisition or maintenance of verbal behavior.[16] Skinner's use of the term 'conditioning' suffers from a similar difficulty. Pavlovian and operant conditioning are processes about which psychologists have developed real understanding. Instruction of human beings is not. The claim that instruction and imparting of information are simply matters of conditioning (357-66) is pointless. The claim is true, if we extend the term 'conditioning' to cover these processes, but we know no more about them after having revised this term in such a way as to deprive it of its relatively clear and objective character. It is, as far as we know, quite false, if we use 'conditioning' in its literal sense. Similarly, when we say that 'it is the function of predication to facilitate the transfer of response from one term to another or from one object to another' (361), we have said nothing of any significance. In what sense is this true of the predication *Whales are mammals*? Or, to take Skinner's example, what point is there in saying that the effect of *The telephone is out of order* on the listener is to bring behavior formerly controlled by the stimulus *out of order* under control of the stimulus *telephone* (or the telephone itself) by a process of simple conditioning (362)? What laws of conditioning hold in this case? Furthermore what behavior is 'controlled' by the stimulus *out of order*, in the abstract? Depending on the object of which this is predicated, the present state of motivation of the listener, etc., the behavior may vary from rage to pleasure, from fixing the object to throwing it out, from simply not using it to trying to use it in the normal way (e.g. to see if it is really out of order), and so on. To speak of 'conditioning' or 'bringing previously available behavior under control of a new stimulus' in such a case is just a kind of play-acting at science. Cf. also footnote 43.

5. The claim that careful arrangement of contingencies of reinforcement by the verbal community is a necessary condition for language learning has appeared, in one form or another, in many places.[17] Since it is based not on actual observation, but on analogies to laboratory study of lower organisms, it is important to determine the status of the underlying assertion within experimental psychology proper. The most common characterization of reinforcement (one which Skinner explicitly rejects, incidentally) is in terms of drive reduction. This characterization can be given substance by defining drives in some way independently of what in fact is learned. If a drive is postulated on the basis of the fact that learning takes place, the claim that reinforcement is necessary for learning will again become as empty as it is in the Skinnerian framework. There is an extensive literature on the question of whether there can be learning without drive-reduction (latent learning). The 'classical' experiment of Blodgett indicated that rats who had explored a maze without reward showed a marked drop in number of errors (as compared to a control group which had not explored the maze) upon introduction of a food reward, indicating that the rat had learned the structure of the maze without reduction of the hunger drive. Drive-reduction theorists countered with an exploratory drive which was reduced during the prereward learning, and claimed that a slight decrement in errors could be noted before food reward. A wide variety of experiments, with somewhat conflicting results, have been carried out with a similar design.[18] Few investigators still doubt the existence of the phenomenon. Hilgard, in his general review of learning theory,[19] concludes that 'there is no longer any doubt but that, under appropriate circumstances, latent learning is demonstrable.'

More recent work has shown that novelty and variety of stimulus are sufficient to arouse curiosity in the rat and to motivate it to explore (visually), and in fact, to learn (since on a presentation of two stimuli, one novel, one repeated, the rat will attend to the novel one);[20] that rats will learn to choose the arm of a single-choice maze that leads to a complex maze, running through this being their only 'reward';[21] that monkeys can learn object discriminations and maintain their performance at a high level of efficiency with visual exploration (looking out of a window for 30 seconds) as the only reward;[22] and, perhaps most strikingly of all, that monkeys and apes will solve rather complex manipulation problems that are simply placed in their cages, and will solve discrimination problems with only exploration and manipulation as incentives.[23] In these cases, solving the problem is apparently its own 'reward'. Results of this kind can be handled by reinforcement theorists only if they are willing to set up curiosity, exploration, and manipulation drives, or to speculate somehow about acquired drives[24] for which there is no evidence outside of the fact that learning takes place in these cases.

There is a variety of other kinds of evidence that has been offered to challenge the view that drive-reduction is necessary for learning. Results on sensory-sensory conditioning have been interpreted as demonstrating learning without drive-reduction.[25] Olds has reported reinforcement by direct stimulation of the brain, from which he concludes that reward need not satisfy a physiological need or withdraw a drive stimulus.[26] The phenomenon of imprinting, long observed by zoologists, is of particular interest in this connection. Some of the most complex patterns of behavior of birds, in particular, are directed towards objects and animals of the type to which they have been exposed at certain critical early periods of life.[27] Imprinting is the most striking evidence for the innate disposition of the animal to learn in a certain direction, and to react appropriately to patterns and objects of certain restricted types, often only long after the original learning has taken place. It is, consequently, unrewarded learning, though the resulting patterns of behavior may be refined through reinforcement. Acquisition of the typical songs of song birds is, in some cases, a type of imprinting. Thorpe reports studies that show 'that some characteristics of the normal song have been learnt in the earliest youth, before the bird itself is able to produce any kind of full song'.[28] The phenomenon of imprinting has recently been investigated under laboratory conditions and controls with positive results.[29]

Phenomena of this general type are certainly familiar from everyday experience. We recognize people and places to which we have given no particular attention. We can look up something in a book and learn it perfectly well with no other motive than to confute reinforcement theory, or out of boredom, or idle curiosity. Everyone engaged in research must have had the experience of working with feverish and prolonged intensity to write a paper which no one else will read or to solve a problem which no one else thinks important and which will bring no conceivable reward—which may only confirm a general opinion that the researcher is wasting his time on irrelevancies. The fact that rats and monkeys do likewise is interesting, and important to show in careful experiment. In fact, studies of behavior of the type mentioned above have an independent and positive significance that far outweighs their incidental importance in bringing into question the claim that learning is impossible without drive-reduction. It is not at all unlikely that insights arising from animal behavior studies with this broadened scope may have the kind of relevance to such complex activities as verbal behavior that reinforcement theory has, so far, failed to exhibit. In any event, in the light of presently available evidence, it is difficult to see how anyone can be willing to claim that reinforcement is necessary for learning, if reinforcement is taken seriously as something identifiable independently of the resulting change in behavior.

Similarly, it seems quite beyond question that children acquire a good deal of their verbal and nonverbal behavior by casual observation and imitation of adults and other children.[30] It is simply not true that children can learn language only through 'meticulous care' on the part of adults who shape their verbal repertoire through careful differential reinforcement, though it may be that such care is often the custom in academic families. It is a common observation that a young child of immigrant parents may learn a second language in the streets, from other children, with amazing rapidity, and that his speech may be completely fluent and correct to the last allophone, while the subtleties that become second nature to the child may elude his parents despite high motivation and continued practice. A child may pick up a large part of his vocabulary and 'feel' for sentence structure from television, from reading, from listening to adults, etc. Even a very young child who has not yet acquired a minimal repertoire from which to form new utterances may imitate a word quite well on an early try, with no attempt on the part of his parents to teach it to him. It is also perfectly obvious that, at a later stage, a child will be able to construct and understand utterances which are quite new, and are, at the same time, acceptable sentences in his language. Every time an adult reads a newspaper, he undoubtedly comes upon countless new sentences which are not at all similar, in a simple, physical sense, to any that he has heard before, and which he will recognize as sentences and understand; he will also be able to detect slight distortions or misprints. Talk of 'stimulus generalization' in such a case simply perpetuates the mystery under a new title. These abilities indicate that there must be fundamental processes at work quite independently of 'feedback' from the environment. I have been able to find no support whatsoever for the doctrine of Skinner and others that slow and careful shaping of verbal behavior through differential reinforcement is an absolute necessity. If reinforcement theory really requires the assumption that there be such meticulous care, it seems best to regard this simply as a reductio ad absurdum argument against this approach. It is also not easy to find any basis (or, for that matter, to attach very much content) to the claim that reinforcing contingencies set up by the verbal community are the single factor responsible for maintaining the strength of verbal behavior. The sources of the 'strength' of this behavior are almost a total mystery at present. Reinforcement undoubtedly plays a significant role, but so do a variety of motivational factors about which nothing serious is known in the case of human beings.

As far as acquisition of language is concerned, it seems clear that reinforcement, casual observation, and natural inquisitiveness (coupled with a strong tendency to imitate) are important factors, as is the remarkable capacity of the child to generalize, hypothesize, and 'process information' in a variety of very special and apparently highly complex ways which we cannot yet describe or begin to understand, and which may be largely innate, or may develop through some sort of learning or through maturation of the nervous system. The manner in which such factors operate and interact in language acquisition is completely unknown. It is clear that what is necessary in such a case is research, not dogmatic and perfectly arbitrary claims, based on analogies to that small part of the experimental literature in which one happens to be interested.

The pointlessness of these claims becomes clear when we consider the well-known difficulties in determining to what extent inborn structure, maturation, and learning are responsible for the particular form of a skilled or complex performance.[31] To take just one example,[32] the gaping response of a nestling thrush is at first released by jarring of the nest, and, at a later stage, by a moving object of specific size, shape, and position relative to the nestling. At this later stage the response is directed towards the part of the stimulus object corresponding to the parent's head, and characterized by a complex configuration of stimuli that can be precisely described. Knowing just this, it would be possible to construct a speculative, learning-theoretic account of how this sequence of behavior patterns might have developed through a process of differential reinforcement, and it would no doubt be possible to train rats to do something similar. However, there appears to be good evidence that these responses to fairly complex 'sign stimuli' are genetically determined and mature without learning. Clearly, the possibility cannot be discounted. Consider now the comparable case of a child imitating new words. At an early stage we may find rather gross correspondences. At a later stage, we find that repetition is of course far from exact (i.e. it is not mimicry, a fact which itself is interesting), but that it reproduces the highly complex configuration of sound features that constitute the phonological structure of the language in question. Again, we can propose a speculative account of how this result might have been obtained through elaborate arrangement of reinforcing contingencies. Here too, however, it is possible that ability to select out of the complex auditory input those features that are phonologically relevant may develop largely independently of reinforcement, through genetically determined maturation. To the extent that this is true, an account of the development and causation of behavior that fails to consider the structure of the organism will provide no understanding of the real processes involved.

It is often argued that experience, rather than innate capacity to handle information in certain specific ways, must be the factor of overwhelming dominance in determining the specific character of language acquisition, since a child speaks the language of the group in which he lives. But this is a superficial argument. As long as we are speculating, we may consider the possibility that the brain has evolved to the point where, given an input of observed Chinese sentences, it produces (by an 'induction' of apparently fantastic complexity and suddenness) the 'rules' of Chinese grammar, and given an input of observed English sentences, it produces (by, perhaps, exactly the same process of induction) the rules of English grammar; or that given an observed application of a term to certain instances it automatically predicts the extension to a class of complexly related instances. If clearly recognized as such, this speculation is neither unreasonable nor fantastic; nor, for that matter, is it beyond the bounds of possible study. There is of course no known neural structure capable of performing this task in the specific ways that observation of the resulting behavior might lead us to postulate; but for that matter, the structures capable of accounting for even the simplest kinds of learning have similarly defied detection.[33]

Summarizing this brief discussion, it seems that there is neither empirical evidence nor any known argument to support any SPECIFIC claim about the relative importance of 'feedback' from the environment and the 'independent contribution of the organism' in the process of language acquisition.

6. We now turn to the system that Skinner develops specifically for the description of verbal behavior. Since this system is based on the notions 'stimulus', 'response', and 'reinforcement', we can conclude from the preceding sections that it will be vague and arbitrary. For reasons noted in Section 1, however, I think it is important to see in detail how far from the mark any analysis phrased solely in these terms must be and how completely this system fails to account for the facts of verbal behavior.

Consider first the term 'verbal behavior' itself. This is defined as 'behavior reinforced through the mediation of other persons' (2). The definition is clearly much too broad. It would include as 'verbal behavior', for example, a rat pressing the bar in a Skinner-box, a child brushing his teeth, a boxer retreating before an opponent, and a mechanic repairing an automobile. Exactly how much of ordinary linguistic behavior is 'verbal' in this sense, however, is something of a question: perhaps, as I have pointed out above, a fairly small fraction of it, if any substantive meaning is assigned to the term 'reinforced'. This definition is subsequently refined by the additional provision that the mediating response of the reinforcing person (the 'listener') must itself 'have been conditioned *precisely in order to reinforce* the behavior of the speaker' (225, italics his). This still covers the examples given above, if we can assume that the 'reinforcing' behavior of the psychologist, the parent, the opposing boxer, and the paying customer are the result of appropriate training, which is perhaps not unreasonable. A significant part of the fragment of linguistic behavior covered by the earlier definition will no doubt be excluded by the refinement, however. Suppose, for example, that while crossing the street I hear someone shout *Watch out for the car* and jump out of the way. It can hardly be proposed that my jumping (the mediating, reinforcing response in Skinner's usage) was conditioned (that is, I was trained to jump) precisely in order to reinforce the behavior of the speaker. Similarly for a wide class of cases. Skinner's assertion that with this refined definition 'we narrow our subject to what is traditionally recognized as the verbal field' (225) appears to be grossly in error.

7. Verbal operants are classified by Skinner in terms of their 'functional' relation to discriminated stimulus, reinforcement, and other verbal responses. A *mand* is defined as 'a verbal operant in which the response is reinforced by a characteristic consequence and is therefore under the functional control of relevant conditions of deprivation or aversive stimulation' (35). This is meant to include questions, commands, etc. Each of the terms in this definition raises a host of problems. A mand such as *Pass the salt* is a class of responses. We cannot tell by observing the form of a response whether it belongs to this class (Skinner is very clear about this), but only by identifying the controlling variables. This is generally impossible. Deprivation is defined in the bar-pressing experiment in terms of length of time that the animal has not been fed or permitted to drink. In the present context, however, it is quite a mysterious notion. No attempt is made here to describe a method for determining 'relevant conditions of deprivation' independently of the 'controlled' response. It is of no help at all to be told (32) that it can be characterized in terms of the operations of the experimenter. If we define deprivation in terms of elapsed time, then at any moment a person is in countless states of deprivation.[34] It appears that we must decide that the relevant condition of deprivation was (say) salt-deprivation, on the basis of the fact that the speaker asked for salt (the reinforcing community which 'sets up' the mand is in a similar predicament). In this case, the assertion that a mand is under the control of relevant deprivation is empty, and we are (contrary to Skinner's intention) identifying the response as a mand completely in terms of form. The word 'relevant' in the definition above conceals some rather serious complications.

In the case of the mand *Pass the salt*, the word 'deprivation' is not out of place, though it appears to be of little use for functional analysis. Suppose however that the speaker says *Give me the book*, *Take me for a ride*, or *Let me fix it*. What kinds of deprivation can be associated with these mands? How do we determine or measure the relevant deprivation? I think we must conclude in this case, as before, either that the notion 'deprivation' is relevant at most to a minute fragment of verbal behavior, or else that the statement 'X is under Y-deprivation' is just an odd paraphrase for 'X wants Y', bearing a misleading and unjustifiable connotation of objectivity.

The notion 'aversive control' is just as confused. This is intended to cover threats, beating, and the like (33). The manner in which aversive stimulation functions is simply described. If a speaker has had a history of appropriate reinforcement (e.g. if a certain response was followed by 'cessation of the threat of such injury—of events which have previously been followed by such injury and which are therefore conditioned aversive stimuli') then he will tend to give the proper response when the threat which had previously been followed by the injury is presented. It would appear to follow from this description that a speaker will not respond properly to the mand *Your money or you life* (38) unless he has a past history of being killed. But even if the difficulties in describing the mechanism of aversive control are somehow removed by a more careful analysis, it will be of little use for identifying operants for reasons similar to those mentioned in the case of deprivation.

It seems, then, that in Skinner's terms there is in most cases no way to decide whether a given response is an instance of a particular mand. Hence it is meaningless, within the terms of his system, to speak of the *characteristic* consequences of a mand, as in the definition above. Furthermore, even if we extend the system so that mands can somehow be identified, we will have to face the obvious fact that most of us are not fortunate enough to have our requests, commands, advice, and so on characteristically reinforced (they may nevertheless exist in considerable 'strength'). These responses could therefore not be considered mands by Skinner. In fact, Skinner sets up a category of 'magical mands' (48-9) to cover the case of 'mands which cannot be accounted for by showing that they have ever had the effect specified or any similar effect upon similar occasions' (the word 'ever' in this statement should be replaced by 'characteristically'). In these pseudo mands, 'the speaker simply describes the reinforcement appropriate to a given state of deprivation or aversive stimulation'. In other words, given the meaning that we have been led to assign to 'reinforcement' and 'deprivation', the speaker asks for what he wants. The remark that 'a speaker appears to create new mands on the analogy of old ones' is also not very helpful.

Skinner's claim that his new descriptive system is superior to the traditional one 'because its terms can be defined with respect to experimental operations' (45) is, we see once again, an illusion. The statement 'X wants Y' is not clarified by pointing out a relation between rate of bar-pressing and hours of food-deprivation; replacing 'X wants Y' by 'X is deprived of Y' adds no new objectivity to the description of behavior. His further claim for the superiority of the new analysis of mands is that it provides an objective basis for the traditional classification into requests, commands, etc. (38-41). The traditional classification is in terms of the intention of the speaker. But intention, Skinner holds, can be reduced to contingencies of reinforcement, and, correspondingly, we can explain the traditional classification in terms of the reinforcing behavior of the listener. Thus a question is a mand which 'specifies verbal action, and the behavior of the listener permits us to classify it as a request, a command, or a prayer' (39). It is a request if 'the listener is independently motivated to reinforce the speaker'; a command if 'the listener's behavior is ... reinforced by reducing a threat'; a prayer if the mand 'promotes reinforcement by generating an emotional disposition'. The mand is advice if the listener is positively reinforced by the consequences of mediating the reinforcement of the speaker; it is a warning if 'by carrying out the behavior specified by the speaker the listener escapes from aversive stimulation'; and so on. All this is obviously wrong if Skinner is using the words 'request', 'command', etc., in anything like the sense of the corresponding English words. The word 'question' does not cover commands. *Please pass the salt* is a request (but not a question), whether or not the listener happens to be motivated to fulfill it; not everyone to whom a request is addressed is favorably disposed. A response does not cease to be a command if it is not followed; nor does a question become a command if the speaker answers it because of an implied or imagined threat. Not all advice is good advice, and a response does not cease to be advice if it is not followed. Similarly, a warning may be misguided; heeding it may cause aversive stimulation, and ignoring it might be positively reinforcing. In short, the entire classification is beside the point. A moment's thought is sufficient to demonstrate the impossibility of distinguishing between requests, commands, advice, etc., on the basis of the behavior or disposition of the particular listener. Nor can we do this on the basis of the typical behavior of all listeners. Some advice is never taken, is always bad, etc., and similarly with other kinds of mands. Skinner's evident satisfaction with this analysis of the traditional classification is extremely puzzling.

8. Mands are operants with no specified relation to a prior stimulus. A *tact*, on the other hand, is defined as 'a verbal operant in which a response of given form is evoked (or at least strengthened) by a particular object or event or property of an object or event' (81). The examples quoted in the discussion of stimulus control (Section 3) are all tacts. The obscurity of the notion 'stimulus control' makes the concept of the tact rather mystical. Since, however, the tact is 'the most important of verbal operants', it is important to investigate the development of this concept in more detail.

We first ask why the verbal community 'sets up' tacts in the child—that is, how the parent is reinforced by setting up the tact. The basic explanation for this behavior of the parent (85-6) is the reinforcement he obtains by the fact that his contact with the environment is extended; to use Skinner's example, the child may later be able to call him to the telephone. (It is difficult to see, then, how first children acquire tacts, since the parent does not have the appropriate history of reinforcement). Reasoning in the same way, we may conclude that the parent induces the child to walk so that he can make some money delivering newspapers. Similarly, the parent sets up an 'echoic repertoire' (e.g. a phonemic system) in the child because this makes it easier to teach him new vocabulary, and extending the child's vocabulary is ultimately useful to the parent. 'In all these cases we explain the behavior of the reinforcing listener by pointing to an improvement in the possibility of controlling the speaker whom he reinforces' (56). Perhaps this provides the explanation for the behavior of the parent in inducing the child to walk; the parent is reinforced by the improvement in his control of the child when the child's mobility increases. Underlying these modes of explanation is a curious view that it is somehow more scientific to attribute to a parent a desire to control the child or enhance his own possibilities for action than a desire to see the child develop and extend his capacities. Needless to say, no evidence is offered to support this contention.

Consider now the problem of explaining the response of the listener to a tact. Suppose, for example, that B hears A say *fox* and reacts appropriately, looks around, runs away, aims his rifle, etc. How can we explain B's behavior? Skinner rightly rejects analyses of this offered by Watson and Bertrand Russell. His own equally inadequate analysis proceeds as follows (87-8). We assume (1) 'that in the history of [B] the stimulus *fox* has been an occasion upon which looking around has been followed by seeing a fox' and (2) 'that the listener has some current "interest in seeing foxes"—that behavior which depends upon a seen fox for its execution is strong, and that the stimulus supplied by a fox is therefore reinforcing'. B carries out the appropriate behavior, then, because 'the heard stimulus *fox* is the occasion upon which turning and looking about is frequently followed by the reinforcement of seeing a fox'; i.e. his behavior is a discriminated operant. This explanation is unconvincing. B may never have seen a fox and may have no current interest in seeing one, and yet may react appropriately to the stimulus *fox*.[35] Since exactly the same behavior may take place when neither of the assumptions is fulfilled, some other mechanism must be operative here.

Skinner remarks several times that his analysis of the tact in terms of stimulus control is an improvement over the traditional formulations in terms of reference and meaning. This is simply not true. His analysis is fundamentally the same as the traditional one, though much less carefully phrased. In particular, it differs only by indiscriminate paraphrase of such notions as denotation (reference) and connotation (meaning), which have been kept clearly apart in traditional formulations, in terms of the vague concept 'stimulus control'. In one traditional formulation a descriptive term is said to denote a set of entities and to connote or designate a certain property or condition that an entity must possess or fulfill if the term is to apply to it.[36] Thus the term *vertebrate* refers to (denotes, is true of) vertebrates and connotes the property 'having a spine' or something of the sort. This connoted defining property is called the meaning of the term. Two terms may have the same reference but different meanings. Thus it is apparently true that the creatures with hearts are all and only the vertebrates. If so, then the term *creature with a heart* refers to vertebrates and designates the property 'having a heart'. This is presumably a different property (a different general condition) from having a spine; hence the terms *vertebrate* and *creature with a heart* are said to have different meanings. This analysis is not incorrect (for at least one sense of meaning), but its many limitations have frequently been pointed out.[37] The major problem is that there is no good way to decide whether two descriptive terms designate the same property.[38] As we have just seen, it is not sufficient that they refer to the same objects. *Vertebrate* and *creature with a spine* would be said to designate the same property (distinct from that designated by *creature with a heart*). If we ask why this is so, the only answer appears to be that the terms are synonymous. The notion 'property' thus seems somehow language-bound, and appeal to 'defining properties' sheds little light on questions of meaning and synonymy.

Skinner accepts the traditional account in toto, as can be seen from his definition of a tact as a response under control of a property (stimulus) of some physical object or event. We have found that the notion 'control' has no real substance, and is perhaps best understood as a paraphrase of 'denote' or 'connote' or, ambiguously, both. The only consequence of adopting the new term 'stimulus control' is that the important differences between reference and meaning are obscured. It provides no new objectivity. The stimulus controlling the response is determined by the response itself; there is no independent and objective method of identification (see Section 3 above). Consequently, when Skinner defines 'synonymy' as the case in which 'the same stimulus leads to quite different responses' (118), we can have no objection. The responses *chair* and *red* made alternatively to the same object are not synonymous, because the stimuli are called different. The responses *vertebrate* and *creature with a spine* would be considered synonymous because they are controlled by the same property of the object under investigation; in more traditional and no less scientific terms, they evoke the same concept. Similarly, when metaphorical extension is explained as due to 'the control exercised by properties of the stimulus which, though present at reinforcement, do not enter into the contingency respected by the very community' (92; traditionally, accidental properties), no objection can be raised which has not already been leveled against the traditional account. Just as we could 'explain' the response *Mozart* to a piece of music in terms of subtle properties of the controlling stimuli, we can, with equal facility, explain the appearance of the response *sun* when no sun is present, as in *Juliet is [like] the sun*. 'We do so by noting that Juliet and the sun have common properties, at least in their effect on the speaker' (93). Since any two objects have indefinitely many properties in common, we can be certain that we will never be at a loss to explain a response of the form A *is like* B, for arbitrary A and B. It is clear, however, that Skinner's recurrent claim that his formulation is simpler and more scientific than the traditional account has no basis in fact.

Tacts under the control of private stimuli (Bloomfield's 'displaced speech') form a large and important class (130-46), including not only such responses as *familiar* and *beautiful*, but also verbal responses referring to past, potential, or future events or behavior. For example, the response *There was an elephant at the zoo* 'must be understood as a response to current stimuli, including events within the speaker himself' (143).[39] If we now ask ourselves what proportion of the tacts in actual life are responses to (descriptions of) actual current outside stimulation, we can see just how large a role must be attributed to private stimuli. A minute amount of verbal behavior, outside the nursery, consists of such remarks as *This is red* and *There is a man*. The fact that 'functional analysis' must make such a heavy appeal to obscure internal stimuli is again a measure of its actual advance over traditional formulations.

9. Responses under the control of prior verbal stimuli are considered under a different heading from the tact. An *echoic operant* is a response which 'generates a sound pattern similar to that of the stimulus' (55). It covers only cases of immediate imitation.[40] No attempt is made to define the sense in which a child's echoic response is 'similar' to the stimulus spoken in the father's bass voice; it seems, though there are no clear statements about this, that Skinner would not accept the account of the phonologist in this respect, but nothing else is offered. The development of an echoic repertoire is attributed completely to differential reinforcement. Since the speaker will do no more, according to Skinner, than what is demanded of him by the verbal community, the degree of accuracy insisted on by this community will determine the elements of

the repertoire, whatever these may be (not necessarily phonemes). 'In a verbal community which does not insist on a precise correspondence, an echoic repertoire may remain slack and will be less successfully applied to novel patterns'. There is no discussion of such familiar phenomena as the accuracy with which a child will pick up a second language or a local dialect in the course of playing with other children, which seem sharply in conflict with these assertions. No anthropological evidence is cited to support the claim that an effective phonemic system does not develop (this is the substance of the quoted remark) in communities that do not insist on precise correspondence.

A verbal response to a written stimulus (reading) is called 'textual behavior'. Other verbal responses to verbal stimuli are called 'intraverbal operants'. Paradigm instances are the response *four* to the stimulus *two plus two* or the response *Paris* to the stimulus *capital of France*. Simple conditioning may be sufficient to account for the response *four* to *two plus two*, [41] but the notion of intraverbal response loses all meaning when we find it extended to cover most of the facts of history and many of the facts of science (72, 129); all word association and 'flight of ideas' (73-6); all translations and paraphrase (77); reports of things seen, heard, or remembered (315); and, in general, large segments of scientific, mathematical, and literary discourse. Obviously the kind of explanation that might be proposed for a student's ability to respond with *Paris* to *capital of France*, after suitable practice, can hardly be seriously offered to account for his ability to make a judicious guess in answering the questions (to him new) *What is the seat of the French government*?,... *the source of the literary dialect*?, ...*the chief target of the German blitzkrieg*?, etc., or his ability to prove a new theorem, translate a new passage, or paraphrase a remark for the first time or in a new way.

The process of 'getting someone to see a point', to see something your way, or to understand a complex state of affairs (e.g. a difficult political situation or a mathematical proof) is, for Skinner, simply a matter of increasing the strength of the listener's already available behavior.[42] Since 'the process is often exemplified by relatively intellectual scientific or philosophical discourse', Skinner considers it 'all the more surprising that is may be reduced to echoic, textual, or intraverbal supplementation' (269). Again, it is only the vagueness and latitude with which the notions 'strength' and 'intraverbal response' are used that save this from absurdity. If we use these terms in their literal sense, it is clear that understanding a statement cannot be equated to shouting it frequently in a high-pitched voice (high response strength), and a clever and convincing argument cannot be accounted for on the basis of a history of pairings of verbal responses.[43]

10. A final class of operants, called *autoclitics*, includes those that are involved in assertion, negation, quantification, qualification of responses, construction of sentences, and the 'highly complex manipulations of verbal thinking'. All these acts are to be explained 'in terms of behavior which is evoked by or acts upon other behavior of the speaker' (313). Autoclitics are, then, responses to already given responses, or rather, as we find in reading through this section, they are responses to covert or incipient or potential verbal behavior. Among the autoclitics are listed such expressions as *I recall*, *I imagine*, *for example*, *assume*, *let X equal* ..., the terms of negation, the *is* of predication and assertion, *all*, *some*, *if*, *then*, and, in general, all morphemes other than nouns, verbs, and adjectives, as well as grammatical processes of ordering and arrangement. Hardly a remark in this section can be accepted without serious qualification. To take just one example, consider Skinner's account of the autoclitic *all* in *All swans are white* (329). Obviously we cannot assume that this is a tact to all swans as stimulus. It is suggested, therefore, that we take *all* to be an autoclitic modifying the whole sentence *Swans are white*. *All* can then be taken as equivalent to *always*, or *always it is possible to say*. Notice, however, that the modified sentence *Swans are white* is just as general as *All swans are white*. Furthermore, the proposed translation of *all* is incorrect if taken literally. It is just as possible to say *Swans are green* as to say *Swans are white*. It is not always possible to say either (e.g. while you are saying something else or sleeping). Probably what Skinner means is that the sentence can be paraphrased '*X is white* is true, for each swan X'. But this paraphrase cannot be given within his system, which has no place for *true*.

Skinner's account of grammar and syntax as autoclitic processes (Chapter 13) differs from a familiar traditional account mainly in the use of the pseudoscientific terms 'control' or 'evoke' in place of the traditional 'refer'. Thus in *The boy runs*, the final *s* of *runs* is a tact under control of such 'subtle properties of a situation' as 'the nature of running as an *activity* rather than an object or property of an object'.[44] (Presumably, then, in *The attempt fails*, *The difficulty remains*, *His anxiety increases*, etc., we must also say that the *s* indicates that the object described as the attempt is carrying out the activity of failing, etc.) In *the boy's gun*, however, the *s* denotes possession (as, presumably, in *the boy's arrival*, ... *story*, ... *age*, etc.) and is under the control of this 'relational aspect of the situation' (336). The 'relational autoclitic of order' (whatever it may mean to call the order of a set of responses a response to them) in *The boy runs the store* is under the control of an 'extremely complex stimulus situation', namely, that the boy is running the store (335). *And* in *the hat and the shoe* is under the control of the property 'pair'. *Through* in *the dog went through the hedge* is under the control of the 'relation between the going dog and the hedge' (342). In general, nouns are evoked by objects, verbs by actions, and so on.

Skinner considers a sentence to be a set of key responses (nouns, verbs, adjectives) on a skeletal frame (346). If we are concerned with the fact that Sam rented a leaky boat, the raw responses to the situation are *rent*, *boat*, *leak*, and *Sam*. Autoclitics (including order) which qualify these responses, express relations between them, and the like, are then added by a process called 'composition' and the result is a grammatical sentence, one of many alternatives among which selection is rather arbitrary. The idea that sentences consist of lexical items placed in a grammatical frame is of course a traditional one, within both philosophy and linguistics. Skinner adds to it only the very implausible speculation that in the internal process of composition, the nouns, verbs, and adjectives are chosen first and then are arranged, qualified, etc., by autoclitic responses to these internal activities.[45]

This view of sentence structure, whether phrased in terms of autoclitics, syncategorematic expressions, or grammatical and lexical morphemes, is inadequate. *Sheep provide wool* has no (physical) frame at all, but no other arrangement of these words is an English sentence. The sequences *furiously sleep ideas green colorless* and *friendly young dogs seem harmless* have the same frames, but only one is a sentence of English (similarly, only one of the sequences formed by reading these from back to front). *Struggling artists can be a nuisance* has the same frame as *marking papers can be a nuisance*, but is quite different in sentence structure, as can be seen by replacing *can be* by *is* or *are* in both cases. There are many other similar and equally simple examples. It is evident that more is involved in sentence structure than insertion of lexical items in grammatical frames; no approach to language that fails to take these deeper processes into account can possibly achieve much success in accounting for actual linguistic behavior.

11. The preceding discussion covers all the major notions that Skinner introduces in his descriptive system. My purpose in discussing the concepts one by one was to show that in each case, if we take his terms in their literal meaning, the description covers almost no aspect of verbal behavior, and if we take them metaphorically, the description offers no improvement over various traditional formulations. The terms borrowed from experimental psychology simply lose their objective meaning with this extension, and take over the full vagueness of ordinary language. Since Skinner limits himself to such a small set of terms for paraphrase, many important distinctions are obscured. I think that this analysis supports the view expressed in Section 1 above, that elimination of the independent contribution of the speaker and learner (a result which Skinner considers of great importance, cf. 311-2) can be achieved only at the cost of eliminating all significance from the descriptive system, which then operates at a level so gross and crude that no answers are suggested to the most elementary questions.[46] The questions to which Skinner has addressed his speculations are hopelessly premature. It is futile to inquire into the causation of verbal behavior until much more is known about the specific character of this behavior; and there is little point in speculating about the process of acquisition without much better understanding of what is acquired.

Anyone who seriously approaches the study of linguistic behavior, whether linguist, psychologist, or philosopher, must quickly become aware of the enormous difficulty of stating a problem which will define the area of his investigations, and which will not be either completely trivial or hopelessly beyond the range of present-day understanding and technique. In selecting functional analysis as his problem, Skinner has set himself a task of the latter type. In an extremely interesting and insightful paper,[47] K. S. Lashley has implicitly delimited a class of problems which can be approached in a fruitful way by the linguist and psychologist, and which are clearly preliminary to those with which Skinner is concerned. Lashley recognizes, as anyone must who seriously considers the data, that the composition and production of an utterance is not simply a matter of stringing together a sequence of responses under the control of outside stimulation and intraverbal association, and that the syntactic organization of an utterance is not something directly represented in any simple way in the physical structure of the utterance itself. A variety of observations lead him to conclude that syntactic structure is 'a generalized pattern imposed on the specific acts as they occur', and that 'a consideration of the structure of the sentence and other motor sequences will show ... that there are, behind the overtly expressed sequences, a multiplicity of integrative processes which can only be inferred from the final results of their activity'. He also comments on the great difficulty of determining the 'selective mechanisms' used in the actual construction of a particular utterance.

Although present-day linguistics cannot provide a precise account of these integrative processes, imposed patterns, and selective mechanisms, it can at least set itself the problem of characterizing these completely. It is reasonable to regard the grammar of a language L ideally as a mechanism that provides an enumeration of the sentences of L in something like the way in which a deductive theory gives an enumeration of a set of theorems. ('Grammar', in this sense of the word, includes phonology.) Furthermore, the theory of language can be regarded as a study of the formal properties of such grammars, and, with a precise enough formulation, this general theory can provide a uniform method for determining, from the process of generation of a given sentence, a structural description which can give a good deal of insight into how this sentence is used and understood. In short, it should be possible to derive from a properly formulated grammar a statement of the integrative processes and generalized patterns imposed on the specific acts that constitute an utterance. The rules of a grammar of the appropriate form can be subdivided into the two types, optional and obligatory; only the latter must be applied in generating an utterance. The optional rules of the grammar can be viewed, then, as the selective mechanisms involved in the production of a particular utterance. The problem of specifying these integrative processes and selective mechanisms is nontrivial and not beyond the range of possible investigation. The results of such a study might, as Lashley suggests, be of independent interest for psychology and neurology (and conversely). Although such a study, even if successful, would by no means answer the major problems involved in the investigation of meaning and the causation of behavior, it surely will not be unrelated to these. It is at least possible, furthermore, that such notions as 'semantic generalization', to which such heavy appeal is made in all approaches to language in use, conceal complexities and specific structure of inference not far different from those that can be studied and exhibited in the case of syntax, and that consequently the general character of the results of syntactic investigations may be a corrective to oversimplified approaches to the theory of meaning.

The behavior of the speaker, listener, and learner of language constitutes, of course, the actual data for any study of language. The construction of a grammar which enumerates sentences in such a way that a meaningful structural description can be determined for each sentence does not in itself provide an account of this actual behavior. It merely characterizes abstractly the ability of one who has mastered the language to distinguish sentences from nonsentences, to understand new sentences (in part), to note certain ambiguities, etc. These are very remarkable abilities. We constantly read and hear new sequences of words, recognize them as sentences, and understand them. It is easy to show that the new events that we accept and understand as sentences are not related to those with which we are familiar by any simple notion of formal (or semantic or statistical) similarity or identity of grammatical frame. Talk of generalization in this case is entirely pointless and empty. It appears that we recognize a new item as a sentence not because it matches some familiar item in any simple way, but because it is generated by the grammar that each individual has somehow and in some form internalized. And we understand a new sentence, in part, because we are somehow capable of determining the process by which this sentence is derived in this grammar.

Suppose that we manage to construct grammars having the properties outlined above. We can then attempt to describe and study the achievement of the speaker, listener, and learner. The speaker and the listener, we must assume, have already acquired the capacities characterized abstractly by the grammar. The speaker's task is to select a particular compatible set of optional rules. If we know, from grammatical study, what choices are available to him and what conditions of compatibility the choices must meet, we can proceed meaningfully to investigate the factors that lead him to make one or another choice. The listener (or reader) must determine, from an exhibited utterance, what optional rules were chosen in the construction of the utterance. It must be admitted that the ability of a human being to do this far surpasses our present understanding. The child who learns a language has in some sense constructed the grammar for himself on the basis of his observation of sentences and nonsentences (i.e. corrections by the verbal community). Study of the actual observed ability of a speaker to distinguish sentences from nonsentences, detect ambiguities, etc., apparently forces us to the conclusion that this grammar is of an extremely complex and abstract character, and that the young child has succeeded in carrying out what from the formal point of view, at least, seems to be a remarkable type of theory construction. Furthermore, this task is accomplished in an astonishingly short time, to a large extent independently of intelligence, and in a comparable way by all children. Any theory of learning must cope with these facts.

It is not easy to accept the view that a child is capable of constructing an extremely complex mechanism for generating a set of sentences, some of which he has heard, or that an adult can instantaneously determine whether (and if so, how) a particular item is generated by this mechanism, which has many of the properties of an abstract deductive theory. Yet this appears to be a fair description of the performance of the speaker, listener, and learner. If this is correct, we can predict that a direct attempt to account for the actual behavior of speaker, listener, and learner, not based on a prior understanding of the structure of grammars, will achieve very limited success. The grammar must be regarded as a component in the behavior of the speaker and listener which can only be inferred, as Lashley has put it, from the resulting physical acts. The fact that all normal children acquire essentially comparable grammars of great complexity with remarkable rapidity suggests that human beings are somehow specially designed to do this, with data-handling or 'hypothesis-formulating' ability of unknown character and complexity.[48] The study of linguistic structure may ultimately lead to some significant insights into this matter. At the moment the question cannot be seriously posed, but in principle it may be possible to study the problem of determining what the built-in structure of an information-processing (hypothesis-forming) system must be to enable it to arrive at the grammar of a language from the available data in the available time. At any rate, just as the attempt to eliminate the contribution of the speaker leads to a 'mentalistic' descriptive system that succeeds only in blurring important traditional distinctions, a refusal to study the contribution of the child to language learning permits only a superficial account of language acquisition, with a vast and unanalyzed contribution attributed to a step called 'generalization' which in fact includes just about everything of interest in this process. If the study of language is limited in these ways, it seems inevitable that major aspects of verbal behavior will remain a mystery.

Footnotes

[1]Skinner's confidence in recent achievements in the study of animal behavior and their applicability to complex human behavior does not appear to be widely shared. In many recent publications of confirmed behaviorists there is a prevailing note of skepticism with regard to the scope of these achievements. For representative comments, see the contributions to *Modern learning theory* (by Estes et al.; New York, 1954); Burgelski, *Psychology of learning* (New York, 1956); Koch, in *Nebraska symposium on motivation* 58 (Lincoln, 1956); Verplanck, Learned and innate behavior, *Psych. rev*. 52.139 (1955). Perhaps the strongest view is that of Harlow, who has asserted (Mice, monkeys, men, and motives, *Psych. rev*. 60.23-32 [1953]) that 'a strong case can be made for the proposition that the importance of the psychological problems studied during the last 15 years has decreased as a negatively accelerated function approaching an asymptote of complete indifference.' Tinbergen, a leading representative of a different approach to animal behavior studies (comparative ethology), concludes a discussion of 'functional analysis' with the comment that 'we may now draw the conclusion that the causation of behavior is immensely more complex than was assumed in the generalizations of the past. A number of internal and external factors act upon complex central nervous structures. Second, it will be obvious that the facts at our disposal are very fragmentary indeed'—*The study of instinct* 74 (Oxford, 1951).

[2]In *Behavior of organisms* (New York, 1938), Skinner remarks that 'although a conditioned operant is the result of the correlation of the response with a particular reinforcement, a relation between it and a discriminative stimulus acting prior to the response is the almost universal rule' (178-9). Even emitted behavior is held to be produced by some sort of 'originating force' (51) which, in the case of operant behavior is not under experimental control. The distinction between eliciting stimuli, discriminated stimuli, and 'originating forces' has never been adequately clarified, and becomes even more confusing when private internal events are considered to be discriminated stimuli (see below).

[3]In a famous experiment, chimpanzees were taught to perform complex tasks to receive tokens which had become secondary reinforcers because of association with food. The idea that money, approval, prestige, etc. actually acquire their motivating effects on human behavior according to this paradigm is unproved, and not particularly plausible. Many psychologists within the behaviorist movement are quite skeptical about this (cf. fn. 23). As in the case of most aspects of human behavior, the evidence about secondary reinforcement is so fragmentary, conflicting, and complex that almost any view can find some support.

[4]Skinner's remark quoted above about the generality of his basic results must be understood in the light of the experimental limitations he has imposed. If it were true in any deep sense that the basic processes in language are well understood and free of species restrictions, it would be

extremely odd that language is limited to man. With the exception of a few scattered observations (cf. his article, A case history in scientific method, *The American psychologist* 11.221-33 [1956]), Skinner is apparently basing this claim on the fact that qualitatively similar results are obtained with bar-pressing of rats and pecking of pigeons under special conditions of deprivation and various schedules of reinforcement. One immediately questions how much can be based on these facts, which are in part at least an artifact traceable to experimental design and the definition of 'stimulus' and 'response' in terms of 'smooth dynamic curves' (see below). The dangers inherent in any attempt to 'extrapolate' to complex behavior from the study of such simple responses as bar-pressing should be obvious, and have often been commented on (cf. e.g. Harlow, op.cit.). The generality of even the simplest results is open to serious question. Cf. in this connection Bitterman, Wodinsky, and Candland, Some comparative psychology, *Am. jour. of psych.* 71.94-110 (1958), where it is shown that there are important qualitative differences in solution of comparable elementary problems by rats and fish.

[5]An analogous argument, in connection with a different aspect of Skinner's thinking, is given by Scriven in *A study of radical behaviorism = Univ. of Minn. studies in philosophy of science*, Vol. 1. Cf. Verplanck's contribution to *Modern learning theory* (283-8) for more general discussion of the difficulties in formulating an adequate definition of 'stimulus' and 'response'. He concludes, quite correctly, that in Skinner's sense of the word, stimuli are not objectively identifiable independently of the resulting behavior, nor are they manipulable. Verplanck presents a clear discussion of many other aspects of Skinner's system, commenting on the untestability of many of the so-called 'laws of behavior' and the limited scope of many of the others, and the arbitrary and obscure character of Skinner's notion of 'lawful relation'; and, at the same time, noting the importance of the experimental data that Skinner has accumulated.

[6]*In Behavior of organisms*, Skinner apparently was willing to accept this consequence. He insists (41-2) that the terms of casual description in the popular vocabulary are not validly descriptive until the defining properties of stimulus and response are specified, the correlation is demonstrated experimentally, and the dynamic changes in it are shown to be lawful. Thus, in describing a child as hiding from a dog, 'it will not be enough to dignify the popular vocabulary by appealing to essential properties of "dogness" or "hidingness" and to suppose them intuitively known.' But this is exactly what Skinner does in the book under review, as we will see directly.

[7]253 f. and elsewhere, repeatedly. As an example of how well we can control behavior using the notions developed in this book, Skinner shows here how he would go about evoking the response *pencil*. The most effective way, he suggests, is to say to the subject 'Please say *pencil'* (our chances would, presumably, be even further improved by use of 'aversive stimulation', e.g. holding a gun to his head). We can also 'make sure that no pencil or writing instrument is available, then hand our subject a pad of paper appropriate to pencil sketching, and offer him a handsome reward for a recognizable picture of a cat.' It would also be useful to have voices saying *pencil* or *pen and* … in the background; signs reading *pencil* or *pen and* …; or to place a 'large and unusual pencil in an unusual place clearly in sight'. 'Under such circumstances, it is highly probable that our subject will say *pencil.*' 'The available techniques are all illustrated in this sample.' These contributions of behavior theory to the practical control of human behavior are amply illustrated elsewhere in the book, as when Skinner shows (113-4) how we can evoke the response *red* (the device suggested is to hold a red object before the subject and say 'Tell me what color this is').

In fairness, it must be mentioned that there are certain nontrivial applications of 'operant conditioning' to the control of human behavior. A wide variety of experiments have shown that the number of plural nouns (for example) produced by a subject will increase if the experimenter says 'right' or 'good' when one is produced (similarly, positive attitudes on a certain issue, stories with particular content, etc.; cf. Krasner, Studies of the conditioning of verbal behavior, *Psych. bull.*, Vol. 55 [1958], for a survey of several dozen experiments of this kind, mostly with positive results). It is of some interest that the subject is usually unaware of the process. Just what insight this gives into normal verbal behavior is not obvious. Nevertheless, it is an example of positive and not totally expected results using the Skinnerian paradigm.

[8]Are theories of learning necessary?, *Psych. rev.* 57.193-216 (1950).

[9]And elsewhere. In his paper Are theories of learning necessary?, Skinner considers the problem how to extend his analysis of behavior to experimental situations in which it is impossible to observe frequencies, rate of response being the only valid datum. His answer is that 'the notion of probability is usually extrapolated to cases in which a frequency analysis cannot be carried out. In the field of behavior we arrange a situation in which frequencies are available as data, but we use the notion of probability in analyzing or formulating instances of even types of behavior which are not susceptible to this analysis' (199). This are, of course, conceptions of probability not based directly on frequency, but I do not see how any of these apply to the cases that Skinner has in mind. I see no way of interpreting the quoted passage other than as signifying an intention to use the word 'probability' in describing behavior quite independently of whether the notion of probability is at all relevant.

[10]Fortunately, 'In English this presents no great difficulty' since, for example, 'relative pitch levels … are not … important' (25). No reference is made to the numerous studies of the function of relative pitch levels and other intonational features in English.

[11]The vagueness of the word 'tendency', as opposed to 'frequency', saves the latter quotation from the obvious incorrectness of the former. Nevertheless, a good deal of stretching is necessary. If 'tendency' has anything like its ordinary meaning, the remark is clearly false. One may believe strongly the assertion that Jupiter has four moons, that many of Sophocles' plays have been irretrievably lost, that the earth will burn to a crisp in ten million years, etc., without experiencing the slightest tendency to act upon these verbal stimuli. We may, of course, turn Skinner's assertion into a very unilluminating truth by defining 'tendency to act' to include tendencies to answer questions in certain ways, under motivation to say what one believes is true.

[12]One should add, however, that it is in general not the stimulus as such that is reinforcing, but the stimulus in a particular situational context. Depending on experimental arrangement, a particular physical event or object may be reinforcing, punishing, or unnoticed. Because Skinner limits himself to a particular, very simple experimental arrangement, it is not necessary for him to add this qualification, which would not be at all easy to formulate precisely. But it is of course necessary if he expects to extend his descriptive system to behavior in general.

[13]This has been frequently noted.

[14]See, for example, Are theories of learning necessary? 199. Elsewhere, he suggests that the term 'learning' be restricted to complex situations, but these are not characterized.

[15]'A child acquires verbal behavior when relatively unpatterned vocalizations, selectively reinforced, gradually assume forms which produce appropriate consequences in a given verbal community' (31). 'Differential reinforcement shapes up all verbal forms, and when a prior stimulus enters into the contingency, reinforcement is responsible for its resulting control … The availability of behavior, its probability or strength, depends on whether reinforcements *continue* in effect and according to what schedules' (203-4). Elsewhere, frequently.

[16]Talk of schedules of reinforcement here is entirely pointless. How are we to decide for example, according to what schedules covert reinforcement is 'arranged', as in thinking or verbal fantasy, or what the scheduling is of such factors as silence, speech, and appropriate future reactions to communicated information?

[17]See, for example, Miller and Dollard, *Social learning and imitation* 82-3 (New York, 1941), for a discussion of the 'meticulous training' that they seem to consider necessary for a child to learn the meanings of words and syntactic patterns. The same notion is implicit in Mowrer's speculative account of how language might be acquired, in *Learning theory and personality dynamics*, Chapter 23 (New York, 1950). Actually, the view appears to be quite general.

[18]For a general review and analysis of this literature, see Thistlethwaite, A critical review of latent learning and related experiments, *Psych. bull.* 48.97-129 (1951). MacCorquodale and Meehl, in their contribution to *Modern learning theory*, carry out a serious and considered attempt to handle the latent learning material from the standpoint of drive-reduction theory, with (as they point out) not entirely satisfactory results. Thorpe reviews the literature from the standpoint of the ethologist, adding also material on homing and topographical orientation (*Learning and instinct in animals* [Cambridge, 1956]).

[19]*Theories of learning* 214 (1956).

[20]Berlyn, Novelty and curiosity as determinants of exploratory behavior, *Brit. jour. of psych.* 41.68-80 (1950); id., Perceptual curiosity in the rat, *Jour. of comp. physiol. psych.* 48.238-46 (1955); Thompson and Solomon, Spontaneous pattern discrimination in the rat, ibid. 47.104-7 (1954).

[21]Montgomery, The role of the exploratory drive in learning, ibid. 60-3. Many other papers in the same journal are designed to show that exploratory behavior is a relatively independent primary 'drive' aroused by novel external stimulation.

[22]Butler, Discrimination learning by Rhesus monkeys to visual-exploration motivation, ibid. 46.95-8 (1953). Later experiments showed that this 'drive' is highly persistent, as opposed to derived drives which rapidly extinguish.

[23]Harlow, Harlow, and Meyer, Learning motivated by a manipulation drive, *Journ. exp. psych.* 40.228-34 (1950), and later investigations initiated by Harlow. Harlow has been particularly insistent on maintaining the inadequacy of physiologically based drives and homeostatic need states for explaining the persistence of motivation and rapidity of learning in primates. He points out, in many papers, that curiosity, play, exploration, and manipulations are, for primates, often more potent drives than hunger and the like, and that they show none of the characteristics of acquired drives. Hebb also presents behavioral and supporting neurological evidence in support of the view that in higher animals there is a positive attraction in work, risk, puzzle, intellectual activity, mild fear and frustration, etc. (Drives and the CNS, *Psych. rev.* 62.243-54 [1955]). He concludes that 'we need not work out tortuous and improbably ways to explain why men work for money, why children learn without pain, why people dislike doing nothing.'

In a brief note (Early recognition of the manipulative drive in monkeys, *British journal of animal behavior* 3.71-2 [1955]), W. Dennis calls attention to the fact that early investigators (Romanes, 1882; Thorndike, 1901), whose 'perception was relatively unaffected by learning theory, did note the intrinsically motivated behavior of monkeys', although, he asserts, no similar observations on monkeys have been made until Harlow's experiments. He quotes Romanes (*Animal intelligence* [1882]) as saying that 'much the most striking feature in the psychology of this animal, and the one which is least like anything met with in other animals, was the tireless spirit of investigation.' Analogous developments, in which genuine discoveries have blinded systematic investigators to the important insights of earlier work, are easily found within recent structural linguistics as well.

[24]Thus J. S. Brown, in commenting on a paper of Harlow's in *Current theory and research in motivation* (Lincoln, 1953), argues that 'in probably every instance [of the experiments cited by Harlow] an ingenious drive-reduction theorist could find some fragment of fear, insecurity, frustration, or whatever, that he could insist was reduced and hence was reinforcing' (53). The same sort of thing could be said for the ingenious phlogiston or ether theorist.

[25]Cf. Birch and Bitterman, Reinforcement and learning: The process of sensory integration, *Psych. rev.* 56.292-308 (1949).

[26]See, for example, his paper A physiological study of reward in McClelland (ed.), *Studies in motivation* 134-43 (New York, 1955).

[27]See Thorpe, op.cit., particularly 115-8 and 337-76, for an excellent discussion of this phenomenon, which has been brought to prominence particularly by the work of K. Lorenz (cf. Der Kumpan in der Umwelt des Vogels, parts of which are reprinted in English translation in Schiller (ed.), *Instinctive behavior* 83-128 (New York, 1957).

[28]Op.cit. 372.

[29]See e.g. Jaynes, Imprinting: Interaction of learned and innate behavior, *Jour. of comp. physiol. psych.* 49.201-6 (1956), where the conclusion is reached that 'the experiments prove that without any observable reward young birds of this species follow a moving stimulus object and very rapidly come to prefer that object to others.'

[30]Of course it is perfectly possible to incorporate this fact within the Skinnerian frame work. If, for example, a child watches an adult using a comb and then, with no instruction tries to comb his own hair, we can explain this act by saying that he performs it because he finds it reinforcing to do so, or because of the reinforcement provided by behaving like a person who is 'reinforcing' (cf. 164). Similarly, an automatic explanation is available for any other behavior. It seems strange at first that Skinner pays so little attention to the literature on latent learning and related topics, considering the tremendous reliance that he places on the notion of reinforcement; I have seen no reference to it in his writings. Similarly, Keller and Schoenfeld, in what appears to be the only text written under predominantly Skinnerian influence, *Principles of psychology* (New York, 1950), dismiss the latent-learning literature in one sentence as 'beside the point', serving only 'to obscure, rather than clarify, a fundamental principle' (the law of effect, 41). However, this neglect is perfectly appropriate in Skinner's case. To the drive-reductionist, or anyone else whom the notion 'reinforcement' has some substantive meaning, these experiments and observations are important (and often embarrassing). But in the Skinnerian sense of the word, neither these results nor any conceivable others can cast any doubt on the claim that reinforcement is essential for the acquisition and maintenance of behavior. Behavior certainly has some concomitant circumstances, and whatever they are, we can call them 'reinforcement'.

[31]Tinbergen (op. cit., Chapter VI) reviews some aspects of this problem, discussing the primary role of maturation in the development of many complex motor patterns (e.g. flying, swimming) in lower organisms, and the effect of an 'innate disposition to learn' in certain specific ways and at certain specific times. Cf. also Schiller, *Instinctive behavior* 265-88, for a discussion of the role of maturing motor patterns in apparently insightful behavior in the chimpanzee.

Lenneberg (*Language, evolution, and purposive behavior*, unpublished) presents a very interesting discussion of the part that biological structure may play in the acquisition of language, and the dangers in neglecting this possibility.

[32]From among many cited by Tinbergen, op.cit. (this on page 85).

[33]Cf. Lashley, In search of the engram, *Symposium of the Society for Experimental Biology* 4.454-82 (1950). Sperry, On the neural basis of the conditioned response, *British journal of animal behaviour* 3.41-4 (1955), argues that to account for the experimental results of Lashley and others, and for other facts that he cites, it is necessary to assume that high-level cerebral activity of the type of insight, expectancy, etc. is involved even in simple conditioning. He states that 'we still lack today a satisfactory picture of the underlying neural mechanism' of the conditioned response.

[34]Furthermore, the motivation of the speaker does not, except in the simplest cases, correspond in intensity to the duration of deprivation. An obvious counter-example is what Hebb has called the 'salted-nut phenomenon' (*Organization of behavior* 199 [New York, 1949]). The difficulty is of course even more serious when we consider 'deprivations' not related to physiological drives.

[35]Just as he may have the appropriate reaction, both emotional and behavioral, to such utterances as *The volcano is erupting* or *There's a homicidal maniac in the next room* without any previous pairing of the verbal and the physical stimulus. Skinner's discussion of Pavlovian conditioning in language (154) is similarly unconvincing.

[36]Mill, *A system of logic* (1843). Carnap gives a recent reformulation in Meaning and synonymy in natural languages, *Phil. studies* 6.33-47 (1955), defining the meaning (intension) of a predicate 'Q' for a speaker X as 'the general condition which an object y must fulfill in order for X to be willing to ascribe the predicate "Q" to y'. The connotation of an expression is often said to constitute its 'cognitive meaning' as opposed to its 'emotive meaning', which is, essentially, the emotional reaction to the expression.

Whether or not this is the best way to approach meaning, it is clear that denotation, cognitive meaning, and emotive meaning are quite different things. The differences are often obscured in empirical studies of meaning, with much consequent confusion. Thus Osgood has set himself the task of accounting for the fact that a stimulus comes to be a sign for another stimulus (a buzzer becomes a sign for food, a word for a thing, etc.). This is clearly (for linguistic signs) a problem of denotation. The method that he actually develops for quantifying and measuring meaning (cg. Osgood, Suci, Tannenbaum, *The measurement of meaning* [Urbana, 1957]) applies, however, only to emotive meaning. Suppose, for example, that A hates both Hitler and science intensely, and considers both highly potent and 'active', while B, agreeing with A about Hitler, likes science very much, although he considers it rather ineffective and not too important. Then A may assign to 'Hitler' and 'science' the same position on the semantic differential, while B will assign 'Hitler' the same position as A did, but 'science' a totally different position. Yet A does not think that 'Hitler' and 'science' are synonymous or that they have the same reference, and A and B may agree precisely on the cognitive meaning of 'science'. Clearly it is the attitude toward the things (the emotive meaning of the words) that is being measured here. There is a gradual shift in Osgood's account from denotation to cognitive meaning to emotive meaning. The confusion is caused, no doubt, by the fact that the term 'meaning' is used in all three senses (and others). [See Carroll's review of the book by Osgood, Suci, and Tannenbaum in this number of LANGUAGE.]

[37]Most clearly by Quine. See *From a logical point of view* (Cambridge, 1953), especially Chapters 2, 3, and 7.

[38]A method for characterizing synonymy in terms of reference is suggested by Goodman, On likeness of meaning, *Analysis* 10.1-7 (1949). Difficulties are discussed by Goodman, On some differences about meaning, ibid. 13.90-6 (1953). Carnap (op.cit.) presents a very similar idea (section 6), but somewhat misleadingly phrased, since he does not bring out the fact that only extensional (referential) notions are being used.

[39]In general, the examples discussed here are badly handled, and the success of the proposed analyses is overstated. In each case, it is easy to see that the proposed analysis, which usually has an air of objectivity, is not equivalent to the analyzed expression. To take just one example, the response *I am looking for my glasses* is certainly not equivalent to the proposed paraphrases: 'When I have behaved in this way in the past, I have found my glasses and have them stopped behaving in this way', or 'Circumstances have arisen in which I am inclined to emit any behavior which in the past has led to the discovery of my glasses; such behavior includes the behavior of looking in which I am now engaged.' One may look for one's glasses for the first time; or one may emit the same behavior in looking for one's glasses as in looking for one's watch, in which case *I am looking for my glasses* and *I am looking for my watch* are equivalent, under the Skinnerian paraphrase. The difficult questions of purposiveness cannot be handled in this superficial manner.

[40]Skinner takes great pains, however, to deny the existence in human beings (or parrots) of any innate faculty or tendency to imitate. His only argument is that no one would suggest an innate tendency to read, yet reading and echoic behavior have similar 'dynamic properties'. This similarity, however, simply indicates the grossness of his descriptive categories.

In the case of parrots, Skinner claims that they have no instinctive capacity to imitate, but only to be reinforced by successful imitation (59). Given Skinner's use of the word 'reinforcement', it is difficult to perceive any distinction here, since exactly the same thing could be said of any other instinctive behavior. For example, where another scientist would say that a certain bird instinctively builds a nest in a certain way, we could say in Skinner's terminology (equivalently) that the bird is instinctively reinforced by building the nest in this way. One is therefore inclined to dismiss this claim as another ritual introduction of the word 'reinforce'. Though there may, under some suitable clarification, be some truth in it, it is difficult to see how many of the cases reported by competent observers can be handled if 'reinforcement' is given some substantive meaning. Cf. Thorpe, op. cit. 353 f.; Lorenz, *King Solomon's ring* 85-8 (New York, 1952); even Mowrer, who tries to show how imitation might develop through secondary reinforcement, cites a case, op. cit. 694, which he apparently believes, but where this could hardly be true. In young children, it seems most implausible to explain imitation in terms of secondary reinforcement.

[41]Though even this possibility is limited. If we were to take these paradigm instances seriously, it should follow that a child who knows how to count from one to 100 could learn an arbitrary 10 X 10 matrix with these numbers as entries as readily as the multiplication table.

[42]Similarly, 'the universality of a literary work refers to the number of potential readers inclined to say the same thing' (275; i.e. the most 'universal' work is a dictionary of clichés and greetings); a speaker is 'stimulating' if he says what we are about to say ourselves (272); etc.

[43]Similarly, consider Skinner's contention (362-5) that communication of knowledge or facts is just the process of making a new response available to the speaker. Here the analogy to animal experiments is particularly weak. When we train a rat to carry out some peculiar act, it makes sense to consider this a matter of adding a response to his repertoire. In the case of human communication, however, it is very difficult to attach any meaning to this terminology. If A imparts to B the information (new to B) that the railroads face collapse, in what sense can the response *The railroads face collapse* be said to be now, but not previously, available to B? Surely B could have said it before (not knowing whether it was true), and known that it was a sentence (as opposed to *Collapse face railroads the*). Nor is there any reason to assume that the response has increased in strength, whatever this means exactly (e.g. B may have no interest in the fact, or he may want it suppressed). It is not clear how we can characterize this notion of 'making a response available' without reducing Skinner's account of 'imparting knowledge' to a triviality.

[44]On the next page, however, the *s* in the same example indicates that 'the object described as *the boy* possesses the property of running.' The difficulty of even maintaining consistency with a conceptual scheme like this is easy to appreciate.

[45]One might just as well argue that exactly the opposite is true. The study of hesitation pauses has shown that these tend to occur before the large categories—noun, verb, adjective; this finding is usually described by the statement that the pauses occur where there is maximum uncertainty or information. Insofar as hesitation indicates on-going composition (if it does at all), it would appear that the 'key responses' are chosen only after the 'grammatical frame'. Cf. C. E. Osgood, unpublished paper; Goldman-Eisler, Speech analysis and mental processes, *Language and speech* 1.67 (1958).

[46]E.g. what are in fact the actual units of verbal behavior? Under what conditions will a physical event capture the attention (be a stimulus) or be a reinforcer? How do we decide what stimuli are in 'control' in a specific case? When are stimuli 'similar'? And so on. (It is not interesting to be told e.g. that we say *Stop* to an automobile or billiard ball because they are sufficiently similar to reinforcing people [46].)

The use of unanalyzed notions like 'similar' and 'generalization' is particularly disturbing, since it indicates an apparent lack of interest in every significant aspect of the learning or the use of language in new situations. No one has ever doubted that in some sense, language is learned by generalization, or that novel utterances and situations are in some way similar to familiar ones. The only matter of serious interest is the specific 'similarity'. Skinner has, apparently, no interest in this. Keller and Schoenfeld (op. cit.) proceed to incorporate these notions (which they identify) into their Skinnerian 'modern objective psychology' by defining two stimuli to be similar when 'we make the same sort of *response* to them' (124; but when are responses of the 'same sort'?). They do not seem to notice that this definition converts their 'principle of generalization' (116), under any reasonable interpretation of this, into a tautology. It is obvious that such a definition will not be of much help in the study of language learning or construction of new responses in appropriate situations.

[47]The problem of serial order in behavior, in Jeffress (ed.), *Hixon symposium on cerebral mechanisms in behavior* (New York, 1951).

[48]There is nothing essentially mysterious about this. Complex innate behavior patterns and innate 'tendencies to learn in specific ways' have been carefully studied in lower organisms. Many psychologists have been inclined to believe that such biological structure will not have an important effect on acquisition of complex behavior in higher organisms, but I have not been able to find any serious justification for this attitude. Some recent studies have stressed the necessity for carefully analyzing the strategies available to the organism, regarded as a complex 'information-processing system' (cf. Bruner, Goodnow, and Austin, *A study of thinking* [New York, 1956]; Newell, Shaw, and Simon, Elements of a theory of human problem solving, *Psych. rev.* 65.151-66 [1958]), if anything significant is to be said about the character of human learning. These may be largely innate, or developed by early learning processes about which very little is yet known. (But see Harlow, The formation of learning sets, *Psych. rev.* 56.51-65 (1949), and many later papers, where striking shifts in the character of learning are shown as a result of early training; also Hebb, *Organization of behavior* 109 ff.) They are undoubtedly quite complex. Cf. Lenneberg, op. cit., and Lees, review of Chomsky's *Syntactic structures* in *Lg.* 33.406f. (1957), for discussion of the topics mentioned in this section.

THE MISBEHAVIOR OF ORGANISMS

Keller Breland and Marian Breland . *American Psychologist, 16,* 681-684.

This article significantly altered the basic assumptions behaviorists held concerning operant conditioning in animals. Breland and Breland exposed a phenomenon they named instinctive drift, which demonstrates the impact an organism's biology has on learned behaviors. Predicting species behavior can only be obtained through knowing and fully understanding the very organism being studied. Without this foundational comprehension of the organism's inheritance researchers often inappropriately use the principles of operant conditioning. At the time the article was published it was given scant attention or even scoffed at as an, "animal tricks" article rather than a laboratory experiment; however the veracity of phenomena the Brelands identified has stood the test of time.

There seems to be a continuing realization by psychologists that perhaps the white rat cannot reveal everything there is to know about behavior. Among the voices raised on this topic, Beach (1950) has emphasized the necessity of widening the range of species subjected to experimental techniques and conditions. However, psychologists as a whole do not seem to be heeding these admonitions, as Whalen (1961) has pointed out.

Perhaps this reluctance is due in part to some dark precognition of what they might find in such investigations, for the ethologists Lorenz (1950, p. 233) and Tinbergen (1951, p. 6) have warned that if psychologists are to understand and predict the behavior of organisms, it is essential that they become thoroughly familiar with the instinctive behavior patterns of each new species they essay to study. Of course, the Watsonian or neobehavioristically oriented experimenter is apt to consider "instinct" an ugly word. He tends to class it with Hebb's (1960) other "seditious notions" which were discarded in the behavioristic revolution, and he may have some premonition that he will encounter this bete noir in extending the range of species and situations studied.

We can assure him that his apprehensions are well grounded. In our attempt to extend a behavioristically oriented approach to the engineering control of animal behavior by operant conditioning techniques, we have fought a running battle with the seditious notion of instinct. It might be of some interest to the psychologist to know how the battle is going and to learn something about the nature of the adversary he is likely to meet if and when he tackles new species in new learning situations.

Our first report (Breland & Breland, 1951) in the *American Psychologist*, concerning our experiences in controlling animal behavior, was wholly affirmative and optimistic, saying in essence that the principles derived from the laboratory could be applied to the extensive control of behavior under nonlaboratory conditions throughout a considerable segment of the phylogenetic scale.

When we began this work, it was our aim to see if the science would work beyond the laboratory, to determine if animal psychology could stand on its own feet as an engineering discipline. These aims have been realized. We have controlled a wide range of animal behavior and have made use of the great popular appeal of animals to make it an economically feasible project. Conditioned behavior has been exhibited at various municipal zoos and museums of natural history and has been used for department store displays, for fair and trade convention exhibits, for entertainment at tourist attractions, on television shows, and in the production of television commercials. Thirty-eight species, totaling over 6,000 individual animals, have been conditioned, and we have dared to tackle such unlikely subjects as reindeer, cockatoos, raccoons, porpoises, and whales.

Emboldened by this consistent reinforcement, we have ventured further and further from the security of the Skinner box. However, in this cavalier extrapolation, we have run afoul of a persistent pattern of discomforting failures. These failures, although disconcertingly frequent and seemingly diverse, fall into a very interesting pattern. They all represent breakdowns of conditioned operant behavior. From a great number of such experiences, we have selected, more or less at random, the following examples.

The first instance of our discomfiture might be entitled, What Makes Sammy Dance? In the exhibit in which this occurred, the casual observer sees a grown bantam chicken emerge from a retaining compartment when the door automatically opens. The chicken walks over about 3 feet, pulls a rubber loop on a small box which starts a repeated auditory stimulus pattern (a four-note tune). The chicken then steps up onto an 18-inch, slightly raised disc, thereby closing a timer switch, and scratches vigorously, round and round, over the disc for 15 seconds, at the rate of about two scratches per second until the automatic feeder fires in the retaining compartment. The chicken goes into the compartment to eat, thereby automatically shutting the door. The popular interpretation of this behavior pattern is that the chicken has turned on the "juke box" and "dances."

The development of this behavioral exhibit was wholly unplanned. In the attempt to create quite another type of demonstration which required a chicken simply to stand on a platform for 12-15 seconds, we found that over 50% developed a very strong and pronounced scratch pattern, which tended to increase in persistence as the time interval was lengthened. (Another 25% or so developed other behaviors—pecking at spots, etc.) However, we were able to change our plans so as to make use of the scratch pattern, and the result was the "dancing chicken" exhibit described above.

In this exhibit the only real contingency for reinforcement is that the chicken must depress the platform for 15 seconds. In the course of a performing day (about 3 hours for each chicken) a chicken may turn out over 10,000 unnecessary, virtually identical responses. Operant behaviorists would probably have little hesitancy in labeling this an example of Skinnerian "superstition" (Skinner, 1948) or "mediating" behavior, and we list it first to whet their explanatory appetite.

However, a second instance involving a raccoon does not fit so neatly into this paradigm. The response concerned the manipulation of money by the raccoon (who has "hands" rather similar to those of the primates). The contingency for reinforcement was picking up the coins and depositing them in a 5-inch metal box.

Raccoons condition readily, have good appetites, and this one was quite tame and an eager subject. We anticipated no trouble. Conditioning him to pick up the first coin was simple. We started out by reinforcing him for picking up a single coin. Then the metal container was introduced, with the requirement that he drop the coin into the container. Here we ran into the first bit of difficulty: he seems to have a great deal of trouble letting go of the coin. He would rub it up against the inside of the container, pull it back out, and clutch it firmly for several seconds. However, he would finally turn it loose and receive his food reinforcement. Then the final contingency: we put him on a ration of 2, requiring that he pick up both coins and put them in the container.

Now the raccoon really had problems (and so did we). Not only could he not let go of the coins, but he spent seconds, even minutes, rubbing them together (in a most miserly fashion), and dipping them into the container. He carried on this behavior to such an extent that the practical application we had in mind—a display featuring a raccoon putting money in a piggy bank—simply was not feasible. The rubbing behavior became worse and worse as time went on, in spite of nonreinforcement.

For the third instance, we return to the gallinaceous birds. The observer sees a hopper full of oval plastic capsules which contain small toys, charms, and the like. When the S_D (a light) is presented to the chicken, she pulls a rubber loop which releases one of these capsules onto a slide, about 16 inches long, inclined at about 30 degrees. The capsule rolls down the slide and comes to rest near the end. Here one or two sharp, straight pecks by the chicken will knock it forward off the slide and out to the observer, and the chicken is then reinforced by an automatic feeder. This is all very well—most chickens are able to master these contingencies in short order. The loop pulling presents no problems; she then has only to peck the capsule off the slide to get her reinforcement.

However, a good 20% of all chickens tried on this set of contingencies fail to make the grade. After they have pecked a few capsules off the slide, they begin to grab at the capsules and drag them backwards into the cage. Here they pound them up and down on the floor of the cage. Of course, this results in no reinforcement for the chicken, and yet some chickens will pull in over half of all the capsules presented to them.

Almost always this problem behavior does not appear until after the capsules begin to move down the slide. Conditioning is begun with stationary capsules placed by the experimenter. When the pecking behavior becomes strong enough, so that the chicken is knocking them off the slide and getting reinforced consistently, the loop pulling is conditioned to the light. The capsules then come rolling down the slide to the chicken. Here most chickens, who before did not have this tendency, will start grabbing and shaking.

The fourth incident also concerns a chicken. Here the observer sees a chicken in a cage about 4 feet long which is placed alongside a miniature baseball field. The reason for the cage is the interesting part. At one end of the cage is an automatic electric feed hopper. At the other is an opening through which the chicken can reach and pull a loop on a bat. If she pulls the loop hard enough the bat (solenoid operated) will swing, knocking a small baseball up the playing field. If it gets past the miniature toy players on the field and hits the back fence, the chicken is automatically reinforced with food at the other end of the cage. If it does not go far enough, or hits one of the players, she tries again. This results in behavior on an irregular ratio. When the feeder sounds, she then runs down the length of the cage and eats.

Our problems began when we tried to remove the cage for photography. Chickens that had been well conditioned in this behavior became wildly excited when the ball started to move. They would jump up on the playing field, chase the ball all over the field, even knock it off on the floor and chase it around, pecking it in every direction, although they had never had access to the ball before. This behavior was so persistent and so disruptive, in spite of the fact that it was never reinforced, that we had to reinstate the cage.

The last instance we shall relate in detail is one of the most annoying and baffling for a good behaviorist. Here a pig was conditioned to pick up large wooden coins and deposit them in a large "piggy bank." The coins were placed several feet from the bank and the pig required to carry them to the bank and deposit them, usually four or five coins for one reinforcement. (Of course, we started out with one coin, near the bank.)

Pigs condition very rapidly, they have no trouble taking ratios, they have ravenous appetites (naturally), and in many ways are among the most tractable animals we have worked with. However, this particular problem behavior developed in pig after pig, usually after a period of weeks or months, getting worse every day. At first the pig would eagerly pick up one dollar, carry it to the bank, run back, get another, carry it rapidly and neatly, and so on, until the ratio was complete. Thereafter, over a period of weeks the behavior would become slower and slower. He might run over eagerly for each dollar, but on the way back, instead of carrying the dollar and depositing it simply and cleanly, he would repeatedly drop it, root it, drop it again, root it along the way, pick it up, toss it up in the air, drop it, root it some more, and so on.

We thought this behavior might simply be the dilly-dallying of an animal on a low drive. However, the behavior persisted and gained in strength in spite of a severely increased drive—he finally went through the ratios so slowly that he did not get enough to eat in the course of a day. Finally it would take the pig about 10 minutes to transport four coins a distance of about 6 feet. This problem behavior developed repeatedly in successive pigs.

There have also been other instances: hamsters that stopped working in a glass case after four or five reinforcements, porpoises and whales that swallow their manipulanda (balls and inner tubes), cats that will not leave the area of the feeder, rabbits that will not go to the feeder, the great difficulty in many species of conditioning vocalization with food reinforcement, problems in conditioning a kick in a cow, the failure to get appreciably increased effort out of the ungulates with increased drive, and so on. These we shall not dwell on in detail, nor shall we discuss how they might be overcome.

These egregious failures came as a rather considerable shock to us, for there was nothing in our background in behaviorism to prepare us for such gross inabilities to predict and control the behavior of animals with which we had been working for years.

The examples listed we feel represent a clean and utter failure of conditioning theory. They are far from what one would normally expect on the basis of the theory alone. Furthermore, they are definite, observable; the diagnosis of theory failure does not depend on subtle statistical interpretations or on semantic legerdemain—the animal simply does not do what he has been conditioned to do.

It seems perfectly clear that, with the possible exception of the dancing chicken, which could conceivably, as we have said, be explained in terms of Skinner's superstition paradigm, the other instances do not fit the behavioristic way of thinking. Here we have animals, after having been conditioned to a specific learned response, gradually drifting into behaviors that are entirely different from those which were conditioned. Moreover, it can easily be seen that these particular behaviors to which the animals drift are clear-cut examples of instinctive behaviors having to do with the natural food getting behaviors of the particular species.

The dancing chicken is exhibiting the gallinaceous birds' scratch pattern that in nature often precedes ingestion. The chicken that hammers capsules is obviously exhibiting instinctive behavior having to do with breaking open of seed pods or the killing of insects, grubs, etc. The raccoon is demonstrating so-called "washing behavior." The rubbing and washing response may result, for example, in the removal of the exoskeleton of a crayfish. The pig is rooting or shaking—behaviors which are strongly built into this species and are connected with the food getting repertoire.

These patterns to which the animals drift require greater physical output and therefore are a violation of the so-called "law of least effort." And most damaging of all, they stretch out the time required for reinforcement when nothing in the experimental setup requires them to do so. They have only to do the little tidbit of behavior to which they were conditioned—for example, pick up the coin and put it in the container—to get reinforced immediately. Instead, they drag the process out for a matter of minutes when there is nothing in the contingency which forces them to do this. Moreover, increasing the drive merely intensifies this effect.

It seems obvious that these animals are trapped by strong instinctive behaviors, and clearly we have here a demonstration of the prepotency of such behavior patterns over those which have been conditioned.

We have termed this phenomenon "instinctive drift." The general principle seems to be that wherever an animal has strong instinctive behaviors in the area of the conditioned response, after continued running the organism will drift toward the instinctive behavior to the detriment of the conditioned behavior and even to the delay or preclusion of the reinforcement. In a very boiled-down, simplified form, it might be stated as "learned behavior drifts toward instinctive behavior."

All this, of course, is not to disparage the use of conditioning techniques, but is intended as a demonstration that there are definite weaknesses in the philosophy underlying these techniques. The pointing out of such weaknesses should make possible a worthwhile revision in behavior theory.

The notion of instinct has now become one of our basic concepts in an effort to make sense of the welter of observations which confront us. When behaviorism tossed out instinct, it is our feeling that some of its power of prediction and control were lost with it. From the foregoing examples, it appears that although it was easy to banish the Instinctivists from the science during the Behavioristic Revolution, it was not possible to banish instinct so easily.

As if, as Hebb suggests, it is advisable to reconsider those things that behaviorism explicitly threw out, perhaps it might likewise be advisable to examine what they tacitly brought in—the hidden assumptions which led most disastrously to these breakdowns in the theory.

Three of the most important of these tacit assumptions seem to us to be: that the animal comes to the laboratory as a virtual *tabula rasa*, that species differences are insignificant, and that all responses are about equally conditionable to all stimuli.

It is obvious, we feel, from the foregoing account, that these assumptions are no longer tenable. After 14 years of continuous conditioning and observation of thousands of animals, it is our reluctant conclusion that the behavior of any species cannot be adequately understood, predicted, or controlled without knowledge of its instinctive patterns, evolutionary history, and ecological niche.

In spite of our early successes with the application of behavioristically oriented conditioning theory, we readily admit now that ethological facts and attitudes in recent years have done more to advance our practical control of animal behavior than recent reports from American "learning labs."

Moreover, as we have recently discovered, if one begins with evolution and instinct as the basic format for the science, a very illuminating viewpoint can be developed which leads naturally to a drastically revised and simplified conceptual framework of startling explanatory power (to be reported elsewhere).

It is hoped that this playback on the theory will be behavioral technology's partial repayment to the academic science whose impeccable empiricism we have used so extensively.

References

Beach, F. A. The snark was a boojum. *American Psychologist*, 1950, 5, 115-124.

Breland, K. & Breland, M. A field of applied animal psychology. *American Psychologist*, 1951, 6, 202-204.

Hebb, D. O. The American revolution. *American Psychologist*, 1960, 15, 735-745.

Lorenz, K. Innate behaviour patterns. *In Symposia of the Society for Experimental Biology.* No. 4 *Physiological mechanism in animal behaviour.* New York: Academic Press, 1950.

Skinner, B. F. Superstition in the pigeon. *Journal of Eexperimental Psychology*, 1948, 38, 168-172.

Tinbergen, N. *The study of instinct.* Oxford Clarendon, 1951.

Whalen, R. E. Comparative psychology. *Amer. Psychologist*, 1961, 16, 84.

AUTO-SHAPING OF THE PIGEON'S KEY-PECK

Paul L. Brown and Herbert M. Jenkins. *Journal of the Experimental Analysis of Behavior, 11(1), 1-8 16,* 1-8.

In this remarkable experiment a plastic disk (key) was illuminated for approximately eight-seconds and was immediately followed by a four-second presentation of food. After only a few pairings the pigeons began pecking the key shortly before the delivery of food. Brown and Jenkins were able to classically condition the pigeon's behavior by lighting up a key (conditioned stimulus) temporarily and then delivering food (unconditioned stimulus). The delivery of food was completely independent of the pigeon's response to the key. The food was delivered regardless. This behavior is quite astonishing because it suggests a degree of preparedness to respond in certain ways to certain stimuli in the natural environment and is completely at odds with the doctrine of equal-potentiality.

Reliable acquisition of the pigeon's key-peck response resulted from repeated unconditional (response-independent) presentations of food after the response key was illuminated momentarily. Comparison groups showed that acquisition was dependent upon light-food pairings, in that order

In the usual arrangement of discriminative operant conditioning, reinforcement is conditional on a stimulus and on a response. Food may be delivered to a hungry pigeon only when it pecks a key and only when the key is lighted. By relaxing, in different ways, the conditionality in the rule for delivering food, three other conditioning arrangements of interest can be generated. The delivery of food may be entirely unconditional, *i.e.*, without regard to the stimulus that is present or to behavior; the delivery of food may be conditional on behavior (e.g., the pigeon must peck a key) but unconditional with respect to stimuli; or the delivery of food may be conditional on the stimulus (*e.g.*, food is delivered only when the key is lighted) but unconditional with respect to responses. Following Skinner, behavior acquired under these arrangements may be characterized as superstitious.

In the classic experiment on superstitious conditioning (Skinner, 1948), the rule of reinforcement was entirely unconditional. The delivery of food was governed only by a temporal schedule and was therefore without regard to behavior. Since food was delivered in an unchanging environment, it can be regarded as unconditional with respect to stimuli, although holding the stimulus constant yields a special case of unconditionality. It would more closely parallel the sense in which food delivery is unconditional on behavior had a stimulus been switched between two or more values independently of food delivery. In any case, the well known result of Skinner's experiment was the development of stereotyped, although idiosyncratic, movement patterns.

An arrangement of the second type, in which reinforcement is conditional on responses but unconditional on stimuli, was investigated by Morse and Skinner (1957). The pigeon's key-peck was reinforced at variable intervals (reinforcement conditional on responses). Once during each hour the color of the key was changed for a 4-min period independently of the program of reinforcement (reinforcement unconditional on stimuli). Some birds developed an especially high rate during the 4-min stimulus while others developed an especially low rate. The direction of change in rate reversed for some birds in the course of long exposure to the procedure. Although the key-peck was conditioned before the stimulus changes were introduced in the Morse and Skinner experiment, that is not an essential feature of the second type of superstitious conditioning. Had a response with an appreciable operant level been chosen, the strengthening of the response through conditional reinforcement, and the acquisition of control by stimuli programmed independently of reinforcement, might have proceeded together. The essential feature of an arrangement of the second type is independence of the program of stimulus changes from the program of reinforcement, coupled with the dependence of reinforcement on responses.

An arrangement of the third type, in which reinforcement is conditional on stimulus values but not on responses, was used in the present experiment. A standard pigeon key was lighted just before food was delivered. The repeated pairing of light with food conditioned a variety of movements to the lighted key. Among these movements was a peck at the lighted key. Because the key-peck is normally shaped by the use of response conditional reinforcement, its emergence under the present circumstances is especially interesting. We have therefore concentrated on analyzing the conditions responsible for the emergence of the first key-peck rather than on other movements that develop in the presence of the stimulus that precedes reinforcement.

Types of superstitious conditioning are classified in terms of procedures, not in terms of behavioral outcomes. The classification does not imply that the behavioral effects observed in each case arise from the same conditioning process. To say that all three procedures produce superstitious conditioning points only to their common feature; namely, that they entail certain unconditional relations among stimuli, responses, and reinforcements. The present experiments show that the emergence of the key-peck when a key-light is repeatedly paired with food presentation is the result of a conditioning process of some sort. Critical questions remain, however, as to what kind of conditioning is at work.

METHOD

The following features were common to the several experiments.

Subjects

Experimentally naïve male White King pigeons. 5 to 6 yr old upon arrival in the laboratory, were maintained at 80% of their free-feeding weight.

Apparatus

A single-key operant conditioning box for pigeons (Lehigh Valley Electronics Model 1519C) was used. The center of the translucent plastic disc that served as the key was located in the center of the working panel 10 in. above the floor. The center of the opening to the food tray was located 5 in. directly below the key. Reinforcement was 4-sec. access to the grain tray. The general illumination of the box, backlighting of the key, and lighting of the food-tray opening during reinforcement were provided by supplying 5 vac to miniature lamps (No. 1820). The compartment light was mounted in a housing, above the key, which directed the light toward the ceiling. It remained on throughout all sessions. A steady masking noise was used in the box. Automatic programming and recording equipment was located in a separate room.

Recording

The basic datum was the occurrence of the first key-peck. An Esterline-Angus operations recorder provided a continuous record of stimulus presentations and responses.

Pretraining

Subjects were trained to approach quickly and to eat from the lighted food tray. Initially the tray was held in the up position and the food-tray opening was filled to the brim with grain. After the pigeon had eaten for 10 to 15 sec, the tray was lowered. On subsequent presentations, the tray was held until the pigeon ate from it. By the end of 10 tray operations all pigeons were reaching the tray and eating within a 4-sec tray-up interval. The key was unlighted during this phase. The tray was raised without knowledge of the bird's position.

EXPERIMENT 1

The basic paradigm consisted of the repeated pairing of a stimulus with the delivery of food. If the emergence of a key-peck under this regime were the result of some form of conditioning, the order in which stimulus and food appeared should be critical. In Exp. 1 the results of forward pairings (stimulus then food) were compared with the result of reverse pairings (food then stimulus).

Procedure

Forward Pairing. Thirty-six subjects received two sessions, each consisting of 80 pairings of an 8-sec white key-light followed immediately, at the offset of the key-light, by a 4-sec tray operation. Between trials the key was unlighted. The intertrial intervals varied randomly from 30 to 90 sec in 5-sec steps. All values were equally represented, yielding a mean intertrial duration of 60 sec. Two other conditions that had no effect on the emergence of the *first* key peck were introduced to maintain the peck to the lighted key for use in subsequent experiments. A peck during the 8-sec light-on period turned the light off and operated the tray immediately. A peck in an intertrial period prevented the appearance of a trial for the next 60 sec.

Reverse Pairing. Twelve subjects received the same treatment except that the order of tray operation and key-light was reversed. The tray operated for 4 sec and then the key-light came on for 8 sec. As in the forward pairing case, although irrelevant to the emergence of the first key-peck, a response on the trial turned the light off and operated the tray.

Results

A schema of the experimental arrangements and summary results are shown for the two groups of Exp. 1 and for those in subsequent experiments in Table 1. All 36 subjects in the forward-pairing group made a key-peck during the 8-sec trial at some point within the series of 160 trials. The mean and the range of the trial number of first peck are given in Table 1. For all but one subject the first peck was made during the trial. An average of only 3.8 intertrial responses were made per session. Discriminative control by the key-light was unmistakable.

Direct observation and a study of motion pictures made of pigeons that were not part of the present group showed the following gross stages in the emergence of the key-peck: first, a general increase of activity, particularly during the trial-on period; second, a progressive centering of movements around the area of the key when lighted; and, finally, pecking movements in the direction of the key. As would be expected, the conditioning of recognizable movement patterns to the light occurred well before the key-peck. In almost all cases it became evident after 10 to 20 pairings that the lighted key occasioned specific movements, oriented to the key, that did not appear in the intertrial interval.

In the reverse-pairing condition only two of the 12 subjects struck the key within 160 trials; far less activity was directed toward the key. After two sessions, the 10 pigeons which failed to peck under the reverse-pairing procedure were placed on the forward-pairing procedure. Eight acquired the key-peck within an average of 59 trials (range of 13 to 88

TABLE 1 Summary of Results

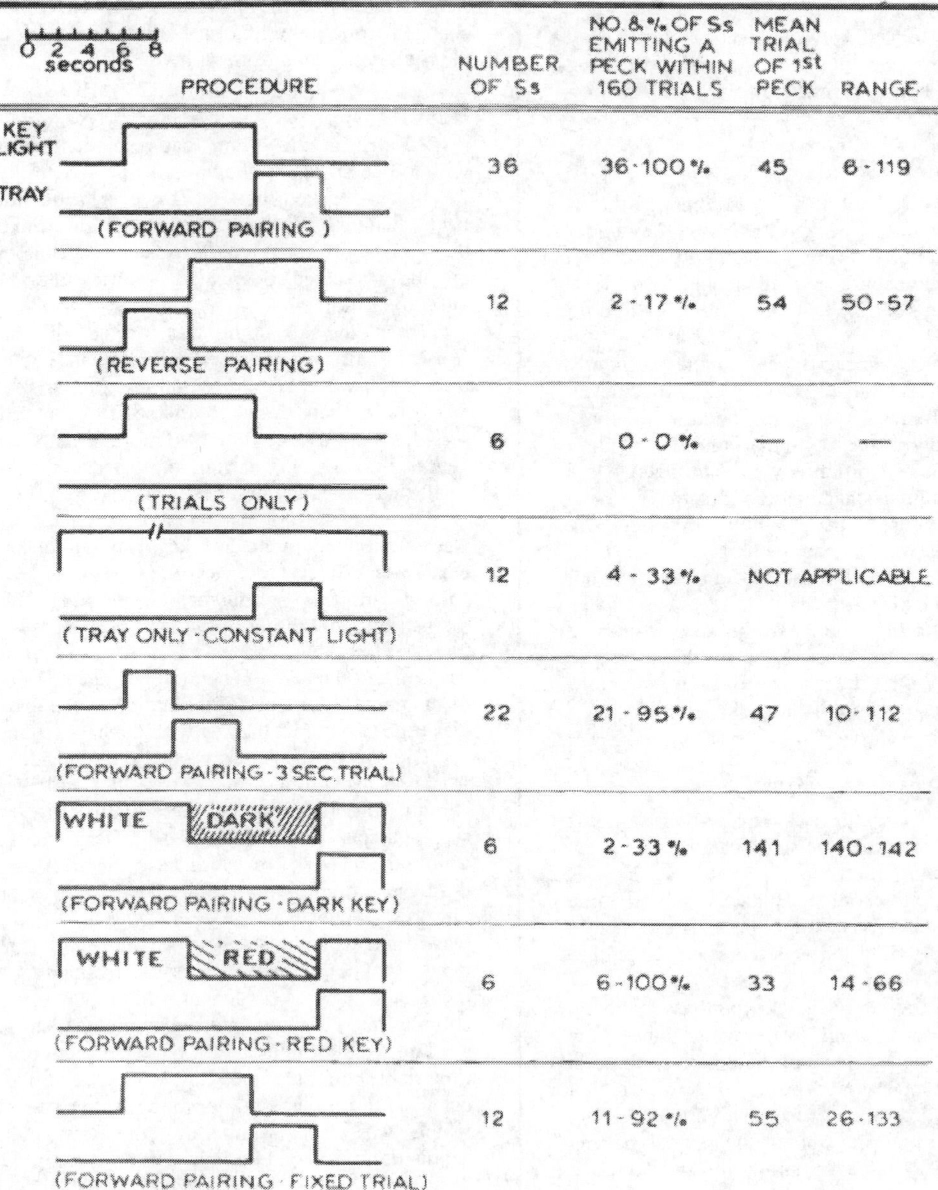

PROCEDURE	NUMBER OF Ss	NO. & % OF Ss EMITTING A PECK WITHIN 160 TRIALS	MEAN TRIAL OF 1st PECK	RANGE
(FORWARD PAIRING)	36	36 - 100%	45	6 - 119
(REVERSE PAIRING)	12	2 - 17%	54	50 - 57
(TRIALS ONLY)	6	0 - 0%	—	—
(TRAY ONLY - CONSTANT LIGHT)	12	4 - 33%	NOT APPLICABLE	
(FORWARD PAIRING - 3 SEC. TRIAL)	22	21 - 95%	47	10 - 112
(FORWARD PAIRING - DARK KEY)	6	2 - 33%	141	140 - 142
(FORWARD PAIRING - RED KEY)	6	6 - 100%	33	14 - 66
(FORWARD PAIRING - FIXED TRIAL)	12	11 - 92%	55	26 - 133

pairings). The remaining two showed clear conditioning of some form of response occasioned by the lighted key but did not peck within a total of 160 forward-pairings.

EXPERIMENT 2

The results of the previous experiment demonstrate the importance of the order of the pairings. It is possible, however, that the comparison of the two orders exaggerates the efficacy of the forward-pairing arrangement because the reverse-pairing may work against the occurrence of movements toward the lighted key (*cf.* Rescorla, 1967). A group of subjects was therefore run with trial presentations but no tray operations in order to estimate the operant level of response to brief key-lights. There is also a practical question. If one is simply interested in conditioning a key-peck, is it helpful to use a momentary illumination of the key in conjunction with tray operations or would steady illumination of the key do as well in producing the first peck? To answer that question, a group was run with a steady key-light and intermittent tray operations.

Procedure

Trials Only. Six subjects received a program identical to that in the forward-pairing condition of Exp. 1 except that the tray did not operate.

Tray Operation Only. Twelve subjects received tray operations on the same schedule as in the forward-pairing condition of Exp. 1. The key-light, however, remained on throughout the sessions.

Results

From the summary data for these conditions in Table 1, it can be seen that no animal pecked the lighted key under the trials-only condition. All were subsequently placed on the forward-pairing procedure and all acquired the key-peck within an average of 23 trials and a range of 6 to 45 trials.

The time available to make a peck at the constantly lighted key in the tray-only condition was about seven times longer than in the forward-pairing condition, but only four of the 12 subjects in the tray-only condition made a peck at any time. This proportion is very significantly less than the 36 of 36 animals that made a first peck in the forward-pairing procedure. The tray-only procedure did produce superstitious movement patterns of the kind described by Skinner (1948) but the movements were not as a rule oriented to the key.

The results attest to the efficacy of the forward-pairing procedure and show it to be superior to the use of a constantly lighted key with intermittent food presentations for the practical purpose of establishing a key-peck.

EXPERIMENT 3

The effects of three variations on the key-light stimulus were examined in the forward-pairing procedure.

If orienting toward and looking at the key is concentrated at the onset of the light, a shorter time between onset and food delivery might produce more rapid acquisition of the peck. A group was therefore run with a shorter trial stimulus.

The similarity of the white-lighted food-tray opening, in which the bird pecks at grain, to the white-lighted key might contribute to the occurrence of the key-peck through stimulus generalization. It should be noted, however, that the presumed effect of stimulus generalization would apply equally to the forward-pairing and to the reverse-pairing condition. Conceivably, however, similarity and forward-pairing interact to produce the result in the forward-pairing condition. The similarity of the trial stimulus to the tray light was reduced in different ways in two separate groups in order to examine the contribution of stimulus generalization.

Procedure

Forward Pairing—3-Sec Trial. Twenty-two subjects were trained under the forward-pairing procedure with a 3-sec trial rather than the 8-sec trial used in the previous forward-pairing groups.

Forward Pairing—Dark Key. Six subjects received the standard forward-pairing program except that the key was lighted (white) during the intertrial period and was turned off on the 8-sec trial that preceded tray operation.

Forward Pairing—Red Key. Six subjects received the same program as the previous group except that the key changed from white, during the intertrial period, to red on the trial, rather than from white to off.

Results

Results for the group that received forward pairings with a 3-sec trial are shown in Table 1. All but one of the 22 subjects pecked the key. However, acquisition was not faster than with the 8-sec trial. The shorter trial does reduce the opportunity for the peck to occur and this may balance out the advantage, if any, of a shorter interval from trial onset to reinforcement.

When the key-light was turned off on the trial (forward-pairing—dark-key condition in Table 1) two of the six subjects made a peck on the trial, and in both cases this occurred late in the second session. An additional two sessions were carried out. Two more birds pecked the dark key, one on the 195th pairing, the other on the 249th pairing. In all four cases, the first peck was made on the trial.

Direct observation showed that a special movement was conditioned on the dark-key trial, but the key-peck was clearly less likely to emerge, or at least required more pairings, in this arrangement than when the trial was marked by the lighting of the key. It is perhaps remarkable that the dark key was pecked at all, since during the trial the key had the same general appearance as the remainder of the panel. In the dim illumination of the enclosure there was little to contrast the key with the background.

The use of the red key on the trial made it stand out from the background on the trial, but still made the trial stimulus dissimilar to the white-lighted tray opening. All six subjects in the forward-pairing—red-key group acquired the peck. In every case the first peck occurred during the trial period. Subsequently an average of 41 intertrial responses per session occurred, a higher rate than was found with the standard forward-pairing arrangement (Exp. 1). The increase in intertrial responding is probably the result of greater generalization between a red trial stimulus and the white intertrial stimulus than is found with a white trial stimulus and a dark key between trials. The important point to note, however, is that the first peck occurred to the red key, not to the white intertrial stimulus which was more similar to the tray light. Further, acquisition with red key-light was no less rapid (average of 33 trials) than with a white key-light. Stimulus generalization from the tray-light to the key-light does not appear to contribute significantly to the present result.

EXPERIMENT 4

In the previous experiments the first key-peck brought an immediate operation of the food tray. Consequently the routine maintenance of responding after the first peck was not of special interest. In the present experiment key-pecks did not affect the trial duration nor the operation of the tray. It is of interest to examine the course of responding beyond the first peck for this arrangement.

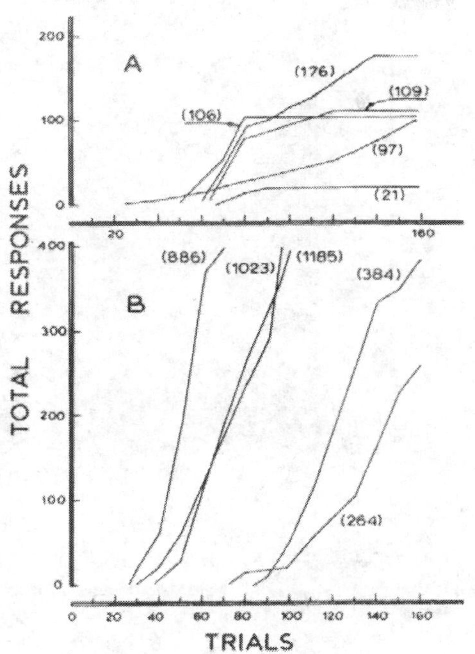

FIG. 1 Cumulative responses for individual birds in Exp. 4 in which a key-peck did not terminate the trial. Numbers in parentheses indicate total key-pecks by the 160th trial. For purposes of presentation the five subjects with a low rate of responding are shown in Panel A and the five with a high rate of responding are shown in Panel B.

Procedure

Forward Pairing—Fixed Trial. Twelve subjects received the standard forward-pairing procedure with an 8-sec trial which now remained fixed in duration throughout 160 pairings in two sessions.

Results

As shown in Table 1, all but one of the 12 subjects made at least one key-peck. One pigeon made only a single key-peck. Cumulative response curves for the remaining 10 birds are shown in Fig. 1. Five subjects developed and maintained a high rate throughout the 8-sec trial. The others showed an appreciably lower level of responding and several stopped pecking the key before the end of the second session. One animal continued pecking during the trial but the location of the peck drifted away from the key. As would be expected, the arrangement does not guarantee a stable performance, but it is capable of generating a surprisingly high level of maintained key-pecking in a substantial percentage of cases. Again, intertrial key responses were infrequent (mean of 5.8 per session for the 11 subjects represented in Fig. 1).

In terms of the appearance of the first key-peck, the results for the fixed-trial group were similar to those obtained in the standard forward-pairing condition and in the forward-pairing—3-sec trial condition.

COLLECTED RESULTS FOR ACQUISITION

A frequency distribution of trial number on which the first peck occurred is shown in Fig. 2 for the 70 pigeons run under the three forward-pairing—3-sec trial group in Exp. 3 and the forward-pairing—fixed-trial group in Exp. 4. The mode of the distribution lies between the 21st and the 40th pairings.

DISCUSSION

The experiments have shown the reliable emergence of a key-peck as the result of unconditional forward pairings of a key-light stimulus and food. Some of the conditions for the occurrence of this response have been explored, but the present arrangement contains other features whose contribution to the result is unknown. Experiments in progress show that the location of the key near the food tray is not a critical feature, although it no doubt hastens the process. Several birds have acquired the peck to a key located on the wall opposite the tray opening or on a side wall. On the other hand, the use of a key-light as a stimulus is undoubtedly a critical feature. It could hardly be expected that an auditory stimulus or variations in overall illumination would yield a key-peck with the present procedure. For reasons shortly to be discussed, a question

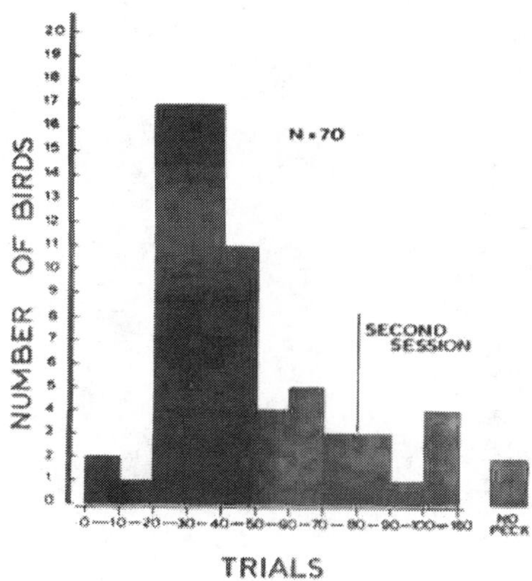

FIG. 2 Frequency distribution showing trials on which birds in certain forward-pairing groups (see text) emitted the first peck.

of particular interest is whether the use of grain as a reinforcer is essential to the emergence of the peck.

In our present view, the emergence of the key-peck may be characterized as a process of auto-shaping on which a direction is imposed by the species-specific tendency of the pigeon to peck at the things it looks at. The bird notices the onset of the light and perhaps makes some minimal motor adjustment to it. The temporal conjunction of reinforcement with noticing leads to orienting and looking toward the key. The species-specific look-peck coupling eventually yields a peck to the trial stimulus.

An appeal to some species-specific predispositions with respect to the stimulus is made necessary by the progressive change in behavior that leads up to the peck. It is not the initial behavior to the lighted key that is established by reinforcement. The progression would appear to be toward more rather than less effortful forms.

With the exception of the species-specific component, our account essentially parallels the accounts offered by Skinner (1948) and by Skinner and Morse (1957) for the first and second types of superstitious behavior. It relies on the shaping action of reinforcement and on the acquisition of discriminative control over the shaped response as a result of the joint presence of the stimulus and the reinforced response. However, what we have called a third type of superstition is also the standard arrangement for classical conditioning and that suggests the possibility of classically conditioned effects arising directly from the repeated pairing of a stimulus with food. Although we agree completely with Kimble's comment (1964) on a paper by Longo, Klempay, and Bitterman (1964) that the use of a classical conditioning procedure in no way guarantees that any response that becomes conditioned is a classically conditioned response, we nevertheless think it unwise to ignore the possibility that some form of classical conditioning contributes to the result.

There are two ways in which this might occur. First, classical conditioning could produce the response through stimulus substitution. The CS (lighted key) comes to evoke the response (peck) elicited by the UCS (grain). That seems unlikely because the peck appears to grow out of and depend upon the development of other motor responses in the vicinity of the key that do not themselves resemble a peck at grain. Even so, it will be of interest to see whether the use of water as a reinforcer, at which birds do not peck, will also condition the key peck.

Second, there is now a considerable number of experiments showing that classical pairings of a stimulus with food make the stimulus capable of affecting operant responses that were not occurring and could not have been shaped or specifically reinforced during the pairings (Bower and Grusec, 1964; Bower and Kaufman, 1963; Estes, 1943; Estes, 1948; Morse and Skinner, 1958; Trapold and Fairlie, 1965; Trapold and Odom, 1965; Walker, 1942). Clearly, there are stimulus effects resulting from pairing that are not specific to whatever responses may be concurrent with the pairing. Would not the same type of effect be involved in the acquisition of responses that are being made concurrently with the pairings as in the present arrangement? A general excitatory effect of the key-light resulting from the pairing of light and food may facilitate the general activity out of which the shaping produces a particular form of movement. While it is hard to see how an effect of this sort could not be involved, untangling a classical component from the response-specific action of reinforcement is extremely difficult, as the literature on the distinction between classical and operant conditioning so amply demonstrates.

Although the emergence of the key-peck as the result of response-independent pairings of the key-light with food raises several as yet unanswered questions about underlying processes, it does produce the key-peck with surprising regularity. When a large number of birds is to be used, the procedure saves time and labor. It no doubt results in idiosyncratic movement patterns associated with the peck itself, but is probably no worse in this respect than is hand-shaping. The procedure is easier to specify and to standardize. Further, it is free from the systematic effects that might be expected to result from individual differences among experimenters in the art of handshaping.

References

Bower, G. and Grusec, T. Effect of prior Pavlovian discrimination training upon training an operant discrimination. *J. exp. Anal. Behav.*, 1964, *7*, 401-404.

Bower, G. and Kaufman, R. Transer across drives of the discriminative effect of a Pavlovian conditioned stimulus.
J. exp. Anal. Behav., 1963, *6*, 445-448.

Estes, W. K. Discriminative conditioning I. A discriminative property of conditioned anticipation. *J. exp. Psychol.*, 1943, *32*, 152-155.

Estes, W. K. Discriminative conditioning II. Effects of a Pavlovian conditioned stimulus upon a subsequently stablished operant response. *J. exp. Psychol.*, 1948, *38*, 173-177.

Kimble, G. A. Comment. *Psychon. Sci.*, 1964, *1*, 40.

Longo, N., Klempay, S., and Bitterman, M. E. Classical appetitive conditioning in the pigeon. *Psychon. Sci.*, 1964, *1*, 19-20.

Morse, W. H., and Skinner, B. F. A second type of superstition in the pigeon. *Amer. J. Psychol.*, 1957, *70*, 308-311.

Morse, W. H., and Skinner, B. F. Some factors involved in the stimulus control of behavior. *J. exp. Anal. Behav.*, 958, *1*, 103-107.

Rescorla, R. A. Pavlovian conditioning and its proper control procedures. *Psychol. Rev.*, 1967, *74*, 71-80.

Skinner, B. F. "Superstition" in the pigeon. *J. exp. Psychol.*, 1948, *38*, 168-172.

AUTO-MAINTENANCE IN THE PIGEON: SUSTAINED PECKING DESPITE CONTINGENT NON-REINFORCEMENT

David R. Williams and Harriet Williams. (1969) *Journal of the Experimental Analysis of Behavior, 12(4),* 511-520.

Williams and Williams elaborated on Brown and Jenkins study by arranging for the key pecks to omit food presentation. Key pecking actually worked against the pigeons by causing the removal of food presentation. What they really needed to learn was to not peck the key, but they could not do it. This study demonstrated that accidental correlations must be taken into account in operant research. Demonstrating the essential role of a researcher's decisions regarding methodology and the importance of remaining objective and not drawing immediate conclusions based upon stereotyped response patterns that emerge. One cannot read this study without wondering why is pecking so important to the pigeon even when it eliminates the possibility of reinforcement? Jenkins and Moore (1973) tackled this question by pairing a lighted key with food in one group and water with another group. Pigeons respond to food and water quite differently. Pigeons peck at food with their beck open and their eyes shut. When presented with water pigeons partially shut their mouth using their tongue to pump up the water while their eyes remain open. The results indicate the pigeons tried to eat the key paired with food and tried to drink the key paired with water. What appears to be happening is the pigeon's response is based upon the type of reinforcement.

Brown and Jenkins (1968) reported a method for automatically and rapidly establishing key pecking in pigeons. Although their "shaping" procedure was carried out without reference to the birds' behavior, it led uniformly to the development of key pecking. Brown and Jenkins suggested that adventitious reinforcement of key-orienting behavior, aided by a tendency for birds to peck at things they look at, might provide a full account of their findings. The consistent success of their procedure with a large number of subjects, however, suggests the operation of a more deterministic mechanism than one based primarily on adventitious reinforcement. The present experiments were carried out to explore the possibility that the auto-shaping procedure directly and actively engenders pecking.

The basic procedure of the present experiments was a variant of Brown and Jenkins' procedure in which pecks prevented reinforcement. As in their method, a response key was illuminated for several seconds before grain was presented. In the present experiment, key pecking turned off the key and blocked presentation of the reinforcer, so that pecking actually prevented the reinforcing event. Because the effect of key pecking under this procedure was not irrelevant to reinforcement but rather reduced it, persistent responding would raise a strong presumption that key pecking can be directly maintained by variables which do not involve response-reinforcer relationships of either deliberate or accidental origin.

(Williams & Williams report the results from four different experiments each designed to tease out some of the subtle nuances of the methodology they had developed. These specifics are beyond the scope of interest here and have been omitted. Only the method for the first experiment is reported)

EXPERIMENT 1

Method

Subjects. Thirteen naïve Silver King pigeons, deprived to 80% of their free-feeding weight, served.

Apparatus. The pigeon chamber was 13 by 13 by 12 in.; one wall housed a standard three-key Lehigh Valley pigeon panel with keys which could be transilluminated by colored lights and vertical and horizontal striped patterns. The house-light and the keys used #1829 bulbs operated at 20 v dc. The keys were 8.5 in. above the floor of the compartment, and the grain hopper was centered 5 in. below the middle key.

Procedure. Upon initial placement in the experimental space, an experimentally naïve bird was confronted by a raised grain hopper filled to the top with grain. The bird was allowed to eat for about 20 sec, after which the hopper was withdrawn. Over the course of several further presentations, which took place without reference to the bird's behavior, eating time was reduced to 4 sec. After these initial unsignalled presentations, birds were either placed directly on the negative procedure or first treated as described in Table 1, and then place on the negative procedure.

TABLE 1 Number of Sessions During Which the Procedures Indicated Were in Force

Bird	Hand-Shaping	Auto-Shaping	FR 1 Timeout
P-16	1	0	1
P-17	0	2	1
P-18	0	4	2
Procedures to the left were carried out first.			

Auto-shaping: positive response contingency. Trials consisted of a 6-sec illumination of the center key, after which the key and the houselight were turned off, and the hopper was presented for 4 sec. Trials were separated by an intertrial interval averaging 30 sec, and ranging from 3 to 180 sec. Each peck on the lighted key turned off the key and the houselight, and presented the feeder directly. Intertrial pecks were recorded but had no scheduled consequences.

Auto-shaping: negative response contingency. The negative auto-shaping procedure exactly duplicated the positive auto-shaping procedure described above, except on trials where the lighted key was pecked. On those trials, the peck turned off the key, but the grain hopper was not presented. Neither the intertrial interval nor the onset of the next trial was altered by a peck; the key was simply darkened and the grain hopper was not presented. Intertrial pecks had no scheduled consequences.

Hand-shaping. After the general pretraining trials, the magazine was presented 50 additional times without warning on each of two successive days. The times between presentations were similar to the intertrial intervals in the auto-shaping procedure, but the response key was never illuminated. On the third experimental day, the key was illuminated on a trials basis, as in the auto-shaping procedure. The key remained on until the reinforcer was presented according to the method of successive approximations described in Ferster and Skinner (1957). A total of 50 reinforcers was presented on this day.

FR 1 Timeout. Under this procedure, the key was illuminated for a 6-sec period, unless a peck occurred. If a peck occurred, the house-light and key light were turned off and the reinforcer was presented. If the key was not pecked, it was turned off and no reinforcer was presented. Intertrial intervals were the same as in the positive auto-shaping procedure.

GENERAL DISCUSSION

Successful auto-maintenance—persistent, directed key pecking despite contingent non-reward—does not seem to be a natural implication of either operant or respondent principles. Because actual pecking of the negative key produces nonreinforcement, it cannot be directly maintained by adventitious relationships. If it is supposed that unobserved behaviors preceding the actual striking of the key are adventitiously maintained, then either (a) one must assume that the adventitiously maintained precursors are inflexibly linked to pecking and account for why they are not extinguished or replaced by precursors for other responses, or (b) one must suppose that the precursors do not invariably lead to pecking but can precede other behaviors as well. If the latter assumption is made, then it is difficult to see why, by operant principles, the precursors do not become closely linked to some other behavior because of the consistent reinforcement such linkage would produce. Even if attention—heightened and directed by adventitious reinforcement and giving rise to behavior through a look-peck coupling—is assumed to be responsible for the initial pecks (Brown and Jenkins), it is difficult to see why the continual extinction of a specific response component would not lead to an operant shift in attention and inconsequential responding (when the negative key comes on, look at the continuous key and peck it). It is, for example, very difficult to see how the continuous key could ultimately control pecking but not compete with the negative key. It seems clear that stimulus-reinforcer relationships, and not only response-reinforcer interactions, play a special role in this phenomenon. Such a conclusion, of course, takes the phenomenon out of reach of a standard operant analysis, where the influence of stimuli depends on their discriminative function with regard to experimental contingencies.

Similarities to the respondent domain are easy to recognize: indeed, the auto-maintenance procedure is formally identical to the "omission training" procedure of Sheffield (1965) except that a key peck substitutes for a saliva drop. In the present case, the response at issue is topographically similar to the response made to food. However, even if one ignores the usual application of respondent analyses to autonomic rather than skeletal behavior, the directed quality of the induced pecking does not follow naturally from respondent principles (see also Brown and Jenkins, 1968). It is unclear, for example, why pecking would be directed at the key rather than the feeder, or indeed why it would be directed anywhere at all. Although respondent laws (which deal with laws of stimulus-reinforcer pairings) are no doubt pertinent to the present phenomenon, a detailed account of this phenomenon would seem to demand a serious augmentation of respondent principles to account for the directed quality of the response.

The most direct empirical precedent for the present phenomena is provided by the work of Breland and Breland (1961), who found, in several species, that response patterns that were related to a reinforcer could "drift" into a situation even though they delayed and interfered with actual production of the reinforcer. As in the present case, such behaviors were intrusive, counterproductive, and uncontrolled by their contingencies. In addition, it has been shown that pigeons trained to peck at other pigeons develop far more elaborate patterns of "aggressive" behavior than the actual contingency demands; the behavior is sometimes so vigorous that it continues into the period when reinforcement is available (Skinner, 1959; Reynolds, Catania, and Skinner, 1963; Azrin and Hutchinson, 1967). Similar effects have been reported in rats (Ulrich, Johnston, Richardson, and Wolff, 1963). When rats' running is reinforced, the speed at which they run is governed directly by the magnitude of the reinforcer, and fast running develops whether or not it produces more rapid reinforcement (Williams, 1966). These examples make it clear that contingencies of reinforcement alone do not determine when or how strongly some behaviors occur, even if the behaviors appear to be skeletal or "voluntary". As an instance of such direct control, the present phenomenon does not appear to be an isolated curiosity.

The place of this phenomenon in the general operant framework deserves explicit consideration. While it has always been recognized that many aspects of experiments, such as deprivation or physical details of the experimental space, influence the "operant level" of some responses, it now appears that many other variables, such as stimulus-reinforcer relationships, can also have an important influence on the unreinforced level of occurrence of some responses. That the stimulus-reinforcer pairing overrode opposing effects of differential reinforcement indicates that the effect was a powerful one, and demonstrates that a high level of responding does not imply the operation of explicit or even adventitious reinforcement. This point should be taken into careful account when effects of reinforcing contingencies *per se* are under investigation (see, for example, Herrnstein, 1966).

To relate the present work to the concept of "operant level" furnishes a context but does not provide an account. In further work, the concept of "arbitrariness", which is so frequently claimed for operants, will require close attention: is the action of reinforcement—direct or contingent—different when a response is "naturally" in the organism's repertory, or when it bears a special relationship to the reinforcer? More broadly, consideration should be given to ascertaining how frequently direct, as opposed to contingent, influences of reinforcers enter into the determination of "skeletal" or "voluntary" behavior in natural environments.

References

Azrin, N. H. and Hutchinson, R. R. Conditioning of the aggressive behavior of pigeons by a fixed-interval schedule of reinforcement. *Journal of the Experimental Analysis of Behavior*, 1967, *10*, 395-402.

Breland, K. and Breland, M. The misbehavior of organisms. *American Psychologist*, 1961, *16*, 681-684.

Brown, P. L. and Jenkins, H. M. Auto-shaping of the pigeon's key-peck. *Journal of the Experimental Analysis of Behavior*, 1968, *11*, 1-8.

Ferster, C. B. and Skinner, B. F. *Schedules of reinforcement.* New York: Appleton-Century-Crofts, 1957.

Herrnstein, R. J. Superstition: a corollary of the principles of operant conditioning. In W. K. Honig (Ed.), *Operant behavior: area of research and application.* New York: Appleton-Century-Crofts, 1966, pp. 33- 51.

Reynolds, G. S., Catania, A. C., and Skinner, B. F. Conditioned and unconditioned aggression in pigeons. *Journal of the Experimental Analysis of Behavior*, 1963, *6*, 73-74.

Sheffield, F. D. Relation between classical conditioning and instrumental learning. In W. F. Prokasy (Ed.), *Classical conditioning.* New York: Appleton-Century-Crofts, 1965. Pp. 302-322.

Skinner, B. F. An experimental analysis of certain emotions. *Journal of the Experimental Analysis of Behavior*, 1959, *2*, 265. (Abstract).

Ulrich, R., Johnston, M., Richardson, J., and Wolff, P. The operant conditioning of fighting behavior in rats. *Psychology Records*, 1963, *13*, 465-470.

Williams, D. R. Relation between response amplitude and reinforcement. *Journal of Experimental Psychology*, 1966, *71*, 634-641.

The Phylogeny and Ontogeny of Behavior

Contingencies of reinforcement throw light on contingencies of survival in the evolution of behavior

B. F. Skinner (1966). *Science, 153,* 1205- 1213.

"Behave, damn you! Behave as you ought!" B. F. Skinner wrote these words for a character in his novel Walden Two, expressing the irritation of a scientist when his experimental expectations have gone awry. The animosity directed at the lab animal is of course a result of the scientist's frustration with his own ignorance. The experiment was so elegant in its design, the theoretical predictions so tightly reasoned, so why didn't the animal behave the way I thought it would? What is wrong with the mental model I have built of how the world around me works? This is a common reaction that all of us experience, whether in the laboratory or living our everyday lives; our expectations dashed against the rocky shores of reality. We are angry when our subjectively constructed maps fail to navigate us through objective terrain. The good news is that being "lost" necessitates exploration, discovery, and new more accurate "maps". What does all of this have to do with this particular article? At the time the article was written it did not have much of an impact. Skinner presents considerable evidence that we can model the mechanisms of selection from ontogeny to phylogeny, but he does so in a very defensive and condescending manner, addressing many of the ethological attacks on the experimental analysis of behavior. The article seemed to be little more than a behaviorist with a tabula rasa *belief system paying lip service to the relevance of genetic predispositions. In rereading the article I was amazed at how much of a precursor it was for evolutionary psychology to come. Skinner's main argument is that phylogeny and ontogeny (nature and nurture) are both main effects and both contribute to the behavior of organisms. Much more importantly, however, a careful reading reveals that he implicitly argues for an understanding of behavior as the product of the interaction of phylogeny and ontogeny. In doing so he anticipates the work of others, particularly Seligman, and Bolles who explicitly make the same argument regarding the interaction of evolved predispositions and environmental experience. The battle cry of the ethologists has long been, "know your organism". Translation: studying the environmental experience of organisms makes very little sense if not understood in the context of the evolved "nature" of the organism. It is ironic that this is exactly what Skinner is advocating. "Behave, damn you! Behave as you ought!" reveals the frustration of not, "knowing your organism". Most often our failed experimental expectations result from too much ontogeny and not enough phylogeny x ontogeny in our computations.*

Parts of the behavior of an organism concerned with the internal economy, as in respiration or digestion, have always been accepted as "inherited," and there is no reason why some responses to the external environment should not also come ready-made in, the same sense. It is widely believed that many students of behavior disagree. The classical reference is to John B. Watson (1):

I should like to go one step further now and say, "Give me a dozen healthy infants, well-formed, and my own specified world to bring them up in and I'll guarantee to take any one at random and train him to become any type of specialist I might select—doctor, lawyer, artist, merchant-chief and, yes, even beggarman and thief, regardless of his talents, penchants, tendencies, abilities, vocations, and race of his ancestors." I am going beyond my facts and I admit it, but so have the advocates of the contrary and they have been doing it for many thousands of years.

Watson was not denying that a substantial part of behavior is inherited. His challenge appears in the first of four chapters describing "how man is equipped to behave at birth." As an enthusiastic specialist in the psychology of learning he went beyond his facts to emphasize what could be done in spite of genetic limitations. He was actually, as Gray (2) has pointed out, "one of the earliest and one of the most careful workers in the area of animal ethology." Yet he is probably responsible for the persistent myth of what has been called "behaviorism's counterfactual dogma" (3). And it is a myth. No reputable student of animal behavior has ever taken the position "that the animal comes to the laboratory as a virtual *tabula rasa*, that species' differences are insignificant, and that all responses are about equality conditionable to all stimuli" (4).

But what does it mean to say that behavior is inherited? Lorenz (5) has noted that ethologists are not agreed on "the concept of 'what we formerly called innate.'" Insofar as the behavior of an organism is simply the physiology of an anatomy, the inheritance of behavior is the inheritance of certain bodily features, and there should be no problem concerning the meaning of "innate" that is not raised by any genetic trait. Perhaps we must qualify the statement that an organism inherits a visual reflex, but we must also qualify the statement that it inherits its eye color.

If the anatomical features underlying behavior were as conspicuous as the wings of *Drosophila*, we should describe them directly and deal with their inheritance in the same way, but at the moment we must be content with so called behavioral manifestations. We describe the behaving organism in terms of its gross anatomy, and we shall no doubt eventually describe the behavior of its fine structures in much the same way, but until then we analyze behavior without referring to fine structures and are constrained to do so even when we wish to make inferences about them.

What features of behavior we eventually yield a satisfactory genetic account? Some kind of inheritance is implied by such concepts as "racial memory" or "death instinct," but a sharper specification is obviously needed. The behavior observed in mazes and similar apparatuses may be "objective," but it is not described in dimensions which yield a meaningful genetic picture. Tropisms and taxes are somewhat more readily quantified, but not all behavior can be thus formulated, and organisms selected for breeding according to tropestic or taxic performances may still differ in other ways (6).

The experimental analysis of behavior has emphasized another property. The probability that an organism will behave in a given way is a more valuable datum than the mere fact that it does so behave. Probability may be inferred from frequency of remission. It is a basic datum, in a theoretical sense because it is related to the question: Why does an organism behave in a given way at a given time? It is basic in a practical sense because frequency has been found to vary in an orderly way with many independent variables. Probability of response is important in examining the inheritance, not only of specific forms of behavior but of behavioral processes and characteristics often described as traits. Very little has been done in studying the genetics of behavior in this sense. Modes of inheritance are not, however, the only issue. Recently advances in the formulation of learned behavior throw considerable light on other genetic and evolutionary problems.

The Provenance of Behavior

Upon a given occasion we observe that an animal displays a certain kind of behavior—learned or unlearned. We describe its topography and evaluate its probability. We discover variables, genetic or environmental, of which the probability is a function. We then undertake to predict or control the behavior. All this concerns a current state of the organism. We have still to ask where the behavior (or the structures which thus behave) came from.

The provenance of the learned behavior has been thoroughly analyzed. Certain kinds of events function as "reinforcers," and, when such an event follows a response, similar responses are more likely to occur. This is operant conditioning. By manipulating the ways in which reinforcing consequences are contingent upon behavior, we generate complex forms of response and bring them under the control of subtle features of the environment. What we may call the ontogeny of behavior is thus traced to contingencies of reinforcement.

In a famous passage Pascal (7) suggested that ontogeny and phylogeny have something in common. "Habit," he said, "is a second nature which destroys the first. But what is this nature? Why is habit not natural? I am very much afraid that nature is itself only first habit as habit is second nature." The provenance of "first habit" has an important place in theories of the evolution of behavior. A given response is in a sense strengthened by consequences which have to do with the survival of the individual and species. A given form of behavior leads not to reinforcement but to procreation. (Sheer reproductive activity does not, of course, always contribute to the survival of a species, as the problems of overpopulation remind us. A few well-fed breeders presumably enjoy an advantage over a larger but impoverished population. The advantage may also be selective. It has recently been suggested (8) that some forms of behavior such as the defense of a territory have an important effect in restricting breeding. Several practical problems raised by what may be called contingencies of selection are remarkably similar to problems which have already been approached experimentally with respect to contingencies of reinforcement.

An identifiable unit. A behavioral process, as a change in frequency of response, can be followed only if it is possible to count responses. The topography of an operant need not be completely fixed, but some defining property must be available to identify instances. An emphasis upon the occurrence of a repeatable unit distinguishes an experimental analysis of behavior from historical or anecdotal accounts. A similar requirement is recognized in ethology. As Julian Huxley has said, "This concept .... of unit releasers which act as specific key stimuli unlocking genetically determined unit behavior patterns ... is probably the most important single contribution of Lorenzian ethology to the science of behavior" (9).

The action of stimuli. Operant reinforcement not only strengthens a given response, it brings the response under the control of a stimulus. But the stimulus does not elicit the response as in a reflex: it merely sets the occasion upon which the response is more likely to occur. The ethologists' "releaser" also simply sets an occasion. Like the discriminative stimulus, it increases the probability of occurrence of a unit of behavior but does not force it. The principal difference between a reflex and an instinct is not in the complexity of the response but in respectively, the eliciting and releasing actions of the stimulus.

Origins of variations. Ontogenic contingencies remain ineffective until a response has occurred. In a familiar experimental arrangement, the rat must press the lever at least once "for other reasons" before it presses it "for food." There is a similar limitation in phylogenic contingencies. An animal must emit a cry at least once for other reasons before they cry can be selected as a warning because of the advantage to the species. It follows that the entire repertoire of an individual or species must exist prior to ontogenic or phylogenic selection, but only in the form of minimal units. Both phylogenic and ontogenic contingencies "shape" complex forms of behavior from relatively undifferentiated material. Both processes are favored if the organism shows an extensive, undifferentiated repertoire.

Programmed contingencies. It is usually not practical to condition a complex operant by waiting for an instance to occur and then reinforcing it. A terminal performance must be reached through intermediate contingencies (perhaps best exemplified by programmed instruction). In a demonstration experiment a rat pulled a chain to obtain a marble from a rack, picked up the marble with its forepaws, carried it to a tube projecting two inches above the floor of its cage, lifted it to the top of the tube, and dropped it inside. "Every step in the process had to be worked out through a series of approximations since the component responses were not in the original repertoire of the rat" (10). The "program" was as follows. The rat was reinforced for any movement which caused a marble to roll over any edge of the floor of its cage, then only over the edge on one side of the cage, then over only a small section of the edge, then over only that section slightly raised, and so on. The raised edge became a tube of gradually diminishing diameter and increasing height. The earlier member of the chain, release of the marble from the rack, was added later. Other kinds of programming have been used to establish subtle stimulus control (11), to sustain behavior in spite of infrequent reinforcement (12), and so on.

A similar programming of complex phylogenic contingencies is familiar in evolutionary theory. The environment may change, demanding that behavior which contributes to survival for a given reason become more complex. Quite different advantages may be responsible for different stages. To take a familiar example the electric organ of the eel could have become useful in stunning prey only after developing something like its present power. Must we attribute the completed organ to a single complex mutation, or were intermediate stages developed because of other advantages? Much weaker currents, for example, may have permitted the eel to detect the nature of objects with which it was in contact. The same question may be asked about behavior. Pascal's "first habit" must often have been the product of "programmed instruction." Many of the complex phylogenic contingencies which now seem to sustain behavior must have been reached through intermediate stages in which less complex forms had lesser but still effective consequences.

The need for programming is a special case of a more general principle. We do not explain any system of behavior simply by demonstrating that is works to the advantage of, or has "net utility" for, the individual or species. It is necessary to show that a given advantage is contingent upon behavior in such a way as to alter its probability.

Adventitious contingencies. It is not true, as Lorenz (5) has asserted, that "adaptiveness is always the irrefutable proof that this process [of adaptation] has taken place." Behavior may have advantages which have played no role in its selection. The converse is also true. Events which follow behavior but are not necessarily produced by it may have a selective effect. A hungry pigeon placed in an apparatus in which a food dispenser operates every 20 seconds regardless of what the pigeon is doing acquires a stereotyped response which is shaped and sustained by wholly coincidental reinforcement (13). The behavior is often "ritualistic;" we call it superstitious. There is presumably a phylogenic parallel. All current characteristics of an organism do not necessarily contribute to its survival and procreation, yet they are all nevertheless "selected." Useless structures with associated useless functions are as inevitable as superstitious behavior. Both become more likely as organisms become more sensitive to contingencies. It should occasion no surprise that behavior has not perfectly adjusted to either ontogenic or phylogenic contingencies.

Unstable and intermittent contingencies. Both phylogenic and ontogenic contingencies are effective even though intermittent. Different schedules of reinforcement generate different patterns of changing probabilities. If there is a phylogenic parallel, it is obscure. A form of behavior generated by intermittent selective contingencies is presumably likely to survive a protracted period in which the contingencies are not in force, because it has already proved powerful enough to survive briefer periods, but this is only roughly parallel with the explanation of the greater resistance to extinction of intermittently reinforced operants.

Contingencies also change, and the behaviors for which they are responsible then change too. When ontogenic contingencies specifying topography of response are relaxed, the topography usually deteriorates, and when reinforcements are no longer forthcoming the operant undergoes extinction. Darwin discussed phylogenic parallels in *The Expression of Emotions in Man and Animals*. His "serviceable associated habits" were apparently both learned and unlearned, and he seems to have assumed that ontogenic contingencies contribute to the inheritance of behavior, at least in generating responses which may then have phylogenic consequences. The behavior of the domestic dog in turning around before lying down on a smooth surface may have been selected by contingencies under which the behavior made a useful bed in grass or brush. If dogs now show this behavior less frequently, it is presumably because a sort of phylogenic extinction has set in. The domestic cat shows a complex response of covering feces which must once have had survival value with respect to predation or disease. The dog has been more responsive to the relaxed contingencies arising from domestication or some other change in predation or disease, and shows the behavior in vestigial form.

Multiple contingencies. An operant may be affected by more than one kind of reinforcement, and a given form of behavior may be traced to more than one advantage to the individual or the species. Two phylogenic or ontogenic consequences may work together or oppose each other in the development of a given response and presumably show "algebraic summation" when opposed.

Social contingencies. The contingencies responsible for social behavior raise special problems in both phylogeny and ontogeny. In the development of a language the behavior of a speaker can become more elaborate only as listeners become sensitive to elaborated speech. A similarly coordinated development must be assumed in the phylogeny of social behavior. The dance of the bee returning from a successful foray can have advantageous effects for the species only when other bees behave appropriately with respect to it, but they cannot develop the behavior until the dance appears. The terminal system must have required a kind of subtle programming in which the behaviors of both "speaker" and "listener" passed through increasingly complex stages. A bee returning from a successful foray may behave in a special way because it is excited or fatigued, and it may show phototropic responses related to recent visual stimulation. If the strength of the behavior varies with the quantity or quality of food the bee has discovered and with the distance and direction it has flown, then the behavior may serve as an important stimulus to other bees, even though its characteristics have not yet been affected by such consequences. If different bees behave in different ways, then more effective versions should be selected. If the behavior of a successful bee evokes behavior on the part of "listeners" which is reinforcing to the "speaker," then the "speaker's" behavior should be ontogenically intensified. The phylogenic development of responsive behavior in the "listener" should contribute to the final system by providing for immediate reinforcement of conspicuous forms of the dance.

The speaker's behavior may become less elaborate if the listener continues to respond to less elaborate forms. We stop someone who is approaching us by pressing our palm against his chest, but he eventually learns to stop upon seeing our outstretched palm. The practical response becomes a gesture. A similar shift in phylogenic contingencies may account for the "intentional movements" of the ethologists.

Behavior may be intensified or elaborated under differential reinforcement involving the stimulation either of the behaving organism or of others. The more conspicuous a superstitious response, for example, the more effective the adventitious contingencies. Behavior is especially likely to become more conspicuous when reinforcement is contingent on the response of another organism. Some ontogenic instances, called "ritualization," are easily demonstrated. Many elaborate rituals of primarily phylogenic origin have been described by ethologists.

Some Problems Raised by Phylogenic Contingencies

Lorenz has recently argued that "our absolute ignorance of the physiological mechanisms underlying learning makes our knowledge of the causation of phyletic adaptation seem quite considerable by comparison" (5). But genetic and behavioral processes are studied and formulated in a rigorous way without reference to the underlying biochemistry. With respect to the provenance of behavior we know much more about ontogenic contingencies than phylogenic. Moreover, phylogenic contingencies raise some very difficult problems which have no ontogenic parallels.

The contingencies responsible for unlearned behavior acted a very long time ago. The natural selection of a given form of behavior, no matter how plausibly argued, remains an inference. We can set up phylogenic contingencies under which a given property of behavior arbitrarily selects individuals for breeding, and thus demonstrate modes of behavioral inheritance, but the experimenter who makes the selection is performing a function of the natural environment which also needs to be studied. Just as the reinforcements arranged in an experimental analysis must be shown to have parallels in "real life" if the results of the analysis are to be significant or useful, so the contingencies which select a given behavioral trait in a genetic experiment must be shown to play a plausible role in natural selection.

Although ontogenic contingencies are easily subjected to an experimental analysis, phylogenic contingencies are not. When the experimenter has shaped a complex response, such as dropping a marble into a tube, the provenance of the behavior raises no problem. The performance may puzzle anyone seeing it for the first time, but it is easily traced to recent, possibly recorded, events. No comparable history can be invoked when a spider is observed to spin a web. We have not seen the phylogenic contingencies at work. All we know is that spiders of a given kind build more or less the same kind of web. Our ignorance often adds a touch of mystery. We are likely to view inherited behavior with a kind of awe not inspired by acquired behavior of similar complexity.

The remoteness of phylogenic contingencies affects our scientific methods, both experimental and conceptual. Until we have identified the variables of which an event is a function, we tend to invent causes. Learned behavior was once commonly attributed to "habit," but an analysis of contingencies of reinforcement has made the term unnecessary. "Instinct," as a hypothetical cause of phylogenic behavior, has had a longer life. We no longer say that our rat possesses a marble-dropping habit, but we are still likely to say that our spider has a web-spinning instinct. The concept of instinct has been severely criticized and is now used with caution or altogether avoided, but explanatory entites serving a similar function still survive in the writings of many ethologists.

A "mental apparatus," for example, no longer finds a useful place in the experimental analysis of behavior, but it survives in discussions of phylogenic contingencies. Here are a few sentences from the writings of prominent ethologists which refer to consciousness or awareness: "The young gosling...gets imprinted upon its mind the image of the first moving object is sees" (W. H. Thorpe. 14): "the infant expresses the inner state of contentment by smiling" (Julian Huxley, 9): "[herring gulls show a] lack of insight into the ends served by their activities" (Tinbergen, 15); "[chimpanzees were unable] to communicate to others the unseen things in their minds" (Kortlandt, 16).

In some mental activities awareness may not be critical, but other cognitive activities are invoked. Thorpe (14) speaks of a disposition "which leads the animal to pay particular attention to objects of a certain kind." What we observe is simply that objects of a certain kind are especially effective stimuli. We know how ontogenic contingencies work to produce such an effect. The ontogenic contingencies which generate the behavior called "paying attention" also presumably have phylogenic parallels. Other mental activities frequently mentioned by ethologists include "organizing experience" and "discovering relations." Expressions of all these sorts show that we have not yet accounted for behavior in terms of contingencies, phylogenic or ontogenic. Unable to show how the organism can behave effectively under complex circumstances, we endow it with a special cognitive ability which permits it to do so. Once the contingencies are understood, we no longer need to appeal to mentalistic explanations.

Other concepts replaced by a more effective analysis include "need" or "drive" and "emotion." In ontogenic behavior we no longer say that a given set of environmental conditions first gives rise to an inner state which the organism then expresses or resolves by behaving in a given way. We no longer represent relations among emotional and motivational variables as relations among such states, as in saying that hunger overcomes fear. We no longer use dynamic analogies or metaphors, as in explaining sudden action as the overflow on bursting out of dammed-up needs or drives. If these are common practices in ethology, it is evidently because the functional relations they attempt to formulate are not clearly understood.

Another kind of innate endowment, particularly likely to appear in explanations of human behavior, takes the form of "traits" or "abilities." Though often measured quantitatively, their dimensions are meaningful only in placing the individual with respect to a population. The behavior measured is almost always obviously learned. To say that intelligence is inherited is not to say that specific forms of behavior are inherited. Phylogenic contingencies conceivably responsible for "the selection of intelligence" do not specify responses. What has been selected appears to be a susceptibility to ontogenic contingencies, leading particularly to a greater speed of conditioning and the capacity to maintain a larger repertoire without confusion.

If is often said that an analysis of behavior in terms of ontogenic contingencies "leaves something out of account," and this is true. It leaves out of account habits, ideas, cognitive processes, needs, drives, traits, and so on. But it does not neglect the facts upon which these concepts are based. It seeks a more effective formulation of the very contingencies to which those who use such concepts must eventually turn to explain their explanations. The strategy has been highly successful at the ontogenic level, where the contingencies are relatively clear. As the nature and mode of operation of phylogenic contingencies come to be better understood, a similar strategy should yield comparable advantages.

Identifying Phylogenic and Ontogenic Variables

The significance of ontogenic variables may be assessed by holding genetic conditions as constant as possible—for example, by studying "pure" strains or identical twins. The technique has a long history. According to Plutarch (*De Puerorum Educatione*) Licurgus, a Spartan, demonstrated the importance of environment by raising two puppies from the same litter so that one became a good hunter while the other preferred food from a plate. On the other hand, genetic variables may be assessed either by studying organisms upon which the environment has had little opportunity to act (because they are newborn or have been reared in a controlled environment) or by comparing groups subject to extensive, but on the average probably similar, environmental histories. The technique also has a long history. In his journal for the 24th of January 1805, Stendahl refers to an experiment in which two birds taken from the nest after hatching and raised by hand exhibited their genetic endowment by eventually mating and building a nest two weeks before the female laid eggs. Behavior exhibited by most of the members of a species is often accepted as inherited if it is unlikely that all the members could have been exposed to relevant ontogenic contingencies.

When contingencies are not obvious, it is perhaps unwise to call any behavior either inherited or acquired. Field observations, in particular, will often not permit a distinction. Friedmann (17) has described the behavior of the African honey guide as follows:

When the bird is ready to begin guiding, it either comes to a person and starts a repetitive series of churring notes, or it stays where it is and begins calling...

As the person comes to within 15 or 20 feet... the bird flies off with an initial conspicuous downward dip, and then goes off to another tree, not necessarily in sight of the follower, in fact more often out of sight than not. Then it waits there, churring lously until the follower again nears it, when the action is repeated. This goes on until the vicinity of the bees' nest is reached. Here the bird suddenly ceases calling and perches quietly in a tree nearby. It waits there for the follower to open the hive, and it usually remains there until the person has departed with his loot of honey-comb, when it comes down to the plundered bees' nest and begins to feed on the bits of comb left strewn about.

The author is quoted as saying that the behavior is "purely instinctive," but it is possible to explain almost all of it in other ways. If we assume that honey guides eat broken bees' nests and cannot eat unbroken nests, that men (not to mention baboons and ratels) break bees' nests, and that birds more easily discover unbroken nests, then only one other assumption is needed to explain the behavior in ontogenic terms. We must assume that the response which produces the churring note is elicited either (i) by any stimulus which frequently precedes the receipt of food (comparable behavior is shown by a hungry dog jumping about when food is being prepared for it) or (ii) when food, ordinarily available, is missing (the dog jumps about when food is not being prepared for it on schedule). An unconditioned honey guide occasionally sees men breaking nests. It waits until they have gone, and then eats the remaining scraps. Later it sees men near but not breaking nests, either because they have not yet found the nests or have not yet reached them. The sight of a man near a nest, or the sight of man when the buzzing of bees around a new can be heard, begins to function in either of the ways just noted to elicit the churring response. The first step in the construction of the final pattern is thus taken by the honey guide. The second step is taken by the man (or baboon or ratel, as the case may be). The churring sound becomes a conditioned stimulus in the presence of which a search for bees' nests is frequently successful. The buzzing of bees would have the same effect if the man could hear it.

The next change occurs in the honey guide. When a man approaches and breaks up a next, his behavior begins to function as a conditioned reinforcer which, together with the fragments which he leaves behind, reinforces churring, which then becomes more probable under the circumstances and emerges primarily as an operant rather than as an emotional response. When this has happened, the geographical arrangements work themselves out naturally. Men learn to move toward the churring sound, and they break nests more often after walking toward nests than after walking in other directions. The honey guide is therefore differentially reinforced when it takes a position which induces men to walk toward a nest. The contingencies may be subtle, but the final topography is often far from perfect.

As we have seen, contingencies which involve two or more organisms raise special problems. The churring of the honey guide is useless until men respond to it, but men will not respond in an appropriate way until the churring is related to the location of bees' nests. The conditions just described compose a sort of program which could lead to the terminal performance. It may be that the conditions will not often arise, but another characteristic of social contingencies quickly takes over. When one honey guide and one man have entered into the symbiotic arrangement, conditions prevail under which other honey guides and other men will be much more rapidly conditioned. A second man will more quickly learn to go in the direction of the churring sound because the sound is already spatially related to bees' nests. A second honey guide will more readily learn to churr in the right places because men respond in a way which reinforces that behavior. When a large number of birds have learned to guide and a large number of men have learned to be guided, conditions are highly favorable for maintaining the system. (It is said that where men no longer bother to break bees' nests, they no longer comprise an occasion for churring, and the honey guide turns to the ratel or baboon. The change in contingencies has occurred too rapidly to work through natural selection. Possibly an instinctive response has been unlearned, but the effect is more plausibly interpreted as the extinction of an operant.)

Imprinting is another phenomenon which shows how hard it is to detect the nature and effect of phylogenic contingencies. In Thomas More's *Utopia*, eggs were incubated. The chicks "are no sooner out of the shell, and able to stir about, but they seem to consider those that feed them as their mothers and follow them as other chickens do the hen that hatched them." Later accounts of imprinting have been reviewed by Gray (2). Various facts suggest phylogenic origins: the response of following an imprinted object appears at a certain age; if it cannot appear then, it may not appear at all; and so on. Some experiments by Peterson (18), however, suggest that what is inherited is not necessarily the behavior of following but a susceptibility to reinforcement by proximity to the mother or mother surrogate. A distress call reduces the distance between mother and chick when the mother responds appropriately, and walking toward the mother has the same effect. Both behaviors may therefore be reinforced (19), but they appear before these ontogenic contingencies come into play and are, therefore, in part at least phylogenic. In the laboratory, however, other behaviors can be made effective which phylogenic contingencies are unlikely to have strengthened. A chick can be conditioned to peck a key, for example, by moving an imprinted object toward it when it pecks or to walk away from the object if, through a mechanical arrangement, this behavior actually brings the object closer. To the extent that chicks follow an imprinted object simply because they thus bring the object closer or prevent it from becoming more distant the behavior could be said to be "species-specific" in the unusual sense that it is the product of *ontogenic* contingencies which prevail for most members of the species.

Ontogenic and phylogenic behaviors are not distinguished by any essence or character. Form of response seldom if ever yields useful classifications. The verbal response *Fire!* may be a command to a firing squad, a call for help, or an answer to the question, *What do you see?* The topography tells us little, but the controlling variables permit us to distinguish three very different verbal operants (20). The sheer forms of instinctive and learned behaviors also tell us little. Animals court, mate, fight, hunt, and rear their young, and they use the same effectors in much the same way in all sorts of learned behavior. Behavior is behavior whether learned or unlearned; it is only the controlling variables which make a difference. The difference is not always important. We might show that a honey guide is controlled by the buzzing of bees rather than by the sight of a nest, for example, without prejudice to the question of whether the behavior is innate or acquired.

Nevertheless the distinction is important if we are to undertake to predict or control the behavior. Implications for human affairs have often affected the design of research and the conclusions drawn from it. A classical example concerns the practice of exogamy. Popper (21) writes:

> *Mill and his psychologistic school of sociology...would try to explain [rules of exogamy] by an appeal to 'human nature,' for instance to some sort of instinctive aversion against incest (developed perhaps through natural selection...): and something like this would also be the naïve or popular explanation. [From Marx's] point of view...however, one could ask whether it is not the other way round, that is to say, whether the apparent instinct is not rather a product of education, the effect rather than the cause of the social rules and traditions demanding exogamy and forbidding incest. It is clear that these two approaches correspond exactly to the very ancient problem whether social laws are 'natural' or 'conventions'...*

Much earlier, in his *Supplement to the Voyage of Bougainville*, Diderot (22) considered the question of whether there is a natural basis for sexual modesty or shame (*pudeur*). Though he was writing nearly a hundred years before Darwin, he pointed to a possible basis for natural selection. "The pleasures of love are followed by a weakness which puts one at the mercy of his enemies. That is the only natural thing about modesty; the rest is convention." Those who are preoccupied with sex are exposed to attack (indeed, may be stimulating attack): hence, those who engage in sexual behavior under cover are more likely to breed successfully. Here are phylogenic contingencies which either make sexual behavior under cover stronger than sexual behavior in the open or reinforce the taking of cover when sexual behavior is strong. Ontogenic contingencies through which organisms seek cover to avoid disturbances during sexual activity are also plausible.

The issue has little to do with the character of incestuous or sexual behavior, or with the way people "feel" about it. The basic distinction is between provenances. And provenance is important because it tells us something about how behavior can be supported or changed. Most of the controversy concerning heredity and environment has arisen in connection with the practical control of behavior through the manipulation of relevant variables.

Interrelations Among Phylogenic and Ontogenic Variables

The ways in which animals behave compose a sort of taxonomy of behavior comparable to other taxonomic parts of biology. Only a very small percentage of existing species has as yet been investigated. (A taxonomy of behavior may indeed by losing ground as new species are discovered.) Moreover, only a small part of the repertoire of any species is every studied. Nothing approaching a fair sampling of species-specific behavior is therefore ever likely to be made.

Specialists in phylogenic contingencies often complain that those who study learned behavior neglect the genetic limitations of their subjects, as the comparative anatomist might object to conclusions drawn from the intensive study of a single species. Beach, for example, has written (23): "Many...appear to believe that in studying the rat they are studying all or nearly all that is important in behavior... How else are we to interpret...[a],457-page opus which is based exclusively upon the performance of rats in bar-pressing situations but is entitled simply *The Behavior of Organisms*?" There are many precedents for concentrating on one species (or at most a very few species) in biological investigations. Mendel discovered the basic laws of genetics—in the garden pea. Morgan worked out the theory of the gene—for the fruitfly. Sherrington investigated the integrative action of the nervous system—in the dog and cat. Pavlov studied the physiological activity of the cerebral cortex—in the dog.

In the experimental analysis of behavior many species differences are minimized. Stimuli are chosen to which the species under investigation can respond and which do not elicit or release disrupting responses: visual stimuli are not used if the organism is blind, nor very bright lights if they evoke evasive action. A response is chosen which may be emitted at a high rate without fatigue and which will operate recording and controlling equipment: we do not reinforce a monkey when it pecks a disk with its nose or a pigeon when it trips a toggle switch—though we might do so if we wished. Reinforcers are chosen which are indeed reinforcing, either positively or negatively. In this way species differences in sensory equipment, in effector systems, in susceptibility to reinforcement, and in possible disruptive repertoires are minimized. The data then show an extraordinary uniformity over a wide range of species. For example, the processes of extinction, discrimination, and generalization, and the performances generated by various schedules of reinforcement are reassuringly similar. (Those who are interested in fine structure may interpret these practices as minimizing the importance of sensory and motor areas in the cortex and emotional and motivational areas in the brain stem, leaving for study the processes associated with nerve tissue as such, rather than with gross anatomy.) Although species differences exist and should be studied, an exhaustive analysis of the behavior of a single species is as easily justified as the study of the chemistry or microanatomy of nerve tissue in one species.

A rather similar objection has been lodged against the extensive use of domesticated animals in laboratory research (24). Domesticated animals offer many advantages. They are more easily handled, they thrive and breed in captivity, they are resistant to the infections encountered in association with men, and so on. Moreover, we are primarily interested in the most domesticated of all animals—man. Wild animals are, of course, different—possibly as different from domesticated varieties as some species are from others, but both kinds of differences may be treated in the same way in the study of basic processes.

The behavioral taxonomist may also argue that the contrived environment of the laboratory is defective since it does not evoke characteristic phylogenic behavior. A pigeon in a small enclosed space pecking a disk which operates a mechanical food dispenser is behaving very differently from pigeons at large. But in what sense is this behavior not "natural"? If there is a natural phylogenic environment, it must be the environment in which a given kind of behavior evolved. But the phylogenic contingencies responsible for current behavior lie in the distant past. Within a few thousand years—a period much too short for genetic changes of any great magnitude—all current species have been subjected to drastic changes in climate, predation, food supply, shelter, and so on. Certainly no land mammal is now living in the environment which, selected its principle genetic features, behavioral or otherwise. Current environments are almost as "unnatural" as a laboratory. In any case, behavior in a natural habitat would have no special claim to genuineness. What an organism does is a fact about that organism regardless of the conditions under which it does it. A behavioral process is none the less real for being exhibited in an arbitrary setting.

The relative importance of phylogenic and ontogenic contingencies cannot be argued from instances in which unlearned or learned behavior intrudes or dominates. Breland and Breland (4) have used operant conditioning and programming to train performing animals. They conditioned a pig to deposit large wooden coins in a "piggy bank." The coins were placed several feet from the bank and the pig required to carry them to the bank and deposit them...At first the pig would eagerly pick up one dollar, carry it to the bank, run back, get another, carry it rapidly and neatly, and so on....Thereafter, over a period of weeks the behavior would become slower and slower. He might run over eagerly for each dollar, but on the way back, instead of carrying the dollar and depositing it simply and clearly, he would repeatedly drop it, root it, drop it again, root it along the way, pick it up, toss it up in the air, drop it, root it some more, and so on. They also conditioned a chicken to deliver plastic capsules containing small toys by moving them toward the purchaser with one or two sharp straight pecks. The chickens began to grab at the capsules and "pound them up and down on the floor of the cage" perhaps as if they were breaking seed pods or pieces of food too large to be swallowed. Since other reinforcers were not used, we cannot be sure that these phylogenic forms of food-getting behavior appeared because the objects were manipulated under food-reinforcement. The conclusion is plausible, however, and not disturbing. A shift in controlling variables is often observed. Under reinforcement on a so-called "fixed-interval schedule" competing behavior emerges at predictable points (25). The intruding behavior may be learned or unlearned. It may disrupt a performance or, as Kelleher (26) has shown, it may not. The facts do not show an inherently greater power of phylogenic contingencies in general. Indeed, the intrusions may occur in the other direction. A hungry pigeon which was being trained to guide missiles (27) was reinforced with food on a schedule which generated a high rate of pecking at a target projected on a plastic disk. It began to peck at the food as rapidly as at the target. The rate was too high to permit it to take grains into its mouth, and it began to starve. A product of ontogenic contingencies had suppressed one of the most powerful phylogenic activities. The behavior of civilized man shows the extent to which environmental variables may mask an inherited endowment.

Misleading Similarities

Since phylogenic and ontogenic contingencies act at different times and shape and maintain behavior in different ways, it is dangerous to try to arrange their products on a single continuum or to describe them with a single set of terms.

An apparent resemblance concerns intention or purpose. Behavior which is influenced by its consequences seems to be directed toward the future. We say that spiders spin webs in order to catch flies and that men set nets in order to catch fish. The "order" is temporal. No account of either form of behavior would be complete if it did not make some reference to its effects. But flies or fish which have not yet been caught cannot affect behavior. Only past effects are relevant. Spiders which have built effective webs have been more likely to leave offspring, and a way of setting a net that has effectively caught fish has been reinforced. Both forms of behavior are therefore more likely to occur again, but for very different reasons.

The concept of purpose has had, of course, an important place in evolutionary theory. It is still sometimes said to be needed to explain the variations upon which natural selection operates. In human behavior a "felt intention" or "sense of purpose" which precedes action is sometimes proposed as a current surrogate for future events. Men who set nets "know why they are doing so," and something of the same sort may have produced the spider's web-spinning behavior which then became subject to natural selection. But men behave because of operant reinforcement even though they cannot "state their purpose"; and when they can, they may simply be describing their behavior and the contingencies responsible for its strength. Self-knowledge is at best a by-product of contingencies; it is not a cause of the behavior generated by them. Even if we could discover a spider's felt intention or sense of purpose, we could not offer it as a cause of the behavior.

Both phylogenic and ontogenic contingencies may seem to "build purpose into" an organism. It has been said that one of the achievements of cybernetics has been to demonstrate that machines may show purpose. But we must look to the construction of the machine, as we look to the phylogeny and ontogeny of behavior, to account for the fact that an ongoing system acts as if it had a purpose.

Another apparent characteristic in common is "adaptation." Both kinds of contingencies change the organism so that it adjusts to its environment in the sense of behaving in it more effectively. With respect to phylogenic contingencies, this is what is meant by natural selection. With respect to ontogeny, it is what is meant by operant conditioning. Successful responses are selected in both cases, and the result is adaptation. But the processes of selection are very different, and we cannot tell from the mere fact that behavior is adaptive which kind of process has been responsible for it.

More specific characteristics of behavior seem to be common products of phylogenic and ontogenic contingencies. Imitation is an example. If we define imitation as behaving in a way which resembles the observed behavior of another organism, the term will describe both phylogenic and ontogenic behavior. But important distinctions need to be made. Phylogenic contingencies are presumably responsible for well-defined responses released by similar behavior (or its products) on the part of others. A warning cry is taken up and passed along by others: one bird in a flock flies off and the others fly off, one member of a herd starts to run, and the others start to run. A stimulus acting upon only one member of a group thus quickly affects other members with plausible phylogenic advantages.

The parrot displays a different kind of imitative behavior. Its vocal repertoire is not composed of inherited responses, each of which, like a warning cry, is released by the sound of a similar response in others. It acquires its imitative behavior ontogenically, but only through an apparently inherited capacity to be reinforced by hearing itself produce familiar sounds. Its responses need not be released by immediately preceding stimuli (the parrot speaks when not spoken to): but an echoic stimulus is often effective, and the response is then a sort of imitation.

A third type of imitative contingency does not presuppose an inherited tendency to be reinforced by behaving as others behave. When other organisms are behaving in a given way, similar behavior is likely to be reinforced, since they would not be behaving in that way if it were not. Quite apart from any instinct of imitation, we learn to do what others are doing because we are then likely to receive the reinforcement they are receiving. We must not overlook distinctions of this sort if we are to use or cope with imitation in a technology of behavior.

Aggression is another term which conceals differences in provenance. Inherited repertoires of aggressive responses are elicited or released by specific stimuli. Azrin, for example, has studied the stereotyped, mutually aggressive behavior evoked when two organisms receive brief electric shocks. But he and his associates have also demonstrated that the opportunity to engage in such behavior functions as a reinforcer and, as such, may be used to shape an indefinite number of "aggressive" operants of arbitrary topographies (28). Evidence of damage to others may be reinforcing for phylogenic reasons because it is associated with competitive survival. Competition in the current environment may make it reinforcing for ontogenic reasons. To deal successfully with any specific aggressive act we must respect its provenance. (Emotional responses, the bodily changes we feel when we are aggressive, like sexual modesty or aversion to incest, may conceivably be the same whether of phylogenic or ontogenic origin: the importance of the distinction is not thereby reduced.) Konrad Lorenz's recent book *On Aggression* (29) could be seriously misleading if it diverts our attention from relevant manipulable variables in the current environment to phylogenic contingencies which, in their sheer remoteness, encourage a nothing-can-be-done-about-it-attitude.

The concept of territoriality also often conceals basic differences. Relatively stereotyped behavior displayed in defending a territory, as a special case of phylogenic aggression, has presumably been generated by contingencies involving food supplies, breeding, population density, and so on. But cleared territory, associated with these and other advantages, becomes a conditioned reinforcer and as such generates behavior much more specifically adapted to clearing a given territory. Territorial behavior may also be primarily ontogenic. Whether the territory defended is as small as a spot on a crowded beach or as large as a sphere of influence in international politics, we shall not get far in analyzing the behavior if we recognize nothing more than "a primary passion for a place of one's own" (30) or insist that "animal behavior provides prototypes of the lust for political power" (31).

Several other concepts involving social structure also neglect important distinctions. A hierarchical "pecking order" is inevitable if the members of a group differ with respect to aggressive behavior in any of the forms just mentioned. There are therefore several kinds of pecking orders, differing in their provenances. Some dominant and submissive behaviors are presumably phylogenic stereotypes; the underdog turns on its back to escape further attack, but it does not follow that the vassal prostrating himself before king or priest is behaving for the same reasons. The ontogenic contingencies which shape the organization of a large company or governmental administration show little in common with the phylogenic contingencies responsible for the hierarchy in the poultry yard. Some forms of human society may resemble the anthill or beehive, but not because they exemplify the same behavioral processes (32).

Basic differences between phylogenic and ontogenic contingencies are particularly neglected in theories of communication. In the inherited signal systems of animals the behavior of a "speaker" furthers the survival of the species when it affects a "listener." The distress call of a chick evokes appropriate behavior in the hen; mating calls and displays evoke appropriate responses in the opposite sex; and so on. De Laguna (33) suggested that animal calls could be classified as declarations, commands, predictions, and so on, and Sebeok (34) has recently attempted a similar synthesis in modern linguistic terms, arguing for the importance of a science of zoosemiotics.

The phylogenic and ontogenic contingencies leading, respectively, to instinctive signal systems and to verbal behavior are quite different. One is not an early version of the other. Cries, displays, and other forms of communication arising from phylogenic contingencies are particularly insensitive to operant reinforcement. Like phylogenic repertoires in general, they are restricted to situations which elicit or release them and hence lack the variety and flexibility which favor operant conditioning. Vocal responses which at least closely resemble instinctive cries have been conditioned, but much less easily than responses using other parts of the skeletal nervous system. The vocal responses in the human child which are so easily shaped by operant reinforcement are not controlled by specific releasers. It was the development of an undifferentiated vocal repertoire which brought a new and important system of behavior within range of operant reinforcement through the mediation of other organisms (20).

Many efforts have been made to represent the products of both sets of contingencies in a single formulation. An utterance, gesture, or display, whether phylogenic or ontogenic, is said to have a referent which is its meaning, the referent or meaning being inferred by a listener. Information theory offers a more elaborate version: the communicating organism selects a message from the environment, reads out relevant information from storage, encodes the message, and emits it; the receiving organism decodes the message, relates it to other stored information, and acts upon it effectively. All these activities, together with the storage of material, may be either phylogenic or ontogenic. The principal terms in such analyses (input, output, sign, referent, and so on) are objective enough, but they do not adequately describe the actual behavior of the speaker or the behavior of the listener as he responds to the speaker. The important differences between phylogenic and ontogenic contingencies must be taken into account in an adequate analysis. It is not true, as Sebeok contends, that "any viable hypothesis about the origin and nature of language will have to incorporate the finds of zoosemiotics." Just as we can analyze and teach imitative behavior without analyzing the phylogenic contingencies responsible for animal mimicry, or study and construct human social systems without analyzing the phylogenic contingencies which lead to the social life of insects, so we can analyze the verbal behavior of man without taking into account the signal systems of other species.

Purpose, adaptation, imitation, aggression, territoriality, social structure, and communication—concepts of this sort have, at first sight, an engaging generality. They appear to be useful in describing both ontogenic and phylogenic behavior and to identify important common properties. Their very generality limits their usefulness, however. A more specific analysis is needed if we are to deal effectively with the two kinds of contingencies and their products.

References and Notes

1. J. B. Watson, *Behaviorism* (W. W. Norton, New York, 1924).
2. P. H. Gray, J. *Gen Psychol.* 68, 333 (1963).
3. J. Hirsch, *Science* 142, 1436 (1963).
4. K. Breland and M. Breland, *Amer. Psychologist* 16, 681 (1961).
5. K. Lorenz, *Evolution and Modification of Behavior* (Univ. of Chicago Press, Chicago. 1965).
6. E. Erienmeyer-Kiming, J. Hirsch, J. M. Weiss, J. *Comp. Physiol. Psychol.* 55, 722 (1962).
7. B. Pascal, *Pensee* (1670).
8. V. C. Wynne-Edwards, *Science* 147, 1543 (1965).
9. J. Huxley, *Perspectives Biol. Med.* 7, 4 (1964).
10. B. F. Skinner, *The Behavior of Organisms* (Appleton-Century-Crofts, New York. 1938).
11. H. S. Terrace, J. *Exp. Anal Behavior* 6, 223 (1963).
12. C. B. Ferster and B. F. Skinner, *Schedules of Reinforcement* (Appleton-Century-Crofts, New York. 1957).
13. B. F. Skinner, J. *Exp Psychol.* 38, 168 (1948).
14. W. H. Thorpe, *Ibis* 93, 1 (1951).
15. N. Tinbergen, *The Herring-Gull's World* (Collins, London, 1953).
16. A. Kortlandt, *Current Anthropol.* 6, 320 (1965).
17. H. Friedmann quoted in *Science* 123, 55 (1956).
18. N. Peterson, *Science* 132, 1395 (1960).
19. H. S. Hoffman, D. Schiff, J. Adams, J. L. Searle, *ibid.* 151, 352 (1966).

20. B. F. Skinner, *Verbal Behavior* (Appleton-Century, Crofts, New York. 1957).
21. K. R. Popper, *The Open Society and Its Enemies* (Routledge & Kegan Paul, London. 1957).
22. D. Diderot, *Supplement as Voyage de Bougainville* (written in 1774, published in 1796).
23. F. Beach, *Amer. Psychologist* 5, 115 (1950).
24. J. L. Kavanau, *Science* 143, 490 (1964).
25. W. H. Morse and B. F. Skinner, J. *Comp. Physiol. Psychol*. 50, 279 (1957).
26. R. T. Kelleher, *Amer. Psychologist* 17, 659 (1962).
27. B. F. Skinner, *ibid.* 15, 28 (1960).
28. N. H. Arzin, R. R. Hutchinson, R. McLaughlin, J. *Exp. Anal. Behav*. 8. 171 (1965).
29. K. Lorenz, *On Aggression* (Harcourt, Brace & World, New York. 1966. German ed. 1963).
30. R. Ardrey, *African Genesis* (Atheneum, New York. 1961).
31. R. Dubos, *Amer. Scientists* 53, 4 (1965).
32. W. C. Allee, *Cooperation Among Animals* (Abelard-Schuman, New York, 1938).
33. G. DeLaguna, *Speech: Its Function and Development* (Yale University Press, New Haven, 1927).
34. T. A. Sebeok, *Science* 147, 1006 (1965).
35. This article was prepared with the help of the NIH grant K6-MH-21, 775 and the Aaron E. Norman Fund.

FOOD REINFORCEMENT AND THE ORGANIZATION OF BEHAVIOUR IN GOLDEN HAMSTERS

Sara J. Shettleworth (1975). *Journal of Experimental Psychology: Animal Behavior Processes, 1(1),* 56-87.

Shettleworth's research was very effective in building a bridge between the naturalistic observation techniques of the ethologists and the laboratory experimental techniques of mainstream learning theory. She began her research as any good ethologist would, by learning the naturally occurring behavioral characteristics of the hamsters she wanted to understand. From this she identified six different response classes. She then experimentally food reinforced these behaviors when the hamsters were food deprived. Interesting the three behaviors which she had previously observed to occur when the animals were hungry and anticipating food were easily conditioned, while the behaviors that naturally decreased when they were hungry showed no conditioning, demonstrating that the hamsters were prepared to learn some associations and contra-prepared to learn others.

Introduction

Not everything an animal does can be modified equally readily by reinforcement. There seem to be constraints on at least the performance of some elements of behaviour as operants, if not on their reinforceability, i.e. on learning *per se*. The existence of such constraints raises the question whether there is some way to classify responses *a priori* according to whether or how they will be affected by reinforcement.

A number of dichotomous schemes for classifying responses have been suggested in the past. All of them implicitly recognize that not all identifiable responses can be conditioned using operant methods, but most of them have been effectively undermined by evidence that at least one member of the "not conditionable" class can be conditioned. For example, Miller's (1969) work has forced abandonment of the notion that autonomic responses cannot be operantly conditioned while skeletal responses can. Skinner's (1938) classification in terms emitted and elicited responses, that in terms of voluntary and involuntary responses (Vanderwolf, 1971), and others have had similar fates (Black and Young, 1972). Nevertheless, there remains a small body of evidence (reviewed by Shettleworth, 1972) that reward or punishment do not have the same effects on all responses. The frequency of some responses may not be modifiable at all, and the frequency of others may be modifiable only with some reinforcers or only to a limited extent. This evidence comes mainly from attempts to use operant techniques to condition the spontaneously occurring action patterns of various animals.

The first attempt to reinforce something other than an "arbitrary operant" seems to have been made by Thorndike (1911), who put a domestic chick into a box and allowed it to rejoin its companions whenever it preened itself. He also released cats from boxes whenever they licked or scratched themselves. Unlike topographically novel responses such as bar-pressing, which can never have had any role in the animal's pre-experimental life, such responses are already being performed by the animal "for other reasons", with some definite function or potential function. It would not be surprising to find that there are limits on the extent to which such units of behaviour can be altered in frequency or intensity by consequences that may have little relationship to their normal function or causation. And in fact the scattered reports of experiments on various species in which such responses have been rewarded or punished do contain some rather strange findings.

For example, one recurrent observation is that rewarded action patterns may become quite minimal in form even as they increase in frequency (e.g. Thorndike, 1911; Hogan, 1964; Konorski, 1967). Thorndike's cats and chicks, for example, eventually gave only the merest suggestion of the rewarded lick, scratch, or preening movement and did not always repeat the response immediately if reward was withheld. However, these responses may have become so perfunctory as a direct result of the reinforcement contingencies and not because of their special nature. If the animal is reinforced each time it begins to engage in some behaviour, it will never have a chance to perform or to be reinforced for more than a minimal form of it. In support of this explanation is Hogan's (1964) finding that although pigeons reinforced with food for preening did show rather abnormal preening behaviour when they were reinforced for each preening movement, preening became less abnormal when reinforcement was given on a variable interval schedule and in extinction.

Contrasting with these reports that minimal responses develop are a number of reports that a reinforced action pattern develops into a high-intensity form exceeding what is required for reinforcement. This has been reported several times for the operant conditioning of fighting behaviour in pigeons for food (Skinner, 1959; Reynolds *et al*., 1963; Azrin and Hutchinson, 1967) and also for fighting in rats for water reward (Ulrich *et at*., 1963). In such experiments, a minimal form of attack, such as exerting a given force against a conspecific, often develops into full-blown fighting including many movements other than that originally reinforced. The subjects may even fight to the extent that they fail to collect reinforcements. Nevertheless, at least in pigeons, fighting is still under the control of the reinforcement schedule (Azrin and Hutchinson, 1967). Similar behaviour in excess of the requirements of reinforcement contingencies was observed also by Breland and Breland (1966) in some situations. In the case of conditioned aggressive behaviour it may appear simply because the shaping procedure brings the animal into contact with stimuli eliciting unconditioned aggression (Reynolds *et al*., 1963; Azrin and Hutchinson, 1967).

Surprisingly, a survey of the rather limited literature (cf. Shettleworth, 1972) reveals few outright failures of reinforcement to affect the frequency of a species-typical action pattern on which it was made contingent. It may be instructive that such failures have been reported more with negative reinforcers (i.e. in escape, avoidance, or punishment paradigms) than with positive reinforcers. Indeed, it has been observed quite often that an avoidance contingency which is demonstrably effective with some responses is quite ineffective with others, even responses which can be affected by other reinforcement contingencies. Findings of this sort have inspired an account of avoidance learning (Bolles, 1970) which states that the only readily acquired avoidance responses are those that are species-specific defence reactions or slight modifications of such responses.

Although reinforcement may almost always have some effect, its effect on some responses can be quite limited. In all the literature in this area, two of the most thoroughly analysed examples (Black and Young, 1972; Sevenster, 1968 and Chapter 12) seem to reveal a constraint purely on the performance of a reinforced response. Both of them show that to understand what happens when reinforcement is made contingent on performance of a species-typical action pattern it may be necessary to take into account the relationship of the normal causal factors for the reinforced response to the conditions present in the learning situation. Although reinforcement may bring it under the control of new causal factors, a response may remain under the control of its original ones as well. This can lead to apparent failures of reinforcement or apparent response-reinforcer interactions when the learning situation itself contains factors that normally inhibit the response. The internal state necessary to make the reinforcer effective and presentation of the reinforcer *per se* seem to be particularly important among such factors.

Black and Young, as well as Sevenster, suggest that it may be impossible for reinforcement to overcome factors inhibiting the reinforced response, and Black and Young were able to show this directly for drinking as an avoidance response in rats. They trained rats to drink water to avoid shocks in the presence of one discriminative stimulus and to press a lever to avoid shocks in the presence of a second stimulus. If the rats were water-deprived or if the water was sweetened, lever pressing and drinking were under stimulus control, and the rats avoided most of the shocks. But when the same rats were satiated and required to drink tap water to avoid, they responded only at a low rate in the presence of the stimulus signaling that drinking should avoid shocks. The constraint on conditioning here, and in the similar example reported by Sevenster, thus seems to be not a constraint on learning in the sense of failure of the to-be-conditioned response to be reinforced, but rather a failure of reinforcement to overcome other, specifically motivational, factors in the situation.

In contrast to these examples of continued control of a response by its normal causal factors, Konorski (1967) describes some results which seem to indicate that a response may be gradually weaned away from the control of its original eliciting factors. There may be a continuum of such effects (cf. Black and Young, 1972), since the sorts of cumulative records presented by Skinner (1938) show that a relatively "neutral" response like bar-pressing can be brought under the control of experimental factors almost immediately, in that it is performed at a nearly maximum rate as soon as it has been reinforced a few times. However, there may also be important differences between learning to perform a response in the absence of its original eliciting factors and performing it in the presence of inhibitory factors.

Although many of the anomalous results of reinforcing species-typical action patterns can be accounted for in terms of motivational factors like those already discussed (Shettleworth, 1972), in most cases there has not been enough experimental analysis to rule out other possibilities. For example, there may be responses which are refractory to all kinds of reward or punishment, as Konorski (1967) suggest, or to particular ones. Analysis might be helped in some cases by considering the normal consequences as well as the normal cause of a to-be-conditioned response in relation to the reinforcer. And something might be learned by considering how the response develops in the normal behaviour of the species in question.

A fairly comprehensive study of what happens when various elements of a single species' behaviour are reinforced with various reinforcers might be expected to show what, if anything, responses that are difficult or impossible to condition have in common in other respects. Thus it might help to show why conditionability may be limited. To make it possible to examine the role of purely motivational factors, such an investigation should include observations of the direct, as opposed to contingent, effects of the reinforcers. I will describe here the first stages of a programme of this sort using golden hamsters (*Mesocricetus auratus*). The experiments so far have dealt with the effects of reinforcement with food. The first one I shall describe provides background data on the effects of hunger and the presentation of food on the behaviour of hamsters in an open field, and the second deals with the effects of food reinforcement on several behaviour patterns the hamsters display in the open field.

Effects of Food and Hunger on the Behaviour of Hamsters in an Open Field

General method. The subjects in all the work to be reported were adult golden hamsters of both sexes, born and reared in the laboratory and at least three months old at the start of an experiment. They were observed in an open field, a two-foot square topless plywood box with one Plexiglas side, sides 18 inches high and sawdust about ½ inch deep on the metal floor. A standard Gerbrands lever for rats and a dipper for delivering food pellets were close together on one wall. The hamsters lived under a reversed light cycle and were observed during the last hour of light or the first four hours of darkness.

All the data to be reported are based on 20-minute one-daily observation sessions during which a hamster's behaviour was recorded continuously in 18 mutually exclusive categories on a keyboard. This was attached to relay circuitry in another room which was programmed to record the number of one-second intervals in which each behaviour occurred. For some behaviours, this measure was recorded separately for each four-minute interval and the number of times the key was pressed (i.e. the number of continuous bouts) was also recorded.

The behaviours which will be of concern here are the following: grooming face and head with forepaws; grooming belly or sides with mouth and/or forepaws; scratching with a hind leg; scent marking; digging; rearing in the open ("open rearing"); rearing with forepaw(s) against the metal panel holding the feeder and lever, including times when the lever was being pressed; and scrabbling, a behaviour in which the hamster claws at the wall, often hopping up and down and moving along the wall as if trying to climb out. Depressions of the lever sufficient to activate a micro-switch (about 23g force) and presentations of food pellets were recorded automatically.

Method: effects of food and hunger. A preliminary experiment, the "baseline experiment", was done to find out what hamsters did in the open field, how their behaviour changed with repeated experience there, and how hunger and/or the availability of food in the open field changed what they did. Thus it provided basic data against which to evaluate the effects of reinforcement with food, particularly because it included a group that received food periodically no matter what they did. Four groups of five experimentally naïve hamsters that were either hungry or not and either received no food in the open field or received 45 milligrammes of food pellets on a VI 30-second schedule were observed for nine 20-minute sessions. The food-deprived hamsters were also observed for an additional two sessions, during which those that had been receiving food in the open field no longer received it, and those that had not been receiving food did receive it, again on a VI 30-second schedule independently of their behaviour. A tone sounded whenever and for as long as a pellet was available in the dipper. "Hunger" in these experiments refers to a condition in which the hamster was gradually reduced to 80-85% of its weight and kept there by being given a measured amount of food one to two hours after the daily session. The undeprived animals were also handled and weighed daily.

Effect of Food Reinforcement on Bar-Pressing and Six Action Patterns

Bar-Pressing, open rearing, scrabbling, digging, and face-washing reinforced with food

Initially, bar-pressing and four action patterns were chosen for reinforcement with food. The four reinforced action patterns were face-washing (grooming face or head with forepaws), open rearing, scrabbling, and digging. All the action patterns were performed by hungry hamsters receiving food in the baseline experiment on an average of between 3 and 10 percent of the one-second intervals, and all typically had bout lengths in excess of one second. Since it is not possible to reinforce successive approximations to (i.e. shape) such responses as one would shape bar-pressing, it seemed important to avoid, at least initially, responses with operant levels so low as possibly to limit reinforceability in and of themselves. These five responses were affected in various ways by hunger in the baseline experiment: open rearing and scrabbling tended to be increased by hunger; face-washing; decreased; and digging and bar-pressing, not changed.

The procedure for reinforcing these responses was designed to avoid specifically reinforcing a form of the response so perfunctory and minimal as to be almost unrecognizable. It also included a minimum number of sessions with continuous reinforcement so that behaviour would be interrupted with food presentation no more than necessary to maintain the reinforced response and so that it would be possible to observe excessive forms of the response that might develop, including increases in behaviours related to the reinforced response.

Method. Accordingly, the procedure was as follows: 15 naïve food-deprived hamsters, about the same ages as those in the first experiment, were observed in the same way for ten sessions in the open field. Each of the five responses was reinforced in three different hamsters. During the first two sessions animals were given food on a VI 30-second schedule so that they would learn to approach the feeder when a pellet was presented. For the animals to be reinforced for bar-pressing, the next two sessions consisted of a small amount of shaping followed by continuous reinforcement for pressing the bar. They then had reinforcement on a VI 20-second schedule for four sessions and two sessions of extinction. During the first session of reinforcement for the hamsters reinforced for scrabbling, digging, open rearing, or face-washing, the recording device was wired to that a food pellet would be delivered whenever the selected response had occurred for 0.2 seconds, i.e. essentially as soon as it began. For the second session of continuous reinforcement and the four sessions on VI 20-second reinforcement that followed, the response requirement was 0.5 seconds. (It was possible to record responses shorter than this.) The six sessions of reinforcement were followed by two sessions of extinction, as in the case of bar-pressing. Throughout all of the sessions with reinforcement, each food pellet remained available until the hamster collected it, unless he did not immediately orient towards the feeder after performing the reinforced response.

(The results in the article are presented in a series of graphs which are summarized here in a single figure from Bower's Theories of Learning)

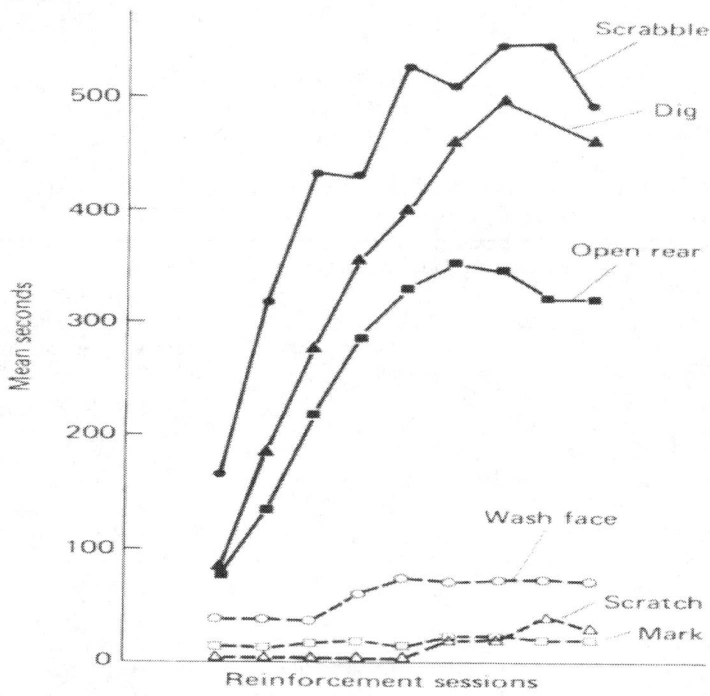

Mean time of a 20-minute session spent performing the rewarded response for one of six different behaviors

General Discussion and Conclusions

Of course prolonged exposure to some reinforcement contingency might cause face-washing, scent marking, or scratching with a hind leg to be performed as regularly and to take up as much of the time as the other responses that were reinforced in these experiments, but the relatively small effect of food reinforcement on these responses suggests that they are limited by some constraint that bar-pressing, scrabbling, digging, and open rearing are free of. The fact that face-washing and scratching with a hind leg, if not scent marking, do increase somewhat, suggests that this constraint may act on the performance of the response rather than on learning itself.

In the case of face-washing, the constraint could be a rather trivial one; namely, the animal needs a supply of saliva before it will lick its paws and rub them over its face and it cannot secrete enough saliva to support a very high rate of face-washing. One problem with this explanation is that since rats, at least, can be operantly conditioned to salivate (Miller, 1969), one would expect salivation to become part of the whole operant face-washing response. Furthermore, the paws are only licked very briefly if at all in the displacement face-washing in the open field (cf. also Dieterlen, 1959). Reinforcing grooming with water should provide a test of the importance of oral factors. To the extent that hamsters need a wet mouth to groom, the provision of water after each grooming bout should increase grooming more and more.*

*Although other species may groom after feeding (cf. Bolles, 1960) and hamsters sometimes do so after a long meal in the home cage, analysis of the session-by-session temporal distribution of grooming for two animals from each group in the baseline experiment showed that grooming in the open field had no particular relationship to eating there.

A second possible explanation for the constraint on face-washing derives from observations that grooming in many species is easily inhibited by tendencies to perform other behaviour (e.g. Andrew, 1956: Rowell, 1961). Observations like that of the difference between grooming in the home cage and grooming in the open field, and those by Dieterlen (1959) and Daly (1971), suggest that this is the case in hamsters as well. It could be that while food does directly reinforce face-washing, the reinforcement procedure also results in anticipation of food or of approaching the feeder being classically conditioned to the overt, or even unobservable, initiation of face-washing.

Such a conditioned anticipation of food might be especially likely to inhibit grooming responses. It is significant in this regard that when face-washing was reinforced the other, unreinforced, forms of grooming did not decrease noticeably in bout length as they became more frequent. The notion that face-washing is inhibited as soon as it begins by an expectation of food that becomes conditioned to it predicts that any form of grooming would be affected by food reinforcement in the same way as face washing. The abortive scratching with the hind leg that developed when that response was reinforced could be taken as evidence that this is so.

Differential effects of interrupting the various behaviours could also have played a role in their apparently different reinforceability. McFarland (in press) has shown that sub-dominant behaviours are less likely to be resumed after a neutral interruption than are dominant behaviours. Selective interruption by reinforcement delivery could tend to mask a facilitatory effect of reinforcement on sub-dominant behaviours, of which grooming and scent marking might be examples. The baseline experiment provides some evidence against this in that the over-all frequencies of the various behaviours in undeprived animals tended to be the same whether or not food pellets and the accompanying tone were presented periodically. Furthermore, in extinction, when the reinforced responses were no longer interrupted by food presentations, the rate of face-washing, scratching, or scent marking remained low (see figures).

The accounts of the present results suggested so far resemble the accounts of Sevenster's and Black and Young's work discussed in the introduction in that they attribute the limited conditioning of certain responses to some inhibitory factor preventing the full effect of reinforcement from manifesting itself. However, associative interpretations of the present findings are also possible. For example the hypothesis, that responses that could not normally function to obtain food are reinforced by food much more weakly than those which could, readily encompasses the differences in the effects of food reinforcement on digging, scrabbling, open rearing, and bar-pressing, on the one hand, and face-washing, scratching with a hind leg, and scent marking, on the other. Bolles (1970) seems to suggest a similar thing for avoidance responses, and, as a more remote example, stimuli that would not normally be relevant to the consequences of feeding are not readily associated with those consequences (Chapter 7). In this case the minimal grooming responses that developed under reinforcement must be interpreted as evidence of a weak effect of reinforcement.

The chief problem with this type of hypothesis for any reinforcer lies in the difficulty of identifying responses that are and are not relevant to the reinforcer. Bolles' suggestion that only species-specific defence reactions are readily acquirable as avoidance responses is relatively free of this criticism because the species-specific defence reactions can be identified as the responses elicited by the aversive stimulus, e.g. freezing to electric shock. Analogously, the responses least affected by food reinforcement might be those decreased by hunger, these might be the same responses that could not normally function in finding food, and the reverse. Similar generalizations might presumably apply to other reinforcers. However, in the present experiments the responses increased to high levels by food reinforcement included some that were not increased by food deprivation, and, in any case, food deprivation does not restrict the range of behaviour nearly so much as do the aversive stimuli used in the sorts of experiments discussed by Bolles.

A further problem with the hypothesis that responses are best reinforceable by functionally related reinforcers is that this possibility may be difficult to distinguish experimentally from the alternative that some responses are just not readily modifiable by reinforcement at all, since it may be difficult to devise experimental consequences appropriate to responses like grooming or scent marking. It must also be kept in mind that different responses can show only limited conditioning for different reasons. For example, grooming in hamsters might be constrained by motivational factors like those suggested previously while scent marking might be refractory to reinforcement *per se*.

Further experiments involving such things as different reinforcers for the same set of responses should help to distinguish among the various mechanisms that could be involved in the constraints on conditioning described here. Detailed sequential analysis of the behaviour of golden hamsters under various conditions might suggest why various behaviours were affected differently by food reinforcement. More precise quantitative information is also needed on the distributions of bout lengths of the various responses both unreinforced and under various reinforcement regimes. Using an "arbitrary operant" which can vary in duration like touching the bar might help to show whether changes in bout length distributions are restricted to certain reinforced action patterns. But it is especially important to inquire how far the cases of limited conditionability described here, whatever their nature, are specific to a free operant situation. In the free operant situation the effect of reinforcement is judged to be stronger the more the animal performs the reinforced response to the exclusion of other behaviour. Since grooming is apparently organized so that it is easily inhibited by other activities, examining its reinforceability in a situation which does not impose this requirement might better allow assessment of the relative contributions of associative and motivational factors to the constraint on its conditioning. For example, in a go- no-go discrimination the measure of learning could be the relative frequency of the reinforced response during the stimulus signaling availability of reinforcement. The ability to withhold the response during the stimulus signaling no reinforcement would also be important here, but the measure of learning would be relatively independent of absolute response rate.

Here I have emphasized the limited operant conditionability of some action patterns of golden hamsters with food reinforcement. In trying to understand how a response's pre-existing role in the animal's behaviour interacts with its acquisition as a operant it may be equally important to focus on why some responses were acquired so rapidly. In these experiments, scrabbling presents some problems because in the baseline experiment it reached its highest levels when food was withdrawn from the hungry hamsters, and dropped almost to zero in the hungry hamsters given food after nine sessions in the open field.

* studied natural behaviors & deduced theories of learning. *

Thus in a sense the more a hamster scrabbled for food reinforcement the more it produced the conditions under which it normally would not scrabble. This may just show that we do not understand the motivation of scrabbling very well. The problem could also be resolved by saying that since scrabbling is basically a form of locomotion, thwarted climbing (Daly, 1971), it is likely not to be tied to a fixed function or set of causal factors (cf. Black and Young, 1972). To do so is to underline the fact that our notions about when and how readily responses can be acquired as operants are still very poorly developed. We still know very little about what aspects of responses can predict to what degree their operant conditionability will be limited, or for what reinforcers. And even if a satisfactory account of such constraints can be developed for a single species, its extension to other species will doubtless raise many new problems.

References

Andrew, R. J. (1956). Normal and irrelevant toilet behaviour in *Emberiza* spp. *Anim. Behav.* 4, 85-91.

Azrin, N. H. and Hutchinson, R. R. (1967). Conditioning of the aggressive behavior of pigeons by a fixed-interval schedule of reinforcement. *F. exp. Anal. Behav.* 10, 395-402.

Black, A. H. and Young, G. A. (1972). Constraints on the operant conditioning of drinking. *In* "Reinforcement: Behavioral Analyses", (R M. Gilbert and J. R. Millenson, eds.) pp. 35-50. Academic Press, New York.

Bolles, R. C. (1960). Grooming behavior in the rat. *F. comp physiol. Psychol.* 53, 306-310.

Bolles, R. C. (1970). Species-specific defense reactions and avoidance learning. *Psychol. Rev.* 77, 32-48.

Breland, K. and Breland, M. (1966). "Animal Behavior." The Macmillan Company, New York.

Daly, J. M. (1971). Behavioural development, early experience, and maternal behaviour in golden hamsters. (*Mesocricetus auratus*) Ph.D. thesis, University of Toronto.

Dieterlen, F. (1959). Des Verhalten des syrischen Goldhamsters (*Mesocricetus auratus*, Waterhouse). Untersuchen zur Frage seiner Entwicklung und seiner angeborene Anteile durch geruchsisolierte Aufzuchten. *Zeits. fur Tierpsychol.* 16, 47-103.

Ewer, R. F. (1968). "Ethology of Mammals." Logos Press, London.

Hogan, J. A. (1964). Operant control of preening in pigeons. *F. exp. Anal. Behav.* 7, 351-354.

Konorski, J. (1967). "Integrative Activity of the Brain." University of Chicago Press, Chicago.

McFarland, D. J. (In press). Time-sharing as a behavioural phenomenon. *Adv. Study Behav.* 5.

Miller, N. E. (1969). Learning of visceral and glandular responses. *Science* 163, 434-445.

Mrosovsky, N. (1964). The performance of dormice and other hibernators on tests of hunger motivation. *Anim. Behav.* 12, 454-469.

Prescott, R. G. W. (1970). Some behavioral effects of variables which influence the "general level of activity" of rats. *Anim. Behav.* 18, 791-796.

Ralls, K. (1971). Mammalian scent-marking. *Science* 171, 443-449.

Reynolds, G. S., Catania, A. C. and Skinner, B. F. (1963). Conditioned and unconditioned aggression in pigeons. *F. exp. Anal. Behav.* 6, 73-74.

Rowell, C. H. F. (1961). Displacement grooming in the chaffinch. *Anim. Behav.* 9, 38-63.

Sevenster, P. (1968). Motivation and learning in sticklebacks. *In* "The Central Nervous System and Fish Behaviour", (D. Ingle, ed.) pp. 233-245. University of Chicago Press.

Shettleworth, S.J. (1972). Constraints on learning. *Adv. Study Behav.* 4, pp. 1-68. Academic Press, New York.

Skinner, B. F. (1938). "The Behavior of Organisms." Appleton-Century, New York.

Skinner, B. F. (1959). An experimental analysis of certain emotions. *F. exp. Anal. Behav.* 2, 264.

Thorndike, E. L. (1911). "Animal Intelligence." The Maccmilan Company, New York.

Ulrich, R., Johnston, M., Richardson, J. and Wolff, P. (1963). The operant conditioning of fighting behavior in rats. *Psychol. Rec.* 13, 465-470.

Vanderwolf, C. H. (1971). Limbic-diencephalic mechanisms of voluntary movement. *Psychol. Rev.* 78, 83-113.

SPECIES-SPECIFIC DEFENSE REACTIONS AND AVOIDANCE LEARNING

Robert C. Bolles (1970). *Psychological Review, 77(1),* 32-48.

Robert Bolles research showed similar anomalous results to those of Shettleworth. In laboratory experiments on avoidance conditioning animals most readily acquired responses that resemble in topology one of their SSDRs and little success in learning avoidance responses that were dissimilar to their SSDRs. Bolles at his most acerbic observed that the two-factor account of avoidance learning, where the animal is suppose to learn about danger signals is, "utter nonsense... No real life predator is going to present cues just before it attacks. What keeps our little friends alive in the forest has nothing to do with avoidance learning as we ordinarily conceive of it or investigate it in the laboratory .... What keeps animals alive in the wild is that they have very effective innate defense reactions which occur when they encounter any kind of new or sudden stimulus. (pp32-33).

The prevailing theories of avoidance learning and the procedures that are usually used to study it seem to be totally out of touch with what is known about how animals defend themselves in nature. This paper suggests some alternative concepts, starting with the assumption that animals have innate species-specific defense reactions (SSDRs) such as fleeing, freezing, and fighting. It is proposed that if a particular avoidance response is rapidly acquired, then that response must necessarily be an SSDR. The learning mechanism in this case appears to be suppression of nonavoidance behavior by the avoidance contingency. The traditional approaches to avoidance learning appear to be slightly more valid in the case of responses that are slowly acquired, although in this case, too the SSDR concept is relevant, and reinforcement appears to be based on the production of a safety signal rather than the termination of an aversive conditioned

Avoidance learning as we know it in the laboratory has frequently been used to "explain" how animals survive in the wild. The purpose of this paper is to turn this inferential process around and use the limited knowledge of natural defensive behavior to help account for some of the anomalies that have been found in laboratory studies of avoidance learning. Let us begin by recalling a little fable. It is a very familiar fable. It was already part of our lore when Hull gave his version of it in 1929, and the story has been told again many times since then. It goes something like this: Once upon a time there was a little animal who ran around in the forest. One day while he was running around, our hero was suddenly attacked by a predator. He was hurt and, of course, frightened, but he was lucky and managed to escape from the predator. He was able to get away and safely back to his home. The fable continues: Some time later our furry friend was again running around in the forest, which was his custom, when suddenly he perceived a conditioned stimulus. He heard or saw or smelled some stimulus which on the earlier occasion had preceded the attack by the predator. Now on this occasion our friend became frightened, he immediately took flight as he had on the previous occasion, and quickly got safely back home. So this time our hero had managed to avoid attack (and possibly worse) by responding appropriately to a cue which signaled danger; he did not have to weather another attack. And from that day hence the little animal who ran around in the forest continued to avoid the predator because the precariousness of his situation prevented, somehow, his becoming careless or forgetful.

The moral of this tale, we are told, is that little animals survive in nature because they learn to avoid big dangerous animals. The ability to learn to avoid has such obviously great survival value, we are told, that we should surely expect the higher animals to have evolved this ability. We should also expect animals to be able to learn to avoid in the laboratory, and we should expand our theories of behavior to encompass such learning.

I propose that this familiar fable with its happy ending and plausible moral is utter nonsense. The parameters of the situation make it impossible for there to be any learning. Thus, no real-life predator is going to present cues just before it attacks. No owl hoots or whistles 5 seconds before pouncing on a mouse. And no owl terminates his hoots or whistles just as the mouse gets away so as to reinforce the avoidance response. Nor will the owl give the mouse enough trials for the necessary learning to occur. What keeps our little friends alive in the forest has nothing to do with avoidance learning as we ordinarily conceive of it or investigate it in the laboratory.

Species-Specific Defense Reactions

What keeps animals alive in the wild is that they have very effective *innate* defensive reactions which occur when they encounter any kind of new or sudden stimulus. These defensive reactions vary somewhat from species to species, but they generally take one of three forms: Animals generally run or fly away, freeze or adopt some type of threat, that is, pseudo-aggressive behavior. These defensive reactions are elicited by the appearance of the predator and by the sudden appearance of innocuous objects. These responses are always near threshold so that the animal will take flight, freeze, or threaten whenever any novel stimulus event occurs. It is not necessary that the stimulus event be paired with shock or pain, or some other unconditioned stimulus. The mouse does not scamper away from the owl because it has learned to escape the painful claws of the enemy; it scampers away from anything happening in its environment, and it does so merely because it is a mouse. The gazelle does not flee from an approaching lion because it has been bitten by lions; it runs away from any large object that approaches it, and it does so because this is one of its species-specific defense reactions. Neither the mouse nor the gazelle can afford to *learn* to avoid; survival is too urgent, the opportunity to learn is too limited and the parameters of the situation make the necessary learning impossible. The animal which survives is one which comes into its environment with defensive reactions already a prominent part of its repertoire.

There is, or course, a considerable gulf between the wild animal of the field and forest and the domesticated animal of the laboratory. Our laboratory rats and dogs and monkeys are relatively approachable and are on relatively friendly term with us. However, this good relationship changes as soon as the animal is placed in a box and given a few electric shocks. When shocked, the normally friendly, inquisitive laboratory animal shows a dramatic change in behavior. Exploration and grooming drop out; so does all of its previously acquired appetitive behavior—bar pressing, etc. Instead of its normal range of highly flexible, adaptive, and outgoing behavior, its behavior is severely restricted to those defensive reactions that characterize the wild animals. It is furtive, hostile, and will flee if given the opportunity to do so.

In short, I am suggesting that the immediate and inevitable effect of severe aversive stimulation on a domesticated animal is to convert it, at least temporarily, into a wild animal by restricting its response repertoire to a narrow class of species-specific defense reactions (SSDRs). I am suggesting further that this sudden, dramatic restriction of the subject's (*S*'s) behavioral repertoire is of the utmost importance in the proper understanding of avoidance learning.

The concept of the SSDR repertoire enables one to make sense of what is one of the most challenging problems in avoidance learning, namely, that some responses either cannot be learned at all or are learned only occasionally after extensive training. A particular *S* may be able to learn one avoidance response (R_a) with great facility and be quite unable to learn another R_a. In the latter case the response may occur frequently, the presumed reinforcement contingencies may be regularly applied, and yet R_a fails to gain in strength. Such failures of learning indicate either that some responses are not acquirable or that the reinforcement contingencies are not what they were thought to be.

These failures of *S*'s to learn in situations where the theories require them to, pose a serious challenge to contemporary behavior theory. Is it possible that some responses in *S*'s repertoire actually are not acquirable as R_as? Such a conception defies one of the principal tenets of operant conditioning theory. The present paper argues for just this conclusion. I suggest that there is a restricted class of behaviors that can be readily acquired as R_as. Specifically, I am proposing that *an* R_a *can be rapidly acquired only if it is an SSDR*.

Is it possible, on the other hand, that the events which are ordinarily assumed to reinforce R_a actually are not effective in that capacity? I will argue that this is indeed the case, and that *an* R_a *is rapidly acquired only by the suppression of other SSDRs*. In other words, I propose that the primary effect of avoidance training is to get rid of competing behavior, and that this is accomplished mainly by the avoidance contingency.

The frequently reported failures of rats to learn certain R_as, such as wheel turning and bar pressing (e.g., D'Amato & Schiff, 1964; Meyer, Cho, & Wesemann, 1960; Smith, McFarland, & Taylor, 1961); should not be regarded as peculiar or as exceptions to the general applicability of operant conditioning principles but rather as one end of a continuum of difficulty of learning. Learning the R_a in a shuttle box is likely to require about 100 trials and a few rats apparently never acquire the response (Brush, 1966). Learning to run in a wheel proceeds considerably faster and more surely. All S_s learn the R_a within 40 trials (Bolles; Stokes, & Younger, 1966). But if we let the rat run down an alley to avoid shock, it may learn to do so in half a dozen trials (Theios, 1963). At the other extreme, if we place a rat in a box and shock it there, it may learn in one trial to jump out of the box (e.g., Maatsch, 1959). There is a continuum of difficulty here and the parameter that is involved, what R_a the situation requires, is an enormously important one which accounts for more of the variance than any other so far discovered in avoidance learning. Indeed, the response requirement is the only really impressive parameter we know of and it is a serious indictment of our major behavior theories that they pay no systematic attention to it.

By contrast, the SSDR hypothesis takes the fact that there are great differential rates of learning as its first principle. If we assume that the rat's SSDR repertoire consists of freezing, fleeing, or fighting (threat behavior), then it is clear why the jump-out box and the one-way apparatus should lead to such rapid acquisition. First, these situations provide abundant stimulus support for fleeing; more importantly, since freezing and aggressive behavior lead only to shock (because they fail to avoid it), these behaviors will be rapidly suppressed and the remaining SSDR, fleeing, will rapidly emerge as the most likely response in the situation. Running in the wheel and in the shuttle box are similar in that again freezing and fighting are punished by the paravoidance(pg 34) of shock, but there is the difference that *S* cannot flee the situation. The *S* can make the right kind of response, but its effectiveness is compromised by the fact that in the wheel *S* does not actually change its environment, while in the shuttle box *S* must return to a place it has just left.

Bar pressing is certainly not an SSDR and, accordingly, we would have to predict that it cannot be learned as an R_a. The truth is that it frequently is not learned. It is also true, however, that it sometimes is learned and this fact has to be dealt with. I suggest that when bar pressing is learned, the course of learning must necessarily be slow and uncertain because the processes involved are slow and uncertain. What is involved, apparently, is a stage of acquisition in which *S* freezes while holding onto the bar. Bolles and McGillis (1968) measured the latency of the bar-press escape response (R_a) and found that within 40 trials it fell to values in the order of .05 second. Such short shocks appear to be the result of very fast "reflexive" presses which occur, and which can only occur, if *S* is freezing on the bar. This behavior then has the effect of limiting the total amount of shock received to a value which does not disrupt *S's* ongoing behavior. Freezing anywhere else in the box or in any other posture will be disrupted by unavoided shocks and punished by these shocks, and so too will any consistent efforts to get out of the box. In effect, the rat must end up freezing on the bar because that is the only response which on the one hand is an SSDR, and on the other hand can continuously survive the avoidance contingency. The observation of rats in this situation indicates that this is what happens. Even the attempts to "shape" the bar-press R_a in the manner that pressing for food is commonly shaped must start with *S* freezing on the bar (D'Amato, Fazzaro, & Etkin, 1968; Feldman & Bremner, 1963; Keehn & Webster, 1968). Thus, freezing on the bar appears to be a necessary stage in the acquisition of the bar-press R_a just as the SSDR hypothesis suggests. How operant R_as can sometimes gradually emerge from this stage of respondent R_es is another story which will have to be considered later. The present discussion merely establishes that the SSDR hypothesis makes sense of the fact that some R_as are trivially easy to acquire while others evidently tax the limits of a particular species, and it provides, as far as I know, the first systematic account of these huge differences.

There is a trivial sense in which the SSDR hypothesis must be true, namely that if the SSDR repertoire includes all of *S*'s behavior in the aversive situation, then no other responses will occur there so no other responses can be reinforced there. The SSDR hypothesis is intended to mean something much more subtle and important than the obvious truth that a response must occur before it can be reinforced however. When appetitive behavior is reinforced with food, it is profitable and convenient to define specific responses in terms of the movements involved, for example, when we "shape" the bar-press response. It is also convenient to define specific responses in terms of their effects on the environment, for example, whether or not it causes a bar to be depressed. These response-class definitions are serviceable because food reinforcement appears to have equivalent effects on all members of these classes. But we will shortly turn to data which indicate that neither of these kinds of response classes, equivalent movements or equivalent environmental effects, holds together in the case of avoidance learning, at least not with respect to the reinforcement operation. Consider the acquisition of a jumping R_a. It appears to be relatively difficult to establish a particular jump topography, and relatively difficult to train the rat to jump if jumping avoids shock and terminates the conditioned stimulus (discussed subsequently), but it is very easy to teach the rat to jump out of a box where it has been shocked (Maatsch, 1959). The critical feature of jumping as a flight response appears to be whether it is *functionally effective* in the sense that it actually makes flight possible. The possibility of flight appears to be much more important in establishing a flight response than either its topographical features or even whether it is effective in avoiding shock.

Consider running which is also sometimes rapidly learned and sometimes is not. We must classify running as an SSDR because we observe that the rat runs in aversive situations (and out of them if it can). We can arrange aversive situations that provide different amounts of stimulus support for running, that is, we can change its operant rate and alter the whole SSDR repertoire by varying the situation. We can also arrange to make running effective in the sense that its occurrence prevents shock. But I contend that no matter how we arrange the situation, running will not be acquired as an R_a, at least not very readily, unless the running response is effective for flight, that is, effective in the functional sense that it takes the rat out of the situation. With other animals we should expect the case to be different if flight is functionally different. For example, whereas the rat and other small rodents flee from predators by getting completely away from them, an animal such as the dog needs to, and typically does, only stand off at some distance. From such observations the SSDR hypothesis suggests the inference that dogs might be much better than rats at learning to run in the shuttle box. Under some circumstances they are evidently quite good at it (e.g., Solomon & Wynne, 1953).

The argument so far can be summarized by giving an explicit statement of the SSDR hypothesis: For an R_a to be rapidly learned in a given situation, the response must be an effective SSDR in that situation and when rapid learning does occur, it is primarily due to the suppression of ineffective SSDRs.

The Escape Contingency

One implication of the SSDR hypothesis is that the contingencies which have traditionally borne the theoretical burden of reinforcing avoidance behavior, namely, the escape contingency and the conditioned stimulus (CS) termination contingency, are relatively ineffectual. There is now considerable evidence suggesting that this is the case and indicating that neither of these familiar aspects of the normal avoidance training procedure is crucial for the establishment of avoidance behavior. Let us look briefly at some of this evidence.

At first, the phenomenon of defensive learning was viewed as an example of Pavlovian conditioning, and the earliest experimental procedures reflected this kind of theoretical orientation. Thus, there was no escape contingency; it was the unconditioned response (UCR) that was *elicited* by a brief inescapable shock that was supposed to become conditioned to the CS. Instrumental avoidance learning procedures arose from the discovery that Pavlovian techniques only seemed to work with autonomic responses and with reflexes. Other techniques had to be developed to train instrumental or operant defensive behavior. The Pavlovian heritage was still apparent however. An avoidance response was first conditioned to the shock as an escape response (R_a) and it was called a UCR at this stage. Then, as it became conditioned to the CS, as it "gradually emerged," it was called a conditioned response (CR) (Solomon & Brush, 1956). In this view the escape contingency was a necessary part of the avoidance training procedure; it was essential for the maintenance of the UCR. This interpretation prevailed until Brogden, Lipman, and Culler (1938) and Mowrer (1939) began to demonstrate its inadequacy. Then, although a pure contiguity account of avoidance could no longer be defended a semicontiguity or compromise position began to prevail. According to this view, which is still probably the predominant view today, R_a gains *some* of its strength by generalization or through conditioning from the strength of R_e. In practical terms the escape contingency was supposed to help establish R_a and accordingly it became a regular part of the avoidance training procedure.

(The remainder of this section of the paper presents the results of several experiments testing the escape contingency hypothesis).

To return to the escape contingency, there have been a number of studies in which it has been eliminated in other ways. Bolles et al. (1966) trained *S*s with shocks of .1-second duration, that is too short to be response terminated, and found very little decrement relative to *S*s that were required to terminate shock in the usual manner. Similar results have been reported by D'Amato, Keller, and DiCara (1964), Hurwitz (1964), and Sidman (1953) in the bar-press situation although there is some question about whether there may still be some possibility of escape with the short shocks that were used. There are also a few instances in which negative transfer from R_e to R_a has been reported (Turner & Solomon, 1962; Warren & Bolles, 1967).

So much for the escape contingency. Knowledge about the escapability of shock does not permit us to predict how fast an animal will learn a particular R_a or whether R_a will be learned at all. Other considerations are much more important and one of the most important of these appears to be what the R_a is. The data suggest that R_a will be rapidly acquired if and only if it permits *S* to flee, freeze, or fight, and that whether there is an escape contingency is relatively inconsequential.

The CS-Termination Contingency

Another regular part of most avoidance experiments is the warning stimulus, or CS. Both its name and part of its assumed function derive from the Pavlovian tradition. The CS was assumed to be the stimulus to which the R_a (or CR) became conditioned. It has become fairly common in recent years to incorporate various control procedures for sensitization effects in order to determine if R_a is under the associative control of the CS. "Real" avoidance is attributed to performance beyond that displayed by sensitization control *S*s. There is some irony in the fact that what counts in nature is not an animal's ability to learn this kind of discrimination but rather that it be subject to these sensitization effects! As observed in the introductory section, what keeps animals alive in nature is that they display SSDRs whenever there any stimulus change in the environment. Some investigators have begun to suggest that perhaps in the laboratory too the stuff of which avoidance behavior is really made is rather indiscriminant defensive behavior. (Bolles et. al. 1966; D'Amato, 1967).

The major theoretical emphasis on the CS of course is not its discriminative function but the reinforcement that is widely assumed to result from its termination. Some theorists introduce the additional element of fear; termination of the CS is assumed to lead to a reduction of fear which is reinforcing (e.g., Miller, 1961; Mowrer, 1939). Others contend that the fear construct is gratuitous here, and that it is sufficient to assume that because the CS is paired with shock, it will become a conditioned negative reinforcer (e.g, Dinsmoor, 1954; Schoenfeld, 1950). According to either version of the story, however, termination of the CS is held to be an essential ingredient in avoidance learning. Hence, the termination of the CS is usually made contingent on the occurrence of R_a and under these circumstances it is easy to point to CS termination as the source of reinforcement when learning occurs.

The argument gained considerable support from Mowrer and Lamoreaux's (1942) early demonstration that making CS termination coincident with the occurrence of R_a led to much faster acquisition than having it go off automatically before R_a occurred or having its termination delayed for some seconds after R_a occurred. There was a little room for concern that any learning was found under the latter conditions, but Kamin (1956) was able to account for it in terms of delay of reinforcement effects, and at this point the CS-termination hypothesis appeared to be quite secure.

(Bolles summarizes several experiments showing that the inadequacy of the CS-termination hypothesis and concludes as follows)

So much for the CS-termination contingency. It is clear that while the CS-termination contingency is of some importance in some situations, it is of little consequence in situations such as the one-way runway and the running wheel where R_a is very rapidly acquired. If we wish to predict whether R_a will be acquired, or how fast it will be acquired, then knowledge about the CS-termination contingency will not give us nearly as much information as knowing what the R_a is. Moreover, even in those situations where CS termination is important, it turns out that it can be replaced by an entirely different kind of response contingency which produces learning just as effectively. It is becoming increasingly difficult to believe that avoidance learning occurs because the CS elicits fear or because it is aversive.[3] Let us look briefly at an alternative view of the role of the CS.

The Safety Signal Effect

The previous section suggested one interpretation of the CS-termination effect, namely, that termination of the CS serves as a source of feedback or stimulus change. This is an attractive hypothesis and it is supported by some evidence (Bolles & Grossen, 1969; Bower et al., 1965; D'Amato et al., 1968). Bolles and Grossen have suggested that the reason some situations lead to such rapid avoidance learning may be that they furnish *S* with a great deal of *intrinsic* feedback. Accordingly, the addition of *extrinsic* feedback provided by the experimenter in the form of lights out or tone termination contributes relatively little to that already resulting from the occurrence of R_a. As we move on to situations which involve little intrinsic feedback, for example, the bar press, which requires little effort and which does not change *S's* environment, the acquisition of the response may depend on there being some extrinsic feedback. With the assumption that intrinsic feedback has greater weight (or a higher sampling probability) than extrinsic feedback, we would be in a good position to explain many of the findings that have been discussed above. The rate-of-learning effect, the CS-termination effect, and the FS-presentation effect would all fall neatly into line.

There are, however, some difficult problems with this interpretation and some of the evidence does not fall into line so readily: (a) Why should intrinsic feedback be inherently more important than an arbitrarily selected external stimulus change, such as the termination of a tone? It is easy to argue that flight reactions necessarily produce a lot of stimulus change, but flight is not the only SSDR, and there is reason to believe that other SSDRs are also very rapidly acquired. For example, the author's observations, as well as those of Keehn (1967), indicate that freezing is acquired in very few trials, even though it is not a vigorous kind of behavior and does not change the situation. The rapid learning of the pseudo-flight response in the running wheel also indicates that the character of the response may be much more important than the simple quantity of stimulus change it produces. (b) Why does the rate of acquisition depend on the direction of stimulus change, that is, whether the stimulus goes on or off, and on its quality and modality (e.g., Myers, 1960, 1964)? Why is a change in geographical location such a particularly effective stimulus change? (c) Why does FS presentation or CS termination appear to be effective only with extended training? That is, if stimulus change is the critical factor then why doesn't it seem to have an effect in a rapidly acquired R_a or in the early trials of a slowly acquired R_a?

This last point needs some illustration. The data shown at the far right in Figure 2 represent life performance of rats with an FS in the shuttle box. Over the course of 80 trials, these *S*s avoided nearly as well as those under the usual CS-termination condition. But the learning curves for the two groups were markedly different; the FS group showed a serious decrement during the first 40 trials, but then caught up with the CS group and eventually surpassed it. In short, the FS condition is not completely equivalent to the CS condition it only produces the same mean performance over the course of the right number of trials. There seems to be a delay in the action of the FS contingency, such that it begins to be effective only after *S* has been in the situation for a number of trials, perhaps 40 or 50. D'Amato et al. (1968) found in their bar-press study that there was no FS effect during the first several hundred trials; it materialized only with continued training. One possibility is that the CS has functions beyond those it shares with the FS. It certainly has a discriminative function, and it may have others, including even an acquired aversiveness function.

A second possibility that is more interesting and more compelling is that the FS does more than provide information. Perhaps it actively reinforces R_a and perhaps 40 or 50 trials (or more depending on the situation) are required for its reinforcing powers to be established. What I am suggesting is that the response-contingent FS acts as a *safety signal* of the sort that Rescorla and LoLordo (1965) have described.

Rescorla and LoLordo gave dogs a number of sessions in which one stimulus was repeatedly paired with unavoidable shock independently of the dogs' behavior, and a second contrasting stimulus was explicitly paired with the absence of shock. The one stimulus thus became a danger signal (DS) while the second became a safety signal (SS). (It is difficult to know how to label these stimuli without begging the question of how they function; there is no intention to imply anything by the designation DS and SS beyond the procedural fact that the one stimulus is correlated with shock while the other is correlated with the absence of shock.) Several procedures were used in these sessions, and it seemed to make little difference precisely how the DS-SS contrast was made as long as the SS consistently predicted the absence of shock. Following this training, the stimuli were introduced momentarily while *S* was performing a previously well-established shuttle-box R_a. The DS was found to produce a short-term elevation in the rate of the R_a, whereas the SS was found to depress the rate of the R_a.

These dramatic results lend themselves to a variety of possible interpretations, but the one favored by Rescorla and LoLordo is that (a) the SS and DS acquire their behavioral effects through Pavlovian conditioning processes, and (b) the DS increases *S's* fear motivation, whereas the SS inhibits fear. They propose that fear is conditioned to the DS by a Pavlovian excitatory mechanism, and that in the test situation the momentary DS provides additional short-term motivation for the previously learned R_a. Similarly, the inhibition of fear by SS is assumed to be produced by a Pavlovian inhibitory mechanism so that brief presentation of the SS in the test situation provides a momentary reduction in *S's* prevailing fear motivation (also see Rescorla & Solomon, 1967).

Without necessarily denying the validity of this interpretation, I want to call attention to other potential properties of these DS and SS stimuli. I would emphasize that the presentation of a DS may be punishing and that the presentation of an SS may be positively reinforcing. Rescorla and LoLordo could not find such effects because their experimental situation was set up to demonstrate motivational and de-motivational effects. But Rescorla (1969) has subsequently found that an SS established in the same noncontingent manner can serve to reinforce an R_a when it is later introduced as a consequence of that R_a, that is, when it is made contingent on it. Similarly, Weisman and Litner (1968) have shown that an SS can be used as a reinforcer to produce either a high or a low rate of responding by making its occurrence differentially contingent on a high or low rate. Hendry (1967) has reported a related reinforcement effect in a conditioned suppression situation.

Let us make a logical extension: think of the R_a produced feedback stimulus in the avoidance learning situation as gradually acquiring safety signal properties. Include among these properties the ability to reinforce R_a. A number of parallels may already be noted between the FS and the SS. For example, if there is an instrumental avoidance contingency, then the FS is surely correlated with the absence of shock, just as the SS is in Rescorla and LoLordo's noncontingent training sessions. The main difference is that the FS is by definition contingent on the occurrence of the response while (at least so far) the SS is established independently of *S's* behavior. The non-contingent procedure provides a vivid demonstration that the DS and SS stimuli can acquire their behavioral powers independently of *S's* behavior. DiCara and Miller (1968) have reported an even more vivid demonstration of what appear to be SS and DS effects by using rats that were deeply curarized. But the possibility of establishing an SS independently of *S's* behavior does not mean that an SS cannot be established when it is response contingent. Indeed a response-produced SS might be more discriminable and more readily established than if the stimulus was scheduled to appear intermittently without any antecedents. There have been no direct comparisons of SS and FS effects, but a comparison across studies using SS and FS techniques is suggestive. Thus, we have seen that establishing an effective FS seems to require 40 or 50 trials or perhaps more in some situations, while from the fact that the SS effect is typically reported in studies that involve 90 or so pairings of the SS with the absence of shock, we may presume that the effect requires approximately the same number Hammond (1966) has claimed to have shown a more rapidly established SS effect in a conditioned suppression situation, but this interpretation seems doubtful in view of the transitory nature of the effect.

The author and his colleagues have recently conducted a series of studies with SS and DS procedures to determine if the SS and DS effects vary across situations with different R_a requirements in the same manner as we had previously found the FS and CS effects to vary. The results have been rather encouraging. Thus, in the one-way runway, where there was no CS-termination or FS-presentation effect, a total absence of SS and DS effects was found. In the running wheel, where the former effects had been found to be small (see Figure 2), the latter were found to be small too, and unimpressive statistically. Then with the shuttle box, in the only one of these studies that has been published (Grossen & Bolles, 1968) large and highly reliable effects which mirrored the size of the CS and FS effects in that situation were found. In all of these studies, procedures like those of Rescorla (1966) were used, including 90 noncontingent pairings. The chief difference in procedure was that we used rats, whereas Rescorla used dogs.

So far, then, the parallel between FS and SS effects suggests that they may be equivalent. The bar-press situation is critical however, and our results there have unfortunately been largely negative. However, Weisman and Litner (1968) obtained impressive SS effects with a wheel-turn R_a, which is comparable to the bar-press R_a in a number of other respects. Perhaps there are unique features of the bar-press R_a that we have not sufficiently allowed for; perhaps its initial dependence on freezing is relevant; or perhaps there is a critical element of the SS-DS procedure that remains to be isolated. For example, it is not clear why SS effects have been reported thus far only in free-operant situations where the rate of responding is measured. We do not know if the effect is limited to rate measures of nondiscriminated avoidance or whether it can be obtained as well with other response measures in discriminated avoidance situations.

In spite of a number of such unanswered questions, it is tempting to hypothesize that the CS termination effect, the FS presentation effect, and the SS reinforcing effect are all functionally equivalent. I propose that this is indeed the case, and further, that in those situations where CS termination is effective in strengthening an R_a, it is effective because it serves as response feedback, and that such feedback is positively reinforcing because it functions as a safety signal. CS termination tells the animals, in effect, that shock is not going to occur.

It should be emphasized that this SS mechanism appears to be limited to learning situations in which the R_a is acquired relatively slowly, for example, in 40 trials or more. The reason for this limitation is evidently that to become established, the SS mechanism requires a number of the pairings of the SS with the absence of shock. The implication of this limitation is that whenever an R_a is rapidly acquired for example, in 40 trials or less, its acquisition must be based on mechanisms that have little to do with the SS, the response-contingent FS, or the CS-termination contingency.

Relation to Other Accounts of Avoidance Learning

The arguments that have been advanced here have been based in part on the finding that the escape contingency is not essential for the acquisition of avoidance learning. This finding is not new, of course, it has been known and widely accepted ever since Mowrer and Lamoreaux's (1946) classic study, and a purely Pavlovian or contiguity interpretation of avoidance has not been seriously advocated for some years. The prevailing accounts of avoidance learning appear to cast the escape contingency in the simple but not altogether bad role of increasing the operant rate of R_a . The question of choosing the right R_a involves much more than obtaining a suitably high operant rate however. Thus, the data shown in Figure 1 indicate what happened with three R_as with nearly equal operant rates. With one the escape contingency was apparently an essential ingredient in learning, with a second R_a it was unimportant because learning was so rapid without it, but with the third R_a the escape contingency was unimportant because neither it nor any other contingency produced learning. Meyer et al. (1960) suggested the appropriate conclusion some years ago: "However inconvenient the general implication, operants are *not* arbitrary; in avoidance learning, their selection is perhaps the most important of considerations [p. 227]."

The argument with regard to the CS-termination contingency is similar, but in the case of CS termination, it is nearly always cast in the leading role in avoidance learning. Fear-reduction theorists and operant theorists alike usually attribute the learning of R_a to response-contingent CS termination. The situation is only slightly complicated by the fact that some theorists attribute reinforcement to the reduction of the fear that is commonly assumed to become classically conditioned to the CS; CS termination is still assumed to be a critical agent in reinforcing R_a. The situation is complicated just a little more by the necessity to invent (or more politely, to hypothesize the existence of) suitable CSs to explain the acquisition of avoidance when there is no observable CS. Sidman (1953) showed that rats could learn to avoid unsignaled shock, and it therefore became necessary to hypothesize that there were *implicit* CSs the termination of which could be said to reinforce the R_a. This need was all the more urgent because, presumably, Sidman's situation provided *S* with no escape contingency.

The argument is now quite familiar: the proproceptive and kinesthetic feedback from nonavoidance behavior serves as the needed CS. If S persists in some response, R, which fails to avoid shock, then the feedback from this behavior, S_1, will be paired with shock. After a number of such trials, S_1 will acquire conditioned, or secondary, aversiveness so that the subject will be reinforced for discontinuing R_1 and initiating some alternative response, R_2. If R_2 also fails to avoid shock the story will be repeated. Only R_a is exempt from the action of the avoidance contingency. The stimuli which earlier occasioned R_1, R_2... must gradually gain discriminative control over R_a as the repeated transitions from the various R_a to R_a and the consequent terminations of the various S_1 reinforce R_a. This theoretical mechanism, originally proposed by Schoenfeld (1950), Sidman (1953), and Dinsmoor (1954); has been subsequently elaborated by Anger (1963). Anger noted that while one stage of acquisition may depend on the aversiveness of S_1, S_2..., there must come a point at which the principal discriminative control and the principal source of reinforcement for R_a is the lapse of time since the last preceding R_a. Only in this way, Anger argued, can one explain the temporal distribution of R_as, or the continued improvement in performance as the subject becomes more proficient. So although there may be some question regarding just which implicit CSs are involved, there is rather widespread agreement that there are some implicit, response-produced stimuli, the termination of which reinforces avoidance learning.

I have no basic fault to find with the postulation of implicit CSs, but I think it important to point out that this conceptual scheme leads to some logical and empirical difficulties. One difficulty is that this account of avoidance involves a peculiar superfluity of explanatory mechanisms. The most common interpretation (e.g., Dinsmoor, 1954) involves what is basically an escape paradigm. While the avoidance contingency is clearly implicated as the principal contract of the situation with S's behavior, the S is not usually assumed to be avoiding in any real sense but escaping. The assumed reinforcement mechanism is the termination of implicit CSs, the stimuli, S_1, S_2..., that have been paired with shock.

Alternatively, we can think in terms of a punishment paradigm. We might suppose that the avoidance contingency is effective, not because it permits S to escape from the various S_1, but because it directly punishes, or suppresses, the various R_1. Dinsmoor (1954) has argued quite rightly that the punishment effect itself needs explication. He has attempted to reduce the phenomena of punishment to avoidance terms, and then to reduce the avoidance to escape from S_1. This tactic is certainly defensible, but is it superior to taking the phenomena of punishment as primary and using them to explain those of avoidance and perhaps even escape? I have tried to show that in the special case of a very rapidly acquired R_a, that is, when R_a is an effective SSDR, the punishment paradigm is uniquely able to handle the facts. In the case of a rapidly acquired R_a, there hardly seems time to make all the necessary S_1 aversive, especially if we cannot show that an environmental CS affects the behavior in the same amount of time. A much faster and more direct mechanism is needed in this case, and the punishment of competing SSDRs is such a mechanism.

The agreed upon importance of the avoidance contingency in unsignaled avoidance suggests another interpretation: an avoidance paradigm. We might suppose that S really is avoiding shock. Although recognizing that it is difficult to put such a concept into precise behavioral terms, some writers have argued that this is the best conception of the problem (e.g., D'Amato et al. 1968; Keehn, 1966). Other theorists (e.g., Herrnstein & Hineline, 1966; Sidman, 1966) have recently come to the similar conclusion that what really reinforces avoidance behavior is the overall reduction in shock density it produces. In the situations that are described, S is not able to avoid shock, or escape it, or to terminate CSs; S merely receives fewer shocks when R_a occurs. Under these conditions the rate of R_a increases. It should be emphasized, however, that the effects described by Herrnstein and Hineline and by Sidman are found after very extensive training. When Herrnstein and Hineline (1966) carefully eliminated all other sources of reinforcement besides reduction in shock density, the bar-press R_a only *began* to emerge after tens of thousands of shocks had been administered. Are we to believe then that this is the source of the reinforcement by which rats can learn other R_as in 100 trials, or 10 trials, or by which they learn to survive in nature? What Herrnstein and Hineline seem to have shown, quite to the contrary, is that avoidance itself, or response-contingent shock density reduction, *cannot* be the mechanism that produces the faster acquisition of R_a generally found under other conditions. We may marvel that such subtle control of the rat's behavior is possible, and we must admire the diligence of the experimenters who brought it about. But just because behavior can eventually be brought under the control of some stimulus and maintained by some contingency, it certainly does not follow that this stimulus controls the behavior under other circumstances or that the contingency is effective when others are available. Nor is there any reason to believe that the factors which can ultimately be used to govern some behavior are necessarily the same as those that were important in establishing it originally. We must look elsewhere for mechanisms to explain how the rat does most of its avoidance learning.

As a final alternative to the CS-termination hypothesis, we can consider an appetitive paradigm. The S learns to avoid shock, not because termination of S_1 (or an explicit CS) is negatively reinforcing, but because R_a and the production of its feedback. S_a is positively reinforcing. Denny and his students are among the few who have defended an appetitive paradigm (e.g., Denny & Weisman, 1964). Although Denny's relaxation theory emphasizes the response which becomes conditioned to the safety signal, whereas I am more concerned with the safety signal itself, there are many striking points of similarity between relaxation theory and the SSDR hypothesis, and both accounts generate similar predictions about avoidance behavior.

I have tried to show that the safety signal interpretation is especially able to handle the data in those cases where R_a is relatively slowly acquired, that is, when R_a is not an SSDR. In this case I assume that during the initial trials, S's behavior is restricted to a small set of SSDRs, and that learning will occur only if a number of rather delicate conditions are fulfilled. The first is that one of S's. SSDRs (e.g., freezing) must be topographically compatible with the required R_a (e.g., bar pressing). Then shock must elicit enough reflexive bar presses so that S can either ??? some shocks (the postshock burst in Sidman's situation) or minimize their duration (when there is an escape contingency). Whit the minimization of shock we may expect a gradual return of S's normal response repertoire, so that it is no longer restricted to SSDRs. This recovery process may be facilitated in the manner that Rescorla and LoLordo have suggested, that is, the R_a contingent FS may become a safety signal and inhibit fear.[4] Finally, I assume that the safety signal actively reinforces R_a, and that eventually R_a may come under the control of still another, more subtle stimuli as their safety-signal properties gradually become discriminated. At this point we may be able to find S quite proficiently performing an R_a which is as unlikely and as unnatural as pressing a bar.

It is clear that an animal's defensive repertoire can be extended beyond the narrow limits set by its SSDRs. But it is unfortunate that our theoretical predilections have led us to be preoccupied with the ultimate limits to which this extension can be carried and with defending CS termination as the reinforcement mechanism. In retrospect, it hardly seems possible that the acquisition of the bar-press R_a could ever have been seriously attributed simply to the action of CS termination, but it was. These preoccupations have not really advanced our understanding of how such extensions occur, how other, more natural R_as are learned, or for that matter how animals survive in nature.

References

ANGER, D. The role of temporal discrimination in the reinforcement of Sidman avoidance behavior. *Journal of the Experimental Analysis of Behavior*, 1963, **6**, 477-506.

BOLLES, R.C. Avoidance and escape learning: Simultaneous acquisition of different responses. *Journal of Comparative and Physiological Psychology*, 1969, **68**, 355-358.

BOLLES, R.C., & GROSSEN, N.E. Effects of an informational stimulus on the acquisition of avoidance behavior in rats. *Journal of Comparative and Physiological Psychology*, 1969, **68**, 90-99.

BOLLES, R.C., & McGILLIS, D.B. The non-operant nature of the bar-press escape response, *Psychonomic Science*, 1968, **11**, 261-262.

BOLLES, R.C., & POPP, R.J. Parameters affecting the acquisition of Sidman avoidance. *Journal of the Experimental Analysis of Behavior*, 1964, **7**, 315-321.

BOLLES, R.C., STOKES, L. W., & YOUNGER, M.S. Does CS termination reinforce avoidance behavior? *Journal of Comparative and Physiological Psychology*. 1966, **62**, 201-207.

BOWER, G., STARR, R., & LAZAROVITZ, L. Amount of response-produced change in the CS and avoidance learning. *Journal of Comparative and Physiological Psychology*, 1965, **59**, 13-17.

BROGDEN, W. J., LIPMAN, E.A., & CULLER, E. The role of incentive in conditioning and learning. *American Journal of Psychology*, 1938, **51**, 109-117.

BRUSH, F.R. On the differences between animals that learn and do not learn to avoid electric shock. *Psychonomic Science*, 1966, **5**, 123-124.

COLE, M., & WAHLSTEN, D. Response-contingent CS termination as a factor in avoidance conditioning. *Psychonomic Science*, 1968, **12**, 15-16.

D'AMATO, M.R. Role of anticipatory responses in avoidance conditioning: An important control. *Psychonomic Science*, 1967, **8**, 191-192

D'AMATO, M.R., FAZZARO, J., & ETKIN, M. Anticipatory responding and avoidance discrimination as factors in avoidance conditioning. *Journal of Experimental Psychology*, 1968, **77**, 41-47.

D'AMATO, M.R., KELLER, D., & DiCARA, L. Facilitation of discriminated avoidance learning by discontinuous shock. *Journal of Comparative and Physiological Psychology*, 1964, **58**, 344-349.

D'AMATO, M.R., & SCHIFF, D. Long-term discriminated avoidance performance in the rat. *Journal of Comparative and Physiological Psychology*, 1964, **57**, 123-126.

DENNY, M.R., & WEISMAN, R.G. Avoidance behavior as a function of length of nonshock confinement. *Journal of Comparative and Physiological Psychology*, 1964, **58**, 252-257.

DiCARA, L.V., & MILLER, N.E. Changes in heart rate instrumentally learned by curarized rats as avoidance responses. *Journal of Comparative and Physiological Psychology*, 1968, **65**, 8-12.

DINSMOOR, J.A. Punishment: I. The avoidance hypothesis. *Psychological Review*, 1954, **61**, 34-46.

FELDMAN, R.S., & BREMNER, F.J. A method for rapid conditioning of stable avoidance bar pressing behavior. *Journal of the Experimental Analysis of Behavior*, 1963, **6**, 393-394.

GROSSEN, N.E., & BOLLES, R.C. Effects of a classical conditioned fear signal and safety signal on nondiscriminated avoidance behavior. *Phychonomic Science*, 168, **11**, 321-322.

HAMMOND, L.J. Increased responding to CS in differential CER. *Psychonomic Science*, 1966, **5**, 337- 338.

HENDRY, D.P. Conditioned inhibition of conditioned suppression. *Psychonomic Science*, 1967, **9**, 261- 262.

HERRNSTEIN, R.J., & HINELINE, P.N. Negative reinforcement as shock-frequency reduction. *Journal of the Experimental Analysis of Behavior*, 1966, **9**, 421-430.

HULL, C.L. A functional interpretation of the conditioned reflex. *Psychological Review*, 1929, **36**, 498-511.

HURWITZ, H. M.B. Method for discriminative avoidance training. *Science*, 1964, **145**, 1070-1071.

KAMIN, L.J. The effects of termination of the CS and avoidance of the US on avoidance learning. *Journal of Comparative and Physiological Psychology*, 1956, **49**, 420-424.

KEEHN, J.D. Avoidance responses as discriminated operants. *British Journal of Psychology*, 1966, **57**, 375-380.

KEEHN, J.D. Running and bar pressing as avoidance responses. *Psychological Reports*, 1967, **20**, 591-602.

KEEHN, J.D., & WEBSTER, C.D. Rapid discriminated bar-press avoidance through avoidance shaping. *Psychonomic Science*, 1968, **10**, 21-22.

LOCKARD, J.S. Choice of a warning signal or no warning signal in an unavoidable shock situation. *Journal of Comparative and Physiological Psychology*, 1963, **56**, 526-530.

MAATSCH, J.L. Learning and fixation after a single shock trial. *Journal of Comparative and Physiological Psychology*, 1959, **52**,408-410.

MEYER, D.R., CHO, C., & WESEMANN, A.F. On problems of conditioning discriminated lever-press avoidance responses. *Psychological Review*, 1960, **67**, 224-228.

MILLER, N.E. Learnable drives and rewards In S.S. Stevens (Ed.) *Handbook of experimental psychology*. New York: Wiley, 1951.

MOGENSON, G.J., MULLIN, A.D., & CLARK, E.A. Effects of delayed secondary reinforcement and response requirements on avoidance learning. *Canadian Journal of Psychology*, 1965, **19**, 61-73.

MOWRER, O. H. A stimulus-response analysis of anxiety and its role as a reinforcing agent. *Psychological Review*, 1939, **46**, 563-565.

MOWRER, O. H. , & LAMOREAUX, R.R. Avoidance conditioning and signal duration—a study of secondary motivation and reward. *Psychological Monographs*, 1942, **54** (5, Whole No. 247).

MOWRER, O. H., & LAMOREAUX, R.R. Fear as an intervening variable in avoidance conditioning. *Journal of Comparative Psychology*, 1946, **39**, 29-50.

MYERS, A.K. Onset vs. termination of stimulus energy as the CS in avoidance conditioning and pseudoconditioning. *Journal of Comparative and Physiological Psychology*, 1960, **53**, 72-78.

MYERS, A.K. Discriminated operant avoidance learning in Wistar and G-4 rats as a function of type of warning stimulus. *Journal of Comparative and Physiological Psychology*, 1964, **58**, 453-455.

RESCORLA, R.A. Predictability and number of pairings in Pavlovian fear conditioning. *Psychonomic Science*, 1966, **4**, 383-384.

RESCORLA, R.A. Establishment of a positive reinforcer through contrast with shock. *Journal of Comparative and Physiological Psychology*, 1969, **67**, 260-263.

RESCORLA, R.A., & LoLORDO, V.M. Inhibition of avoidance behavior. *Journal of Comparative and Physiological Psychology*, 1965, **59**, 406-412.

RESCORLA, R.A., & SOLOMON, R.L. Two process learning theory: Relationships between Pavlovian conditioning and instrumental learning. *Psychological Review*, 1967, **74**, 151-182.

SCHOENFELD, W.N. An experimental approach to anxiety escape and avoidance behavior. In P.H. Hock & J. Zubin (Eds.) *Anxiety*. New York: Grune & Stratton, 1950.

SIDMAN, M. Two temporal parameters of the aintenance of avoidance behavior by the white rat. *Journal of Comparative and Physiological Psychology*, 1953, **46**, 253-261.

SIDMAN, M. Some properties of the warning stimulus in avoidance behavior. *Journal of Comparative and Physiological Psychology*, 1955, **48**, 444-450.

SIDMAN, M. Avoidance behavior. In W. K. Honig (Ed.), *Operant behavior: Areas of research and application*. New York: Appleton-Century-Crofts, 1966.

SMITH, O.A., JR., McFARLAND, W.L., & TAYLOR, E. Performance in a shock-avoidance conditioning situation interpreted as pseudoconditioning. *Journal of Comparative and Physiological Psychology*, 1961, **54**, 154-157.

SOLOMON, R.L., & BRUSH, E.S. Experimentally derived conceptions of anxiety and aversion. In M.R. Jones (Ed.), *Nebraska Symposium on Motivation*, 1956, **4**, 212-305.

SOLOMON, R.L., & WYNNE, L.C. Traumatic avoidance learning: Acquisition in normal dogs. *Psychological Monographs*, 1953, **67** (4, Whole No. 354).

THEIOS, J. Simple conditioning as two-stage all-or-none learning. *Psychological Review*, 1963, **70**, 403- 417.

TURNER, L.H., & SOLOMON, R.L. Human traumatic avoidance learning: Theory and experiments on the operant-respondent distinction and failures to learn. *Psychological Monographs*, 1962, **76** (40, Whole No. 559).

WARREN, L.A., JR., & BOLLES, R.C. A reevaluation of simple contiguity interpretation of avoidance learning. *Journal of Comparative and Physiological Psychology*, 1967, **64**, 179-182.

WEISMAN, R.G., & LITNER, J.S. Positive conditioned reinforcement of Sidman avoidance behavior in rats. *Journal of Comparative and Physiological Psychology*, 1969, **68**, 597-603.

THE "SUPERSTITION" EXPERIMENT: A REEXAMINATION OF ITS IMPLICATIONS FOR THE PRINCIPLES OF ADAPTIVE BEHAVIOR

J.E.R. Staddon & Virginia L. Simmelhag (1971). *Psychological Review, 78(1),* 3-43.

This paper had a tremendous impact for several reasons, but primarily because of its integrative nature, tying together very diverse phenomena, and secondly its emphasis on the parallels between the Law of Effect and evolution through natural selection. Additionally, Staddon & Simmelhag propose a much more parsimonious conceptualization of the classical and operant learning paradigms, where classical conditioning is defined operationally as a schedule of reinforcement that does not prescribe a contingency, that is a correlation between the behavior of the subject and the delivery of reinforcement. Many of the ideas expressed originally here have become commonplace in theories of learning. The article itself contains extensive and detailed results from a number of experiments. The more technical aspects of the methodologies and data analyses have been edited in this annotation.

Replication and extension of Skinner's "superstition" experiment showed the development of two kinds of behavior at asymptote: interim activities (related to adjunctive behavior) occurred just after food delivery; the terminal response (a discriminated operant) occurred toward the end of the interval and continued until food delivery. These data suggest a view of operant conditioning (the terminal response) in terms of two sets of principles: principles of behavioral variation that describe the origins of behavior "appropriate" to a situation, in advance of reinforcement; and principles of reinforcement that describe the selective elimination of behavior so produced. This approach was supported by (a) an account of the parallels between the Law of Effect and evolution by means of natural selection, (b) its ability to shed light on persistent problems in learning (e.g., continuity vs. noncontinuity, variability associated with extinction, the relationship between classical and instrumental conditioning, the controversy between behaviorist and cognitive approaches to learning), and (c) its ability to deal with a number of recent anomalies in the learning literature ("instinctive drift," auto-shaping, and auto-maintenance). The interim activities were interpreted in terms of interactions among motivational systems, and this view was supported by a review of the literature on adjunctive behavior and by comparison with similar phenomena in ethology (displacement, redirection, and "vacuum" activities). The proposed theoretical scheme represents a shift away from hypothetical "laws of learning" toward an interpretation of behavioral change in terms of interaction and competition among tendencies to action according to principles evolved in phylogeny.

The field of learning has undergone increasing fractionation in recent years. Interest in "miniature systems" and exact theories of local effects has grown to the detriment of any attempt at overall integration. Consequently, as one perceptive observer has noted:

> At times, one senses a widespread feeling of discouragement about the prospects of ever getting clear on the fundamentals of conditioning. Attempts to arrive at firm decisions about alternative formulations rarely produce incisive results. Every finding seems capable of many explanations. Issues become old, shopworn, and disappear without a proper burial [Jenkins, 1970, pp. 107-108].

The present article outlines an attempt to redress this imbalance. It is organized around the problem of "superstitious" behavior, originated by Skinner some years ago, which plays a crucial part in the empirical and theoretical foundations of current views of learning. Discussion of a replication of Skinner's original experiment leads to an account of the relationships between evolution and learning, and a system of classification derived there from. The paper concludes with a theoretical account of "superstition" and some related phenomena.

THE "SUPERSTITION" EXPERIMENT

In his classic experiment on "superstitious" behavior, Skinner (1948) showed that the mere delivery of food to a hungry animal is sufficient to produce operant conditioning. The pigeons in that experiment were allowed 5-second access to food every 15 seconds, and food delivery was independent of their behavior. Nevertheless, nearly every pigeon developed a recognizable form of stereotyped, superstitious behavior that became temporally correlated with food delivery as training progressed.

Skinner's (1961) analysis of this phenomenon is a straightforward application of the Law of Effect: The conditioning process is usually obvious. The bird happens to be executing some response as the hopper appears; as a result it tends to repeat this response. If the interval before the next presentation is not so great that extinction takes place, a second "contingency"...is probable. This strengthens the response still further and subsequent reinforcement becomes more probable [p. 405].

Skinner's observations were quickly repeated in a number of laboratories. The apparent simplicity and reliability of the phenomenon, coupled with the plausibility of Skinner's interpretation of it and the more exciting attractions of work on reinforcement schedules then developing, effectively stifled further study of this situation. However, both the experiment and his explication played a crucial role in advancing Skinner's theoretical view of operant behavior as the strengthening of unpredictably generated ("emitted") behavior by the automatic action of reinforcers.

Two kinds of data obtained in recent years raise new questions about "superstition" in this sense. First, experiments with time-related reinforcement schedules have shown the development of so-called "mediating" behavior during the waiting period, when the animal is not making the reinforced response. Thus, on schedules which require the animal to space his responses a few seconds apart if they are to be effective in producing reinforcement (spaced-responding schedules), pigeons often show activities such as pacing and turning circles. Similarly, on fixed-interval schedules, in which the first response t seconds after the preceding reinforcement is effective in producing reinforcement, pigeons may show a similar behavior during the post-reinforcement "pause" when they are not making the reinforced response. Other species show activities of this sort in the presence of appropriate environmental stimuli; for example, schedule-induced polydipsia, in which rats reinforced with food on temporal reinforcement schedules show excessive drinking if water is continuously available (Falk, 1969). None of these activities is reinforced, in the sense of being contiguous with food delivery, yet they are reliably produced in situations similar in many respects to Skinner's superstition procedure. Possibly, therefore, some of the activities labeled superstitious by Skinner, and attributed by him to accidental reinforcement of spontaneously occurring behavior, may instead reflect the same causal factors as these mediating activities.

Second, a number of experiments have demonstrated the development of behavior in operant conditioning situations by a process more reminiscent of Pavlovian (classical) conditioning than Law of Effect learning as commonly understood. Breland and Breland (1961) reported a series of observations showing that with continued operant training, species-specific behavior will often emerge to disrupt an apparently well-learned operant response. In the cases they describe, behavior closely linked to food (presumably reflecting an instinctive mechanism) began to occur in advance of food delivery in the presence of previously neutral stimuli ("instinctive drift"). Since these "irrelevant" activities interfered with food delivery by delaying the occurrence of the reinforced response, they cannot be explained by the Law of Effect. A description in terms of stimulus substitution—a principle usually associated with Pavlovian conditioning—is better, although still not completed satisfactory. More recently, Brown and Jenkins (1968) have shown that hungry pigeons can be trained to peck a lighted response key simply by illuminating the key for a few seconds before food delivery. Fewer than a hundred light-food pairings are usually sufficient to bring about key pecking. The relationship between this "auto-shaping" procedure and Pavlovian conditioning is further emphasized by an experiment reported by Williams and Williams (1969). They found that auto-shaped key pecking is maintained even if the key peck turns off the light on the key and thus prevents food delivery on that occasion. All these experiments show the occurrence of food-related behaviors, in anticipation of food, under conditions more or less incompatible with the Law of Effect.

The auto-shaping procedure is operationally identical to Pavlovian conditioning with short delay (the light-food interval in these experiments is typically 8 seconds). Therefore the eventual emergence of food-related behavior, in anticipation of food delivery, is not altogether surprising—although the directed nature of key pecking has no counterpart in principles of conditioning that take salivation as a model response. The superstition situation is also equivalent to a Pavlovian procedure—in this case temporal conditioning, in which the UCS (food) is simply presented at regular intervals. Perhaps, therefore, prolonged exposure to this situation will also lead to the emergence of food-related behavior in anticipation of food. Possibly the superstitious behavior described by Skinner includes activities of this sort that occur in anticipation of food, as well as mediating activities that occur just after food delivery.

The present experiment affords an opportunity to test these ideas. It provides comparative data on the effect of fixed versus variable interfood intervals on superstitious responding (Skinner used only fixed intervals), as well as allowing a comparison between response-dependent and response-independent fixed-interval schedules. The experiment also extends Skinner's work by recording in some detail both the kind and time of occurrence of superstitious activities. The emphasis is on the steady-state adaptation to the procedures, but some data on the course of development of superstition are presented.

We hope to show that careful study of the superstition situation makes necessary a revision of Skinner's original interpretation and, by extension, requires a shift of emphasis in our view of adaptive behavior.

(Method and Results omitted)

Discussion

The results of this experiment confirm the suggestion that the "superstition" situation generally produces two distinct kinds of activity: interim activities that occur at short and intermediate postfood times, and the terminal response that begins later in the interval and continues until food delivery. It is not always clear from Skinner's original discussion just which kind of behavior he was observing. In one case, he briefly describes an experiment in which the interfood interval was 60 seconds, and the "superstitious" response (a "well-defined hopping step from the right to the left foot") was automatically recorded. In this case, the behavior was evidently a terminal response, since it occurred with increasing frequency through the interval:

The bird does not respond immediately after eating, but when 10 or 15 or even 20 sec. have elapsed it begins to respond rapidly and continues until the reinforcement is received [Skinner, 1961, p. 406].

On other occasions, however, Skinner may have been observing interim activities, as, in our experience, they are sometimes much more striking than the terminal response, especially early in training when they may include actions like jumping in the air, vigorous wing flapping, and idiosyncratic head and limb movements. We have also sometimes observed interim activities during sessions when there was no obvious terminal response.

Nature of the Terminal Response

The data from both FI and VI schedules of food presentation indicate that the probability of the terminal response at different postfood times was a function of the probability of food delivery at those times: the probability of the terminal response increased just in advance of increases in the probability of food delivery, and decreased just after decreases in that probability.

(*Technical details omitted ....)*

This result raises the possibility that the effect of the response-dependency, in operant conditioning experiments using interval reinforcement schedules, may be largely one of determining (perhaps imperfectly) the *location* of pecking, rather than either its form or its frequency of occurrence.

Nature of the Interim Activities

Falk (1969, 1970) has coined the term *adjunctive behavior* for a variety of activities that are induced in a number of different animal species (rats, pigeons, monkeys, chimpanzees) by intermittent schedules of reinforcement. These activities generally occur just after reinforcement, when the reinforced (i.e., terminal) response is not occurring. However, the important variable in determining their temporal location seems to be the low probability of further reinforcement in the immediate postreinforcement period (rather than the interruption of eating)

(....)

The interim activities in the present experiment appear to reflect the same causal factors as adjunctive behavior: they occur at times when reinforcement is not available and the terminal response is not occurring;

(....)

An analogy can be drawn between the terminal and interim activities here and the classical dichotomy between consummatory and appetitive behavior (Craig, 1918). Thus, pecking, the stable terminal response is a food-elicited (consummatory) activity in pigeons, and the interim activities were quite variable, as might be expected of appetitive behavior. Moreoever, the variability of the sequences (as measured by the number of "forks" in the sequence) was greatest at the beginning of the sequence and decreased toward the end (cf. Figure 2). More or less unlearned sequences terminating in consummatory acts show a similar reduction in variability toward the end of the sequence (e.g., Morris, 1958).

In a similar vein, Falk (1970) has compared adjunctive behavior with displacement activities (Tinbergen, 1952):

In both adjunctive behavior and displacement activity situations, the interruption of a consummatory behavior in an intensely motivated animal induces the occurrence of another behavior immediately following the interruption [p. 305].

At the present stage of knowledge, these comparisons do little more than group together a number of puzzling phenomena that cannot as yet be convincingly explained either by ethological principles or by the Law of Effect. We can choose either to accept these behaviors as anomalies within our present conceptual system, hoping that further research will show how to reconcile them, or revise the system in a way that will accommodate them more naturally. The first alternative is becoming increasingly hard to maintain, as it becomes clear that these behaviors are of wide occurrence, and as they continue to resist attempts to explain them in conventional terms. Polydipsia is the most widely studied adjunctive behavior and Falk (1969) summarizes research results as follows:

It is not explicable in terms of any altered state of water balance initiated by the experimental conditions. It cannot be attributed to adventitious reinforcing effects. Since it cannot be related to abnormal water losses, chronic internal stimulation arising from unusual states...or from injury to the central nervous system, the overdrinking would be classified clinically as primary or psychogenic polydipsia [p. 587].

A revision of the conceptual foundations of operant behavior, which will deal naturally with these behaviors, as well as guide research into more profitable channels, seems called for.

Development of the Terminal Response

The development of the terminal response provides some clues toward an alternative conception. Changes in the terminal response throughout acquisition rule out an unqualified application of the Law of Effect as a description of the process. For example, three of the four birds made the response Head in magazine at a higher frequency and for a larger fraction of the total time than any other response, for the first few sessions of exposure to the superstition procedure (either FI or VI, depending on the bird). This behavior was also the one most often contiguous with the delivery of food. Yet during later sessions it dropped out abruptly and was replaced by Pecking. Thus the development of Pecking as terminal response resembles the findings of Williams and Williams and of Breland and Breland, much more than it does the strengthening of an emitted response, in Skinner's terms, by the automatic action of food as a reinforcer. In all these cases, the presentation of food at a predictable time resulted after training in the regular occurrence of a food-related behavior in anticipation of food delivery, quite independently of the demand characteristics of the situation (i.e., the reinforcement schedule). Given that food is a stimulus that elicits pecking by pigeons, the appearance of pecking, in anticipation of food in the present experiment is an instance of the principle of stimulus substitution (Hilgard & Marquis, 1940). The stimulus is of course a temporal one (postfood time), and the situation is analogous, therefore, to Pavlovian temporal conditioning (Pavlov, 1927), both operationally and in its conformity to the substitution principle. Therefore, it is tempting to attribute the appearance of pecking to a classical conditioning mechanism, and leave it at that.

A number of considerations suggest that this explanation will not suffice, however (a) The behavior of one bird (29) is a partial exception. He showed a terminal response (Head in magazine) different from Pecking, although this response was metastable (Staddon, 1965), in the sense that it was displaced by Pecking following a schedule shift. In addition, Skinner's results and informal observations in a number of laboratories indicate that the superstition procedure may generate behaviors other than pecking that persist for considerable periods of time. Presumably, many of these behaviors are terminal responses, in our sense, and, metastable or not, they cannot be dismissed in favor of a Pavlovian account of all terminal responses in superstition situations. (b) The results of Rachlin (1969), who was able to obtain spontaneous key pecking by means of the auto-shaping procedure of Brown and Jenkins, but using electric shock reduction rather than food as the reinforcer, also complicate the picture since it is not clear that pecking is elicited by shock as it is by food. The results of Sidman and Fletcher (1968) who were able to auto shape key pushing in rhesus monkeys, are also not readily explicable by stimulus substitution. (c) Williams and Williams (1969) note that the directed nature of the key peck in the auto-shaping situation is not readily accommodated within a Pavlovian framework:

the directed quality of the induced pecking does not follow naturally from respondent principles (see also Brown and Jenkins, 1968). It is unclear, for example, why pecking would be directed at the key rather than the feeder, or indeed why it would be directed anywhere at all [p. 519].

A similar objection can be raised here, since the terminal response of pecking was always directed at the magazine wall, although it is important to notice that this objection is more damaging to an interpretation in terms of classical conditioning than one couched simply in terms of stimulus substitution. (d) Finally, there is the problem of skeletal nature of pecking. Ever since Skinner's (1938) original suggestion, it has become increasingly common to restrict the concept of classical conditioning to autonomically mediated responses. Some criticisms of this convention are presented below and Staddon (1970a) has argued against the operant/respondent and emitted/elicited dichotomies. For the moment, let it be said that the objection to the skeletal nature of the response is only a problem for an interpretation of the development of pecking in terms of classical conditioning, as traditionally conceived. It does not conflict with a stimulus substitution interpretation.

In summary, it is clear that while the principle of stimulus substitution describes the development of the terminal response in a majority of cases, and is more successful than an appeal to Pavlovian principles modeled on the salivation reference experiment, it is not adequate as a universal account. We turn now to the possibility of a general scheme to deal with these anomalous facts.

EVOLUTION AND LEARNING

Objectively considered, the subject matter of the psychology of animal learning—the behavior of animals—is a part of biology. This commonality does not extend to terms and concept however. Although the ethologists have investigated unlearned behaviors in a variety of species, learning remains almost exclusively the possession of psychologists. Consequently, the theoretical foundations of the study of learning, such as they are, have evolved almost independently of biology. It is not 15 years since Verplanck (1955) wrote: "the structure of the theory of unlearned behavior and that of learned behavior must prove to be similar if not identical [p. 140]," but little progress toward a unified set of concepts has been made. Yet the facts discussed in the previous section seem to demand an interpretation within the context of adaptive behavior as a whole.

`The principles of evolution by natural selection provide a unifying framework for biology. Pfaffman (1970) has recently commented:

I am impressed by the extent to which evolution, the genetic machinery, and biochemistry provide for biologists a common language and unity of theory that overrides the molecular versus organismic debate within biology. In contrast, it is obvious that there is no unified theory of behavior for all students of behavior [p. 438].

These considerations—the commonality of subject matter between biology and animal psychology, the probable common basis of learned and unlearned behavior, the unifying role of evolutionary processes in biology—all suggest the application of evolutionary principles to the psychology of learning in animals. In recent years, several papers have drawn attention to the similarities between evolution and learning (e.g., Breland & Breland, 1966; Broadbent, 1961; Gilbert, 1970; Herrnstein, 1964; Pringle, 1951; Skinner, 1966a, 1966b, 1969), but no version of the evolutionary approach has proved influential as yet. The main reasons for this failure, perhaps, have been the comparative effectiveness of traditional versions of the

Law of Effect in dealing with the limited phenomena of laboratory learning experiments and the lack of a substantial body of facts clearly in conflict with accepted theory. To some extent, of course, the second factor reflects the first—although it would be cynical to speculate that the kind of experiments psychologists do are often such as to preclude data that might go beyond current theory. In any event, neither of these reasons now holds true.

The growing number of facts on autoshaping, instinctive drift, adjunctive, and superstitious behaviors are not readily accommodated within traditional views. In addition, the history of the Law of Effect as a principle of *acquisition* (as opposed to the steady state, i.e., asymptote) has not been a distinguished one. Little remains of the impressive edifice erected by Hull and his followers on this base. We are no longer concerned with the production of learning curves, nor with the measurement of habit strength or reaction potential. Hullian theory has proven effective neither in the elucidation of complex cases nor as an aid to the discovery of new phenomena. Indeed, the opposite has generally been true: new learning phenomena such as schedules of reinforcement, learning, and reversal sets, etc. have typically been the result of unaided curiosity rather than the hypothetico-deductive method, as exemplified by Hull and his students. This represents a failure of Hullian theory rather than a general indictment of the hypothetico-deductive method, which has proven every bit as powerful as Hull believed it to be—when used by others (e.g., Darwin, cf. Ghiselin, 1969). A similar, although less sweeping, verdict must be handed down on stochastic learning theory, which represents perhaps the most direct attempt to translate the Law of Effect into a quantitative principle of acquisition. With the exception of predictions about the steady state, such as Estes' ingenious deduction of probability matching (Estes, 1957), the early promise of this approach as a way of understanding the behavior of individual animals has not been fulfilled. It seems fair to say that the rash of theoretical elaboration that has occupied the years since Thorndike first stated the Law of Effect has told us almost nothing more about the moment-by-moment behavior of a single organism in a learning situation. Although the alternative we will offer may be no better than earlier views, it does accommodate the anomalies we have discussed—and the need for *some* alternative can hardly be questioned.

The close analogy between the Law of Effect and evolution suggests an approach that may be a step toward the general framework which the psychology of learning so obviously lacks. At the present stage of knowledge, this approach is simply an analogy, although a compelling one, and cannot yet be called an evolutionary theory of learning. However, it provides a beginning and may lead to a truly evolutionary account which can securely imbed the study of learning in the broader field of biology.

Behavioral Variation and Reinforcement

The Law of Effect, suitably modified to take account of advances since Thorndike's original formulation, can be stated so as to emphasize acquisition, or the steady state, and learning (e.g., S-R bonds), or performance. We will take as a point of departure a neutral version of the law that emphasizes performance in the steady state, as follows: "If, in a given situation, a positive correlation be imposed between some aspect of an animal's behavior and the delivery of reinforcement, that behavior will generally come to predominate in that situation." The term "correlation" is intended to include cases of delay of reinforcement and experiments in which the response acts on the rate of reinforcement directly (e.g., Herrnstein & Hineline, 1966; Keehn, 1970). This formulation does not take account of more complex situations where more than one behavior and more than one correlation are involved (i.e., choice situations), as these complications do not affect the present argument. A discussion of three aspects of this law—(a) the initial behavior in the situation before reinforcement is introduced, (b) the process whereby this behavior is transformed into the dominant reinforced behavior, and (c) reinforcement—follows:

(a) The behavior in a situation before the occurrence of reinforcement reflects a number of factors, including past experience in similar situations (transfer), motivation, stimulus factors (e.g., novel or sign stimuli), and others. We propose the label "principles of behavioral variation" for all such factors that originate behavior. These principles are analogous to Darwin's laws of variation, corresponding to the modern laws of heredity and ontogeny that provide the phenotypes on which selection (analogous to the principles of reinforcement, see below) can act. Thus, the term "variation" is intended to denote not mere variability, but the organized production of novelty, in the Darwinian sense.

(b) Transition from initial behavior to final behavior is the traditional problem of learning theory and, as we have seen, is essentially unsolved at the level of the individual organism. However, it is at this point that the analogy to the mechanism of natural selection becomes most apparent. Broadbent (1961) makes the parallel quite clear:

> Since individual animals differ, and those with useful characteristics [with respect to a particular niche] survive and pass them on to their children, we can explain the delicate adjustment of each animal's shape to its surroundings without requiring a conscious purpose on the part of the Polar bear to grow a white coat. Equally each individual animal [under the Law of Effect] tries various actions and those become more common which are followed by consummatory acts [i.e., reinforcement] [p. 56].

Thus, the transition from initial to final behavior can be viewed as the outcome of two processes: a process that generates behavior and a process that selects (i.e., selectively eliminates) from the behavior so produced. Since there is no reason to suppose that the process which generates behavior following the first and subsequent reinforcements is different in kind from the process that generated the initial behavior (although the "*effects* will generally be different, see Extinction below), we can include both under the head of principles of behavioral variation. We propose the label "principles of reinforcement" for the second selective process.

(c) As we have seen, the Darwinian principle of selection is analogous to the process that transforms initial behavior into final behavior—the "principles of reinforcement." The notion of reinforcement (more exactly, the schedule of reinforcement) itself is in fact analogous to an earlier concept, one that preceded evolution by natural selection and can be derived from it: the Law of Conditions of Existence, that is, the fact that organisms are adapted to a particular niche. This is apparent in the form of the statements: "The Polar bear has a white coat *because* it is adaptive in his environment." "The pigeon pecks the key *because* he is reinforced for doing so." It is important to emphasize this distinction between *reinforcement* and *principles of reinforcement*, and the analogous distinction between adaptation to a niche and the process of selection by which adaptation comes about. In the case of adaptation, the process of selection involves differential reproduction, either through absence of a mate, infertility, or death before reproductive maturity. In the case of reinforcement, the distinction is less obvious, since the principles of reinforcement refer to the *laws by means of which* behaviors that fail to yield reinforcement are eliminated, rather than the simple fact that reinforced behaviors generally predominate at the expense of unreinforced behaviors.

Thus, both evolution and learning can be regarded as the outcome of two independent processes: a process of variation that generates either phenotypes, in the case of evolution, or behavior, in the case of learning: and a process of selection that acts within the limits set by the first process. In both cases, the actual outcome of the total process is related to, but not identical with, the material acted upon: phenotypes reproduce more or less successfully, but a gene pool is the outcome of selection; similarly, behaviors are more or less highly correlated with reinforcement, but learning (i.e., an alternation in memory) results.

The three aspects of this process—variation, selection, and adaptation—have received differing emphases at different times, depending on the prevailing state of knowledge. Before Darwin, adaptation, in the form of the Law of Conditions of Existence, was emphasized, since the only explanation for it—the design of the Creator—was not scientifically fruitful. Following Darwin, selection, both natural and artificial, received increased attention, in the absence of firm knowledge of the mechanism of variation (i.e., inheritance). With the advent of Mendelian genetics, variation has been most intensively studied (this is one aspect of the "molecular vs. organismic" debate referred to by Pfaffman).

In terms of this development, the study of learning is at a relatively primitive level since the Law of Effect, although a great advance over the level of understanding which preceded it, simply represents the identification of environmental events—reinforcers—with respect to which behavior is adaptive. Lacking is a clear understanding of both selection (the principles of reinforcement) and variation (the principles of variation).

Space precludes-exhaustive elaboration of all the implications of the classificatory scheme we are suggesting. However, in order to provide some context for our account of the facts already discussed, it seems essential to briefly summarize some possible candidates for principles of variation and reinforcement. It should be obvious that current knowledge does not permit the categories used to be either exhaustive or clear-cut.

Principles of behavioral variation. 1. Transfer processes: One of the main sources of behavior in a new situation is obviously past experience in similar situations. Transfer has been most exhaustively studied under the restricted conditions of verbal learning (e.g., Tulving & Madigan, 1970), but the principles of memory thus derived—proactive and retroactive interference, primacy and recency, retrieval factors, etc.—are presumably of general applicability.

With few exceptions (e.g., Gonzales, Behrend, & Bitterman, 1967), these principles have been little used to interpret animal learning experiments. Other principles of transfer are stimulus and response generalization (induction) and what might be called "compositional transfer," in which several past experiences are combined to generate a novel behavior, as in insight learning and other forms of subjective organization of past input.

2. Stimulus substitution: This principle, which is usually identified with Pavlovian conditioning, has already been discussed as a description of the origin of the terminal response of Pecking. It may also describe the origin of the metastable terminal response Head in magazine, since this response is also elicited by food under these conditions, and the animal which showed this response most persistently (Bird 29) had had considerable experimental experience. The difference in the persistence of Head in magazine in the case of this bird, as compared with others, cannot be explained in this way and might reflect a difference in other transfer processes. The final dominance of Pecking, in every case, may reflect a special susceptibility of consummatory responses to the stimulus substitution principle, or the action of other transfer principles in this particular situation in ways that are presently unclear. The indefinite persistence of key pecking following only three peck-contingent reinforcements, found by Neuringer (1970b), tends to support the simpler conclusion, as does the data of Wolin (1968), who reports a similarity between the topography of operant pecking for food or water reinforcers, and the appropriate unconditioned response. We return later to a general discussion of this principle in relation to these data (pp. 33-34).

3. Preparatory responses: This principle is also frequently associated with classical conditioning, and in that sense is related to, and to some extent overlaps with, the stimulus substitution principle. Thus, some conditioned responses, such as salivation, can be equally well described by either principle. Others, also respondents (such as heart rate, which increases following electric shock, but usually decreases in anticipation of it [Zeaman & Smith, 1965]) may be classified as preparatory responses. Skeletal responses observed in classical conditioning situations are often preparatory in nature (see discussion of classical conditioning below).

4. Syntactic constraints: There are often sequential constraints among behaviors, so that a given behavior is determined by some property of the sequence of preceding behaviors. Examples are spontaneous position alternation observed in rats and other rodents, stimulus alternation observed in moneys on learning set problems (e.g., Levine,

1965), and sequential dependencies observed in most species which cause responses to occur in runs rather than alternating randomly (e.g., position habits and other perseverative errors). Human language provides the most developed example of syntactic constraints.

5. Orienting responses: This category includes all those transient behaviors, such as exploration, play, curiosity, etc., that expose the organism to new stimuli and provide the possibility of transfer to future situations.

6. Situation-specific and species-typical responses: Certain situations seem to call forth specific responses, which are often typical of the species rather than the individual and do not seem to depend in any obvious way on any of the other principles of variation such as transfer, etc. Examples are the species-specific defense reactions discussed by Bolles (1970), which occur in fear-producing situations, the tendency to peck bright objects shown by many birds (Breland & Breland, 1966), and the digging shown by small rodents (Fantino & Cole, 1968). Other examples are given by Glickman and Sroges (1966).

Principles of reinforcement. Before the discovery of the mechanism of inheritance, evolution could be explained only in terms of a goal—adaptation—and a means sufficient to reach that goal—variation and selection; the generation-by-generation details of the process were obscure: "Our ignorance of the laws of variation is profound [Darwin, 1951, p. 170]." We are at present equally ignorant of the mechanism of behavioral variation. Since learning usually involve constant interplay between variation and reinforcement, we are not yet in a position to suggest anything specific about the moment-by-moment details of the process, either in its variational or selective aspects. However, just as Darwin was able to say something about selection by pointing out the adaptive role of various structures, so it is possible to learn something about the selective role of reinforcement by looking at steady-state adaptations to fixed conditions of reinforcement, that is, reinforcement schedules. On this basis, we suggest the following tentative generalizations about the effects of reinforcement:

1. Reinforcement acts directly only on the terminal response; activities which occur at other times (interim activities, adjunctive behavior, etc.) must be accounted for in other ways, to be discussed later. This assertion is perhaps closer to a definition than an empirical generalization, since it is equivalent to the assertion that the terminal response may, in general, be *identified* as the activity occurring in closest proximity to reinforcement in the steady state. Identification is, of course, no problem in conditioning situations that *enforce* a contingency between some property of behavior and the delivery of reinforcement. However, we will show later that there is no empirical or logical basis for separating situations that do impose a contingency between response and reinforcement from those that do not (see Classical Conditioning below).

2. Reinforcement acts only to eliminate behaviors that are less directly correlated with reinforcement than others. This generalization, like the first, is also more like a definition, since all that is *observed* (under consistent conditions of reinforcement) is the eventual predominance of one behavior over others—which is consistent with either a suppressive or a strengthening effect. As Skinner (1966a) points out in a summary of the Law of Effect:

> Thorndike was closer to the principle of natural selection than the [usual] statement of his law. He did not need to say that a response which had been followed by a certain kind of consequence was more likely to occur again but simply that it was not less likely. It eventually held the field because responses which failed to have such effects tended, like less favored species, to disappear [p. 13].

Unfortunately, Skinner, and most other behaviorists, elected to follow Thorndike in considering reinforcement to have a positive, strengthening, or "stamping-in" effect. One of the main purposes of the present paper is to suggest that this decision was a mistake and has given rise to a number of problems and controversies that can be avoided if the effects of reinforcement are considered to be purely selective or suppressive.

There are three kinds of argument which support a purely selective role for reinforcement. The first, and most important, is that the overall conceptual scheme which results is simpler and more easily related to biological accounts of behavior than the alternative.

The second point is that situations such as extinction and shaping by successive approximations that might seem to require an active role for reinforcement can be interpreted in a way that does not require anything more than a selective effect. This point is discussed later (see Extinction below).

The third point is that the superstition and related experiments suggest that the response contingency imposed by most reinforcement schedules is not essential for the production of *some* terminal response, but only for the selection of one response over others, or for directing a response which would probably predominate in any case—as in key pecking by pigeons. Our failure to find a consistent difference in rate of observer-defined pecking between the response-dependent and response-independent conditions of the present superstition experiment supports this view, as does a recent finding that the contingency between electric shock and responding is not necessary to the generation of behavior maintained by intermittent shock delivery to squirrel monkeys (Hutchinson, 1970; Stretch, personal communication, 1970).

The usual interpretation of the fact that there is a terminal response in the superstition situation, despite the absence of response-contingency, is the notion of accidental strengthening of a response by contiguity with the delivery of reinforcement. Here we consider the general implications of adventitious reinforcement as an explanation, and its incompatibility with the notion of reinforcement as selection. Other problems related to adventitious reinforcement are discussed later (see Acquisition, Classical Conditioning).

First, adventitious reinforcement implies failure of constancy, in the sense that the animal is presumed to be unable, because of the stamping-in mechanism of reinforcement, to distinguish between real and accidental correlations between his behavior and the occurrence of reinforcement. This is a strong assumption, in view of the adaptive utility of the constancy process and its ubiquity in perceptual and motor mechanisms. In perception, a similar failure to distinguish changes in sensory input that are produced by our own behavior from changes that are independent of behavior might cause us to perceive the world as rotating every time we turn our head. It is of course true that on the basis of one or a few instances the animal may not be in a position to be certain about the reality of a contingent relationship between his behavior and reinforcement—and this kind of sampling limitation might account for a transient superstitious effect. It is less convincing as an account of a long-term effect.

Second, if reinforcement is considered as purely selective, it *cannot* be invoked as an explanation of behavior when *no* imposed contingency exists between reinforcement and behavior (i.e., in the *absence* of selection). To do otherwise would be like taking a population of white mice, breeding them for 20 generations without further selection for color, and then attributing the resulting white population to the results of "accidental selection." In this case, as in the case of response-independent reinforcement, the outcome reflects a characteristic of the initial population (i.e., the mice gene pool, the nature of the organism), and not a nonexistent selection process.

In short, the notion of adventitious reinforcement is not a tenable one. The extent to which reinforcement can be invoked as an explanation for behavior is directly related both to the degree of *imposed contingency* between response and reinforcement and to the opportunities for that contingency to have some selective effect (i.e., the number of contingent reinforcements). If there is no contingency, or if few contingent reinforcements have occurred, the resulting behavior must owe more to principles of variation than to the selective action of reinforcement. On the other hand, if many contingent reinforcements have been delivered during a protracted period of shaping, the final form of behavior is obviously much less dependent on *particular* principles of variation, and the role or reinforcement (selection) may properly be emphasized.

3. There is considerable evidence for the generality of the principle implicating relative rate or proximity of reinforcement as the fundamental independent variable determining the spatial and temporal location of responding in steady-state conditioning situations. Thus, Herrnstein (1970) has recently reviewed a number of operant conditioning experiments involving differential reinforcement of simultaneous (concurrent schedules) and successive (multiple schedules) choices which support the idea of relative reinforcement rate as the independent variable most directly related to the rate of key pecking in pigeons. Shimp (1969) has presented an analysis which is formally different from Herrnstein's, but which also implicates differences in reinforcement rate as the crucial variable. An extensive series of experiments by Catania and Reynolds (1968) suggests a similar (although less exact) relationship between rate of pecking and relative temporal density of reinforcement on interval reinforcement schedules. Jenkins (1970) summarizes a series of studies with a discrete-trials procedure that led him to suggest relative proximity to reinforcement as an important determiner of the tendency to respond in the presence of a stimulus. Staddon (1970a) has suggested a similar principle to account for positive "goal gradients" that underlie the effects of reinforcement omission on a variety of interval schedules.

4. The concept of reinforcement implies a capacity to be reinforced. The fact that a given stimulus may be reinforcing at one time, but not at another, requires the idea of a *state* corresponding to each class of reinforcers. The independent variable of which the strength of most of these states is a function is deprivation with respect to the appropriate class of reinforcers (food deprivation for the hunger state, water for thirst, etc.). This will not do for most negative reinforcers (e.g., the removal of electric shock), however, since there is no obvious counterpart to deprivation in this case. It is also unlikely that deprivation is the only independent variable sufficient to alter the strength of states associated with positive reinforcement. For example, evidence is discussed later in favor of reciprocal inhibitory interaction between states as a possible factor in polydipsia and other adjunctive behavior. Interactions of this sort may also alter the strength of states for which there is no deprivation requirement as in audio anaesthesia (Licklider, 1961).

Thus, one may hope for a set of principles of reinforcement that will deal both with the proper classification of states and with the interactions among them.

The theoretical vocabulary of learning is full of terms with an uneasy conceptual status somewhere between explanation, definition, and category label. This terminology, which is not coherent or internally consistent, makes it difficult to approach particular topics with an open mind. It is too easy to dismiss an experimental result as due to adventitious reinforcement or respondent conditioning without, in fact, having any clear understanding of what has been said. Simply defining everything operationally is of little help in this situation since a set of definitions is not a theory. And a theory, in the sense of system of concepts that is internally consistent and coherent, is what is required if we are to be sure, in particular cases, whether we really understand a phenomenon—or are merely substituting one mystery for another, with the assistance of an opaque vocabulary.

What we are proposing is too primitive to be called a theory in this sense. However, it does offer a system of classification that makes it difficult to have the illusion of understanding a phenomenon if comprehension is really lacking. In the following section, some implications of this scheme are shown in three major areas: acquisition, extinction, and classical conditioning. This is followed by a brief discussion of possible difficulties of this approach. With the aid of this groundwork, it will then be easier to return to a general account of the superstition and related experiments in the concluding section.

Acquisition

The number of trials necessary for learning is one of those perennial problems that seems to defy resolution. Appeal to data is not conclusive because learning curves are sometimes incremental and sometimes step-like. Even in particular cases, theory is not conclusive either, since with sufficient ingenuity, theoretical accounts of both kinds of curve may be constructed on the basis of either one (or a few) trial learning assumptions or incremental assumptions involving thresholds. We turn now to the possibility that the issue is a consequence of the stamping-in view of reinforcement and becomes less urgent once that view is challenged.

A comment by Skinner (1953) on the necessary and sufficient conditions for the development of superstition provides an illustration:

In superstitious operant behavior...the process of conditioning has miscarried. Conditioning offers tremendous advantages in equipping the organism with behavior which is effective in a novel environment, but there appears to be no way of preventing the acquisition of non-advantageous behavior through accident. Curiously, this difficulty must have increased as the process of conditioning was accelerated in the course of evolution. If, for example, three reinforcements were always required in order to change the probability of a response, superstitious behavior would be unlikely. It is only because organisms have reached the point at which a single contingency makes a substantial change that they are vulnerable to coincidences [pp. 86-87].

Even within the framework of the stamping-in view, it is clear that the truth of this statement depends on a tacit assumption that responses will not generally occur more than once unless followed by reinforcement. If a given response can be relied on to occur at least 20 times in succession, even without reinforcement, then 3-trial, or even 10-trial learning might well be sufficient to insure its acquisition under the conditions of the superstition experiment. The assumption that responses will occur only once in the absence of reinforcement is a strong assumption about syntactic constraints, in our terminology. Moreover, it is contradicted by the results of the Williams and Williams study (1969), which show indefinite persistence of pecking in the absence of any contiguous relationship between pecks and reinforcement. There is no reason to suppose that a similar persistence is not characteristic of other behaviors (e.g., position habits), although pecking may be more persistent than most. Thus, the finding of superstitious terminal responses, or of indefinite pecking following just three response-contingent reinforcements (Neuringer, 1970b), need imply nothing about the number of trials necessary for learning.

These considerations suggest, as a minimum, the need to take variation into account in discussions of the "speed of conditioning," since rapid acquisition may either reflect an unpersistent response that is really learned rapidly, or a very persistent one that may be learned quite slowly. No inferences about "speed of conditioning" can be drawn solely on the basis of speed of acquisition without information about the frequency and pattern of a given behavior to be expected in a given situation (which may include predictable delivery of reinforcement) *in the absence of contiguity* between that behavior and reinforcement. In practice, since information of the required sort is rarely, if ever available, it seems wise to defer the issue of speed of learning until behavioral variation has been much more thoroughly studied.

Thus, the moment-by-moment details concerning the effect of reinforcement remain uncertain until much more is known about variation. In the meantime it seems more parsimonious and less likely to lead to fruitless controversies about "speed of conditioning," continuity versus noncontinuity, etc. to assume that the appearance of one behavior, rather than another, at a certain time or place, rather than some other time or place, always requires explanation in terms of principles of variation, with only the *disappearance* of behaviors being attributable to the effects of reinforcement.

This general approach is not novel. It resembles both Harlow's (1959) account of learning-set acquisition in terms of the progressive elimination of error factors, and certain versions of stimulus-sampling theory (Neimark & Estes, 1967). In Harlow's terms, as in ours, one-trial acquisition is a phenomenon that depends on the existence of factors that make the correct behavior much more probable (and persistent) than others (i.e., upon principles of variation). In the learning-set case, these factors are embodied in the prior training procedure, which progressively selects for an initially weak behavior (the "win stay, lose shift" strategy) at the expense of the initially much stronger tendencies to approach particular stimuli. A lengthy process may not be essential, however, for principles of variation involving insight ("compositional transfer." see above) may serve the same function if they are available to the animal. The important point is the shift of emphasis away from the supposed efficacy of some stamping-in-mechanism, the action of which must remain obscure in the absence of knowledge about variation, to the principles of variation that determine the strength of behaviors in advance of contiguity with reinforcement.

Extinction

Extinction is often used as a test for "what is learned" during a training procedure, as in generalization testing (Guttman & Kalish, 1956), and testing for control by temporal factors (Ferster & Skinner, 1957; Staddon, 1970b). Under these conditions it is assumed that behavior is determined almost entirely by transfer from the base-line condition. Providing the difference between the extinction and training conditions is not too great, either in terms of environmental factors (the stimulus situation is not too different) or temporal factors (the extinction is not prolonged), this assumption can be justified by the reliability and predictability of the behavior usually observed.

When these conditions are not satisfied or when the training preceding extinction has not been protracted, this reliability is not usually found. On the contrary, extinction under these conditions is usually associated with an increase in the variability of behavior (Antonitis, 1951; Millenson & Hurwitz, 1961). This increase in variability is exactly what would be expected if, as we have suggested, reinforcement has a purely selective effect: in these terms, training involves a progressive reduction in variability under the selective action of reinforcement (centripetal selection, see below), so that absence of reinforcement (extinction) represents a relaxation of selection—with an attendant rise in variability. We turn now to a brief account of the effects of changes in the amount and direction of selection in evolution, which may shed some further light on the properties of behavioral extinction.

Darwin (1896) comments on the effect of domestication as follows:

From a remote period to the present day, under climates and circumstances as different as it is possible to conceive, organic beings of all kinds, when domesticated or cultivated, have varied... These facts, and innumerable others which could be added, indicate that a change of almost any kind in the conditions of life suffices to cause variability...[Vol. 2, p. 243].

Although Darwin sometimes (erroneously) interpreted this observation as reflecting a direct effect of changed conditions on the reproductive system, it can be interpreted in modern terms as due to a relaxation of selection. This is clear from the concept of *centripetal selection* (Haldane, 1959; Mayr, 1963; Simpson, 1953), which refers to the fact that selection under *un*changing conditions, if long continued, acts to weed out extremes rather than systematically to shift population characteristics in any particular direction:

When adaptation is keeping up, selection at any one time will be mainly in favor of the existing type...In such cases, the intensity of selection tends to affect not the rate of change but the amount of variation [Simpson, 1953, p. 147].

Thus, a *change* in conditions will generally involve a shift *away* from centripetal selection, with its tendency to reduce variability, and will often lead, therefore, to increased variability. The most obvious example of the effects of relaxation of selection in evolution is degenerating or vestigial structures, that are no longer being selected for:

It is so commonly true that degenerating structures are highly variable that this may be advanced as an empirical evolutionary generalization [Simpson, 1953, p. 75].

We have already noted that the onset of variability in extinction is often delayed. A similar delay in the effect of changed conditions is often apparent in evolution, Darwin (1896) notes:

We have good grounds for believing that the influence of changed conditions accumulates, so that no effect is produced on a species until it has been exposed during several generations to continued cultivation or domestication. Universal experience shows us that when new flowers are first introduced into our gardens they do not vary; but ultimately all, with the rarest exceptions, vary to a greater or less extent [Vol. 2, p. 249].

Similar delays have also been reported in experiments on artificial selection (Mayr, 1963). These delays seem to reflect what has been termed "genetic inertia" or "genetic homeostasis" (Mayr, 1963), that is, the tendency for a gene pool which is the result of a long period of consistent selection to resist changes in the direction of selection. A similar mechanism in behavior might account for the dependence of variability in extinction on the duration of the preceding training period, which was referred to earlier: The amount of variability might be expected to be greater and its onset sooner following a brief training period than after one of longer duration. Genetic homeostasis also seems to be involved in the phenomenon of reversion, to be discussed next.

Not all the variation which occurs either in behavioral extinction, or following a change in the conditions of life in evolution, is wholly novel. A relatively common effect, for example, is the reappearance of what Darwin terms "ancestral types," that is, phenotypes which predominated earlier in phylogeny but which have been selected against more recently. This is the phenomenon of reversion which, because of his ignorance concerning heredity, Darwin (1896) found among the most mysterious of evolutionary processes:

But on the doctrine of reversion...the germ [germ plasm] becomes a far more marvelous object, for, besides the visible changes which it undergoes [i.e., phenotypic expressions], we must believe that it is crowded with invisible characters, proper to...ancestors separated by hundreds or even thousands of generations from the present time: and these characters, like those written on paper with invisible ink, lie ready to be evolved whenever the organization is disturbed by certain known or unknown conditions [Vol. 2, pp. 35-36].

Thus, one effect of a relaxation of selection is a more or less transient increase in the relative influence of the distant past at the expense of the immediate past. In behavioral extinction, this should involve the reappearance of old (in the sense of previously extinguished) behavior patterns; that is, transfer from conditions preceding the training condition at the expense of transfer from the training condition. In both cases, evolution and behavior, the effect of the change in conditions may be expected to depend on variables such as the magnitude of the change and the time since the preceding change.

The analogy from Darwin suggests that any considerable change in conditions should increase variability, yet a change in reinforcement schedules that includes an *increase* in reinforcement rate is not usually thought of as producing an increase in variability. This apparent contradiction is resolved by noting that an increase in rate of reinforcement, in addition to changing conditions, also increases the rate of selection (since the analogy assumes reinforcement to have a purely selective effect). Thus, variability may be briefly increased, but since the rapidity of selection is also increased, the net effect may be small. An analogous (but impossible) phenomenon in evolution would be to decrease the time between generations at the same time that conditions are changed. This would speed up the attainment of a new equilibrium and minimize the increase in variability generally associated with changed environment.

The increase in variability due to extinction is most directly put to use in the process of shaping by successive approximations. Frequently, following the first few reinforcements delivered during a "shaping" session, the effect is simply an increase in the range and vigor of behavior. This change can be viewed as being due to the interruption of eating (cf. Mandler, 1964), however, rather than any direct strengthening effect of reinforcement (which we are questioning in any case). In terms of the foregoing analysis, the conditions following the first reinforcement should be optimal for an increase in variability: the change is large (from continuous eating to absence of food) and the training procedure is of short duration (the 3-4 second eating bout), so that time since the preceding change is also short. As food continues to be delivered intermittently, selection occurs and variability decreases.

We have been suggesting a purely selective (rather than strengthening, stamping-in, or energizing) role for reinforcement. The present discussion suggests that such an essentially passive role is compatible with a number of phenomena—extinction, the activating effects of isolated reinforcements—that may appear to demand a more active role for reinforcement. This compatibility was established by drawing attention to similar phenomena in evolution, where the purely selective effect of the conditions of life (analogous to the schedule of reinforcement) is unquestioned. However, no *necessary* identity between the genetic mechanism, which is responsible for the effect of changed conditions on variability in structure, and whatever process is responsible for analogous effects in behavior, is intended. Any process for the production of variation that incorporates some latent memory of past adaptations is likely to show similar effects.

Classical Conditioning

Our scheme has strong implications for the distinction between classical (Pavlovian, respondent) and instrumental (operant) conditioning, to the extent that the distinction goes beyond procedural differences. Classical conditioning is often thought of as a paradigmatic instance of the primary process of learning: "The [learning] process appears to be based entirely on temporal contiguity and to have classical conditioning as its behavioral prototype [Sheffield, 1965, p. 321]." The salivation "reference experiment" can be interpreted as prototypical in at least two ways that are not always kept separate. The first (which has some similarities to our position) is referred to by Sheffield—the notion that learning depends solely on temporal relationships. Guthrie's aphorism that the animal "learns what he does" is a related idea. It is not easy to find a definitive account of this position, but it may perhaps be summarized by saying that reinforcement or reward is simply necessary to ensure that some behavior occurs in a conditioning situation. Principles involving temporal relationships (contiguity) then ensure that whatever occurs will transfer from one occasion to the next.

The second way in which classical conditioning is discussed as prototypical is in the terms of the rule that relates the conditioned and unconditioned responses. Pavlov (1927) emphasized stimulus substitution as the distinctive property of the situation: the response originally elicited only by the UCS is later made to the CS. Subsequently, two kinds of departure from this rule have been pointed out: (a) Even in the salivation experiment, there are other readily identifiable components of the conditioned response that do not fit the stimulus substitution rule. These preparatory responses (Zener, 1937) are largely, but not exclusively, skeletal (rather than autonomic). (b) Even in the case of salivation and other autonomic responses, the CR is rarely identical to the UCR (i.e., a redintegrative response), so that components of the UCR may be missing from the CR. More serious are differences in direction of change between CR and UCR, which may not even be consistent across individuals, as in heart rate and respiratory conditioning (Martin & Levey, 1969; Upton, 1929; Zeaman & Smith, 1965).

Partly because of problems involving preparatory responses, classical conditioning has increasingly been restricted to autonomically mediated responses. There were two bases for this restriction the apparent difficulty of conditioning skeletal responses by the operations of classical conditioning and according to the stimulus substitution principle (cf. Skinner, 1938, p. 115), and the supposed impossibility of conditioning autonomic responses via the Law of Effect. This is clear from Kimble's (1961) comment:

> Obviously the common expression, "the conditioned response," is misleading, and probably in important ways. At the same time it should be recognized that the behavior described by Zener [preparatory responses] was almost certainly instrumentally, rather than classically, conditioned [p. 54].

The force of this argument is lost once the susceptibility of autonomic responses such as salivation to operant conditioning is demonstrated.

The foregoing facts are sufficient to show the error of continuing to regard classical conditioning as a unified process, much less as an explanatory element in accounts of operant conditioning. If classical conditioning is a single process, then it must be describable by principles of operation that apply to every instance. As we have seen, even stimulus substitution, the most general such principle, fails to apply in every case. Many, but not all, the anomalous cases and skeletal responses—which suggested that perhaps the notion of a single process could be preserved by restricting the term to autonomic responses. The only independent basis for this is to segregate skeletal and autonomic responses on the grounds that operant conditioning of autonomic responses is impossible. Since this is now known to be false (Miller, 1969), the only remaining basis for excluding skeletal responses from the class of classically conditionable responses is their failure to conform to the principle of stimulus substitution. But, in addition to being tautologous (classical conditioning simply becomes equivalent to learning via stimulus substitution), this fails because many autonomic responses do not conform to this principle and, based on the work of Brown and Jenkins and of Williams and Williams, at least one skeletal response—pecking in pigeons—does obey it (other possibilities are leg flexion and eyeblink). Thus, the class of classically conditionable responses can be defined neither in terms of the neural mediating system (autonomic vs. skeletal) nor in terms of adherence to a particular principle of learning.

The only remaining feature common to all the situations labeled as classical conditioning is the procedure itself. Research in this area has tended to focus on the properties of the temporal relationship between CS and UCS that are necessary and sufficient for the CS to acquire the power to elicit the conditioned response, and a consensus appears to be emerging that the crucial factor is the extent to which the CS is a predictor of the UCS (Rescorla, 1967). However, the notion of predictiveness does not appear to differ from *relative proximity* (of the CS to the UCS, or of a stimulus to reinforcement) which, as we have seen (Principle of Reinforcement 3, above), is a factor of wide applicability in operant conditioning. Thus, for all practical purposes, classical conditioning may be defined operationally as a class of reinforcement schedules that involve presentation of reinforcement independently of the subject's behavior.

We conclude, therefore, that the division of the field of learning into two classes—classical and instrumental conditioning—each governed by separate sets of principles, has no basis in fact. As an alternative, we suggest an analysis based on the principles of behavioral variation and reinforcement we have already discussed. In terms of this analysis, all adaptive behavior is subsumed under an expanded version of the Law of Effect, and a given situation is to be understood in terms of two factors: (a) the reinforcement schedule, that is, the rule prescribing the delivery of reinforcement, or, more generally, stimuli, in relation to the behavior of the organism, and (b) the nature of the response under consideration. In terms of such an analysis, the properties normally considered as distinctive of classical conditioning may, once attention is directed to the question, be seen as due in part to a reinforcement schedule that happens to prescribe no correlation between the delivery of reinforcement and the subject's behavior, and in part to the special properties of responses such as salivation.

(Discussion of the implications for this proposed interpretation of classical conditioning as a schedule where there is no correlation between the subject's behavior and the delivery of reinforcement, is quite technical and omitted in this annotation)

Difficulties of the Proposed Classification

Science is conservative and, quite correctly, resists most attempts to alter an established theoretical framework. We have already tried to show that the number of anomalies facing current learning theories is sufficient to justify a search for alternatives. Nevertheless, the radical appearance of the scheme we suggest is a substantial obstacle to its consideration. It is important, therefore, to point out that it is little more than an extension and reorganization of familiar concepts, that is, reinforcement S-R behavior units, learning principles such as transfer and ethological observations on species-related behaviors. The difference is therefore largely one of emphasis and selection rather than the introduction of wholly novel ideas.

Any discussion of evolution and learning naturally brings to mind the learning-instinct issue. There is no simple parallel between this dichotomy and anything in the scheme we propose. The origin of every behavior is supposed traceable to principles of variation; if, for example, in a particular case a principle of transfer is involved, one might want to say that the behavior is learned. However, the question must then simply be asked again about the previous situation from which transfer has supposedly occurred. In this way, almost any question about the relative roles of heredity and environment will involve unraveling the whole of ontogeny. This conclusion will not be unfamiliar to ethologists (cf. Beach, 1955).

It is also important to emphasize that we have not been directly concerned with the evolution of the capacity to learn; although it may be that increasing knowledge of variation will shed light on this issue.

One objection that may be raised to the proposed scheme is that it is derived from and deals explicitly only with positive reinforcement. However, a recent account of behavior sustained by negative reinforcement (Bolles, 1970) is in perfect agreement with our position. Bolles points out that some activities are much more easily conditioned than others in avoidance situations, and these are the unconditioned activities that normally occur in a variety of potentially dangerous circumstances. These species-specific defense reaction, in Bolles' terminology, occur in advance of reinforcement (i.e., the avoidance of electric shock) –in our terms, they are determined initially by one of the principles of behavioral variation. The lack of arbitrariness of the response is perhaps more obvious in avoidance than in any other situation because of the complexity of the schedules involved: the animal must usually learn something about the pattern of occurrence of an intermittent aversive event, in the absence of responding, before he is in a position to detect alterations in that pattern correlated with his own behavior. Although a similar situation prevails in all reinforcement schedules, the change to be discriminated seems considerably easier both in appetitive conditioning, where the shift is from zero reinforcement in the absence of responding to reinforcement following every response, and in escape, where it is from continuous presence of the aversive stimulus in the absence of responding to complete absence following each response. Bolles suggests other reasons, related to the limited opportunities for avoidance (in the schedule sense) in the wild life of small mammals, and thus the limited opportunities for the capacity to avoid to be selected in phylogeny.

The strongest point in favor of our proposal is its promise of parsimony. Consequently, the most damaging criticism that can be directed against it is the absence of firm specification of the principles of reinforcement and variation. This appears to allow the creation of such principles at will, enabling us to explain everything—and nothing. There are two defenses against this criticism. First, we again emphasize the tentative nature of the principles we have suggested. The overlap among the principles of variation, particularly, suggests that our list is provisional. Second, there is the strong possibility that clear recognition of the distinction between variation and reinforcement may be essential to further advance. In defense of this proposition, we first briefly discuss some examples from synoptic accounts of current learning theory, which show it to incorporate few safeguards against multiple explanations for phenomena. Since our scheme of classification is at least internally consistent and forces one to relate each new principle of variation to others that already exist, it has some advantages in this respect. Second, we discuss the controversy between cognitive and behavioristic theorists regarding the role of structure in behavior, in relation to a similar controversy in the history of evolutionary thought. The persistence of this controversy and its amenability to analysis in terms of variation and reinforcement suggest that our classification may be of some value despite its incompleteness.

1. Hilgard and Marquis (1940) list as principles of reinforcement: Stimulus substitution, expectancy, and the principle (law) of effect. It should be apparent from the earlier arguments that the Law of Effect is the result of the combined effect of both variation and reinforcement, stimulus substitution is a principle of variation, and expectancy refers to a general characteristic which can be imputed to most learning. Consequently this set of terms allows for considerable uncertainty in application to particular situations. For example, our analysis of the Williams and Williams experiment (see p. 33) makes use of both stimulus substitution and a principle of reinforcement analogous to what Hilgard and Marquis mean by the Law of Effect. Yet the same situation could also be analyzed in terms of expectancy; and it appears to be incompatible with the Law of Effect as traditionally understood. Progress since 1940 has not been dramatic, as illustrated by a list of "elementary conditioning processes" inventoried by Jenkins (1970) in connection with his work on cyclic reinforcement schedules: generalization, delay of reinforcement, conditioned reinforcement, unconditioned effects of eating, frustration effects, effects related to "behavioral contrast." Despite the number of these processes and the lack of any obvious relationship among them, Jenkins finds that they are unable to account for some rather simple features of his data, which require a description in terms of the relative proximity of a stimulus or a response to reinforcement as a major determiner (see Principles of Reinforcement, above).

2. There is a history of fruitless controversy between many behaviorists, who place little emphasis on the structural properties of behavior, and students of cognitive processes, who see structure as the most interesting and important behavioral attribute (cf. Staddon, 1967, 1969, for a discussion in relation to operant conditioning). The distinction between variation and reinforcement can shed some light on this issue, which can be illustrated by briefly considering the contrasting views of Skinner and Chomsky (Chomsky, 1959; MacCorquodale, 1969) on the causation of learned behavior.

Chomsky's major concern is with principles of variation, in our terms, as is clear from his emphasis on the rule-governed nature of language (see Principle of Behavioral Variation 4, above).

Skinner's position is less obvious, but becomes clear from his account of the shaping of behavior (Skinner, 1953); he writes:

Operant conditioning shapes behavior as a sculptor shapes a lump of clay. Although at some point the sculptor seems to have produced an entirely novel object, we can always follow the process back to the original undifferentiated lump, and we can make the successive stages by which we return to this condition as small as we wish. At no point does anything emerge which is very different from what preceded it. The final product seems to have a special unity or integrity of design, but we cannot find a point at which this suddenly appears. In the same sense, an operant is not something which appears full grown in the behavior of the organism. It is the result of a continuous shaping process [p. 91].

For Skinner, apparently, moment-to-moment variation in behavior is small in magnitude and essentially random (in the sense that it is unrelated to the final goal) in direction. Behavior is the result of the "accumulation…of indefinite variations which have proved serviceable" in Darwin's phrase. The similarity to natural selection is further emphasized by Darwin's (1951) account of the evolution of complex structures:

If it could be demonstrated that any complex organ existed, which could not possibly have been formed by numerous, successive, slight modifications, my theory would absolutely break down [p. 191].

In the history of evolution after Darwin, the rediscovery of Mendel's laws led to a retreat from gradualism in favor of a saltationism that traced evolutionary progress (especially evolutionary novelty) to large changes (mutations) of a more purposive sort (cf. Mayr, 1960). This position is closer to the view of Chomsky and other cognitive theorists, who tend to stress the importance of insight and other rules of composition that can produce sudden jumps in behavior.

The history of evolution has not supported the saltationist view. Fisher (1930) showed that large changes are much less likely to be adaptive than small ones, and Haldane and others have shown by a variety of arguments that the time available for evolution by the selection of small variations is more than sufficient to account for the observed differences among taxa: "The saltationism of the early Mendelians has been refuted in all its aspects {Mayr, 1960, p. 350]."

At a superficial level, therefore, these comparisons might appear to favor Skinner's gradualism and emphasis on reinforcement (selection), to the detriment of the cognitive position. This is probably unjustifiable for two main reasons. First, detailed analysis of complex problem solving clearly indicates the insufficiency of random variation as an account of the process (e.g., Neisser, 1967). The heuristics that are employed may, of course, be attributed to past learning based entirely on random variation. However, this suggestion meets with quantitative difficulties when applied to the development of language—the best-studied example of rule-governed behavior. Although calculations in this area are of limited validity in the absence of established principles of variation (analogous to Mendelian genetics), the attempts that have been made seem to indicate that the time available in ontogeny for the development of language is incompatible with any kind of learning by random variation (Chomsky,

1962; McNeill, 1968). This negative result is the opposite of Haldane's affirmative conclusion on the sufficiency of small mutations as a basis for phylogenetic changes. It suggests that neither the heuristics employed in complex problem solving, nor the rules of syntax, need to be built up entirely de novo during ontogeny.

Second, the relationship between evolution and learning is such as to allow greater flexibility to learning. This is because natural selection can only be a response to small differences in "fitness": the most fit genotype will tend to prevail, although the species as a whole may thereby be led into an evolutionary blind alley. In terms of contemporary accounts of goal-directed mechanisms, natural selection represents a hill-climbing process (Minsky, 1961) and has no provision for prediction. This is clean in a familiar analogy due to Sewall Wright (1931) which shows the relationships among selection, structure, and variation. He pictures the field of possible structural variation as a landscape with hills and valleys. The range of variation present in a population of organisms is represented by a closed area on this landscape. Selection pressure is represented by the gradient (upward slope) of the landscape, so that each *peak* is an adaptive optimum for a given constellation of characters; valleys represent unstable equilibria yielding so-called centrifugal selection. If the area representing a given species includes a single adaptive peak, selection will be centripetal, so that the species will tend to cluster more and more closely around the peak. Thus, small mutations are more likely to lead to improvements in fitness than large ones (with a limiting probability of .5, as Fisher, 1930, has shown), and the consequent predominant role of such small differences in fitness in the evolutionary process becomes obvious.

Learning is not so limited, however, because the principles of variation can be weighted to take account of regularities in the past history of the species (these are Skinner's, 1966b, "phylogenic contingencies"); that is, behavior need not occur at random in advance of reinforcement, but can reflect a priori probabilities that have been selected for during phylogency. Other more complex strategies of this sort may also be built up by natural selection, giving learning a predictive capacity largely denied to evolution itself. Thus, although learned behavior reflects differences in reinforcement rate, just as evolution reflects selection on the basis of relative fitness, it need *not* be generally true either that small changes in behavior are more likely to be adaptive than large ones, or that the direction of change is unrelated to the final goal—as Skinner's account implies, and as is usually (although not invariably) the case in evolution. However, since the more elaborate principles of variation must themselves be built up step-by-step by natural selection, it is to be expected that the pattern and range of behavioral variation must bear some relationship to the phylogenetic status of the organism: "higher" organism, such as man, are likely to have developed more complex principles of variation than "lower" organism, such as the pigeon.

Thus, the major focus of the argument between Skinner and Chomsky is not on the importance of reinforcement, but about the complexity of the principles of variation that determine the nature of behavior in advance of reinforcement. Since Skinner derives his ideas from work on rats and pigeons, and Chomsky from the study of human language, there are considerable grounds for a disagreement, especially if its basis is not clearly perceived by either party. Clear conceptual separation of variation from reinforcement makes this kind of confusion much less likely.

Conclusion

The argument so far has served to draw attention to a number of generalizations about steady-state conditioning situations:

1. Most such situations involve some times and stimuli associated with relatively high reinforcement probability (e.g., the period at the end of the interval on fixed-interval schedules), and others associated with relatively low reinforcement probability (e.g., the period at the beginning of the interval).

2. The *terminal response* (a discriminated operant in Skinner's terminology) is restricted to periods of relatively high reinforcement probability. This distribution of the terminal response with respect to time and stimuli corresponds to a principle of reinforcement that relates the strength of a response to the relative frequency, density, or proximity of reinforcement associated with that response (Catania & Reynolds, 1968; Herrnstein, 1970; Jenkins, 1970).

3. The type, as opposed to the temporal and stimulus location, of the terminal response in situations involving both response-dependent and response-independent reinforcement is determined by the interaction between principles of variation (e.g., transfer, stimulus substitution) that describe the occurrence of the response, in advance of reinforcement, and principles of reinforcement that determine whether it will persist or not (selective function of reinforcement).

4. Periods of low reinforcement probability are generally associated with *interim activities*, resembling appetitive behavior. If appropriate stimuli (goal objects) are provided, stereotyped *adjunctive behavior* (e.g., polydipsia, pica; Falk, 1969) takes the place of the more variable and relatively undirected interim activities.

5. Both terminal response and interim activities are more correctly labeled as predisposing conditions or *states* rather than behaviors, since in the absence of response dependency, the type of activity falling into these categories is not fixed. Thus, drinking, wheel running, fighting, pecking, and a number of other activities may be either terminal or adjunctive behaviors, depending on historical and stimulus factors (Segal, 1969b; Skinner, 1959; Skinner & Morse, 1958). Directing factors for adjunctive behavior are the availability of appropriate goal objects (see above), and factors related to reinforcement that render some kinds of activity more probable than others: for example, polydipsia appears to partially displace both adjunctive wheel-running (Segal, 1969a) and chewing-manipulatory behavior (Freed & Hymowitz, 1969) in rats (in situations with food as terminal reinforcer), even when both supporting stimuli are concurrently available.

(Detailed discussions of the terminal response, interim activities and adjunctive behaviors in relation to the proposed system are omitted here)

Epilogue

This ends our outline of conditioning, We have dealt with both terminal periods—which, we suggest, reflect a Law of Effect process that can best be understood by analogy with evolution by means of natural selection—and interim periods—which may reflect a mechanism enabling animals to allocate their activities efficiently. Learned behavior, under the relatively simple conditions of reinforcement schedules at least, is viewed as reflecting the sequencing, with respect to time and stimuli, of terminal and interim periods; and the scheme is therefore potentially comprehensive, although necessarily incomplete as to details.

Our proposal is founded on the belief that the most distinctive thing about living creatures is the balance they maintain among a number of tendencies to action, each one adaptive, yet each destructive if pursued to the exclusion of others. This emphasis on the *integration* of behavior has required that the scheme attempt to be comprehensive and that it relate in a natural way to biological and physiological considerations. Such merits as it possesses lie not in formal elegance or precision but in an ability to organize otherwise unrelated facts and to suggest gaps where others may possibly be found.

References

AKERMAN, B., ANDERSON, E., FABRICIUS, E., & SVENSSON, L. Observations on central regulation of body temperature and of food and water intake in the pigeon (*Columba livia*). *Acta Physiologica, Scandinavica*, 1960, **50**, 328-336

ANDREW, R. J. Some remarks on behaviour in conflict situations, with special reference to *Emberiza* Spp. *British Journal of Animal Behaviour*, 1956, **4**, 41-45.

ANTONITIS, J. J. Response variability in the white rat during conditioning, extinction, and reconditioning. *Journal of Experimental Psychology*, 1951, **42**, 273-281.

AZRIN, N. H. Time-out from positive reinforcement. *Science*, 1961, **133**, 382-383.

AZRIN, N. H Aggression. Paper presented at the meeting of the American Psychological Association, Los Angeles, September 1964.

AZRIN, N. H., HUTCHINSON, R. R., & HAKE, D. F. Extinction-induced aggression. *Journal of the Experimental Analysis of Behavior*, 1966, **9**, 191-204.

BEACH F. A. The descent of instinct. *Psychological Review*, 1955, **62**, 401-410.

BEALE, I. L., & WINTON, A. S, W. Inhibitory stimulus control in concurrent schedules. *Journal of the Experimental Analysis of Behavior*, 1970, **14**, 133-137.

BLACK, A. H. Constraints on the operant conditioning of drinking. In, *Schedule-induced and schedule-dependent phenomena*. Vol. 2. Toronto: Addiction Research Foundation, 1970.

BOLLES, R. C. Species-specific defense reactions and avoidance learning. *Psychological Review*, 1970, **77**, 32-48.

BRELAND, K., & BRELAND, M. The misbehavior of organisms. *American Psychologist*, 1961, **16**, 661-664.

BRELAND, K., & BRELAND, M. *Animal behavior*, New York: Macmillan, 1966.

BROADBENT, D. E. *Behaviour*. London: Methuen, 1961.

BROWN, P.L., & JENKINS, H. M. Auto-shaping of the pigeon's key-peck, *Journal of the Experimental Analysis of Behavior*, 1968, **11**, 1-8.

BURKS, C. D. Schedule-induced polydipsia: Are response-dependent schedules a limiting condition? *Journal of the Experimental Analysis of Behavior*, 1970, **13**, 351-358.

BURKS, C. D., & FISHER, A. E. Anticholinergic blockade of schedule-induced polydipsia. *Physiology and Behavior*, 1970, *5*, 635-640.

CANE, V. Some ways of describing behaviour. In W. H. Thorpe & O. L. Zangwill (Eds.), *Current problems in animalbehaviour*. London: Cambridge University Press, 1961.

CATANIA, A. C. Concurrent performances: Inhibition of one response by reinforcement of another. *Journal of the Experimental Analysis of Behavior*, 1969, **12**, 731-744.

CATANIA, A. C., & REYNOLDS, G. S. A quantitative analysis of the responding maintained by interval schedules of reinforcement. *Journal of the Experimental Analysis of Behavior*, 1968, **11**(Pt. 2), 327-383.

CHAPMAN, H. W. Oropharyngeal determinants of non-regulatory drinking in the rat. Unpublished doctoral dissertation, University of Pennsylvania, 1969.

CHOMSKY, N. A review of B. F. Skinner's *Verbal behavior*. *Language*, 1959, **35**, 26-58.

CHOMSKY, N. Explanatory models in linguistics. In E. Nagel, P. Suppes, & A. Tarski (Eds), *Logic methodology and philosophy of science: Proceedings of the 1960 International Congress*. Stanford: Stanford University Press, 1962.

CRAIG, W. Appetites and aversions as constituents of instincts. *Biological Bulletin of the Marine Biological Laboratory*, Woods Hole, Mass., 1918, **XXXIV**, 91-107.

DARWIN, C. *The origin of species*. Oxford: The University Press, 1951. (Reprinted from the sixth edition, 1872).

DARWIN, C. *The variation of animals and plants under domestication*. New York: Appleton, 1896. 2 vols.

DAVIS, J. D., & KEEHN, J. D. Magnitude of reinforcement and consummatory behavior. *Science*, 1959, **130**, 269- 270.

ESTES, W. K. Of models and men. *American Psychologist*, 1957, **12**, 609-617.

FALK, J. L. Studies on schedule-induced polydipsia. In M. J. Wayner (Ed.), *Thirst: First international symposium on thirst in the regulation of body water*. New York: Pergamon Press, 1964.

FALK, J. L. Schedule-induced polydipsia as a function of fixed interval length. *Journal of the Experimental Analysis of Behavior*, 1966, **9**, 37-39.

FALK, J. L. Control of schedule-induced polydipsia: Type, size, and spacing of meals. *Journal of the Experimental Analysis of Behavior*, 1967, **10**, 199-206.

FALK, J. L. Conditions producing psychogenic polydipsia in animals. *Annals of the New York Academy of Sciences*, 1969, **157**, 569-593.

FALK, J. L. The nature and determinants of adjunctive behavior. In, *Schedule-induced and schedule-dependent phenomena*. Vol. 2. Toronto: Addiction Research Foundation, 1970.

FANTINO, E., & COLE, M. Sand-digging in mice: Functional autonomy? *Psychonomic Science*. 1968, **10**, 29-30.

FERSTER, C. B., & SKINNER, B. F. *Schedules of reinforcement*. New York: Appleton-Century-Crofts, 1957.

FISHER, R. A. *The genetical theory of natural selection*. Oxford: Clarendon Press, 1930.

FLORY, R. Attack behavior as a function of minimum inter-food interval. *Journal of the Experimental Analysis of Behavior*, 1969, **12**, 825-828.

FREED, E. X., & HYMOWITZ, N. A fortuitous observation regarding "psychogenic" polydipsia. *Psychological Reports*, 1969, **24**, 224-226.

GARCIA, J., ERVIN, F. R., & KOELLING, R. Learning with prolonged delay of reinforcement. *Psychonomic Science*, 1966, **5**, 121-122.

GHISELIN, J. T. *The triumph of the Darwinian method*. Berkeley: University of California Press, 1969.

GILBERT, R. M. Psychology and biology. *Canadian Psychologist*, 1970, **11**, 221-238.

GLICKMAN, S. E., & SCHIFF, B. B. A biological theory of reinforcement. *Psychological Review*, 1967, **74**, 81-109.

GLICKMAN, S. E., & SROGES, R. W. Curiosity in zoo animals. *Behaviour*, 1966, **26**, 151-188.

GONZALEZ, R. C., BEHREND, E. R., & BITTERMAN, M. E. Reversal learning and forgetting in bird and fish. *Science*, 1967, **158**, 519-521.

GROSSMAN, S. P. Direct adrenergic and cholinergic stimulation of hypothalamic mechanisms. *American Journal of Physiology*, 1962, **202**, 872-882.

GUTTMAN, N., & KALISH, H. I. Discriminability and stimulus generalization. *Journal of Experimental Psychology*, 1956, **51**, 79-88.

HALDANE, J. B. S. Natural selection. In P. R. Bell (Ed.), *Darwin's biological work*. Cambridge: University Press, 959.

HARLOW, H. F. Learning set and error factor theory. In S. Koch (Ed.), *Psychology: A study of a science*. Vol. 2. New York: McGraw-Hill, 1959.

HAWKINS, T. D., EVERETT, P. B., GITHENS, S. H., & SCHROT, J. F. Adjunctive drinking: A functional analysis of water and alcohol ingestion. In, *Schedule-induced and schedule-dependent phenomena*. Vol. 1. Toronto: Addiction Research Foundation, 1970.

HERRNSTEIN, R. J. "Will." *Proceedings of the American Philosophical Society*, 1964, **108**, 455-458.

HERRNSTEIN, R. J. Superstition: A corollary of the principles of operant conditioning. In W. K. Honig (Ed.), *Operant behavior: Areas of research and application*. New York: Appleton-Century-Crofts. 1966.

HERRNSTEIN, R. J. On the law of effect. *Journal of the Experimental Analysis of Behavior*, 1970, **13**, 243-266.

HERRNSTEIN, R. J., & HINELINE, P. N. Negative reinforcement as shock-frequency reduction. *Journal of Experimental Analysis of Behavior*, 1966, **9**, 421-430.

HILGARD, E. R., & MARQUIS, D. G. *Conditioning and learning*. New York: Appleton-Century, 1940.

HINDE, R. A. *Animal behaviour: A synthesis of ethology and comparative psychology*. New York: McGraw-Hill, 1966.

HUTCHINSON, R. The production and maintenance of behavior by shock and shock-associated stimuli. In R. Ulrich (Chm.), The maintenance of responding through the presentation of electric shocks. Symposium presented at the meeting of the American Psychological Association, Miami, September 1970.

JENKINS, H. M. Sequential organization in schedules of reinforcement. In W. M. Schoenfeld & J. Farmer (Eds.), *Theory of reinforcement schedules*. New York: Appleton-Century-Crofts, 1970.

KALAT, J. W., & Rozin, P. "Salience": A factor which can override temporal contiguity in taste-aversion learning. *Journal of Comparative and Physiological Psychology*, 1970, **71**, 192-197.

KEEHN, J. D. Beyond the law of effect. In, *Schedule-induced and schedule-dependent phynomena*. Vol. 1. Toronto:
Addiction Research Foundation, 1970.

KIMBLE, G. A. *Hilgard and Marquis' conditioning and learning*. New York: Appleton-Century-Crofts, 1961.

LEVINE, M. Hypothesis behavior. In A. M. Schrier, H. F. Harlow, & F. Stollnitz (Eds.), *Behavior of nonhuman primates*. Vol. 1. New York: Academic Press, 1965.

LICKLIDER, J. C. R. On psychophysiological models. In W. A. Rosenblith (Ed.), *Sensory communication*. Cambridge: M.I.T. Press, 1961.

MACCORQUODALE, K. B. F. Skinner's *Verbal behavior*: A retrospective appreciation. *Journal of the Experimental Analysis of Behavior*, 1969, **12**, 831-841.

MANDLER, G. The interruption of behavior. *Nebraska Symposium on Motivation*, 1964, **12**, 163-219.

MARTIN, I., & LEVEY, A. B. *The genesis of the classical conditioned response*. Oxford: Pergamon Press, 1969.

MAYR, E. The emergence of evolutionary novelties. In S. Tax (Ed.), *The evolution of life*. Vol. 1. Chicago: University Press, 1960.

MAYR, E. *Animal species and evolution*. Cambridge: Harvard University Press, 1963.

MCFARLAND, D. J. Hunger, thirst and displacement pecking in the barbary dove. *Animal Behaviour*, 1965, **13**, 293-300.

MCFARLAND, D. J. On the causal and functional significance of displacement activities. *Zeitschrift fur Tierpsychologie*, 1966, **23**, 217-235.

MCNEILL, D. On theories of language acquisition. In T. R. Dixon & D. L. Horton (Eds.), *Verbal behavior and general behavior theory*. Englewood Cliffs, N. J.: Prentice-Hall, 1968.

MILLENSON, J. R., & Hurwitz, H. M. B. Some temporal and sequential properties of behavior during conditioning and extinction. *Journal of the Experimental Analysis of Behavior*, 1961, **4**, 97-106.

MILLER, N. E. Learning of visceral and glandular responses. *Science*, 1969. **163**, 434-445.

MINSKY, M. Steps toward artificial intelligence. *Proceedings of the Institute of Radio Engineers*, 1961, **49**, 10-30.

MORRIS, D. The reproductive behaviour of the Zebra finch (*Poephila guttata*), with special reference to pseudofemale behaviour and displacement activities. *Behaviour*, 1954, **6**, 271-322.

MORRIS, D. The reproductive behaviour of the Ten-spined Stickleback (*Pygosteus pungitius* L.), *Behaviour*, 1958, Supplement VI, 1-154.

NEIMARK, E. D., & ESTES, W. K. *Stimulus sampling theory*. San Francisco: Holden-Day, 1967.

NEISSER, U. *Cognitive psychology*. New York: Appleton-Century-Crofts, 1967.

NEURINGER, A. J. Many responses per food reward with free food present. *Science*, 1970, **169**, 503-504. (a)

NEURINGER, A. J. Superstitious key pecking after three peck-produced reinforcements. *Journal of the Experimental Analysis of Behavior*, 1970, **13**, 127-134.

PAVLOV, I. P. *Conditioned reflexes*. (Trans. by G. V. Anrep.) London: Oxford University Press, 1927.

PFAFFMAN, C. The behavioral science model. *American Psychologist*, 1970, **25**, 437-441.

PRINGLE, J. W. S. On the parallel between learning and evolution. *Behaviour*, 1951, **3**, 174-215.

PRYOR, K. W., HAAG, R., & O'REILLY, J. The creative porpoise: Training for novel behavior. *Journal of the Experimental Analysis of Behavior*, 1969, **12**, 653-661.

RACHLIN, H. Autoshaping of key pecking in pigeons with negative reinforcement. *Journal of the Experimental Analysis of Behavior*, 1969, **12**, 521-531.

RESCORLA, R. A. Pavlovian conditioning and its proper control procedures. *Psychological Review*, 1967, **74**, 71-80.

REVUSKY, S. H., & BEDARF, E. W. Association of illness with prior ingestion of novel foods. *Science*, 1967, **155**, 219-220.

REYNIERSE, J. H., & SPANIER, D. Excessive drinking in rats' adaptation to the schedule of feeding. *Psychonomic Science*, 1968, **10**, 95-96.

ROSENBLITH, J. Z. Polydipsia induced in the rat by a second-order schedule. *Journal of the Experimental Analysis of Behavior*, 1970, **14**, 139-144.

ROWELL, C. H. F. Displacement grooming in the Chaffinch. *Animal Behaviour*, 1961, **9**, 38-63.

ROZIN, P. Central or peripheral mediation of learning with long CS-US intervals in the feeding system. *Journal of Comparative and Physiological Psychology*, 1969, **67**, 421-429.

SCHAEFER, R. W., & PREMACK, D. Licking rates in infant albino rats. *Science*, 1961, **134**, 1980-1981.

SEGAL, E. The interaction of psychogenic polydipsia with wheel running in rats. *Psychonomic Science*, 1969, **14**, 141-144. (a) SEGAL, E. Transformation of polydipsic drinking into operant drinking. A paradign? *Psychonomic Science,* 1969, **16**, 133-135. (b)

SEGAL, E. Speculations on the provenance of operants. In, *Schedule-induced and schedule-dependent phenomena*. Vol. 2. Toronto: Addiction Research Foundation, 1970.

SEGAL, E., & HOLLOWAY, S. M. Timing behavior in rats with water drinking as a mediator. *Science*, 1963, **140**, 888-889.

SEGAL, E., ODEN, D. L., & DEADWYLER, S. A. Determinants of polydipsia: IV. Free-reinforcement schedules. *Psychonomic Science*, 1965, **3**, 11-12.

SEVENSTER, P. A causal analysis of a displacement activity (Fanning in *Gasterosteus Aculeatus* L.). *Behaviour*, 1961, Supplement IX, 1-170.

SHANAB, M. B., & PETERSON, J. L. Polydipsia in the pigeon. *Psychonomic Science*, 1969, **15**, 51-52.

SHEFFIELD, F. S. Relation between classical conditioning and instrumental learning. In W. F. Prokasy (Ed.), *Classical conditioning: A symposium*. New York: Appleton-Century-Crofts, 1965.

SHIMP, C. P. Optimal behavior in free-operant experiments. *Psychological Review*, 1969, **76**, 97-112.

SIDMAN, M., & FLETCHER, F. G. A demonstration of auto-shaping with monkeys. *Journal of the Experimental Analysis of Behavior*, 1968, **11**, 307-309.

SIMMELHAG, V. L. The form and distribution of responding in pigeons on response-independent fixed and variable interval schedules of reinforcement.

Unpublished master's thesis, University of Toronto, 1968.

SIMPSON, G. G. *The major features of evolution*. New York: Columbia University Press, 1953.

SKINNER, B. F. *The behavior of organisms*. New York: Appleton-Century, 1938.

SKINNER, B. F. "Superstition" in the pigeon. *Journal of Experimental Psychology*, 1948, **38**, 168-172.

SKINNER, B. F. *Science and human behavior*. New York: Macmillan, 1953.

SKINNER, B. F. Reinforcement today. *American Psychologist*, 1958, **13**, 94-99.

SKINNER, B. F. An experimental analysis of certain emotions. *Journal of the Experimental Analysis of Behavior* 1959, **2**, 264.

SKINNER, B. F. *Cumulative record.* New York: Appleton-Century-Crofts, 1961.

SKINNER, B. F. Operant behavior. In W. K. Honig (Ed.), *Operant behavior: Areas of research and application.* New York: Appleton-Century-Crofts, 1966. (a)

SKINNER, B. F. The phylogeny and ontogeny of behavior. *Science*, 1966, **153**, 1205-1213. (b)

SKINNER, B. F. *Contingencies of reinforcement*. New York: Appleton-Century-Crofts, 1969.

SKINNER, B. F., & MORSE, W. H. Fixed-interval reinforcement of running in a wheel. *Journal of the Experimental Analysis of Behavior*, 1958, **1**, 371-379.

STADDON, J. E. R. Some properties of spaced responding in pigeons. *Journal of the Experimental Analysis of Behavior*, 1965, **8**, 19-27.

STADDON, J. E. R. Asymptotic behavior: The concept of the operant. *Psychological Review*, 1967, **74**, 377-391.

STADDON, J. E. R. Inhibition and the operant. A review of G. v. Bekesy, *Sensory inhibition*, and F. Ratliff, *Mach bands: Quantitative studies on neural networks in the retina. Journal of the Experimental Analysis of Behavior*, 1969, **12**, 481-487.

STADDON, J. E. R. Reinforcement after-effects. In, *Schedule-induced and schedule-dependent phenomena.* Vol. 2. Toronto: Addiction Research Foundation, 1970.

STADDON, J. E. R. Temporal effects of reinforcement: A negative "frustration" effect. *Learning and Motivation*, 1970, **1**, 227-247. (b)

STEIN, L. Excessive drinking in the rat: Superstition or thirst? *Journal of Comparative and Physiological Psychology*, 1964, **58**, 237-242.

STELLAR, E., & HILL, J. H. The rat's rate of drinking as a function of water deprivation. *Journal of Comparative and Physiological Psychology*, 1952, **45**, 96-102.

STRICKER, E. M., & ADAIR, E. R. Body fluid balance, taste, and postprandial factors in schedule-induced polydipsia. *Journal of Comparative and Physiological Psychology*, 1966, **62**, 449-454.

TERRACE, H. S. Stimulus control. In W. K. Honig (Ed.), *Operant behavior: Areas of research and application.* New York: Appleton-Century-Crofts, 1966.

THOMPSON, D. M. Escape from S^D associated with fixed-ratio reinforcement. *Journal of the Experimental Analysis of Behavior*, 1964, **7**, 1-8.

TINBERGEN, N. "Derived" activities: Their causation, biological significance, origin, and emancipation during evolution. *Quarterly Review of Biology*, 1952, **27**, 1-32.

TULVING, E., & Madigan, S. A. Memory and verbal learning. *Annual Review of Psychology*, 1970, **21**, 437-484.

UPTON, M. The auditory sensitivity of guinea pigs. *American Journal of Psychology*, 1929, **41**, 412-421.

VALENSTEIN, E. S., COX, V. C., & KAKOLEWSKI, J. W. Reexamination of the role of the hypothalamus in motivation. *Psychological Review*, 1970, **77**, 16-31.

VERPLANCK, W. S. Since learned behavior is innate, and vice versa, what now? *Psychological Review*, 1955, **52**, 139-144.

VON HOLST, E., & VON SAINT PAUL, U. On the functional organization of drives. *Animal Behaviour*, 1963, **11**, 1- 20.

WILLIAMS, D. R. Classical conditioning and incentive motivation. In W. F. Prokasy (Ed.), *Classical conditioning: A symposium.* New York: Appleton-Century-Crofts, 1965.

WILLIAMS, D. R., & WILLIAMS, H. Auto-maintenance in the pigeon: Sustained pecking despite contingent non-reinforcement. *Journal of the Experimental Analysis of Behavior*, 1969, **12**, 511-520.

WOLIN, B. R. Difference in manner of pecking a key between pigeons reinforced with food and with water. In A. C. Catania (Ed.), *Contemporary research in operant behavior*. New York: Scott, Foresman, 1968.

WRIGHT, S. Evolution in Mendelian populations, *Genetics*, 1931, **16**, 97-159.

WUTTKE, W. The effects of d-amphetamine on schedule-controlled water licking in the squirrel-monkey. *Psychopharmacologia* (Berlin), 1970, **17**, 70-82.

ZEAMAN, D., & SMITH, R. W. Review of some recent findings in human cardiac conditioning. In W. F. Prokasy (Ed.), *Classical conditioning: A symposium.* New York: Appleton-Century-Crofts, 1965.

ZENER, K. The significance of behavior accompanying conditioned salivary secretion for theories of the conditioned response. *American Journal of Psychology*, 1937, **50**, 384-403.

The Relation of Cue to Consequence in Avoidance Learning

John Garcia and Robert A. Koelling (1966). *Psychonomic Science, 4,* 123- 124.

Following ingestion of poisoned bait which induced illness the rats in the experiment became immediately conditioned to the olfactory and gustatory cues. The rats declined the bait from that moment on; however, they did not exhibit signs of being conditioned to the environment in which they initially received the bait and would return to the place they had been previously poisoned. These results demonstrated that rats have a naturally wired sensitivity to taste and odor which consequently increases their survival rate. This effect has also been called bait shyness, taste aversion mechanism, and the Garcia effect or Garcia-Koelling effect. The fact that species more quickly associate some CS-US (condition stimulus-unconditioned stimulus) combinations than others is known as preparedness, a term coined by Martin Seligman. Preparedness is of extraordinary value to species and can serve as protection from environmental dangers. Identifying how a species learns can be best understood through their evolutionary history. Rats acute keenness to taste and smell is absolutely essential for them to survive and is not of great importance to other species. For instance, birds are visual not gustatory foragers and spotting food easily is necessary for their survival. Studying behavior is founded upon the researcher knowing the very organism they are studying. KNOW YOUR ORGANISM - it is the mantra of the ethologists.

An audiovisual stimulus was made contingent upon the rat's licking at the water spout, thus making it analogous with a gustatory stimulus. When the audiovisual stimulus and the gustatory stimulus were paired with electric shock the avoidance reactions transferred to the audiovisual stimulus, but not the gustatory stimulus. Conversely, when both stimuli were paired with toxin or x-ray the avoidance reactions transferred to the gustatory stimulus, but not the audiovisual stimulus. Apparently stimuli are selected as cues dependent upon the nature of the subsequent reinforcer.

A great deal of evidence stemming from diverse sources suggests an inadequacy in the usual formulations concerning reinforcement. Barnett (1963) has described the "bait-shy" behavior of wild rats which have survived a poisoning attempt. These animals utilizing olfactory and gustatory cues, avoid the poison bait which previously made them ill. However, there is no evidence that they avoid the "place" of the poisoning.

In a recent volume (Haley & Snyder, 1964) several authors have discussed studies in which ionizing radiations were employed as a noxious stimulus to produce avoidance reactions in animals. Ionizing radiation like many poisons produces gastrointestinal disturbances and nausea. Strong aversions are readily established in animals when distinctively flavored fluids are conditionally paired with x-rays. Subsequently, the gustatory stimulus will depress fluid intake without radiation. In contrast, a distinctive environmental complex of auditory, visual, and tactual stimuli does not inhibit drinking even when the compound stimulus is associated with the identical radiation schedule. This differential effect has also been observed following ingestion of a toxin and the injection of a drug (Garcia & Koelling, 1965).

Apparently this differential effectiveness of cues is due either to the nature of the reinforcer, i.e., radiation or toxic effects, or to the peculiar relation which a gustatory stimulus has to the drinking response, i.e., gustatory stimulation occurs if and only if the animal licks the fluid. The environmental cues associated with a distinctive place are not as dependent upon a single response of the organism. Therefore, we made an auditory and visual stimulus dependent upon the animal's licking the water spout. Thus, in four experiments reported here "bright-noisy" water, as well as "tasty" water was conditionally paired with radiation, a toxin, immediate shock, and delayed shock, respectively, as reinforcers. Later the capacity of these response-controlled stimuli to inhibit drinking in the absence of reinforcement was tested.

Method

The apparatus was a light and sound shielded box (7 in. x 7 in. x 7 in.) with a drinking spout connected to an electronic drinkometer which counted each touch of the rat's tongue to the spout. "Bright-noisy" water was provided by connecting an incandescent lamp (5 watts) and a clicking relay into this circuit. "Tasty" water was provided by adding flavors to the drinking supply.

Each experimental group consisted of 10 rats (90 day old Sprague-Dawley males) maintained in individual cages without water, but with *Purina Laboratory chow ad libidum.*

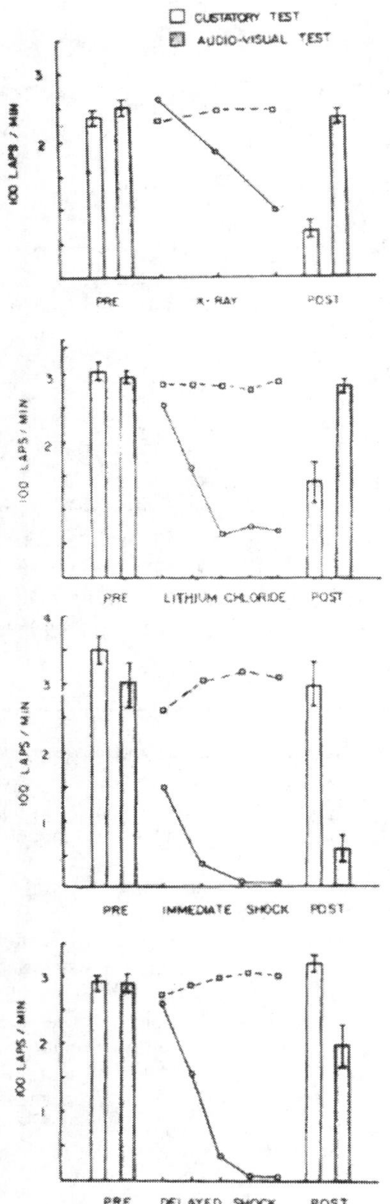

Fig. 1. The bars indicate water intake (±. St. Error) during a gustatory test (a distinctive taste) and an audiovisual test (light and sound contingent upon licking) before and after conditional pairing with the reinforcers indicated. The curves illustrate mean intake during acquisition.

The procedure was: A. One week of habituation to drinking in the apparatus without stimulation. B. Prestests to measure intake of bright-noise water and tasty water prior to training. C. Acquisition training with: (1) reinforced trials where these stimuli were paired with reinforcement during drinking, (2) nonreinforced trials where rats drank water without stimuli or reinforcement. Training terminated when there was a reliable difference between water intake scores on reinforced and nonreinforced trials. D. Post-tests to measure intake of bright-noisy water and tasty water after training.

In the x-ray study an audiovisual group and a gustatory group were exposed to an identical radiation schedule. In the other studies reinforcement was contingent upon the rat's response. To insure that both the audiovisual and the gustatory stimuli received equivalent reinforcement, they were combined and simultaneously paired with the reinforcer during acquisition training. Therefore, one group serving as its own control and divided into equal subgroups, was tested in balanced order with an audiovisual and a gustatory test before and after training with these stimuli combined.

One 20-min. reinforced trial was administered every three days in the x-ray and lithium chloride studies. This prolonged intertrial interval was designed to allow sufficient time for the rats to recover from acute effects of treatment. On each interpolated day the animals received a 20-min. nonreinforced trial. They were post-tested two days after their last reinforced trial. The x-ray groups received a total of three reinforced trials, each with 54 r of filtered 250 kv x-rays delivered in 20 min. Sweet water (1 gm saccharin per liter) was the gustatory stimulus. The lithium chloride group had a total of five reinforced trials with toxic salty water (.12M lithium chloride). Non-toxic salty water (.12M sodium chloride) which rats cannot readily distinguish from the toxic solution was used in the gustatory tests (Nachman, 1963).

The immediate shock study was conducted on a more orthodox avoidance schedule. Tests and trials were 2 min. long. Each day for four consecutive acquisition days, animals were given two nonreinforced and two reinforced trials in an NRRN, RNNR pattern. A shock, the minimal current required to interrupt drinking (0.5 sec. at 0.08-0.20 ma), was delivered through a floor grid 2 sec. after the first lick at the spout.

The delayed shock study was conducted simultaneously with the lithium chloride on the same schedule. Non-toxic salty water was the gustatory stimulus. Shock reinforcement was delayed during first trials and gradually increased in intensity (.05 to .30 ma) in a schedule designed to produce a drinking pattern during the 20-min. period which resembled that of the corresponding animal drinking toxic salty water.

Results and Discussion

The results indicate that all reinforcers were effective in producing discrimination learning during the acquisition phase (see Fig. 1), but obvious differences occurred in the post-tests. The avoidance reactions produced by x-rays and lithium chloride are readily transferred to the gustatory stimulus but not to the audiovisual stimulus. The effect is more pronounced in the x-ray study, perhaps due to differences in dose. The x-ray animals received a constant dose while the lithium chloride rats drank a decreasing amount of the toxic solution during training. Nevertheless, the difference between post-test scores is statistically significant in both experiments ($p < 0.01$ by ranks test).

Apparently when gustatory stimuli are paired with agents which produce nausea and gastric upset, they acquire secondary reinforcing properties which might be described as "conditioned nausea." Auditory and visual stimulation do not readily acquire similar properties even when they are contingent upon the licking response.

In contrast, the effect of both immediate and delayed shock to the paws is in the opposite direction. The avoidance reactions produced by electric shock to the paws transferred to the audiovisual stimulus but not to the gustatory stimulus. As one might expect the effect of delayed shocks was not as effective as shocks where the reinforcer immediately and consistently followed licking. Again, the difference between post-test intake scores is statistically significant in both studies ($p < 0.01$ by ranks test). Thus, when shock which produces peripheral pain is the reinforcer, "conditioned fear" properties are more readily acquired by auditory and visual stimuli than by gustatory stimuli.

It seems that given reinforcers are not equally effective for all classes of discriminable stimuli. The cues, which the animal selects from the welter of stimuli in the learning situation, appear to be related to the consequences of the subsequent reinforcer. Two speculations are offered: (1) Common elements in the time-intensity patterns of stimulation may facilitate a cross modal generalization from reinforcer to cue in one case and not in another. (3) More likely, natural selection may have favored mechanisms which associate gustatory and olfactory cues with internal discomfort since the chemical receptors sample the materials soon to be incorporated into the internal environment. Krechevsky (1933) postulated such a genetically coded hypothesis to account for the predispositions of rats to respond systematically to specific cues in an insoluble maze. The hypothesis of the sick rat, as for many of us under similar circumstances, would be, "It must have been something I ate.

References

Barnett, S. A. *The rat a study in behavior*. Chicago: Aldine Press, 1963.

Garcia, J., & Hoelling, R. A. *A comparison of aversions induced by x-rays, toxins, and drugs in the rat*. Radiat. Res., in press, 1965.

Haley, T. J., & Snyder, R. S. (Eds.) *The response of the nervous system to ionizing radiation*. Boston: Little, Brown & Co., 1964.

Krechevsky, I. *The hereditary nature of 'hypothesis'*. *J. comp Psychol.*, 1932, 16, 99-116.

Nachman, M. *Learned aversion to the taste of lithium chloride and generalization to other salts*. *J. comp physiol. Psychol.*, 1963. 56, 343-349.

Tilting at the Paper Mills of Academe

John Garcia (1981). *American Psychologist, 36(2),* 149-158.

When I teach experimental psychology I always point to the Garcia taste aversion research to exemplify the acquisition of scientific knowledge. In this famous article reviewing his research Garcia laments that the editorial and review process is slow and prodigious. I would point out, however, that in a matter of a few short years Garcia's results went from unimaginable and unpublishable to being referenced in nearly every General Psychology textbook. To me this shows the worth of the scientific enterprise – for in science the truth will out. In science, unlike others ways of knowing, all you have to do is look and see for yourself if you don't believe me. If I am wrong my "truths" are refuted, but if you replicate my observations we gain confidence in the reliability of the knowledge obtained. The more times the experimental phenomenon is reproduced the greater our confidence in its verity. I can think of no better example of this axiom than the research of John Garcia on taste aversion.

Tilting at the Paper Mills of Academe is also a paper about revolution in science. What happens when anomalous data contradict existing theory and why is the establishment so slow to assimilate new findings. Is it an old fogies versus young turks dominance struggle, or is it a virtue of science that it is conservative and cautious, and as a consequence more dependable? Well, you read the article and decide for yourself.

ABSTRACT: Errant authors of empirical learning reports are often dashed to earth by editorial reviewers, who castigate them for trivial departures from the orthodox associative paradigms subserving a vacuous general-process notion, which allows no consideration of specialized structures in humans or in beasts. Paradigmatic illustrations on immediate reinforcement were not subjected to the same zealous scrutiny, thus some classic experiments proved to be classic blunders. Immediate-reinforcement notions owe more to simplistic ideas of profit in a "free-market" economy than to empirical associationism. John Locke did not assume an unstructured neonate mind; he recognized natural connections as well as nurtured ones. He proposed neurological specificity of sensations over a century before J. Muller and noted the existence of specialized taste-illness pathways nearly three centuries before J. Garcia.

My material is drawn from the field of learning and my title from a misadventure of that legendary knight, Don Quixote de la Mancha (Cervantes, 1605/1867?). Sighting 30 or 40 large windmills newly established in South Central Spain during an energy crisis, when long droughts had stilled the waterwheels on the Rio Zancara, Don Quixote perceived them to be giant demons, threatening him with their multiple arms. He spurred his steed, Rocinante, charging the mills in God's good service to wipe so evil a breed off the face of the earth. The errant knight and his noble steed were swept into the air by the giant arms and dashed to earth again. The good squire, Sancho Panza, picked up his befuddled master and offered him a mechanistic and pedestrian explanation: "They are only windmills." But Don Quixote defended his more global dynamic theory, proclaiming, "The same evil influence which reduces my monetary support and denies me books and space would like us to believe that its monstrous lackeys are mere grinders of corn in order to rob us of the glory of exposing their true malignant nature." Some researchers feel the same way about journal editors and their consultants. But, like Sancho Panza, I hold a simpler view. I have studied editorial behavior for years, and I have come to the conclusion that journal editors are neophobic creatures of our own kind.

The author's confrontation with the editors often begins not with paranoid delusions, but with great hope and expectation. The author submits the final product of an arduous writing and rewriting process and receives a warm note of thanks from the editor. Then, after many months, the second editorial response finally arrives. It is apt to be a supercilious sophistry bearing so tenuous a relationship to the manuscript that the author concludes the consultants must have been out to lunch when the paper was being reviewed. Often, the critique is embellished with gratuitous personal insults. One consultant, in an ill-worded passage, informed the editor that one of our recent manuscripts would not have been acceptable even as a term paper in his or her learning class. (Unfortunately, since the review was anonymous, I was unable to properly congratulate the consultant on his or her high academic standards.) The dissonance produced by the first courteous response and the second caustic one leads many authors to believe journals are governed by Janus-faced demons, but I present evidence indicating that journals are actually operated by timid but tractable organisms.

On the Neophobia of Editorial Consultants

After a decade of successful radiobiological research, during which my associates and I published a series of some 20 papers in prestigious journals and volumes without a single rejection, I felt I was ready for the big leagues. Our radiation research convinced me that two classic principles of conditioning were of limited generality; although not wrong, I felt they were simply not necessary for all conditioning. I wanted to record my views for posterity in the annals of my first scientific love, the field of learning.

First, I felt that unconditioned stimuli (or reinforcers) have a selective effect on what is learned. We tested this proposition in a double-dissociation design in which two cues, a sweet taste or a clicking light, were made contingent upon the licking of a drinking spout by thirsty rats. Drinking under these conditions was punished by either shock to the feet or illness produced by X rays. Shock produced an avoidance of bright, noisy water but not of sweet water; conversely, illness produced an aversion for sweet water but not for bright, noisy water (Garcia & Koelling, 1966). Our selectivity hypothesis was supported, but our paper was rejected by several journals. Some editorial consultants said we used too many treatments. Others said we used too few. One said we did not know how X-ray reinforcement worked. Apparently this consultant was satisfied that we all know how shock reinforcement works.

So we went back to the laboratory and repeated the experiment in a different guise. The two cues were now the size or the taste of food pellets presented to hungry rats. The two punishments were the same. So were the results. Shock produced an avoidance reaction to the size cue but not to the taste cue, whereas illness produced an aversion for taste but not for size (Garcia, McGowan, Ervin, & Koelling, 1968). This paper was promptly accepted by a journal that had refused the first paper, indicating that journals are operated by neophobic creatures that habituate in one trial.

The second classical principle that I felt has limited generality is contiguity. Immediate reinforcement is simply not necessary for learning when illness is the reinforcer. We tested this proposition by giving rats a drink of sweet water and injecting them with an emetic drug after various delays. Delays of up to 30 minutes had little effect on the strength of the taste aversion (Garcia, Ervin, & Koelling, 1966). Our hypothesis on the effectiveness of delayed-illness reinforcement was clearly demonstrated, but this paper was also rejected by two journals on the first trial.

Again, we gave the editors a second trial. This time thiamine-deprived rats drank sweet water and then received thiamine after various delays. Because we used a beneficial injection rather than a noxious one, the rats increased their consumption of saccharin, but again delays of 30 minutes had little effect on learning (Garcia, Ervin, Yorke, & Koelling, 1967). This paper was promptly accepted by a journal that had rejected the first paper. Editorial neophobia followed by rapid habituation approached the status of established law.

The Veneration of Procedure

More recently, we discovered some limitations of a third established principle of conditioning called overshadowing or blocking. This phenomenon is observed when two cues are combined into a compound signal; the stronger, more reliable cue usually overshadows, or blocks, conditioning to the weaker, less reliable cue. This makes perfectly good sense; if an animal has valid, reliable information, why should it bother to learn invalid, unreliable information? (I always use anthropomorphism and teleology to predict animal behavior because this works better than most learning theories. I could rationalize this heresy by pointing to our common neurosensory systems or to convergent evolutionary forces. But, in truth, I merely put myself in the animal's place. I cannot think in the cryptic jargon of learning; obviously, neither can editorial consultants.)

In our laboratory, Ken Rusiniak found that when a weak odor cue was combined with a strong taste cue and followed by illness, taste did not overshadow odor. Taste did exactly the opposite, it potentiated odor, converting it into a strong cue (Rusiniak, Hankins, Garcia, & Brett, 1979). Linda Brett observed a similar effect in hawks eating mice. The black color of the mouse's coat was a useless cue for poison. After eating a black mouse and suffering a toxic injection, hawks rejected both black and white mice. However, when the black mouse also tasted different, the poisoned hawk retreated wildly from the next black mouse on sight, but accepted white mice avidly (Brett, Hankins, & Garcia, 1967). Chris Clarke and his associates in Australia designed an elegant experiment using blue and/or salty water to demonstrate the potentiation effect in pigeons (Clarke, Westbrooke, & Irwin, 1979).

The species differences fascinated us and our Australian colleagues, so in our first publication attempt, we combined the rat and pigeon data into one paper and sent it off to a journal. We showed that almond-scented water was a very weak cue for the poisoned rat but that sweet water was a strong cue and that blue water was a poor cue for the poisoned pigeon but that salty water was a good one. When the weak cues were combined with the strong taste cues, however, the rat acquired a strong aversion for almond-scented, unsweetened water, and the pigeon acquired a strong aversion for blue, unsalted water. The data were clear, but the paper was rejected.

The species differences did not fascinate the editorial consultants as much as the methodological differences between the rat and pigeon studies disturbed them. One editorial consultant said we used unorthodox procedures, complaining that our methods were neither blocking nor overshadowing procedures. In the former case, one stimulus is made stronger than the other by prior association with the reinforcing unconditioned stimulus, and in the latter, two stimuli differing in salience are presented together. These procedural criticisms are irrelevant on two grounds. First, the principle of overshadowing and blocking is a general rule that states a relationship between signal elements of different effectiveness. Our study belonged to that category. Second, there are no empirical or theoretical grounds for expecting that our departures from orthodox procedures would turn overshadowing into potentiation, nor did the consultant provide any such evidence or logic.

Another editorial consultant said I had a history of presenting important but flawed research and wrote, "The danger here is not especially severe if the initial report is in error. That will be quickly discovered by others. The real danger comes just when the work is substantially correct but the original work is flawed. For others will lose time and effort tracking down those flaws." Apparently, it never occurred to him that if the research proved to be substantially correct, then the flaws would be proven quite trivial.

The third referee was impressed because we replicated the potentiation phenomena with different species, in different sensory systems, with different methods, and in different laboratories on different continents; all this, he said, attested to the reliability of the phenomena, even if the study was a bit untidy. But we lost the split decision, so we published the rat and pigeon data in separate papers, side by side, in a journal that welcomes species differences and anatomical explanations (Clarke et. al., 1979; Rusiniak et al., 1979).

By this time we had become adept at habituating editors. Claire Palmerino designed an experiment complete enough to satisfy the most fastidious learning methodologist (Palmerino, Rusiniak, & Garcia, 1980). She used a single acquisition trial flanked by pre- and posttests and conducted two experiments employing 28 groups of rats. She balanced order effects and precluded explanations on the basis of prior odor-taste associations (sensory preconditioning) or nonassociative effects of illness (pseudoconditioning), demonstrating that odor alone has a steep delay-of-illness gradient and that odor aversions are possible with immediate reinforcement but are completely abolished by delays of 30 minutes. However, when odor was potentiated by taste, the gradient of odor tested alone in extinction resembled the long delay gradient of taste; a two-hour delay had no effect on the aversive reaction to a potentiated odor. This paper was accepted by a journal after one prior habituation trial.

The Ritual of Quantification

Learning consultants are obsessed with measurement and quantification, often to the detriment of psychological variables. Rats can learn to use flavor to avoid shock, although they use the odor component more effectively than the taste component; in this case, the flavor becomes a sign for shock. When flavor is followed by illness, inhibition of drinking is much simpler because rats simply do not like the flavor; an affective change or hedonic shift occurs (Garcia & Rusiniak, 1980). This distinction cannot be inferred from the quantity of fluid consumed, but it is quite obvious from the behavior of the rat: It gapes, retches, and rubs its chin on the floor. But such vulgarities upset those who prefer pristine numbers. One consultant said that he did not understand the meaning of "hedonic change." I doubt that he was totally ignorant of the long psychological tradition that stretches from Bentham's (1823/1907) hedonic calculus to Young's (1966) elegant isohedonic contours. I suspect he was trying to exorcise the rat's feelings (and sensory physiology) out of the "objective" approach to learning.

The one-bottle taste test is often criticized on the grounds that it is a less sensitive measure than the two-bottle test. This point is trivial and untrue, as a moment's though reveals. While pigeons and other animals are able to make the more direct simultaneous discrimination visually, the rat always makes successive discriminations with its tongue. In the two-bottle test, the rat controls the order and duration of stimulus presentation, and this can be a disadvantage.

Another quantitative criticism reflexively elicited by comparisons of foot shock vis-à-vis internal illness is that the two punishments are not delivered under equivalent stimulus parameters. In other words, internal nausea differs from peripheral shock pain in its quantitative pattern as well as in its sensory properties. A number of researchers have varied the anatomical locus and time-intensity patterning of electrocutaneous shock to mimic the effects of illness on licking, but to no avail; the selective effect of the reinforcers is unchanged (see Garcia, Palmerino, Rusiniak, & Kiefer, in press, for a discussion). Therefore, the logic that calls for equivalent quantitative parameters must be suspect. So is the logic that calls for adherence to orthodox paradigms and procedures. They stem from a compulsion to snare an ephemeral phenomenon called "general-process learning" in a trap composed of operational definitions and control groups without regard to the biological structure of the learning beast.

Pseudoconditioning and Pseudocriticism

By this time it must be obvious that I am peevish about procedures, that I am sensitive about sensitization, and that I am sick of pseudoconditioning. The very term *control group* is a misnomer. All groups are given a specific experimental treatment to establish a specific point.

Not long ago, a taste aversion paper was published which presented findings that were neither novel nor interesting, yet the paper led to a prolonged series of letters to the editor (Mitchell, Scott, & Mitchell, 1977). Almost everyone in taste aversion research got into the act (see Notes and Comments, *Animal Learning & Behavior*, 1978, 6, 115-124; 1979, 7, 562-563). The above authors presented a six-group experimental design. Half the groups received an associative treatment, namely sweet water followed by injection. The other half received a so-called nonassociative treatment, namely, unsweetened water followed by injection. Three injection parameters were employed: a zero dose, an immediate toxic dose, and a delayed toxic dose. Significant differences were claimed for the associative treatment; no significant differences were reported for the so-called nonassociative treatment. What caused the furor was that the authors chided other researchers in the field for failing to use nonassociative control groups.

At about the same time, a similar criticism appeared in a letter to *Science* (see reply by Bitterman in Garcia, Hankins, & Rusiniak, 1976). "There were no pseudocontitioning controls, yet illness might have produced aversion to saccharin, and shock might have produced aversion to the sound of a buzzer, quite independently of pairing (p. 265). Actually, our first paper on taste aversion learning published in *Science* (Garcia, Kimeldorf, & Koelling, 1955), employed the same six-group design; half the groups received an associative treatment (sweet water and radiation), and half the animals had the so-called nonassociative treatment (unsweetened water and radiation). The associative treatment produced a dosage-dependent aversion for the sweet fluid; the so-called nonassociative treatment did not produce a pseudoconditioned saccharin aversion. It should not be surprising that I employed this hackneyed learning design. After all, my professors at Berkely, Tolman, Ritchie, and Krech, insisted that I take elementary experimental design and statistics courses despite all rumors to the contrary.

I say "so-called nonassociative" because nonassociative learning procedures do not prevent the rat from making associations. If an unpaired stimulus is presented to the rat, it will associate that single stimulus with a specific point in time and space, it not with a prior stimulus event. In the study just cited, we tested all groups with two bottles (sweetened *vs.* unsweetened water). And the water groups displayed an aversion for water despite its familiarity, attesting to the prejudicial associative bias of the rat; for them water was, after all, the fluid paired with radiation illness.

At that time, I wanted to point out the water aversion in our report, but a wiser head prevailed. Kimeldorf said that we would have enough difficulty getting editorial consultants to accept a saccharin aversion induced by such low dosages, neither the learning experts nor the radiation experts, he said, were quite ready for a water aversion. Fortunately, no one noticed, or at least no one mentioned, the dosage-dependent increase in the saccharin preference of the water group clearly visible in Table 1, though it was constrained by the high preference ceiling for saccharin (Garcia, Kimeldorf, & Koelling, 1955).

Sensitization is generally assumed to be a nonselective arousal process that primes the animal to learn just about anything that comes its way (Malmo, 1959). However, it seems rather obvious that if an animal has the capacity to selectively connect taste to illness given the impoverished information afforded by a single trial in which the two sensations are separated by hours, it will also be selectively sensitized to novel tastes when that information is reduced even further to illness without prior taste stimulation (Domjan, 1977). After suffering foot shock, rats also prefer familiar surroundings to strange places (Aitken, 1972; Aitken & Sheldon, 1970).

Recently, Miller and Domjan (in press) demonstrated that rats suffering from lithium illness indeed showed a reduced preference for a novel sweet taste but not for a novel noisy light flash contingent upon licking. This taste sensitization was present 35 minutes, but not 6 hours, after the toxic injection. Conversely, shocked animals feared the noisy light flash but not the sweet taste. This external sensitization was present immediately after, but not 5 minutes after, the shock. The selectivity and the temporal relationships of the two forms of sensitization correspond to those of the two forms of conditioning. Both the nonassociative procedures and the associative procedures reveal the selective bias of the rat's mind and/or brain.

Much is made of novelty in taste aversion learning. While it is undoubtedly facilitatory in some cases (e.g., Revusky & Bedarf, 1967), it is no more necessary for taste-illness learning than for any other form of associative learning. Taste aversins for familiar fluids have been demonstrated in rats (Garcia & Koelling, 1967), for familiar prey in coyotes (Gustavson, Kelly, Sweeney, & Garcia, 1976), for familiar prey in hawks (Brett et. al., 1976), and for familiar foods in children (Bernstein, 1978). In fact, animals suffering from chronic illness often exhibit neophilia, a preference for novel diets (Bernstein & Sigmundi, 1980; Rozin & Kalat, 1971). In any case, nonassociative procedures with their impoverished information produce only transient effects compared with the robust effects produced by associative information, as Miller and Domjan (in press) point out. Taste and illness can be separated by hours in a single acquisition trial, and the test can be conducted days after the illness (Garcia, Hankins, & Rusiniak, 1974). In fact, animals tested for the first time one month after illness exhibit no apparent loss in the strength of the aversion (Garcia, McGowan, & Green, 1972).

Uncontrolled Orthodoxy

Control groups do not seems to be required if the experimental results conform to the prevailing zeitgeist of immediate reinforcement and general-process learning. For example, the Guthrie and Horton (1946) experiment with one group of cats became a classic. These authors simply placed a succession of cats in a transparent box with a pole standing upright in the center. Time after time, cats rubbed up against the pole in a stereotypic manner, tripping the latch and releasing themselves from the box. By Guthrie and Horton's account, the rubbing response was an accidental one, learned because it was the last response to the locked box and thus was not subject to interference by further responding to that same situation. On returning to the locked box, the cat merely retrieved the last response made in the situation. By most other instrumental accounts, the rubbing response was learned because it was immediately reinforced by release from annoying confinement.

Both accounts were wrong, but for over 30 years, Guthrie and Horton's cats adorned our learning textbooks in stereotypic outline before Moore and Stuttard (1979) asked what would happen if cats were placed in a transparent box without escape or any palpable reward for rubbing the upright pole. The cats rubbed like all our pet cats do when we come home. Cats rub ecstatically against our shins or displace the greeting onto any pole, edge, or surface that is handy. We had the "control" group before us all those years, but failed to recognize its relevance, so well had the zeitgeist prepared us to accept the general associational power of immediate reinforcement.

The paper by Moore and Stuttard was not actly welcomed by editorial consultants (Moore, Note l). The simplicity and ingenuity of Guthrie and Horton's explanation were said to be convincing, even if their experimental evidence was not. One consultant simply could not understand that the cats in this study had no problem to solve, no response to learn, and no reward for rubbing against the vertical pole. He said that "very few psychologists would be interested in *whether the cat's learning in the puzzle box* is to be explained in terms of a modified law of effect or as a special case of species-specific response emerging in an unusual environment under unusual conditions" (Moore, Note 1, italics added). Another editorial consultant quoted Guthrie and Horton's (1946) comment: "To predict what a cat will do when it is placed in a puzzle box requires familiarity with cats (p. 37)." This damming statement leaves us with two alternatives: Either (a) Guthrie and Horton failed to recognize the most common social response of the cat, or (b) Guthrie and Horton deliberately put an artificial shinbone in the center of the box for the cat to rub against without discussing the expected response or providing a baseline control measure. Others argued that even if the rubbing response was a natural behavioral pattern, its rate of emission was no doubt increased by escape from the box. But as Moore and Stuttard (1979) pointed out, it was the shape of the response pattern that was at issue, not its rate; Guthrie and Horton provided no baseline rate, explaining only that the stereotyped form of the response was stamped into the cat's repertoire by immediate release from the box. "With such a powerful technology," said Revusky (Note 2), "one could, no doubt, teach a fish to swim." Much to their credit, the editors overruled their consultants and published Moore and Stuttard's paper (I feel that our treatment for editorial neophobia may have played a modest role here).

The Alien Wind From the "Free Market"

The prevailing zeitgeist was skillfully harnessed by Skinner (1938) when he rejected classical conditioning in rather blunt tones; real learning could not be studied in a restrained and passive dog whose attention was aroused by a bell and whose saliva was evoked by a squirt of sour water into the mouth. Pavlov, of course, was not primarily interested in drooling behavior. Conditioned saliva evoked by the bell was merely the peripheral evidence that a new element of learning had been established in the recesses of the dog's brain, a new pathway between the auditory analyzer and the salivary mechanism. But Skinner (1950) rejected the need for unspecified biological processes or gratuitous theoretical explanations. Behavioral change was the end point of learning, and reflexes automatically evoked by identifiable stimuli were not important for that end.

Skinner gave us a conceptual organism much more compatible with the active and pragmatic spirit of the American frontier. His pigeon, unrestrained though confined to a box, freely emitted a variety of responses on a stage set by environmental stimuli. The key light signaled only that the food was available. The pigeon had to work for it by depressing the key. The response was defined not by its internal neural connections, but by the excursion of the key, that is, by the effect the pigeon produced in the environment. And the way to modify that response product and its rate of output was to arrange a reinforcing payoff for the desired production goals. If the desired response was not in the array of products originally displayed by the pigeon, it could be shaped by immaculate conception, through reinforcing successive approximations to the desired product. Just as profit operates selectively to produce desired goods and services in a free market according to Smith (1776/1937), so reinforcement selectively shapes the productive behavior of a free organism according to Skinner (1938).

Any stimulus applied immediately after the response which, by empirical test, would increase response production was deemed a reinforcer. The nature of reinforcement and its effect on the pigeon's behavior were left unexamined; this was the fatal flaw that would ultimately dismantle Skinner's system. The general procedures were said to be applicable to any and all reflexes, in any and all organisms. There was no need to concern ourselves with species differences, with brain differences, or with reinforcer differences. The payoff schedule's the thing wherein we'd capture control of the organism.

So pervasive was this wind that blew in from economics that 30 years passed before Brown and Jenkins (1968) pulled the plug connecting the key to the feeder, thereby converting the Skinner box into a Pavlovian chamber. The key light came on and food followed with no work requirement, as in a social welfare program. But the pigeon labored at the lighted key anyway. If grain was signaled, the pigeon pecked at the key as if it were grain, and if water was forthcoming, the pigeon pumped at the key as if it were water. Apparently, Skinner's pigeon could no more resist pecking the signal when grain was imminent any more than Pavlov's dog could stop slobbering when vinegar was signaled (for a review, see Garcia, Clarke, & Hankins, 1973).

I am not arguing that no animal will work for pay. In the wide wide world of animal behavior one can probably find a behavioral metaphor for any socioeconomic system. The name of that game is *sociobiology*, wherein genetic investment strategy is invented for a social trait and the world is then searched for an animal metaphor, preferably an insect (Dawkins, 1976). For the middle-class free enterprise ethic, I recommend the California scrub jay (*Aphelocoma coerulescens*). A pair of these wild blue jays appear promptly when my wife or I open the garden gate in the morning. They work for peanuts. They postpone gratification and save for the future. They match their energy expenditures to value received. Given a small discolored or cracked peanut, they hide it perfunctorily under a nearby leaf. Given a large, clean peanut well suited for storage, they fly off to deposit it in some faraway secret safe. Over the years, they have developed a mystical concept of us as the benign peanut givers and display toward us social behaviors unrelated to peanut acquisition. They greet us on our walks far from home where they never received a goober, and in the evening after work is done, they come to the garden and perch on the back of a chair. They fluff out their feathers in relaxed comfort and join us in conversation with soft chirps and warbles. The two birds have driven off all competitors and formed a stable partnership that has endured for over six years. It is apparently a small "mom and pop" peanut business, but thus far we see no evidence that they are willing to share it with their relatives or that they are preparing to pass it on to their children.

My complaint is that operant conditioning did not teach us much about pigeons. It remained for biologists to investigate the most fascinating behavior of pigeons. When they suspected that birds were using geomagnetic cues to navigate home, a magnetic sensor in the pigeon's brain was sought out (Walcott, Gould, & Kirschvink, 1979). Pavlov certainly would have approved. Those interested in learning should return to Pavlov's task, the search for detailed information on how new connections are made in the brain when an animal is subjected to training procedures. Those interested in unlearned adaptive behavior should search for detailed information on how that specific behavior is articulated to the niche and how that program pf interaction is specifically encoded into the genes. Without such specification, Wilson's (1975) sociobiology is about as useful as McDougall's (1908) socioinstinct theory.

The Nature of John Locke

To resist the alien winds of time, learning psychologists must look to our own historic roots in empirical associationism. There is no better place to begin than in Locke's "An Essay Concerning Human Understanding" (1690/1975). First, let us dispense with the canard that he was a radical environmentalist wedded to the "tabula rasa." This false notion stems from an assumption he made for the sake of argument in a passage in which he stressed that experience stems from two sources, nurture and nature. He wrote,

Let us then suppose the Mind to be, as we say, white Paper, void of all Characters, without an *Ideas*; How comes it to be furnished? .... Whence has it all the materials of Reason and Knowledge? To this I answer, in one word, From *Experience*: .... Our Observation employ'd either about *external, sensible Objects; or about the internal Operations of our Minds, perceived and reflected on by our selves, is that, which supplies our Understandings with all the materials of thinking*. (Locke, 1690/1975, p. 104)

He went on to describe this second "fountain of knowledge" as an internal, natural source that contains the basis for the law of effect:

This source of *Ideas*, every Man has wholly in himself: And though it be not Sense, as having nothing to do with external Objects; yet it is very like it, and might properly enough be call'd internal Sense. But as I call the other *Sensation*, so I call this REFLECTION, the *Ideas* it affords being such only, as the Mind gets by reflecting on its own Operations within it self..... The term *Operations* here, I use in a large sense, as comprehending not barely the Actions of the Mind about its *Ideas*, but some sort of Passions arising sometimes from them, such as is the satisfaction or uneasiness arising from any thought. (p. 105)

When Locke discussed the association of ideas, he distinguished between natural associations and acquired associations:

Some of our *Ideas* have a natural Correspondence and Connexion one with another. It is the Office and Excellency of our Reason to trace these, and hold them together in that Union and Correspondence which is founded in their peculiar Beings. Besides this there is another Connexion of *Ideas* wholly owing to Chance or Custom; *Ideas* that in themselves are not at all of kin, come to be so united in some Mens Minds, that 'tis very hard to separate them...... I say most of the Antipathies, I do not say all, for some of them are truly Natural, depend upon our original Constitution, and are born with us. (pp. 395-396)

The Biology of Empirical Associationism

At times, John Locke wrote like a psychobiologist, anticipating the doctrine of specific energies of nerves over a century before it was elaborated by Johannes Muller and Von Helmholtz. And in the bargain he put forth a kinetic hypothesis of heat nearly half a century before Bernoulli:

If we imagine *Warmth, as it is in our Hands, to be nothing but a certain sort and degree of Motion in the minute Particles of our Nerves, or animal Spirits*, we may understand how it is possible, that the same Water may at the same time produce the Sensation of Heat in one Hand, and Cold in the other;....if the Sensation of Heat and Cold, be nothing but the increase or diminution of the motion of the minute Parts of our Bodies, caused by the Corpuscles of any other Body, it is easie to be understood. That if that motion be greater in one Hand, than in the other; if a Body be applied to the two Hands, which has in its minute Particles a greater motion, than in those of one of the Hands, and a less, than in those of the other, it will increase the motion of the one Hand, and lessen it in the other, and so cause the different Sensations of Heat and Cold, that depend thereon. (Locke, 1690/1975, p. 139)

As one might suspect by this time, John Locke knew a great deal about taste aversion learning. He clearly distinguished between the effect of food on the taste receptors and its effect on the internal visceral receptors:

Ideas of Sickness and Pain are not in the Manna, but Effects of its Operations on us, and are no where when we feel them not...*Sweetness and Whiteness are not really in Manna*, which are but the effects of the operations of *Manna*, by the motion, size, and figure of its Particles on the Eyes and Palate; as the Pain and Sickness caused by *Manna*, are confessedly nothing, but the effects of its operations on the Stomach and Guts by the size, motion, and figure of its insensible parts. (p. 138).

Furthermore, Locke knew that a single taste-illness trial could produce a lasting aversion by operating on the emetic mechanism. And he knew that a conditioned aversion could endure even though the memory of the actual association was beyond recall:

A grown Person surfeiting with Honey, no sooner hears the Name of it, but his Phancy immediately carries Sickness and Qualms to his Stomach, and he cannot bear the very *Idea* of it; other *Ideas* of Dislike and Sickness, and Vomiting presently accompany it and he is disturb'd, but he knows from whence to date this Weakness, and can tell how he got this Indisposition. Had this happen'd to him by an over dose of Honey, when a Child, all the same Effects would have followed but the Cause would have been mistaken and the Antipathy counted Natural. (p. 397)

I am thankful that He left something for us to find; he apparently was not aware that food odors are potentiated by the taste of food. Finally, he warned those who simplistically proclaim "Mankind" as the superior being and apply a general scale of intelligence to all "creatures" in this "Fabrick," by which he meant "this vast and stupendous Universe":

He that will not set himself proudly at the top of all things, but will consider the Immensity of this Fabrick, and the great variety, that is to be found in this little and inconsiderable part of it, which he has to do with, may be apt to think, that in other Mansions of it there may be other, and different intelligent Beings, of whose Faculties, he has as little Knowledge or Apprehension, as a Worm shut up in one drawer of a Cabinet, hath of the Senses or Understanding of a Man. (p. 120)

All this psychobiological structure was wiped away by the alien wind, and what remains of John Locke in our time is the specious and empty tabula rasa. As Sancho Panza might have said to Don Quixote, "Stop, they are but windmills. They flail their arms and crank out gruel in obedience to an ill wind, *el espirtu del tiempo*. In truth's sake, you must level your lance at the wind. Change the wind, Don Quixote, charge the wind!"

References Notes

1. Moore, B.R. Personal communication, March 1980.
2. Revusky, S.H. Personal communication, March 1980.

References

Aitken, P. P. Aversive stimulation and rats' preference for familiarity *Psychonomic Science*, 1972, 28, 281-282.

Aitken, P. P., & Sheldon, J. H. Electric shock and rats' preference for the familiar areas of a maze. *British Journal of Psychology*, 1970, 61, 95-97.

Bentham, J. *An introduction to the principles of morals and legislation*, Oxford, England: Clarendon Press, 1907. (Originally published, 1823).

Bernstein, I. L. Learned taste aversions in children receiving chemotherapy. *Science*, 1978, 200, 1302-1303.

Bernstein, I. L., & Sigmundi, R. A. Tumor anorexia: A learned food aversion? *Science*, 1980, 209, 416-418.

Brett, L. P., Hankins, W. G., & Garcia, J. Prey-lithiumaversions. III: Buteo hawks. *Behavioral Biology*, 1976, 17, 87-98.

Brown, P. L., & Jenkins, H. M. Autoshaping of the pigeon's key-peck *Journal of the Experimental Analysis of Behavior*, 1968, 2, 1-8.

Cervantes Saavedra, M de. *The history of Don Quixote* (J. W. Clarke, Ed; G. Dore, Illus). London: Cassel, Petter & Galpin, 1867? (Originally published, 1605.)

Clarke, J. C., Westbook, R. F., & Irwin, J. Potentiation instead of overshadowing in the pigeon. *Behavioral and Neural Biology*, 1979, 25, 18-29.

Dawkins, R. *The selfish gene*. New York: Oxford University Press, 1976.

Domjan, M. Attenuation and enhancement of neophobia for edible substances. In L. M. Barker, M. R. Best, & M. Domjan (Eds.), *Learning mechanisms in food selection*. Waco, Tex.: Baylor University Press, 1977.

Garcia, J., Clarke, J., & Hankins, W. G. Natural responses to scheduled rewards in P. P. G. Bateson & P. Klopher (Eds.), *Perspectives in ethology*. New York: Plenum Press, 1973.

Garcia, J., Ervin, R. R., & Koelling, R. A. Learning with prolonged delay of reinforcement. *Psychonomic Science*, 1966, 5, 121-122.

Garcia, J., Ervin, F. R., Yorke, C. H., & Koelling, R. A. Conditioning with delayed vitamin injections. *Science*, 1967, 155, 716-718.

Garcia, J., Hankins, W. G., & Rusiniak, K. W. Behavioral regulation of the milieu interne in man and rat. *Science*, 1974, 185, 824-831.

Garcia, J., Hankins, W. G., & Rusiniak, K. W. Flavor aversion studies with reply by M. E. Bitterman). *Science*, 1976,
192, 265-267.

Garcia, J., Kimeldorf, D. J., & Koelling, R. A. A conditioned aversion towards saccharin resulting from exposure to gamma radiation. *Science*, 1955, 122, 157-159.

Garcia, J., & Koelling, R. A. Relation of cue to consequence in avoidance learning. *Psychonomic Science*, 1966, 4, 123-124.

Garcia, J., & Koelling, R. A. A comparison of aversions induced by X-rays, toxins and drugs in the rat. *Radiation Research Supplement*, 1967, 7, 439-450.

Garcia, J., McGowan, B., Ervin, F. R., & Koelling, R. A. Cues: Their relative effectiveness as a function of the reinforcer. *Science*, 1968, 160, 794-795.

Garcia, J., McGowan, B., & Green, K. Biological constraints on conditioning II. In A. Black & W. Prokasy (Eds.), *Classical conditioning: II, Current research and theory*. New York: Appleton-Century-Crofts, 1972.

Garcia, J. Palmerino, C. C., Rusiniak, K. W., & Kiefer, S. W. Taste aversions and the nurture of instinct. In J. L.

McGaugh & R. F. Thompson (Eds.), *The neurobiology of learning and instinct*. New York: Plenum Press in press.

Garcia, J., & Rusiniak, K. W. What the nose learns from the mouth. In D. Miller-Schwarze & R. M. Silverstein (Eds), *Chemical signals*: New York: Plenum Press, 1980.

Gustavson, C. R., Kelly, D. J., Sweeney, J., & Garcia, J. Preylithium aversions I: Coyotes and wolves. *Behaviora Biology*, 1976, 17, 61-72.

Guthrie, E. R., & Barton, G. P. *Cats in a puzzle box*. New York: Rinehart, 1946.

Locke, J. *An essay concerning human understanding* (P. H. Nidditch, Ed). Oxford, England: Clarendon Press, 1975. (Originally published, 1690.)

Malmo, R. B. Activation: A neurophysiological dimension. *Psychological Review*, 1959, 66, 367-386.

McDougall, W. *Introduction to social psychology*. London: Methuen, 1908.

Miller, V., & Domjan, J. Selective sensitization induced by lithium malaise and foot-shock in rats. *Behavioral and Neural Biology*, in press.

Mitchell, D., Scott, D. W., & Mitchell, L. K. Attenuated and enhanced neophobia in the taste-aversion "delay of reinforcement" effect. *Animal Learning & Behavior*, 1977, 5, 99-102

Moore, B. R., & Stuttard, S. Dr. Guthrie and Felis domesticus Or: Tripping over the cat. *Science*, 1979, 205, 1031- 1033.

Notes and comments. *Animal Learning & Behavior*, 1978, 6, 115-124; 1979, 7, 562-563.

Palmerino, C. C., Rusiniak, K. W., & Garcia, J. Flavor-illness aversions: The peculiar roles of odor and taste in memory for poison. *Science*, 1980, 208, 753-755.

Revusky, S., & Bedarf, E. Association of illness with prior ingestion of novel foods. *Science*. 1967, 155, 219-220.

Rozin, F., & Kalat, J. Specific hungers and poison avoidance as adaptive specializations of learning. *Psychological Review*, 1971, 78, 459-486.

Rusiniak, K. W., Hankins, W. G., Garcia, J., & Brett, L. P. Flavor-illness aversions: Potentiation of odor by taste in rats. *Behavioral and Neural Biology*, 1979, 25, 1-17.

Skinner, B. F. *The behavior of organisms: An experimental analysis*. New York: Appleton-Century-Crofts, 1938.

Skinner, B. F. Are learning theories really necessary? *Psychological Review*, 1950, 57, 193-216.

Smith, A. *An inquiry into the nature and causes of the wealth of nations*. (E. Cannan, Ed.). New York: Random House, 1937. (Originally published, 1776).

Walcott, C., Gould, J. A., & Kirschvink, J. A. Pigeons have magnets. *Science*, 1979, 205, 1027-1029.

Wilson, E. O. *Sociobiology: The new synthesis*. Cambridge, Mass.: Harvard University Press, 1975.

Young, P. Hedonic organization and regulation of behavior. *Psychological Review*, 1966, 73, 58-86.

Predictability and Number of Pairings in Pavlovian Fear Conditioning

Robert A. Rescorla (1966). *Psychonomic Science, 4(11),* 383-384.

The prevailing view of regarding Pavlovian conditioning prior to Rescorla's pioneering work was one of stimulus substitution. That is, the close temporal contiguity of the CS and US was believed to produce a physiological connection between them. The reverberating neural circuits resulting from CS excitation were assumed to quite literally become conjoined with those from US excitation. And since the US is innately connected to the UR, the CS, following acquisition, substitutes for the US. This all seemed to make perfect sense until Robert Rescorla comes along and demonstrates the ***associability of a CS and the non-occurrence of a US****. Rescorla's work caused a paradigm shift in the way we think about Pavlovian conditioning. In this elegant little experiment he shows that it is the contingency, i.e. the correlation between the occurrence of the CS and the US that is responsible for their association. Pavlovian conditioning seems to boil down to a question of whether or not one stimulus provides reliable information about another stimulus. It is the predictive value of the stimulus that is important and predictability can be achieved with either a positive or a negative correlation. That is, a CS can, through experience, come to reliably predict the non-occurrence of the US. Using fear conditioning Rescorla showed that a CS that is always followed by an aversive US will come to serve as a* ***danger signal*** *and that a CS that is always followed by the absence of the aversive US will come to serve as a* ***safety signal****; the equivalent of positive and negative correlation. As a control Rescorla used a zero correlation treatment where the CS had no predictive value, because it preceded the US only on occasion and randomly. See what I mean about this being an elegant experiment; simple, straight forward and revolutionary.*

Three groups of dogs were Sidman avoidance trained. They then received different kinds of Pavlovian fear conditioning. For one group CSs and USs occurred randomly and independently; for a second group, CSs predicted the occurrence of USs; for a third group, CSs predicted the absence of the USs. The CSs were subsequently presented while S performed the avoidance response. CSs which had predicted the occurrence or the absence of USs produced, respectively, increases and decreases in avoidance rate. For the group with random CSs and USs in conditioning, the CS had no effect upon avoidance.

Traditional conceptions of Pavlovian conditioning have emphasized the pairing of CS and US as the essential condition for the development of a CR. As long as the CS and US occur in temporal contiguity, the conditions for Pavlovian conditioning are assumed to be met. In contrast, another view of Pavlovian conditioning argues that conditioning depends upon the degree to which the CS allows S to *predict* the occurrence of the US. If the CS is followed by a change in the probability of the US, Pavlovian conditioning will occur. If the CS forecasts an *increased* likelihood of the US, excitatory conditioning will occur; if the CS forecasts a *decreased* likelihood of the US, the CS will take on inhibitory properties. According to this view, the number of CS-US pairings may be irrelevant to the development of a CR if the CS does not predict a change in the probability of occurrence of the US.

The experiment reported here explores the fruitfulness of this second approach to Pavlovian fear conditioning. Three groups of dogs received different kinds of Pavlovian conditioning. For one group, CSs and USs occurred randomly and independently in such a way that CS occurrences provided no information about US occurrences. In a second group, CS occurrences were followed by an increase in the probability of US occurrences; however, Ss in this group received the same number of CS-US pairings as did Ss in the first group. For the third group, CS occurrences predicted the *absence* of USs. These CSs were there presented while S performed a previously trained avoidance response. Increases in the rate of avoidance responding produced by CSs were taken as evidence for excitatory fear conditioning and decreases were taken as indicating inhibition of fear. Such changes in rate of avoidance responding have been shown by Rescorla & LoLordo (1965) to be a sensitive index of the level of conditioned fear.

Method

Ss were 18 mongrel dogs, individually housed and maintained on ad lib food and water throughout the experiment. The apparatus was a two-compartment dog

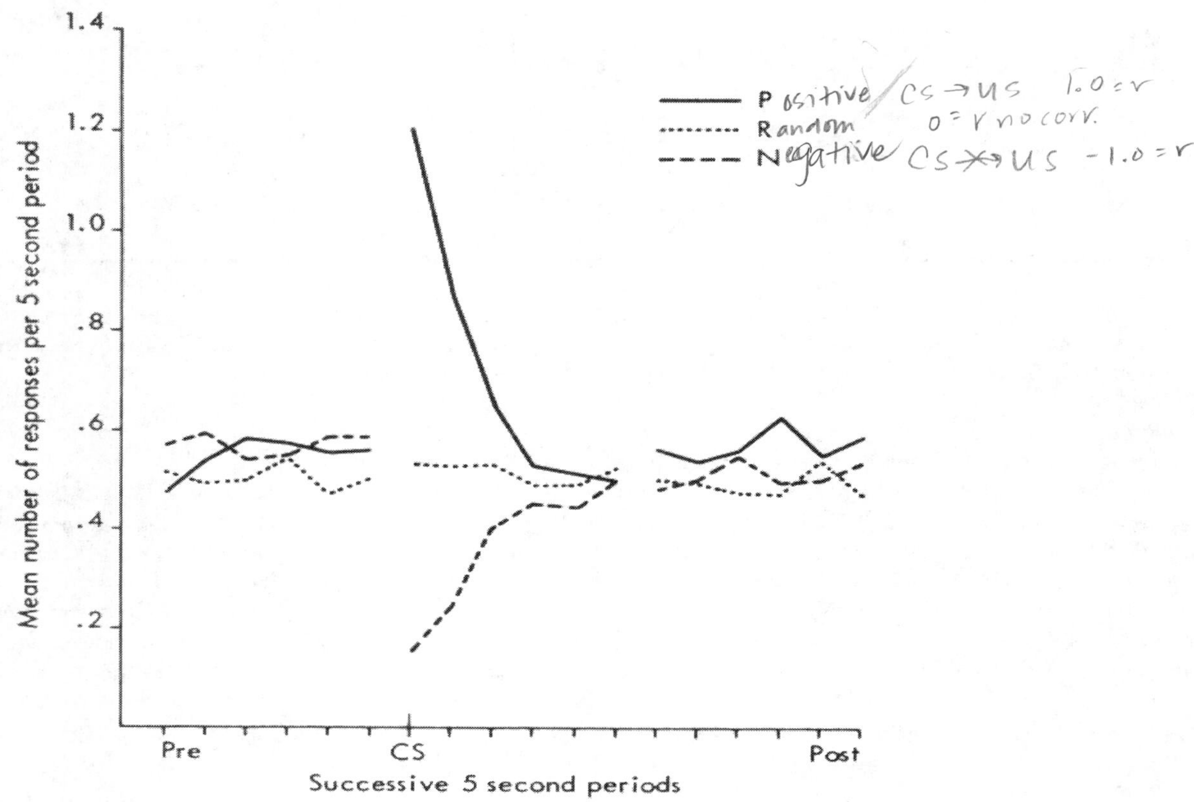

Figure 1. Mean number of responses per 5-sec. Period in successive periods prior to CS onset, during the CS and the subsequent 25 seconds of differential conditioning treatment, and after the expiration of the 25 second period.

shuttlebox described in detail by Solomon & Wynne (1953). The two compartments were separated by a barrier of adjustable height and by a drop gate which, when lowered, prevented S from crossing from one compartment into the other. The floor was composed of stainless steel grids which could be electrified through a scrambler. Speakers, mounted above the hardware-cloth ceiling, provided a continuous white noise background and permitted the presentation of tonal stimuli.

The training procedure was similar to that described by Rescorla & LoLordo (1965). Each S was trained to jump the barrier, separating the two sides of the shuttlebox, to avoid electric shock. Brief shocks, 0.25 sec., were programmed on a Sidman avoidance schedule; the shock-shock interval was 10 sec. and the response-shock interval 30 sec. The Ss received three initial days of avoidance training. On the first day the barrier height was 9 in. and the shock level 6 ma; on all subsequent days, the barrier height was 15 in. and the shock set at 8 ma.

Beginning with the fourth experimental day, S was confined to one-half of the shuttlebox and given Pavlovian fear conditioning. For the six dogs in Group R (random), 24, 5-sec., 3 ma shocks were programmed on a variable interval schedule with a mean of 2.5 min. Twenty-four, 5-sec., 400 cps tones were independently programmed randomly throughout the session in such a way that a tone onset was equiprobable at any time in the session. This was accomplished by a VI timer and a series of tapes. The six dogs in Group P (positive prediction) received a treatment identical to that of Group R except that they received only those shocks which were programmed to occur within 30 sec. after a tone onset. The six dogs in Group N (negative prediction) received a treatment identical to that of Group R except that they received only those shocks which were *not* programmed to occur within 30 sec. after a tone onset. The treatments for Groups P and N were accomplished by having each CS onset reset a 30 sec. timer through which the pre-programmed shocks were gated. Thus, for Group P, CS occurrences predicted US occurrences; and for Group N, CS occurrences predicted absence of USs.

Pavlovian conditioning and Sidman avoidance training days were then alternated until S had received a total of seven avoidance and five conditioning sessions. On day 13 a single test session was given. During this session, S performed the avoidance response with the Sidman schedule remaining in effect. In addition, 24, 5-sec., 400 cps tones were superimposed upon the avoidance behavior with a mean intertribal interval of 2.5 min. Changes in the rate of avoidance induced by these CSs were used as an index of the conditioned excitatory and inhibitory effects of the tones.

Results

The Sidman avoidance response was rapidly acquired by most animals and after several sessions all Ss were reliable responders. Figure 1 shows the results of the test session. Plotted in this figure are the mean number of responses per 5-sec. period of time over successive 5-sec. periods. Prior to the occurrence of a CS, all groups responded at approximately the same rate. However, the occurrence of a CS led to markedly different results in the three groups. For Group P, CS onset produced an abrupt increase in response rate followed by a return to base rate. The rate increase was confined to the first few 5-sec. periods following CS onset. In contrast, the CS produced a sharp decrease in rate in Group N. Again the rate change was maximal immediately following CS onset. For Group R, the occurrence of a CS produced very little effect.

Comparisons among the groups were made with the help of suppression ratios. These ratios are of the form $A/_{(A+B)}$ where B is the mean rate in the 30 sec. prior to CS onset and A is the rate for the period on which the two groups are to be compared. Using this measure, the rate increase during the CS was reliably greater for Group P than for Group R ($U=0$; $p<.01$). Group R, in turn, responded more frequently during CS than did Group N ($U=0$; $p<.01$). Similar conclusions result if the groups are compared on the rate during the entire 30 sec. following CS onset.

Discussion

The results of this experiment indicate that the degree to which a CS allows S to predict US occurrences is an important variable in Pavlovian fear conditioning. Stimuli which signaled increased probability of the US became elicitors of fear, resulting in an increased jumping rate, and stimuli which signaled decreased probability of the US became inhibitors of fear, resulting in a decreased jumping rate. The results, therefore, substantiate the findings of Rescorla & LoLordo (1965), that active inhibition and excitation of fear can be induced by Pavlovian methods. However, these effects seem to be independent of the more traditionally emphasized effects of number of CS-US pairings. Despite the fact that Ss in Group R received at least as many pairings of the CS and US as Ss in Group P, only the Ss in Group P showed evidence of Pavlovian fear conditioning.

The temporal location of the effect produced by the CS is also of interest. The differential effects of the CS for the three groups were primarily confined to the periods immediately following CS onset. Perhaps this happened because shocks were uniformly distributed, and for Group P the probability of a US in the next 30 sec. was maximal just after CS onset and declined as time since the CS increased; but for Group N, the probability of a shock was minimal immediately after CS onset. Another possibility is that the period immediately after CS onset is simply more discriminable from the baseline conditions than are subsequent periods.

These results suggest that we consider as a basic dimension of Pavlovian conditioning the degree to which the US is contingent upon prior CSs. From this point of view, the appropriate control procedure for non-associative effects of Pavlovian conditioning, such as sensitization or pseudoconditioning, is one in which there is *no* contingency between CS and US. The two extremes in which CS predicts either the increased or the decreased probability of a US are seen in the present experiment to produce, respectively, excitation and inhibition. A procedure such as that of Group R in which there is *no contingency* between CS and US provides an appropriate control procedure against which to evaluate both of these effects.

References

Rescorla, R. A., & LoLordo, V. M. Inhibition of avoidance behavior. *J. comp. physiol. Psychol.*, 1965, 59, 406-412.

Soloman, R. L., & Wynne, L. C. Traumatic avoidance learning: Acquisition in normal dogs. *Psychol. Monogr.*, 1953, 67, No. 4 (Whole No. 354).

PAVLOVIAN CONDITIONING
It's Not What You Think It Is

Robert A. Rescorla (1988). *American Psychologist, 43, 3,* 151-160.

After some twenty years and hundreds of experiments Rescorla was in a position to write a review article summarizing what had been learned about Pavlovian conditioning for a more general audience. Hence the publication of this article in the American Psychologist. It is significant not only because it provides a comprehensive review of the literature but because it very succinctly explains the differences between Pavlov's general notions regarding stimulus substitution models and the more contemporary contingency or correlational models. Like the Garcia article "Tilting at the Paper Mills of Academe", Rescorla provides a fascinating historical account of how ideas grow and develop, adapting themselves as it were to an ever changing zeitgeist.

Current thinking about Pavlovian conditioning differs substantially from that of 20 years ago. Yet the changes that have taken place remain poorly appreciated by psychologists generally. Traditional descriptions of conditioning as the acquired ability of one stimulus to evoke the original response to another because of their pairing are shown to be inadequate. They fail to characterize adequately the circumstances producing learning, the content of that learning, or the manner in which that learning influences performance. Instead, conditioning is now described as the learning of relations among events so as to allow the organism to represent its environment. Within this framework, the study of Pavlovian conditioning continues to be an intellectually active area, full of new discoveries and information relevant to other areas of psychology.

Pavlovian conditioning is one of the oldest and most systematically studied phenomena in psychology. Outside of psychology, it is one of our best known findings. But at the same time, within psychology it is badly misunderstood and misrepresented. In the last 20 years, knowledge of the associative processes underlying Pavlovian conditioning has expanded dramatically. The result is that modern thinking about conditioning is completely different from the views psychologists held 20 years ago. Unfortunately, these changes are very poorly appreciated by psychologists at large. The last time many psychologists read anything about Pavlovian conditioning was before these changes took place. Even those more recently education often received that education from textbooks and instructors that had largely ignored the dramatic conceptual changes that had taken place. The result is that many think of Pavlovian conditioning as an obsolete technical field that is intellectually stagnant.

My intention in this article is to show that this view is incorrect. First, I will review some of the changes that have occurred in Pavlovian conditioning in order to give the flavor of its contemporary form. I will argue that it is an intellectually challenging field, in which substantial and exciting progress has been made. Second, I will argue that conditioning continues to have a central place in psychology generally. I will describe how it touches on and informs several related fields that are currently more in vogue.

To begin the discussion, consider how conditioning was described 20 years ago, when those in my generation were students. One popular introductory text put it thus: The essential operation in conditioning is a *pairing* of two stimuli. One, initially neutral in that it elicits no response, is called the *conditioned stimulus (CS)*; the other, which is one that consistently elicits a response, is called the *unconditioned stimulus (US)*. The response elicited by the unconditioned stimulus is the *unconditioned response (UR)*. As a result of the pairing of the conditioned stimulus (CS) and the unconditioned stimulus (US), the previously neutral conditioned stimulus comes to elicit the response. Then it is called the *conditioned response (CR)*. (Morgan & King, 1966, pp. 79-80).

This description is typical of those found in both introductory and advanced textbooks 20 years ago.

Unfortunately, it is also typical of what one finds in textbooks today. One popular introductory text published in 1987 describes conditioning in this way: "The originally neutral conditioned stimulus, through repeated paring with the unconditioned one, acquires the response originally given to the unconditioned stimulus" (Atkinson, Atkinson, Smith, & Hilgard, 1987, p. 658). Students are exposed to similar descriptions in textbooks specializing in allied fields of psychology. In a cognitive textbook, one reads,

We start out by taking an unconditioned stimulus (UCS) that produces the desired response without training… We pair the UCS with a conditioned stimulus (CS)… This procedure, when repeated several times… will ultimately result in the occurrence of the response following the CS alone. (Klatsky, 1980, p. 281).

A widely used developmental text agrees, calling conditioning a "form of learning in which a neutral stimulus, when paired repeatedly with an unconditioned stimulus, eventually comes to evoke the original response" (Gardner, 1982, p. 594). Similarly, a best-selling textbook of abnormal psychology describes a conditioned stimulus as "a stimulus that, because of its having been paired with another stimulus (unconditioned stimulus) that naturally provokes an unconditioned response, is eventually able to evoke that response" (Rosenhan & Seligman, 1984, p. 669).

Of course, textbook descriptions vary widely in their precision and sophistication, but these citations represent a common view. Indeed, these quotations will certainly sound so familiar that many readers may wonder what is wrong with them. I want to suggest that the answer is "almost everything." These descriptions make assertions about what I take to be the primary issues to be addressed in the study of any learning process: What are the circumstances that produce learning? What is the content of the learning? How does that learning affect the behavior of the organism? But they are mistaken or misleading in virtually every assertion they make about each of these. These descriptions in fact capture almost nothing of modern data and theory in Pavlovian conditioning.

I want to illustrate this claim using some data collected in my own laboratory over the years, but first let me make an orienting comment. Descriptions of conditioning, such as those just cited, come from a long and honorable tradition in physiology, the reflex tradition in which Pavlov worked and within which many early behaviorists thought. This tradition sees conditioning as a kind of low-level mechanical process in which the control over a response is passed from one stimulus to another. Much modern thinking about conditioning instead derives largely from the associative tradition originating in philosophy. It sees conditioning as the learning that results from exposure to relations among events in the environment. Such learning is a primary means by which the organism represents the structure of its world. Consequently, Pavlovian conditioning must have considerable richness, both in the relations it represents and in the ways its representation influences behavior, a richness that was not envisioned within the reflex tradition.

Let me now turn to illustrating the difference that this alternative view makes for each of three issues: the circumstances producing learning, the content of learning, and the effects of learning on behavior.

Circumstances Producing Pavlovian Conditioning

Each of the descriptions given earlier cites one major circumstance as responsible for producing Pavlovian conditioning, the pairing or contiguity of two events. To be sure, contiguity remains a central concept, but a modern view of conditioning as the learning of relations sees contiguity as neither necessary nor sufficient. Rather, that view emphasizes the information that one stimulus gives about another. We now know that arranging for two well-processed events to be contiguous need not produce an association between them; nor does the failure to arrange contiguity preclude associative learning.

The insufficiency of contiguity for producing Pavlovian conditioning can be illustrated by results that have been available for almost 20 years (e.g., Rescorla, 1968) but that have apparently failed to be integrated into the view of conditioning held by many psychologists. Consider a learning situation in which a rat is exposed to two prominent events, a tone CS that occurs for two-minute periods and a brief, mild electric shock US applied to a grid on which the animal is standing. Suppose that those two events are uncorrelated in time, such that the tone provides no information about the shock. That relation is schematized in the top of Figure 1. Also schematized in that figure is a variation on that treatment in which only those USs scheduled to occur during the tone are actually applied to the animal. The point to notice about those two treatments is that they share the same contiguity of the tone with the US, but they differ in the amount of information that the tone gives about the US. In the first treatment, the shock is equally likely whether or not the tone is present, and so the tone provides no information; in the second treatment, the shock only occurs during the tone, and so the tone is quite informative about shock occurrence. It turns out that in many conditioning situations learning is determined not by what these treatments share but rather by how they differ. The second group will develop an association between the CS and US, but the first will fail to do so. In effect, conditioning is sensitive to the base rate of US occurrence against which a CS/US contiguity takes place.

Indeed, systematic experiments show that in many situations the amount of conditioning is exquisitely attuned to variations in the base rate of the US. An early illustration of that point is shown in Figure 2, which plots asymptotic levels of fear conditioning (measured by the ability of the CS to interfere with ongoing behavior) as a function in the likelihood of the US during the CS. The parameter in the figure is the base-rate likelihood of the US in the absence of the CS. Each curve shows that conditioning is indeed an increasing function of the likelihood of the shock during the tone. For instance, in the frequently studied case in which the shock likelihood is zero in the absence of the CS, then conditioning is greater the greater the probability of the shock during the tone. This is not a surprising result. What is more interesting is the effect of the base rate of US occurrence in the absence of the CS. At any given likelihood of shock during the CS, conditioning is an inverse function of the base rate. When the CS/US contiguity is held constant, conditioning changes from excellent to negligible simply by increasing the shock base rate. Indeed, when the likelihood of a US is the same in the presence and absence of the CS (as is true of the initial point on each function), there is little evidence of conditioning at all. One description of these results is that conditioning depends not on the contiguity between the CS and the US but rather on the information that the CS provides about the US. These are early data, but the basic results have been observed repeatedly in a variety of conditioning preparations. They strongly suggest that simple contiguity of CS and US fails to capture the relation required to produce an association.

The same conclusion is suggested by various other modern conditioning phenomena, such as the Kamin (1968) blocking effect. That effect has had a profound impact on

Figure 1
Schematic of Two Conditioned Stimulus/ Unconditioned Stimulus (CS/US) Relations That Share the Same Contiguity but Differ in the Information the CS Gives About the US

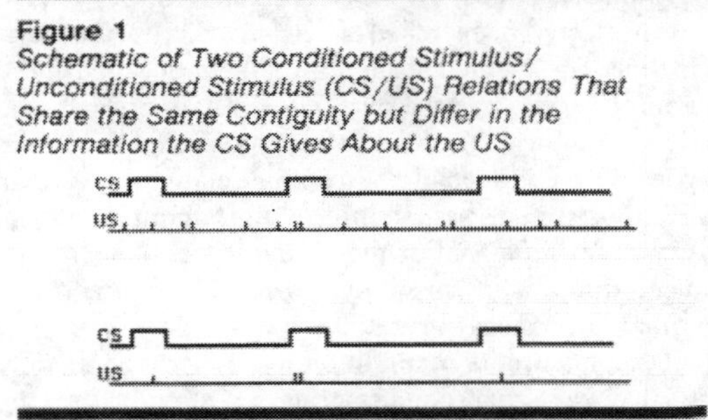

contemporary thinking about Pavlovian conditioning, yet it is unknown to many psychologists. In a simple blocking experiment, two groups of animals receive a compound stimulus (such as a light and tone) signaling a US. Eventually both groups will be tested for their conditioning of one stimulus, say the tone. However, one of the groups has a history of the light alone signaling the US, whereas the other group lacks that history. Notice that the two groups share the same contiguous occurrence of the US with the light/tone compound, but they differ in that for one the prior training of the light makes the tone redundant. The result of interest is that the tone becomes well conditioned in the first group but poorly conditioned in the group with light pretraining. Conditioning is not governed by the contiguity that the groups share but rather by the informational relation on which they differ. Again, simple contiguity of two events fails to capture the results; rather, information seems important. This is a result that has been widely repeated in many conditioning situations.

These two classic experiments illustrate that contiguity is not sufficient to produce Pavlovian conditioning. But neither is contiguity necessary to produce Pavlovian associations. This can be illustrated in a variety of ways, but a simple one makes reference to the treatments in Figure 1. Consider a variation on the first treatment in which, instead of omitting all of the shocks in the absence of the tone, we omit all those in its presence. This variation takes away all of the CS/US contiguities while maintaining a high base rate of US occurrence. Under these circumstances, the organism does not simply fail to learn; rather, it learns that there is a negative relation between the tone and the US. In the jargon of the field, the tone becomes a conditioned inhibitor. Again, this outcome is not intuitively surprising, but neither is it well accommodated by the description of conditioning in which the main circumstance producing learning is contiguity. Yet conditioned inhibition is a major part of modern thinking about Pavlovian conditioning. No theory of conditioning would be considered adequate if it failed to explain a wide variety of inhibitory phenomena (cf. Miller & Spear, 1985).

These kinds of results clearly suggest that the simple pairing of two events cannot be taken as fundamental to the description of Pavlovian conditioning. Instead, they encourage the prevalent modern view that conditioning involves the learning of relations among events. It provides the animal with a much richer representation of the environment than a reflex tradition would ever have suggested. Of course, one cannot leave the analysis at this

Figure 2
Dependence of Conditioning on Both the Likelihood of the US During the CS and the Base Rate of US Occurrence in the Absence of the CS

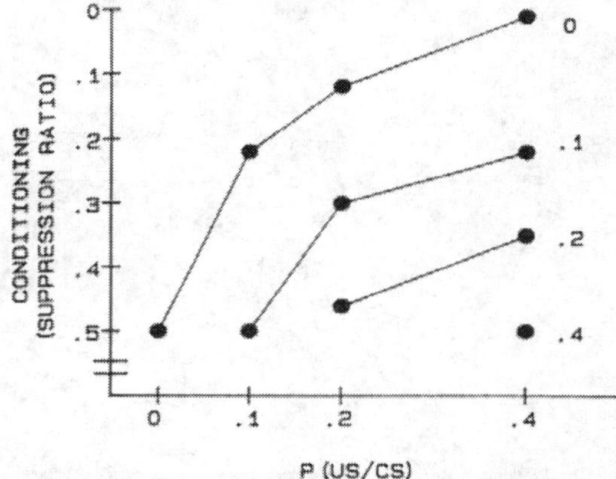

Note. Adapted from "Probability of Shock in the Presence and Absence of CS in Fear Conditioning" by R. A. Rescorla, 1968, *Journal of Comparative and Physiological Psychology, 66*, p. 4. Copyright 1968 by the American Psychological Association. Reprinted by permission. Asymptotic fear conditioning is plotted as a function of shock likelihood during the conditioned stimulus (CS). The parameter is the shock likelihood in the absence of the CS. When the CS/US contiguity [P(US/CS)] is held constant, conditioning varies from substantial to negligible as a function of the US (unconditioned stimulus) base rate. Conditioning is indexed by a ratio comparing responding during the CS with the ongoing response rate. With that ratio, 0.5 indicates no conditioning and 0 indicates excellent conditioning.

level; rather, one needs to provide theories of how these relations are coded by the organism. Such theories are now available, several of which are stated in sufficient quantitative detail to be taken seriously as useful accounts (e.g., Mackintosh, 1975; Pearce & Hall, 1980; Rescorla & Wagner, 1972). These theories emphasize the importance of a discrepancy between the actual state of the world and the organism's representation of that state. They see learning as a process by which the two are brought into line. In effect, they offer a sophisticated reformulation of the notion of contiguity. A useful shorthand is that organisms adjust their Pavlovian associations only when they are "surprised." This is not the place to describe these theories in detail, but they do an excellent job with phenomena like those described in Figure 2.

The importance of relations can be seen in yet another way. It is not only temporal and logical relations among events that are important to conditioning. Conditioning is also sensitive to relations involving the properties of the events themselves. There is a kind of abstractness with which the descriptions of conditioning are often stated, an abstractness that is characteristic of a field seeking general principles. These descriptions suggest that conditioning occurs whenever one arranges a temporal relation among the events, regardless of the other properties of the events. The claim in essence is that the animal comes to conditioning with no preconceptions about the structure of the world, ready to accommodate itself to any world that it faces. Pavlovian conditioning has, of course, served as one of the pillars for radical empiricism. But in modern times it has become clear that this pillar itself is partly built on the existing structure in the organism. Not all stimuli are equally associable; instead, a stimulus may be easier to associate with some signals rather than others. The

Figure 3
Effect of a Part-Whole Relation on Pavlovian Conditioning

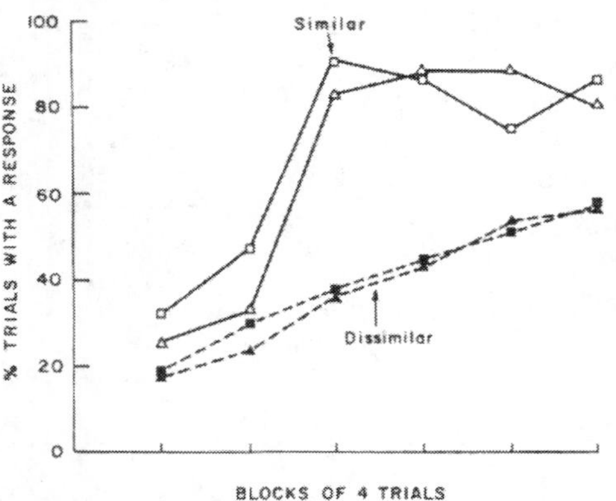

Note. From *Pavlovian Second-Order Conditioning: Studies in Associative Learning* (p. 49) by R. A. Rescorla, 1980, Hillsdale, NJ: Erlbaum. Copyright 1980 by Lawrence Erlbaum Associates. Reprinted by permission. Responding is shown to two second-order stimuli, an outline triangle and outline square, that signaled a colored triangle or a colored square. In the *similar* group, each outline form signaled a colored form of the same shape; in the *dissimilar* group, each signaled a colored form of a different shape.

most well-known demonstration of this, of course, is Garcia and Koelling's (1966) seminal work on the cue-to-consequence effect. They found that an internal distress was easier to associate with a gustatory rather than an auditory—visual stimulus, whereas a peripherally administered pain was more readily associated with the auditory—visual rather than the gustatory stimulus.

But this work is not alone in identifying instances of preferential learning among stimuli bearing qualitative relations to each other. For instance, spatial relationship, a variable important to philosophical associationism but neglected by the reflex tradition, is now known to affect Pavlovian associations (e.g., Rescorla, 1980). Similarly, recent work shows that perceptual relations among events, such as similarity and the part-whole relation, also are important determinants of conditioning.

Figure 3 shows an example of how one perceptual relation (part to whole) affects the results of Pavlovian conditioning. Those results come from an autoshaping experiment in pigeons. Autoshaping is one of the most popular modern Pavlovian preparations, so it is worth mentioning in its own right. In that preparation, birds are exposed to a response-independent signaling relation between an illuminated disc (say, a red square or a red triangle) and food. As the birds learn that relation, they come to peck the disc. That result is worth analysis of its own, but for the present we will simply take it as an index that the birds have associated the red square with food. More important for our present purposes, they will peck not only the red square but also localized stimuli that in turn signal the red square (producing so-called second-order conditioning). Figure 3 shows the development of pecking at two stimuli, colorless outlines of a square and a triangle, when they signal a red square and a red triangle. For the animals having a *similar* relation, each colored figure was signaled by the same-form achromatic figure; each whole was signaled by one of its parts. For the animals having a *dissimilar* relation, the colored figures were also signaled by the achromatic figures except that the forms were mismatched so as to destroy the part-whole relation. It is clear that conditioning proceeded more rapidly in animals who had the part-whole relation. That is, a perceptual relation influenced the formation of an association. This is a particularly interesting perceptual relation because in the natural environment partial information about an object frequently serves as a signal of the entire object. Apparently, Pavlovian conditioning is especially sensitive to that fact.

One final comment needs to be made about the circumstances that produce conditioning. It is a commonly held belief that Pavlovian conditioning is a slow process by which organisms learn only if stimulus relations are laboriously repeated over and over again. Several of the descriptions cites earlier acknowledge this belief by using such terms as *repeatedly* and *eventually*. However, this view is not well supported by modern data. Although conditioning can sometimes be slow, in fact most modern conditioning preparations routinely show rapid learning. One-trial learning is not confined to flavor-aversion learning, and learning in five or six trials is common. In fact, the data displayed in Figure 3 are a good example of learning that is excellent after eight trials. Notice that those data were obtained in a second-order conditioning paradigm, a procedure that itself has an undeserved reputation for being weak and transient (See Rescorla, 1980).

The picture that emerges from this discussion of the circumstances that produce conditioning is quite different from that given by the classical descriptions. Pavlovian conditioning is not a stupid process by which the organism will-nilly forms associations between any two stimuli that happen to co-occur. Rather, the organism is better seen as an information seeker using logical and perceptual relations among events, along with its own preconceptions, to form a sophisticated representation of its world. Indeed, in teaching undergraduates, I favor an analogy between animals showing Pavlovian conditioning and scientists identifying the cause of a phenomenon. If one thinks of Pavlovian conditioning as developing between a CS and a US under just those circumstances that would lead a scientist to conclude that the CS causes the US, one has a surprisingly successful heuristic for remembering the facts of what it takes to produce Pavlovian associative learning (see Dickinson, 1980; Mackintosh, 1983).

Content of Pavlovian Conditioning: What Is Learned

The descriptions of conditioning given earlier imply a highly restricted content in which a single neutral stimulus becomes associated with one that evokes a response. But modern Pavlovian thinking suggests a picture that is richer in two ways.

First, it is clear that in any Pavlovian experiment the animal learns about many different stimuli. Associations are formed not just between the primary events psychologists present, the CS and US. For instance, each of those events also becomes associated with the context in which they are presented (e.g., Balsam & Tomie, 1985). Such associations are one way that organisms use Pavlovian conditioning to

Figure 4
Design of an Experiment Demonstrating Hierarchical Organization

R+	X → RH	RH+, R−, H−	X? Y?
H+	Y → R, Y → H	RH−, R+, H+	

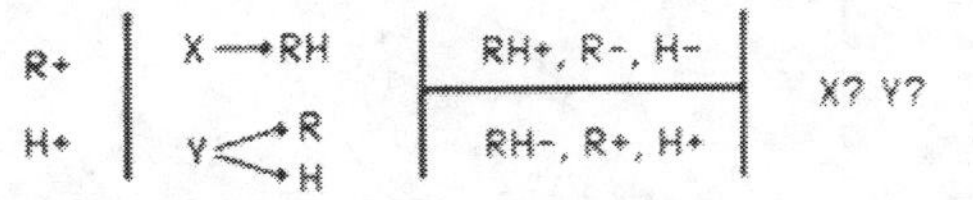

Note. Birds received first-order Pavlovian conditioning of two keylights (R and H) with a food (+) unconditioned stimulus (US). Then one second-order stimulus (*X*) signaled the RH compound, whereas another (*Y*) signaled the elements. Then the birds received one of two conditional discriminations between the RH compound and its elements and were tested for the response to *X* and *Y*. The physical identities of the *X* and *Y* stimuli were counterbalanced as a blue keylight and a black *X* on a white background.

code spatial information. Moreover, associations form not only between events but also within each of the events that the traditional description identifies (e.g., Rescorla & Durlach, 1981). Indeed, considerable effort is going into analyzing the latter learning because within-event associations may be one way that the organism represents individual events. Moreover, many examples of Pavlovian associations involve stimuli that do not evoke an original response. Pavlovian conditioning also encodes the relations among relatively innocuous events. So, modern experimentation supports the proposition that the organism concurrently forms a broad range of associations among a wide variety of stimuli. Moreover, quite powerful procedures have been developed to expose the existence of these associations and to carry out an analysis of their properties.

Second, modern Pavlovian thinking does not envision all of this learning taking place among simple pairs of elements all treated at the same level of analysis by the organism. Rather, as the British associationists claimed years ago, there is good reason to believe that there is a hierarchical organization in which associations among some pairs of items yield new entities that themselves can enter into further associations.

One illustration comes from a recent second-order autoshaping experiment conducted in my laboratory, the experimental design of which is shown in Figure 4. In this experiment, one stimulus *(X)* signaled the occurrence of a compound stimulus composed of a keylight that was red (R) on one half and had horizontal stripes (H) on the other half. The birds were interested in that fact because R and H each had a separate history of signaling the occurrence of food. Previous experiments had demonstrated that the birds would come to peck *X* as a result of its second-order conditioning by the RH compound. The question of interest was what would be the associative structure that supported that pecking. One possibility is that the bird would form two pairwise associations, learning the individual associations of *X* with R and with H. But a more interesting possibility is that the organism would form a representation of the RH event (perhaps using the association we know forms between R and H in such settings) and then use that representation as an element to associate with *X*. Either associative structure would cause the bird to show conditioning to *X*, but the former solution involves two parallel associative connections, whereas the latter involves a hierarchical organization.

The technology of modern Pavlovian conditioning provides a way to separate these two alternatives. In many conditioning preparations, responding to a signal tracks the current state of its associate (e.g., Rescorla, 1980). If the value of a reinforcer is changed after conditioning has been completed, subsequent responding to its associated CSs will also change accordingly. This fact can be used to decide with which stimulus *X* has become associated. In this instance, we deliberately gave the RH compound and its elements different values. For some animals, we extinguished the separately presented R and H elements but reinforced the RH compound; for others, we did the converse. Then we tested responding to *X*. If the animal has only separate associations of *X* with the R and H elements, responding to *X* should track the value of those elements, but if *X* has an association with RH, responding should track the compound's value rather than that of the R and H elements. In order to compare the results from *X* with those from an associative structure that we know to represent simple pairwise associations, we also used R and H to condition another stimulus *(Y)*. Like *X*, *Y* was followed by R and H, but unlike *X*, *Y* received R and H on separate trials, thereby ensuring its having separate associations with those elements. As a result, responding to *Y* should track the current value of the R and H elements, not that of the RH compound.

The results of various stages of this experiment are shown in Figure 5. The first panel shows the level of responding to *X* and *Y* at the end of their second-order conditioning by the RH compound and the R and H elements. Those treatments produced similar levels of conditioning. On that basis alone, one cannot identify any differences in the associations of *X* and *Y*. The middle panel shows the course of the discriminations between RH and its elements. The birds could readily code a compound and its elements differentially, a result of some interest in itself. But the data of most interest are those shown in the final panel, from the testing of the second-order *X* and *Y* stimuli. Consider first the results from *Y*, which had signaled R and H separately. Responding to that stimulus tracked the value of the individual R and H separately. Responding to that stimulus tracked the value of the individual R and H elements, not the value of the RH compound. Under those conditions, individual associations are indeed formed. Quite different are the results of testing *X*, the stimulus that had signaled the RH compound. Responding to that stimulus tracked the current value of the RH compound rather than the value of its elements. Clearly, the animals had not simply coded the RH compound in terms of parallel associations with its elements. Rather, they had engaged in some more hierarchical structuring of the situation, forming a representation of the compound and using it as an associate. This is the kind of hierarchical organization envisioned by the British associationists; it is extremely important because it may provide a means for an associative theory to build complex performances by bootstrapping based on elementary mechanisms. Such hierarchical structures are often discussed in various learning literatures, but they turn out to be very difficult to document definitively. One demonstration, however, can be given within the framework of Pavlovian conditioning.

Another illustration of such a hierarchical structure comes from recent demonstrations of a phenomenon variously called "occasion-setting" and "facilitation" (Holland, 1983; Rescorla, 1985). That phenomenon arises in situations in

Figure 5
Results of an Experiment Demonstrating Hierarchical Organization

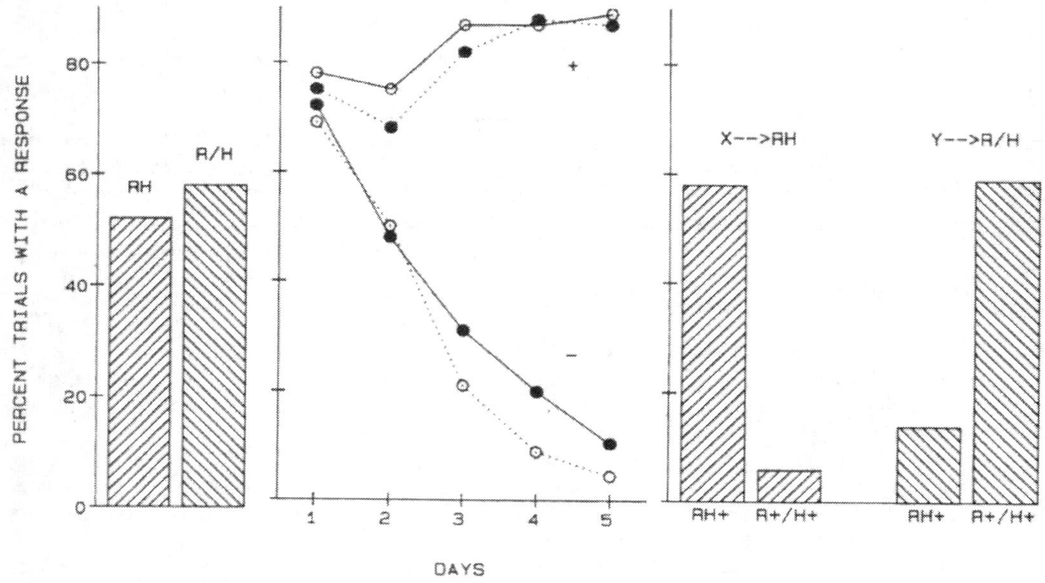

Note. The left panel shows asymptotic second-order conditioning of *X* and *Y* by the RH compound and the R and H elements, respectively. The middle panel shows a conditional discrimination of the form RH+, R−, H− (solid symbols) or RH−, R+, H+ (open symbols). The right panel shows responding to *X* and *Y* as a function of the most recent treatment of the RH compound and its elements. In both cases, responding to *X* and *Y* tracked the current value of the stimulus that it had signaled.

which a Pavlovian stimulus is deliberately arranged to signal not another stimulus but rather a relation between two other stimuli. Under proper conditions, such learning readily develops. Moreover, it can be relatively independent of the learning of separate associations to the elements. For instance, a stimulus that signals a positive relation between two other stimuli can simultaneously have either excitatory or inhibitory associations with the elements themselves.

Several laboratories are currently actively engaged in analyzing this kind of hierarchical relation. Their findings have important general implications for our understanding of Pavlovian conditioning. They suggest that associations may play a modulatory, rather than an elicitive, role. And they are changing the way we think about excitatory and inhibitory associations. Moreover, thinking about this modulatory role is beginning to be brought to bear on the analysis of stimulus control in instrumental learning.

Modern thinking about Pavlovian conditioning views associations as basic, but those associations are formed among representations of multiple events. Moreover, those representations themselves are often complex and include relations generated by other associations .Pavlovian conditioning does not consist simply of learning relations between a neutral event and a valuable event. Many different associations are formed, and the resulting content of learning allows a rich representation of the world.

Influences on Behavior

The descriptions quoted earlier contain a highly restricted view of how conditioning affects behavior. They envision only one way in which performance is generated: The CS becomes capable of evoking the response originally evoked by the US. However, there are very few students of conditioning who would care to defend that claim. There are three reasons why I believe it should be rejected.

First, many of the standard conditioning preparations simply do not show this feature. Consider, for instance, conditioned suppression situations such as those used to collect the data shown in Figure 2. The response to the shock US is abruptly increased activity, whereas the response to a tone signaling that shock is dramatically reduced activity.

Second, there is an important, but poorly appreciated, fact about conditioning that makes nonsense out of any claim that a signal simply acquires the ability to evoke the response to the US: The response observed to a CS often depends not only on the US but also on the perceptual properties of the CS itself. Two different signals of the same US may evoke quite different responses. For instance, for rat subjects a diffuse tone that signals a shock US results in immobility, but a localized prod signaling shock results in attempts to hide the prod from view by covering it with any available material (e.g., Pinel & Treit, 1979). Similarly, different CSs signaling food to a pigeon come to produce quite different response forms. As noted above, a

Figure 6
Dependence of the Form of the Conditioned Response on the Identity of the Signal

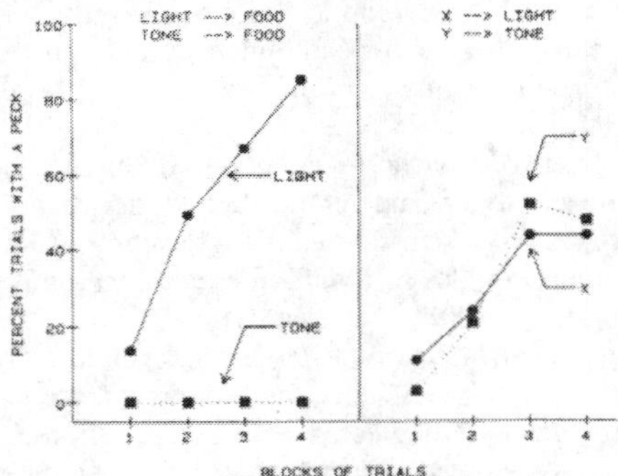

Note. The left panel shows keypecking in birds for whom both a localized keylight and a diffuse tone signaled food. The right panel shows keypecking to two other localized keylights (*X* and *Y*) that signaled the light and tone, respectively. The physical identities of *X* and *Y* were counterbalanced as red and green.

localized visual signal of food evokes directed pecking. However, a diffuse auditory signal of that same food does not evoke pecking but rather enhances general activity. Figure 6 shows a relevant illustration from a recent experiment in our laboratory. The left-hand panel of that figure shows the results of giving the same birds separate keylight and auditory signals for food. It is clear that the birds came to peck during the keylight but not during the tone. But the absence of pecking does not result from a failure of learning about the tone. Direct observation of the bird shows that the tone produces enhanced general activity. Moreover, the right-hand panel of Figure 6 suggests that although the tone and light evoke different responses, the bird has in some sense learned the same thing about the two stimuli. That panel shows the results of a second stage of the experiment in which the light and the tone were each signaled by another keylight *(X and Y)*. Both the tone and the light served as excellent reinforcers, thereby displaying that they had become associated with food. There are two points to note from this demonstration: First, the form of the conditioned response varies from CS to CS, and so it cannot always be like the response to the US. Second, sometimes we have difficulty seeing any evidence of learning if we simply look at the responses elicited by the CS; rather, other measures, such as the ability to serve as a reinforcer, can often provide better evidence of learning.

The third reason to reject the classical notion of how conditioning affects performance is that there is a sense in which the response one sees to a Pavlovian CS can be arbitrarily selected by the experimenter. That is possible because one important feature of Pavlovian conditioning is its involvement in goal-directed instrumental performance. It has been known for years that Pavlovian conditioning makes important contributions to the control of emotions and motivations. Twenty years ago, one of my most respected professors, Frank Irwin, asked me how I could be interested in Pavlovian conditioning, a process that he characterized as being "all spit and twitches" and of little general psychological interest. But it is important to understand that Irwin's characterization was wrong. Conditioning is intimately involved in the control of central psychological processes, such as emotions and motivations. In fact, two-process theories of instrumental performance are built on that proposition (e.g., Mowrer, 1947; Rescorla & Solomon, 1967; Trapold & Overmier, 1972).

In our laboratory, we routinely exploit the effect on instrumental behavior to detect the presence of a Pavlovian association. Figure 7 shows the results of one recent experiment conducted in collaboration with Ruth Colwill. These data come from rat subjects that are making an instrumental choice response, pulling a chain for a pellet or pressing a lever for liquid sucrose. While they were engaging in those performances, we presented a CS that had been made a Pavlovian signal either of food or of sucrose. The result of interest is that presentation of the Pavlovian CS biased the results of the instrumental performance. When the CS signaled the same reinforcer as did the chain pull, it enhanced chain pulling relative to lever pressing; on the other hand, when the CS shared the same reinforcer with the lever press, it enhanced lever pressing (cf. Kruse, Overmier, Konz, & Rokke, 1983). The point is that we can modulate an arbitrarily selected response (chain pulling and lever pressing) by the presentation of a Pavlovian signal. The same Pavlovian conditioning can show up in a broad range of responses depending on the context in which it is assessed. These results are of interest for what they tell us about the animal's knowledge about the consequences of its instrumental responding (see Colwill & Rescorla, 1986), but in the present context they make the point that conditioning can show up in arbitrarily selected behaviors, not just in the response the US evoked.

The implication is that describing Pavlovian conditioning as the endowing of a CS with the ability to evoke the same response as the US is a wholly inadequate characterization. Pavlovian conditioning is not the shifting of a response from one stimulus to another. Instead, conditioning involves the learning of relations among events that are complexly represented, a learning that can be exhibited in various ways. We are badly in need of an adequate theory of performance in Pavlovian conditioning, but the classical notion of a new stimulus taking on the ability to evoke an old response clearly will not do.

Return for a moment to the definitions of conditioning with which we began. They emphasized repeated pairing between two stimuli, one neutral and one valuable, with the result that the neutral one comes to evoke the response of the valuable one. But we have seen that pairing is not central, that all sorts of stimuli become associated in a manner that goes beyond simple dyadic relations, and that the Pavlovian associations influence behavior in many ways other than by the transferring of a response.

Finally, it is worth noting that these changes in our views of Pavlovian conditioning have been accompanied and encouraged by changes in the laboratory preparations used for its study. Many of the early observations in conditioning were made using the salivary preparation, often by Pavlov (1927) himself. But no contemporary American laboratory makes extensive use of that technique. As can be seen from the preceding discussion, modern studies of conditioning use a much more diverse set of

Figure 7

Exhibition of Pavlovian Conditioning in the Control of Instrumental Behavior

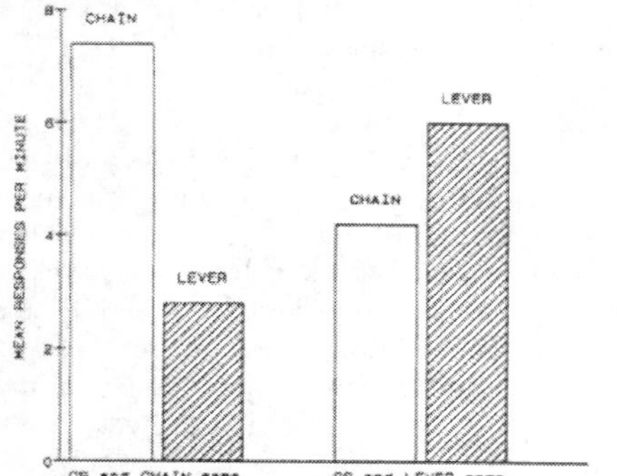

Note. Responding is shown during the presentation of a Pavlovian conditioned stimulus (CS) that signaled the same reinforcer as that earned either by a chain pull or a lever press.

procedures, involving a range of signals, consequences, and behavioral measures, in various species. The flexibility of contemporary thinking is partly an adaptation to that diversity.

The Place of Pavlovian Conditioning in Psychology

It is worth making some comments about the role of Pavlovian conditioning in psychology in general because that has also changed. It is important to realize that those who study this elementary learning process are not nearly as imperialistic as the animal learning psychologists of the 1940s and 1950s. In those days, conditioning was more than a learning process. It was the centerpiece for a set of theories intended to explain all behavior. More than that, it represented a way of doing science. Because conditioning came to psychology at a time when psychologists were working out scientific ways of studying behavior, it became bound up with considerable philosophical baggage. It stood not only for an explanation of psychological phenomena but also for a way of doing psychology altogether. One can still see some of the aftereffects of this heritage in the conservative style of introducing new theoretical concepts and in the commitment to elementarism. But Pavlovian conditioning has largely shed its philosophical role. Those who study conditioning have little interest in recapturing all of psychology in the name of behaviorism. What then is the role of Pavlovian conditioning in psychology? I see three kinds of contributions that it continues to make.

First, it continues to be a sample learning process that admits of careful detailed analysis. It is, of course, only one of a possibly quite large number of learning processes. Few would claim that all improvements from experience are based on a single process. However, Pavlovian conditioning is an important learning process for which the analysis is proceeding apace. As I hope my previous comments have illustrated, important questions are being addressed about what produces learning, about what the products of learning are, and about how organisms can represent their world. Moreover, by working in a relatively constrained domain, we can often better characterize what would be adequate answers to questions about the nature of learning and better develop techniques for providing those answers. So one role for Pavlovian conditioning is as a model for the study of modification by experience generally.

A second role for Pavlovian conditioning is to continue to provide a body of data and developed theory that inform adjacent areas of scientific inquiry. The study of Pavlovian conditioning provides information about a learning process of continuing interest to allied fields. Two of the most intensely pursued current areas of interest provide examples: cognitive science and neuroscience. After a period in which it neglected learning processes, modern cognitive psychology has returned to their study; indeed, even the association has regained some respectability. This is especially obvious in the approach to cognitive processes currently called "parallel distributed processing" or "connectionism." According to this approach (e.g., McClelland & Rumelhart, 1986; Rumelhart & McClelland, 1986), many phenomena can be understood in terms of multiple parallel connections between stimulus input and response output. Although fueled by analogies to neural structures and modern computer design, these connectionistic theories clearly harken back to classical associationism. They appeal to multiple associations interacting to produce complex outputs. In some cases, theories of this sort have attacked apparently complex behaviors with surprisingly promising results. For instance, something of speech perception and production, of category learning, and of place recognition can be captured by such theories. it is still too early to know whether these initial results forecast ultimately successful accounts. But they do belie some widely accepted assertions that certain classes of psychological phenomena are in principle beyond the reach of inherently associationistic theories.

Connectionistic theories of this sort bear an obvious resemblance to theories of Pavlovian conditioning. Both view the organism as using multiple associations to build an overall representation, and both view the organism as adjusting its representation to bring it into line with the worlds, striving to reduce any discrepancies. Indeed, it is striking that often such complex models are built on elements that are tied quite closely to Pavlovian associations. For instance, one of the learning principles most frequently adopted within these models, the so-called delta rule, is virtually identical to one popular theory in Pavlovian conditioning, the Rescorla-Wagner model. Both are error-correction rules, in which the animal uses evidence from all available stimuli and adjusts the strength of reach stimulus based on the total error. Here, then, is a striking point of contact between Pavlovian conditioning and a portion of cognitive science.

The second area of intense activity is neuroscience. Although that area has mushroomed and contains many parts that do not border on psychology, one important subarea is the study of the neural bases of learning processes. Neuroscientists have decided, quite rightly I believe, that Pavlovian conditioning provides one of the best-worked-out learning situations for them to analyze. It has a well-developed data base that can be characterized quite successfully by available theories. The hopeful sign is that, increasingly, neuroscientists are familiarizing themselves with the contemporary state of Pavlovian conditioning and are attempting to account for a host of new results, such as sensitivity to information, inhibitory learning, and so forth. Indeed, many neuroscientists are better acquainted with the modern state of Pavlovian conditioning than are psychologists at large. It is partly through that acquaintance that genuine progress is being made in the biological analysis of learning.

Pavlovian conditioning stands between these two very active areas of research. It provides a context in which to assess some of the assumptions about the elements contributing to more complex cognitive theories. It also provides an organized data base and theoretical structure to help inform and guide the neural analysis of learning. The association is not dead, but rather continues to be a fundamental concept in the analysis of learning processes. Moreover, it is in Pavlovian conditioning that many of the important discoveries are currently being made about associative processes. As a result, allied areas will continue to turn to conditioning for data and theory.

Finally, Pavlovian conditioning continues to play the role of generating practical applications. Of course, an early example was the development of some aspects of behavior therapy. Behavior therapy was spun off early and has now developed its own mature literature. In my view, an unfortunate consequence of that early emergence is that some behavior therapists still view conditioning in the way characterized by the quotations that I have criticized. But there continue to be other instances of applications and potential applications stemming from the laboratory study of Pavlovian conditioning. For instance, recent work suggests that the body's reactions to drugs and some diseases involve Pavlovian conditioning mechanisms. Phenomena such as drug tolerance (e.g., Siegel, 1983), stress-induced analgesia, and immunosuppression (e.g., Ader & Cohen, 1981) seem to involve Pavlovian conditioning. Those observations suggest new instances in which conditioning will have relatively direct practical consequences.

Trends come and go in psychology. Topics that are hot today will be cold in 10 or even 5 years, but some parts of psychology continue to build systematic and important data bases and theories. The study of sensory mechanisms is one example. I think that the study of the associative mechanisms underlying Pavlovian conditioning is another. These fields are enduring and systematic, but I hope it is now obvious that they are also changing and exciting.

References

Ader, R., & Cohen, N. (1981). Conditioned immunopharmacologic responses. In R. Ader (Ed.), *Psychoneuroimmunology*. New York: Academic Press.

Atkinson, R.L., Atkinson, R.C., Smith, E.E., & Hilgard, E.R. (1987*). Introduction to psychology* (9th ed.). New York: Harcourt, Brace, Jovanovich. Balsam, P.D., & Tomie, A. (Eds.). (1985). *Context and learning*. Hillsdale, NJ: Erlbaum.

Colwill, R.M., & Rescorla, R.A. (1986). Associative structures in instrumental learning. In G.H. Bower (Ed.), *The psychology of learning and motivation* (Vol. 20, pp. 55-103). New York: Academic Press.

Dickinson, A. (1980). *Contemporary animal learning theory*. London, England: Cambridge University Press.

Garcia, J., & Koelling, R.A. (1966). Relation of cue to consequence in avoidance learning, *Psychonomic Science, 4,* 123-124.

Gardner, H. (1982). *Developmental psychology* (2nd ed.). Boston: Little, Brown.

Holland, P.C. (1983). "Occasion-setting" in Pavlovian feature positive discriminations. In M.L. Commons, R.J. Herrnstein, & A.R. Wagner (Eds.), *Quantitative analyses of behavior: Volume 4. Discrimination processes* (pp. 183-206). Cambridge, MA: Ballinger.

Kamin, L.J. (1968). Attention-like processes in classical conditioning. In M.R. Jones (Ed.), *Miami symposium on the prediction of behavior: Aversive stimuli* (pp. 9-32). Coral Gables, FL: University of Miami Press.

Klatsky, R. (1980). *Human memory* (2nd ed.). San Francisco: Freeman.

Kruse, J.M., Overmier, J.B., Konz, W.A., & Rokke, E. (1983). Pavlovian conditioned stimulus effects upon instrumental choice behavior are reinforcer specific. *Learning and Motivation, 14*, 165-181.

Mackintosh, N.J. (1975). A theory of attention: Variations in the associability of stimuli with reinforcement. *Psychological Review, 82*, 276-298.

Mackintosh, N.J. (1983). *Conditioning and associative learning*. Oxford, England: Oxford University Press.

McClelland, J.L., & Rumelhart, D.E. (1986). *Parallel distributed processing* (Vol. 2). Cambridge, MA: MIT Press.

Miller, R.R., & Spear, N.E. (Eds.). (1985). *Information processing in animals: Conditioned inhibition.* Hillsdale, NJ: Erlbaum.

Morgan, C.T., & King, R.A. (1966). *Introduction to psychology* (3rd ed.). New York: McGraw-Hill.

Mowrer, O.H. (1947). On the dual nature of learning—a reinterpretation of "conditioning" and "problem solving." *Harvard Educational Review, 17*, 102-148.

Pavlov, I.P. (1927). *Conditioned reflexes*. London: Oxford.

Pearce, J.M., & Hall, G. (1980). A model for Pavlovian conditioning: Variations in the effectiveness of conditioned but not of unconditioned stimuli. *Psychological Review, 87*, 532-552.

Pinel, J.P.J., & Treit, D. (1979). Conditioned defensive burying in rats: Availability of burying materials. *Animal Learning and Behavior, 7*, 392-396.

Rescorla, R.A. (1968). Probability of shock in the presence and absence of CS in fear conditioning. *Journal of Comparative and Physiological Psychology, 66*, 1-5.

Rescorla, R.A. (1980). *Pavlovian second-order conditioning: Studies in associative learning*. Hillsdale, NJ: Erlbaum.

Rescorla, R.A. (1985). Conditioned inhibition and facilitation. In R.R. Miller & N.S. Spear (Eds.),

Information processing in animals: Conditioned inhibition (pp. 299-326). Hillsdale, NJ: Erlbaum.

Rescorla, R.A., & Durlach, P.J. (1981). Within-event learning in Pavlovian conditioning. In N.E. Spear & R.R. Miller (Eds.), *Information processing in animals: Memory mechanisms* (pp. 83-111). Hillsdale, NJ: Erlbaum.

Rescorla, R.A., & Solomon, R.L. (1967). Two-process learning theory: Relationships between Pavlovian conditioning and instrumental learning. *Psychological Review, 74*, 151-182.

Rescorla, R.A., & Wagner, A.R. (1972). A theory of Pavlovian conditioning: Variations in the effectiveness of reinforcement and nonreinforcement. In A. H. Black & W.F. Prokasy (Eds.), *Classical conditioning II: Current research and theory* (pp. 64-99). New York: Appleton-Century-Crofts.

Rosenhan, D.L., & Seligman, M.E.P. (1984). *Abnormal psychology*. New York: Norton.

Rumelhart, D.E., & McClelland, J.L. (1986). *Parallel distributed processing* (Vol. 1). Cambridge, MA: MIT Press.

Siegel, S. (1983). Classical conditioning, drug tolerance, and drug dependence. In R.G. Smart, F.B. Glaser, Y. Isreal, H. Kalant, R.E. Popham, & W. Schmidt (Eds.), *Research advances in alcohol and drug problems* (Vol. 7, pp. 207-246). New York: Plenum.

Trapold, M.A., & Overmier, J.B. (1972). The second learning process in instrumental learning. In A.A. Black & W.F. Prokasy (Eds.), *Classical conditioning II: Current research and theory* (pp. 427-452). New York: Appleton-
Century-Crofts.

TOWARD EMPIRICAL BEHAVIOR LAWS I. POSITIVE REINFORCEMENT[1]

David Premack (1959). *Psychological Review, 66(4),* 219-233.

The Premack Principle states, "given two behaviors which differ in their likely occurrence, the less likely behavior can be reinforced by using the more likely behavior as a reward." In other words, reward yourself for going to the library and studying by permitting yourself to participate in an activity you really enjoy. The Premack Principle is a relationship between two behaviors. The essential ingredient in implementing this behavior modification is to be extremely observant of the individual and thereby recognize what the person does eagerly and what they avoid doing. More probable behaviors reinforce less probable behaviors. This is a good example of common sense or folk psychology, sometimes called Grandma's Rule of behavior modification, "No TV until you do your homework", but even more importantly it revolutionized the way we thought about the nature of reinforcement. The term reinforcer implies a "something" which the organism acquires, a stimulus which is added to the situation. What Premack did was change this perspective. In Premack's view what is reinforcing is not the stimulus but the consummatory response, it is not food the stimulus which reinforces the rat's bar pressing it is eating the activity which does so. Further and perhaps even more significantly Premack forced us to recognize that reinforcement is relative. Eating is only reinforcing if you are hungry. Typically speaking you would use eating to reinforce another activity, but you can imagine a situation where you have eaten too much and been too inactive and the reverse would be true. Imagine Grandma saying, "Nope sorry, you can't go out and play until you finish that last cookie you took even though you didn't really want it." This is a relativity theory of reinforcement and it significantly impacted the way we came to think about reinforcement in relation to the evolutionary and experiential history of the individual organism.

This account of reinforcement is based upon a generalization, not a theory. Few cases underlie the generalization, but that which is generalized to are measurable properties of behavior.

If accurate, the present generalization will provide: first, an explanation of reinforcement; second, a criterion for evaluating the logical need for motivation constructs; and third, a possible basis for an empirical quantitative account of learning. This first paper, however, deals mainly with positive reinforcement. Learning, motivation, and the aversive case require independent treatment, though some reference to these topics will occur here.

THE RATE DIFFERENTIAL: A NECESSARY AND SUFFICIENT CONDITION FOR REINFORCEMENT

The account is based on the assumption that the nature of reinforcement can be discerned by taking two responses (Rs) of the organism, arranging both of the possible contingencies between them, and noting what differentiates between the contingencies in which reinforcement does and does not occur.

A hypothetical example is provided by using a rat, the bar press, and the ingestion of pellets. If by reinforcement we mean, for the moment, the traditional increase in frequency of an R, the experiment will require two preliminary measures: (*a*) the rate of the bar press when the bar is available to the rat, which we will call the *independent rate* of bar pressing; and (*b*) the rate at which pellets are ingested when they are available to the rat, the independent rate of pellet ingestion.

Given the independent rates of both bar pressing and pellet ingestion, the experiment proceeds by arranging both contingencies: (*a*) the availability of a pellet contingent upon a bar press and (*b*) the availability of the bar contingent upon the ingestion of a pellet. Consider that the former produces a rate of bar pressing greater than the independent rate, but that the bar contingent upon ingestion does not produce a rate of ingestion greater than that of the independent rate. What conclusions may be drawn as to the determinants of reinforcement?

Conclusions based upon the literature will include: need reduction, drive reduction, sensory stimulation, ingestive behavior per se, all combinations of the above. If, however, the conclusion is based solely upon the experimental outcome, it may read as follows: *Reinforcement results when an R of a lower independent rate coincides, within temporal limits, with the stimuli governing the occurrence of an R of a higher independent rate.*

A further consideration arises as a result of having measured the independent rates of both the bar press and ingestion. The rate at which pellets were ingested when contingent upon the bar press may approach the independent rate of pellet ingestion; the two rates could not be equal in all cases because of the bar press itself, but the former might approach the latter as the limiting case. Now, if the above were so and each bar press were followed by the ingestion of a pellet, the rate of the pellet-contingent bar pressing would tend to equal the independent rate of pellet ingestion. As it turns out, the proportionality is not that simple; the independent rate of the higher R does *not* limit the contingent rate of the lower-rate R, etc. Nonetheless, the following possibility is of heuristic value: In the idealized case, the dependent or contingent or acquired rate of the lower-rate R tends to equal the independent rate of the higher-rate R.

Are these the only possible conclusions? They may be if only the one case is considered. But if we assign as great a weight to the negative as to the positive finding, and take an inductive leap, we may conclude as follows: *Any response A will reinforce any other response B, if and only if the independent rate of A is greater than that of B.*

This is the induction that will be examined here; not proved, the evidence to be presented is altogether insufficient, but examined for the definition of terms, implications, and, briefly, for quantification possibilities.

TEST METHODS

A test of this account concerns three main questions. First, is a rate differential a sufficient condition for reinforcement? Second, will the effectiveness of the differential vary as different variables constitute the rates of the Rs involved? Third, will the lower-rate R attain exactly the independent rate of the contingent higher-rate R? The latter is not incorporated in the quantitative versions, but is retained here, so as to consider performance factors that may disturb equality between the two Rs.

Tests of these questions require independent measures of both of the Rs involved, but few experiments provide this information. In runway studies there is no measure of the independent rate of the "runway R," no simple way of obtaining such a measure, and typically no measure of the R that terminates the run. Though the Skinner box provides in principle for measures of both Rs, in practice we have no measure of the higher-rate R, viz., ingestion, licking, or, more recently, rising up and sniffing the light source. Methods suited to the present questions are described below. Only the first is adequate, however, and after both are described, advantages of the one will be noted.

Rs Ranked Along a Rate Continuum

If the independent rates of several of an organism's Rs are determined in advance, the Rs can be ranked in terms of rate, and the account tested by arranging all possible contingencies between the ranked Rs. Let A, B, and C represent any three Rs, with independent rates in the order stated. It follows from the account that: A will reinforce both B and C, C will reinforce neither A nor B, and B will reinforce C but not A.

Support for the view of reinforcement as an absolute property is given by both A and C. Since A is and C is not a reinforcer, they exemplify the proposition that some stimuli are and some are not reinforcers—in a broader sense, that species are characterized by a set of stimuli which is and a set which is not reinforcing. The conclusion that reinforcement cannot be explained on the behavior level typically follows from this view, i.e., follows from, first, assigning reinforcement to a set of stimuli, and then noting that the set cannot be physically characterized.

The reinforcement properties of B suggest, however, that the absolute view is based upon failing to consider the rate of the would-be reinforcing R relative to the rate of the to-be-reinforced R. B shows this well since, if the account is accurate, B both is and is not a reinforcer. The reinforcement properties of B suggest, therefore, that "Is this stimulus a reinforcer?" requires the further question "With respect to what Rs?" (In the present terms, if the rate of the R governed by the stimulus in question is greater than that of the to-be-reinforced R, the stimulus can be used as a reinforcer.) But tests that use only one "instrumental" R or that deal solely with rat, ingestion, and usual laboratory parameters are unlikely to show the relativity; this combination assures that the independent rate of the ingestive R will exceed that of the "instrumental" R. Other combinations of species, Rs, and parameters demonstrate the relativity; one which permits reinforcing ingestion is shown in a later section.

The data to be reported here, however, are intended largely as a concrete example; they concern one subject and realize only part of the paradigm. The subject is a Cebus monkey, a species Klüver (1933) has described as being especially manipulative. The Rs ranked in terms of rate are all manipulation Rs; they were used to show the reinforcement of one "instrumental" R by another, i.e., to show that what makes an R "instrumental" is a rate less than that of the contingent R.

An apparatus has been devised which permits giving the subject a number of different manipulanda, either singly or in pairs. When used to determine the independent rate, the different manipulanda are given to the subject, one at a time, under a standard test condition, and with no restrictions upon responding. When the manipulanda are given in pairs, either one can be locked and its operation made contingent upon the prior operation of the other and free manipulandum of the pair. Operation of the free member releases the locked member, and operation of the previously locked member restores its own lock. In this way a consistent schedule is arranged between operation of the free member and release of the locked member. Only one release of the locked member is provided by any number of operations of the free member.

A panel, which holds any one or any pair of manipulanda, is bolted to a port in the monkey's home cage, and all testing is conducted there. Testing is in home cage so as to approximate an environment in which unmeasured Rs are low and stable. The need for a low, asymptotic level of "competing" Rs is emphasized by this account; according to it, a competing R of an independent rate greater than that of the measured R can, by uncontrolled contingencies, reinforce the measured R.

The three Rs used so far are: lever pressing, operation of a horizontally hinged door, and the bin R in which the animal pushes back a light door mounted behind a hole and contacts an empty bin. The independent rates of these Rs were determined by giving the subject the appropriate manipulandum on five to ten 90-minute sessions. The subject was tested daily, but each item was given equally often daily, on alternate days and every third day, so that the mean intertest interval per item was about 48 hours. The long interval was used to maintain R-frequency per item at near maximum from test to test. The independent rate of manipulation Rs varies with several parameters, which will be noted later, but may be kept relatively constant by the usual controls and by avoiding short intertest intervals which result in a cumulative decrement. For the parameters used, the mean frequencies were about 20 for the bin, 50 for the lever, and 100 for the door.

The tests described below followed, by 24 hours, the determination of the independent rates. Six of each kind were given daily in the order described, except for extinction, where only four were run. The tests concern only the door and lever. Because of presenting the same pair of manipulanda at only 24-hour intervals, an over-all decrement occurred. The reinforcement effect occurred despite the decrement.

First, when the subject was given the two manipulanda together, with no contingency between them, so that both the door and lever were free, the lower-rate R appeared to occur at less than its independent rate, while the higher R occurred at about its independent rate. For the six tests, the door averaged about 90, the lever about 36. Whether this kind of situation suppresses the lower-rate R cannot be evaluated because of the decrement associated with an intertest interval less than the one used to determine the independent rates. In the present series, however, this control condition served only to determine if presenting together previously unpaired manipulanda would produce an increment in the lower- rate R. That no increment occurred is the outcome important for the test series.

Second, the lower-rate R was made contingent upon the higher-rate R by now making operation of the lever contingent upon the prior operation of the door. The door averaged about 80, the lever only about 22. Because the higher-rate R tended to occur first and relatively often, the lower-rate manipulandum was actually free both from the outset, and for most, of the test period. However, each lever press left the lever locked. Consequently, the subject could not respond to the lower-rate manipulandum in its customary "bursts," but could make closely spaced lever presses only by alternating higher- with lower-rate Rs. The alternation did not occur, however. Instead, after making a lower-rate R, the subject made varying numbers of higher-rate Rs, after varying intervals, and then returned to the lower-rate R after varying intervals. *Mainly, this lack of alternation between free and locked members demonstrates the failure of a lower-rate R to exert a controlling effect upon a higher-rate R*; it contrasts with the alternation which occurs when the rate differential is in the opposite direction, viz., from low to high. Finally, did the lower-rate R fail to reinforce the higher-rate R because the former did not follow the higher-rate R either sufficiently often or closely? This possibility cannot be ruled out, and finer tests of this point are needed. An important consideration for such tests, however, is that reinforcement is witnessed not by occurrence of an R, but by a rate of occurrence greater than the independent rate.

Third, the rate differential was arranged from low to high by making the higher-rate door R contingent upon the lower-rate lever press. The lever press attained a mean frequency of about 120, which contrasts both with its original independent frequency (about 50) and with that of the door R (about 100). Thus the lower-rate R was not only increased by exceeded the independent frequency of the higher-rate R. On the first two tests the higher-rate R was notably reduced, though it attained its original independent frequency on the last two of the six tests. Three factors are notable here. (*a*) Because of its contingent status, the higher-rate R could not occur in its usual "bursts"; this may account for the reduced rate on the early tests, and an accommodation to this factor, for the steady increase in the higher-rate R that took place across the six tests. (*b*) As the free R, the lever press could and to some extent did occur in "bursts," which may account partly for the fact that on all tests the number of lower-rate Rs exceeded the number of higher-rate Rs. An average of about 80% of individual lever presses were followed by a door R; this represents the alternation between the two Rs. The percentage did not increase across tests, though there were essentially no "bursts" of lever presses in any test not directly followed by a door R. Hurwitz (1958) has reported a case for rats and food-contingent bar pressing where, at an intermediate stage of training, bar presses exceeded pellets ingested, though the two Rs alternated with further training. The ultimate performance proportionality between the two Rs may be affected by the absolute rate of the higher R or by the difference between the rates of the two Rs. (*c*) Responding increased across this series of tests, in contrast to both test conditions above.

Fourth, extinction was run by removing the door from the panel, closing the port which the door had occupied with a blank, and giving the subject only the lever. This is the situation in which the independent rate was originally determined. As an extinction condition it is blunt: the stimuli governing the higher-rate R are grossly absent. Nonetheless, the subject pressed the lever at an elevated rate (78 and 56) on the first two sessions and then dropped progressively on the last two sessions to a level below the original independent rate.

While these data suggest that a rate differential is a sufficient condition for reinforcement, they have been reported as the most concrete means of describing a test method. Comparable tests are being extended to the greater number of Cebus now available.

Measuring Independent Rate in the Context of the Test

In contrast to the method described, where the independent rates are determined in *advance* of the contingency tests, a second method consists in measuring the independent rates in the context of the test. For example, the runway or choice-point can be combined with an apparatus that permits measuring the rate of the Rs that occur in the end boxes. Runway speed can then be examined for its relation to rate of end-box Rs, or choice-behavior for its relation to the difference between the rates of the Rs in the two end boxes. Since, however, this account is stated in terms of rate, it cannot treat either runway speed or percent turns. But even at the level of suggestion, data obtained with the second method may be misleading in their interpretation for this account.

When rates are determined during rather than before the contingency tests, the resulting data will relate *number* of higher-rate Rs to the dependent variable, e.g., number of end-box Rs to speed of the run. If we designate the "runway R" as A, and Rs that terminate runs for groups tested with different end-box items as B and C, the tests will contrast, say, A → BB with A → CCCCC. In the first method, however, not more than one higher-rate R need follow a lower-rate R. In the manipulation case, for example, only one door R followed any lever press. Consequently, the contrast may be between A → B and A → C, where A is a common lower-rate R, and B and C are higher-rate Rs with independent rates determined in advance of the contingency tests. The first method emphasizes, therefore, as the second does not, that in order to produce an increment in the lower-rate R, only *one* higher-rate R need follow the lower-rate R.

In the light of this emphasis, the first method suggests further that one contingency, rather than repeated trials, between Rs of different independent rates will produce an increment in the lower-rate R. That is, is A → B + A → B + A → B, etc., produces an increment in A, so will A → B. In the manipulation example above, this suggests that *one* contingency between the lever press and door R will produce an increment in the lever press, the increment to be evaluated by comparing an extinction measure with the previously determined independent rate. Except as discontinuities are considered either at the level of number of contingencies or interval between contingencies, one contingency between one lower- and one higher-rate R would be considered to produce an increment in the lower-rate R.

Especially for quantification possibilities are these important considerations. If single contingencies are effective, then the differences between *mean* rates, which we are using here, can *not* be made the basis of reinforcement. That is, since the single R cannot have a mean value, a function relating changes in the lower-rate R to some relation between lower- and higher-rate Rs must employ R values other than mean rate. Considerations of this kind, however, concern learning rather than performance. For the data treated here mean rate will suffice; the measure may be viewed as an approximation of whatever R value may serve ultimately to permit the kind of function that is being sought.

REINFORCEMENT OF CONSUMMATORY Rs

It follows from this account that consummatory Rs are reinforcible, provided that a condition can be found in which the organism's rate of, say, ingestion is less than the rate at which it performs some nonconsummatory R. This rate relation, however, is the reverse of the one which obtains in the usual laboratory test. There the "instrumental" R is a noningestive R, the contingent R a consummatory R, and the rate relations such that the latter is substantially higher in independent rate than the former. The food deprivation, which is part of the usual test, assures a high independent rate of ingestion. Though it may also increase the independent rate of the "instrumental" R, the increment given the latter will not offset the advantage of the ingestive R, since particularly the maximum independent rate of ingestion will exceed that of the "instrumental" R. To use ingestion as the "instrumental" R, however, requires that it now have an independent rate less than that of the contingent and would-be reinforcing R. The ease of establishing this condition appears to vary with the species.

In the rat, and perhaps the rodents generally, the difficulty begins with the fact that ad lib. maintenance does not lead to a rate of ingestion which is less than the independent rate of the common and engineerable nonconsummatory Rs. The momentary rate of the rat's ad lib. eating session is unusually constant (Baker, 1952), and this constant tends to be higher than the maximum independent rate of, say, the bar or light-contingent bar press, at least for those values of food, bar, and light intensity which we have tried. While there may be a low-rate food and high-rate light intensity which together will yield a reversal of the customary rate relations between ingestive and noningestive Rs, we have not found the values.

Moreover, reducing the ad lib. eating constant by a deprivation technique does not facilitate the reinforcement of eating. By first depriving the rat of food, a low eating rate can be obtained; following deprivation the rat does not eat at a constant rate, but under some circumstances begins at a value greater than the ad lib. constant and terminates at a very low value (Baker, 1952). However, when the terminal eating rate is low, the independent rates of the other Rs may be equally low. And if satiation effects are broad, reducing the rate of all Rs, little reinforcement of any kind will be possible.

Other techniques may work. For example, the wheel turn which, in the rat, has a substantially higher independent rate than the bar press, and which Kagan and Berkun (1954) have shown to reinforce the bar press, may serve to reinforce ingestion. But the difficulty of finding stimulus pairs and parameters which will provide the desired rate relations in the rat comments merely on a species peculiarity of the rat.

Measures on a Cebus monkey indicate that parameters can be found under which the monkey operates some manipulanda at a rate greater than that at which it ingests most foods. Beyond the Cebus, however, the child may be the ideal subject. For certain age levels and socioeconomic classes, the desired rate relations appear to obtain within the parameters of the child's daily life. The study described below shows that a reversal of the usual laboratory rate relations between eating and noneating Rs can be obtained with the child and, that when it is, eating is reinforcible.

A pinball machine (PBM), rewired for continuous operation, and a candy dispenser, the two placed side by side, comprised the experimental arrangement. A PBM was used instead of the simpler devices in use with the monkeys, since the present purpose was less to analyze manipulation than to obtain as a high a manipulation rate as possible. Candy consisted of constant-size chocolate bits, delivered one at a time by a conveyer belt into a dish each time the child ate the piece in the dish. Thirty-three children, the entire first-grade class of a public school served as subjects. Their average age was 6.7 years.

Each child was tested twice, the first serving to determine the subject's relative R frequency to the candy and the PBM, and the second as the test of the hypothesis. Both tests lasted 15 minutes and used the same materials; the second was given three to four days after the first.

On the first test, both the candy and PBM were unrestrictedly available. The child was led to a position midway between the two devices and told, "We have two games here; you can play both of them as much as you like." After demonstrating both devices, the experimenter said, "I'll be back here sitting down," and then retired behind a one-way viewing screen. Sixty-one per cent of the children made more

PBM responses than they ate pieces of candy. In Table 1, they comprise the larger group labeled "manipulators"; those labeled "eaters" represent the 39% who ate more pieces of candy than the made PBM responses (three ties which occurred were scored as "eaters").

On the second test, the availability of candy and the PBM were made subject to either of two contingency relations, E-M or M-E. For E-M, each operation of the PBM was contingent upon the prior ingestion of a piece of candy, whereas for M-E, each piece of candy was contingent upon the prior operation of the PBM. Both the "manipulators" and the "eaters" were randomly divided, and half of each main group tested under E-M and half under M-E. For "manipulators" E-M was the experimental condition and M-E the control; the reverse held for the "eaters." What characterizes both experimental conditions is that the higher-rate R is contingent upon the lower-rate R ("manipulators" must eat to manipulate; "eaters" must manipulate to eat). Control conditions make the higher-rate R freely available, as in Test 1, and thus provide a measure of changes in the lower-rate R which may occur independent of the rate-differential contingency.

Like the magazine-trained rat that responds to the inoperative magazine rather than pressing the bar, "manipulators" in the experimental condition "fiddled" with the inoperative PBM, ignoring the candy, while "eaters" stood by the empty dish, ignoring the PBM. Consequently, because of the time-limited session, instructions were used to establish the first contingency (defined as a PBM response followed by the ingestion of candy, or vice versa, regardless of the time between the two responses). If three minutes elapsed without a response, the experimenter said, "Remember, there are two games." If this failed, he then said, "I wonder what would happen if you ate a piece of candy? Played the PBM?" according to whichever was appropriate. Once a contingency occurred, nothing further was said.

The results are shown in Table 1 in terms of the increase in the number of lower-rate Rs from the first to the second test. For "manipulators" this is the increase in number of pieces of candy eaten; for "eaters," increase in number of PBM responses. As may be seen in Table 1, control-condition increments are small compared with those for the experimental condition, and the mean differences within both main groups are significant at less than the 1% level of confidence. In both cases, a rate-differential contingency increased the frequency of the lower-rate R: While candy reinforced manipulation for the "eaters," the PBM reinforced eating for the "manipulators."

More elegant demonstrations with nonverbal organisms are needed, but the above results suggest that the uniqueness of consummatory Rs does not consist in their unreinforcibility. They may be distinctive in the high rates which they attain relative to the other Rs, though the rate relations possible for the different Rs appear to vary with the species. For example, Lorenz (1957, pp. 129-175) has noted that stalking in certain predators commonly attains, in present terms, an independent rate greater than that of ingestion. As a survival mechanism, perhaps there may be, however, a number of parameters in all species under which the independent rate of ingestion exceeds that of the other Rs.
Finally, the above study is of interest for its suggestions concerning the relativity of reinforcement. That species are *not* characterized by a specific set of reinforcing stimuli, and

TABLE 1
INCREASE IN LOWER RATE RESPONSE FROM FIRST TO SECOND TEST

Manipulators

Increment in number of pieces of candy eaten per subject

E-M (Exp.)	M-E (Control)
16	0
16	4
19	19
22	0
14	5
14	10
28	0
19	0
26	7
81	a
Mean = 25.5	Mean = 5
Median = 19	Median = 4

Eaters

Increment in number of pieces of PBM responses per subject

M-E (Exp.)	E-M (Control)
10	5
8	0
7	0
1	0
16	7
9	0
16	
Mean = 9.4	Mean = 2
Median =9.0	Median = 0

that this mistaken absolute view has resulted from failing to consider the rate of the would-be-reinforcing R *relative* to that of the to-be-reinforced R, are main suggestions of the study. Indeed, that reinforcement is not only a relative property but, in some instances, a reversible one is also indicated. For example, there would seem little doubt but that with sufficient food deprivation "manipulators" would become "eaters" and, consequently, that the R which had been "instrumental" could be made reinforcing, and vice versa. A comprehensive treatment of both the relativity and reversibility is reserved for a later paper. Here the main point is simply this: Any stimulus to which the species responds can be used as a reinforcer, provided only that the rate of the R governed by the stimulus is greater than that of some other R.

"DRIVE"

Effect of the Intertest Interval

While the broad effects of food deprivation are apparently unique, the effect of the interval between feeding sessions *specifically* upon ingestion may represent a general function, one holding for the independent rate of any movement and the interval between occurrences of the movement.

For example, Butler (1957) has shown visual-contingent responding in the rhesus monkey to increase with deprivation for visual stimuli. Hill (1956) has reported wheel turning in the rat to increase with the confinement interval. For independent groups of rats tested at intervals of 12, 24, and 48 hours, Premack, Collier, and Roberts (1957) found both the bar press and light-contingent bar press to be increasing functions of the intertest interval. For the same group of rats rotated through five intertest intervals ranging from 3 to 48 hours, and tested eight consecutive times at each interval, Premack (1958) found the light-contingent bar press to be an increasing function of the interval. Finally, Premack and Bahwell (in press) found lever pressing in a Cebus monkey to be generally increasing function of deprivation for the lever. Given the same lever on 252 half-hour sessions, an equal number of sessions at about 15-, 39-, and 65-hour intervals, the monkey responded 4,109 times; significantly most often at the largest interval; and showed no decline across the about 5-month test period. Continued examination of species movement may reveal differences in temporal parameters, but a common increasing function for independent rate of all movement and deprivation for the stimuli upon which the movement depends.

As to the general effects of food deprivation, some parallel may possibly be found in depriving the organism of *any* behavior which, like ingestion, has a high independent rate and is recurrent throughout the organism's life. For a nonconsummatory R, the wheel turn tends to have these characteristics of the rat. Slonaker (1927) has reported that rats turn a continuously available wheel at a substantial rate during about two-thirds of their life. Moreover, the decrement in the wheel turn reported to occur across repeated tests (Hill, 1956) does *not* distinguish the wheel turn from ingestion. We have found rats to ingest significantly more of a new food on the first than on succeeding days; when shifted from ad lib. lab food to Gaines dog meal, rats ate a mean of 19.98 grams the first day and only 14.19 grams by Day 14 ($p < .01$, $F = 2.41$, df 13/143); across days decline has been found also for Noyes pellets. On the basis of these parallels, Premack and Premack (1958) studied ad lib. food consumption as a function of deprivation for a continuously available activity wheel. When deprived of the wheel, rats ate significantly more than they had when the wheel was available and than a control maintained without the wheel. In two replications, grams intake attained a maximum on about the third post-wheel deprivation day, and intake did not return to baseline for about 14 days.

What seems most likely to distinguish food deprivation from deprivation for stimuli governing noningestive Rs are the different relations within the stimulus classes. Let A, B, C, and D subsume the members of the food class. Though no data can be found on this point, it seems probable that organisms deprived of the class, and tested on, say, A, would ingest more of A than a control maintained on B, C, and D, and tested on A. In the case of nonfood stimuli, however, depriving for increasing amounts of the stimulus class appears to *reduce* the over-all response level. Ochocki and Premack (1958) maintained one group of rats in the colony, another group in light-tight, sound-treated icebox hulls, and tested subgroups of both main groups on the light-contingent bar press at intervals of 3, 12, and 48 hours. While responding was an increasing function of the intertest interval for both main groups, frequency was significantly lower at all intervals for the stimulus deprived group.

"Drive"

Whereas in the Hull-Spence system, hours of food deprivation is related to D, and D ultimately to performance, in this account hours of food deprivation is first examined for its effect upon the independent rate of ingestion. Subsequently, the independent rate of ingestion is examined for its effect upon lower-rate Rs that lead to ingestion. Though tradition has set the ingestive case off, by calling it "drive" or "motivation," in this account the effect of the ingestive contingency does not differ in modus operandi from that of *any* higher-rate R—manipulative, locomotive, or sensory—upon the paired lower-rate R.

Of the paradigms which can be used to test the reinforcement generalization, the one most relevant to the usual "drive" study is the following: The *same* higher-rate R, when at different values of independent rate, is made contingent upon a common lower-rate R. Thus, in the customary "drive" study the higher-rate R for all groups is ingestion, and the differences in hours of food deprivation represent possible differences in the independent rates of ingestion for the several groups. This paradigm contrasts with one in which *different* higher-rate Rs are made contingent upon a common lower-rate R, but the prediction made by the reinforcement generalization is the same for both paradigms, viz., the increment in the lower-rate R will be greater, the greater the independent rate of the contingent higher-rate R.

Because the intervening variable approach has dominated the field, little data relevant to this account can be found. The literature shows two separate approaches: (*a*) determinants of the independent rate of ingestion, and (*b*) effect of hours of food deprivation upon food-contingent Rs. Tests of this account require that the two approaches be united in the same study.

Consider as a typical "drive" study one in which several groups are differentiated in terms of hours of food deprivation and tested on the same food-contingent, lower-rate R. To convert this study into a test of this account requires two measures, both of which are omitted by the intervening variable approach. First, we require the effect of hours of food deprivation upon the independent rate of ingestion, and second, the effect of hours of food deprivation upon the independent rate of the R that is to be used as the "instrumental" R. Food deprivation may affect the rate of the "instrumental" R *before* it has been made food-contingent in the study, and the effect may be different for the several groups. Moreover, for certain deprivation procedures, hours of food deprivation may affect differently the "instrumental" and ingestive Rs.

A recent study by Birch, Burnstein, and Clark (1958), coupled with a less recent one by Bousfield and Elliott (1934), approximates the methodology of measuring, first, the effect of the independent variable upon ingestion and, second, the effect of the ingestive contingency upon the lower-rate R. Together they also provide a bit of information as to whether the effect of hours of food deprivation is the same for the "instrumental" and ingestive Rs.

In both studies essentially the same independent variable was used. Rats were first maintained for protracted periods on a fixed deprivation schedule and then tested at varying hours after their last feeding. The studies differ in terms of their dependent variables. In what amounts to an extinction measure, Birch et al. found that number of approaches to the empty feeding device was greatest at the previously scheduled feeding time, less for times both greater and less than the scheduled feeding time. Bousfield and Elliott considered the effect of the same variable upon ingestion itself. They found the rate of ingestion, as well as grams intake, to be greatest for the group tested at the scheduled feeding time, less for groups tested at all other times. Thus, the relation to hours of food deprivation was the same, both for the extinction measure of the food-contingent R and the independent rate of ingestion. And in neither case was this the monotonic increasing relation that has been shown, with other deprivation procedures, to hold for grams intake and hours of food deprivation (Lawrence & Mason, 1955).

Birch et al. next tested runway speed as a function of the same variable. On the first trial, *before* a run had led to ingestion, speed and hours of food deprivation were not significantly related, though there was an indication of increased speed with greater deprivation. However, on the second trial, *after* a run had led to ingestion, runway speed was greatest for the group tested at the scheduled feeding time, less for groups tested at all other times. Thus, while comparison of the first-trial results with those by Bousfield and Elliott suggests that, for this deprivation procedure, hours of food deprivation may affect differently the ingestive and "instrumental" Rs, once the "instrumental" R had led to ingestion it was related to hours of food deprivation in the same way as was the independent rate of ingestion. Taken in sum, these results suggest that the independent rate of ingestion is itself the direct determinant of changes in ingestion-contingent lower-rate Rs, in contrast to hours of food deprivation, which acts merely to affect the independent rate of ingestion, as well as possibly the independent rate of the "instrumental" R. Moreover, when compared with the manipulation example, they suggest that the effect of a higher-rate ingestive R upon the paired lower-rate R does not differ in-modus operandi from that of a higher-rate manipulation R upon the paired lower-rate R.

Birch et al. placed only two pellets in the runway end box; if one had been used, we would predict the same group differences. The assumption here, as noted earlier, is that an increment in the lower-rate R, that is some function of the relation between the mean rates of the lower and higher Rs, can be produced though only one higher R follows the lower R. An increment occurred in the lever press, for example, though only one door R followed any lever press. Mean rate is being used as an approximation, however. If contingency changes in the lower-rate R are to be calculated directly from precontingency measures of both lower- and higher-rate Rs, it is already evident that R values other than mean rate will be required.

The broad effects of both food deprivation and satiation are unique, but these distinctions notwithstanding, the ingestive case is subsumed by the reinforcement generalization on the following grounds. First, a rate produced by food deprivation does not differ in its reinforcement effect from a rate produced by any other operation. Second, the modus operandi of the ingestive contingency is the same as that of any higher-rate R. Third, the shape of the function for increments in ingestion-contingent lower-rate Rs and hours of food deprivation is directly predictable from the function for the independent rate of ingestion and hours of food deprivation. If further study bears these considerations out, then for the inferences of the intervening variable approach there may be substituted measurement of the independent rates of the lower- and higher-rate Rs.

COMMENSURABILITY OF BEHAVIOR UNITS

In the tests of independent rate described earlier, the subject was simply given test items under a condition that was the same for all items. No restrictions were placed upon the items, the subject determined its own units of responding, and the records, as measured, consisted of a succession of manipulanda operations, ingestions of food units, and, in some unreported work, succession of wheel revolutions. No criterion for dividing these behavior segments was provided. In effect, each segment of unrestricted responding was divided by the anthropomorphic unit, e.g., "lever press," "pellet ingested," etc. Though, at this stage, the main justification for these R units is that the comparisons "worked," in retrospect it is possible to make explicit the assumptions underlying the choice of units and thus to provide a formal criterion for selecting the R unit by which to count the independent rate of any segment of unrestricted responding.

The assumption which is here applied to all behavior segments generated by unrestricted test items is that each segment contains what might be called a smallest possible unit (spu). The spu *is defined as that unit which gives the same amount of responding as is given by free responding, when in fact stimulus restrictions force the organism to respond by* spu.

In the ingestive case, spu would seem to amount to the intact chain, i.e., to a combination of seizes, bites, chews, and swallows which is recurrent throughout the unrestricted segment, though make-up of the combination may vary with the organism, as well as with degree of food deprivation, size of pellet, consistency, etc. To treat the intact ingestive chain as the spu amounts to considering that: if stimulus restrictions forced the organism to respond by discrete chains, in equal periods of stimulus availability, it would ingest essentially as many pellets as when pellets were free and it responded by its characteristic multiple of intact chains. Tests of this assumption can be made by more complex procedures than were used here; they would involve variously restricting both the number of food units available at any one time and the intervals between their availability. However, the contingency situation itself amounts in part to such a test, since there the occurrence of the lower-rate R imposes intervals between multiples of the organism's free responding units. Consequently, if the single intact chain were made the contingency unit, and the asymptotic amount of pellets ingested in that situation tended to equal the amount ingested in tests of unrestricted responding, evidence would exist for treating the intact chain as the spu.

To perform the above test requires a knowledge of the number of intact chains that occur per pellet or multiple of pellets. Since pellets vary as to size, in order to count the unrestricted ingestive segment by intact chains the pellets would have first to be calibrated in terms of the organism's R units. The independent rate for the segment of unrestricted ingestion would then amount to: number of pellets ingested per unit time by number of chains per pellet or multiple of pellets. Though calibration will make some occasion for the direct observation of behavior unavoidable, calibration is unavoidable; if the experimenter's stimulus-effect measurement unit were simply equated with the R unit, the independent rate of the segment could be made to vary with the choice of food units.

Seizing, biting, chewing, etc., cannot be used to count the independent rate of the unrestricted ingestive segment, except as the correlation between certain of these units and the intact chain is known. In the context of unrestricted ingestion, it may be expected that the smaller units do not occur at their independent rate. Seizing may be affected by biting, biting by chewing, etc., though to determine which reinforce which others would require testing various combinations of them in isolation of the rest, insofar as that is possible. When tested in isolation, each of the smaller units would be expected to stabilize at some value of independent rate, but in each case at values less than that of the intact chain.

In the context of unrestricted ingestion, certain of the smaller units appear to occur multiply within the chain, and thus at a rate greater than that of the intact chain. The within-chain arrangement may be such as to schedule ratios of certain of the smaller units with respect to others; for example, a number of chews may antecede a swallow. But that the within-chain rate of all such units is dependent, not independent, could be shown, presumably, either by testing them in isolation or, what would amount to the same thing, by making any one of them the contingency unit. As contingency units, seizing or biting or chewing, etc., would be expected to fall short of their within-chain rates. And, in general, when the rate of the contingency unit does not approach the rate at which the same unit occurred when the unit was a part of the segment of unrestricted responding, there is evidence that the segment was not counted by the spu, but by some unit of dependent rate.

The manipulation case reported suggests that single operations of the manipulanda may comprise the spu for segments of unrestricted manipulation. Both rats and monkeys appear to manipulate in "bursts," i.e., by multiples of lever presses, etc. Nonetheless, when the Cebus was given the door in contingent status, and thus restricted to discrete operations of the door, the immediate and substantial reduction in the door Rs was transient. By the fifth contingency test, the door R had reacquired its original rate, though it was then limited to discrete occurrences in contrast to the multiples characteristic of unrestricted manipulation.

An essential parallel between intact ingestion and manipulation chains may possibly be shown as follows: for manipulanda which yield different independent rates of operation, *contacts* to the same inoperable manipulanda may vary little and in all cases stabilize at independent rates substantially less than those for operations. Indeed, in the Cebus the generally high manipulation rate may make it possible to schedule, say, lever presses with respect to lever contacts. Though species may adapt to disrupted multiples of intact chains, the adaptability cannot be thoroughgoing. Instead, for repeated tests at the same intertest intervals, different movements of the species may be expected to stabilize at different independent rates. Work of this kind would further the brilliant, pioneer investigations by Schiller (1952) concerning species-specific movements in the chimp, and the relevance of these movements to what has been called insight.

In locomotion a blind, empirical approach is necessitated by the relative absence of anthropomorphic units coupled with the difficulty of observation. With the rat and the activity wheel the spu may possibly be found by testing across a series of decreasing stimulus restrictions. Starting with a small fraction of a revolution, the distance the wheel is made available on any one operation may be gradually increased until a per operation distance is found which, in equal periods of wheel availability, yields a total distance of use equal to that for the unrestricted wheel. If such a unit exists, then the independent rate of the segment for unrestricted wheel turning would amount to: number of revolutions per unit time by number of spu's per revolution or multiples of revolutions. This technique would accommodate differences in wheel diameters, and would not require topographical calibration of the measurement unit.

A different and more general approach to the problem of determining the independent rate for behavior segments lacking in anthropomorphic units has been suggested by MacCorquodale.[2] In brief, the method consists in first ranking Rs that are easily counted. Provided the reinforcement generalization holds across the group of ranked Rs, their rate continuum is then used to locate the independent rate of arbitrary units taken from behavior segments that are difficult to count.

Finally, that rate is a property common to disparate movements and that a method may possibly be found for assigning but one value of independent rate to any segment of unrestricted responding are themselves of little consequence. Advantages depend upon using the common property as the basis for a function, for only then do the disparate movements become commensurable in terms of their values for the common property.

The function that is entailed by the reinforcement generalization is nonspecific, though within the limits of that function there is a definite commensurability between the different Rs. Because the generalization treats a rate differential as a sufficient condition for reinforcement, ranking the Rs of an organism in terms of their independent rates should permit predicting which Rs will reinforce which others. Only the R with the highest independent rate should be a universal reinforcer, only the lowest R fail to reinforce any other R, while those intermediate on the continuum should reinforce all those below themselves and be reinforced in turn by all those above. Moreover, all Rs of like independent rate would be equal; they would reinforce the same lower-rate Rs and be reinforced in turn by a common group of higher-rate Rs. The function is nonspecific, however, in that it does not permit specifying the dependent rate that will be attained by the lower-rate R. And what is being sought is the function that will permit calculating dependent rate from measures of the independent rates of the two Rs involved in any instance of reinforcement.

References

Baker, R.A., Jr. A study of the feeding behavior of laboratory animals. Unpublished doctoral dissertation, Stanford Univer., 1952.

Birch, D., Burnstein, E., & Clark, R.A. Response strength as a function of hours of food deprivation under a controlled maintenance schedule. *J. comp. physiol. Psychol.*, 1958, 51, 350-354.

Bousfield, W.A., & Elliott, M.H. The effect of fasting on the eating behavior of rats. *J. genel. Psychol.,* 1934, 45, 227-237.

Butler, R.A. The effect of deprivation of visual incentives on visual exploration motivation in monkeys. *J. comp. physiol. Psychol.*, 1957, 50, 177-179.

Hill, W.F. Activity as an autonomous drive. *J. comp. physiol. Psychol.*, 1956, 49, 15-19.

Hurwitz, H.M.B. A source of error in estimating the number of reinforcements in a lever-pressing apparatus. *J. exp. Anal. Behav.*, 1958, 1, 149-152.

Kagan, J., & Berkun, M. The reward value of running activity. *J. comp. physiol. Psychol.*, 1954, 47, 108.

Klüver, H. *Behavior mechanisms in monkeys*. Chicago: Univer. Chicago Press, 1933.

Lawrence, D.H., & Mason, W.A. Food intake in the rat as a function of deprivation intervals and feeding rhythms. *J. comp. physiol. Psychol.,* 1955, 48, 267-271.

Lorenz, K. The conception of instinctive behavior. In C. H. Schiller (Ed.), *Instinctive behavior.* New York: International Univer. Press, 1957. Pp. 129-175.

Ochocki, F.J., & Premack, D. The joint effect of stimulus deprivation and the intertest interval on the frequency of light-contingent bar pressing. Paper read at Midwestern Psychological Association, Detroit, May 1958.

Premack, A.J., & Premack, D. Increments in ad libitum eating as a function of deprivation for wheel-turning behavior. Paper read at Midwestern Psychological Association, Detroit, May 1958.

Premack, D. Deprivation-performance function for light-contingent bar pressing as determined by the number of consecutive tests per deprivation interval. Paper read at Midwestern Psychological Association, Detroit, May 1958.

Premack, D., & Bahwell, R. Operant level lever pressing by a monkey as a function of intertest interval. *J. exp. Anal. Behav.*, in press.

Premack, D., Collier, G., & Roberts, C.L. Frequency of light contingent bar pressing as a function of the amount of deprivation for light. *Amer. Psychologist*, 1957, 12, 411. (Abstract).

Schiller, P. von. Innate constituents of complex responses in primates. *Psychol. Rev.*, 1952, 59, 177-191.

Slonaker, J.R. Long fluctuations in voluntary activity of the albino rat. *Amer. J. Physiol.*, 1926, 77, 503-508.

Footnotes:

[1] This paper was prepared during the author's tenure as a USPHS postdoctoral research fellow. Part of this paper was read at the Midwestern Psychological Association, Detroit, May 1958, in a symposium on reinforcement. I am deeply indebted to my wife, Anne James Premack, for her assistance with both the formulation and clarification of this account.

[2] K. MacCorquodale. Personal communication, November 1958.

SELECTION BY CONSEQUENCES

B.F. Skinner (1981). *Science, 213(4507),* 501-504.

In his autobiography Skinner referred to this article as "Life, Mind, and Zeitgeist", echoing what Karl Popper called a three world view, the worlds of genetic, behavioral, and cultural evolution. Skinner's thesis is that there is a unifying interdependence between these three worlds; namely, the Darwinian algorithm of variation, selection, and retention.

The history of human behavior, if we may take it to begin with the origin of life on Earth, is possibly exceeded in scope only by the history of the universe. Like astronomer and cosmologist, the historian proceeds only by reconstructing what may have happened rather than by reviewing recorded facts. The story presumably began, not with a big bang, but with that extraordinary moment when a molecule came into existence which had the power to reproduce itself. It was then that selection by consequences made its appearance as a causal mode. Reproduction was itself a first consequence and it led, through natural selection, to the evolution of cells, organs, and organisms which reproduced themselves under increasingly diverse conditions.

What we call behavior evolved as a set of functions furthering the interchange between organism and environment. In a fairly stable world it could be as much a part of the genetic endowment of a species as digestion, respiration, or any other biological function. The involvement with the environment, however, imposed limitations. The behavior functioned well only under conditions fairly similar to those under which it was selected. Reproduction under a much wider range of conditions became possible with the evolution of two processes through which individual organisms acquired behavior appropriate to novel environments. Through respondent (Pavlovian) conditioning, responses prepared in advance by natural selection could come under the control of new stimuli. Through operant conditioning, new responses could be strengthened ("reinforced") by events which immediately followed them.

A Second Kind of Selection

Operant conditioning is a second kind of selection by consequences. It must have evolved in parallel with two other products of the same contingencies of natural selection—a susceptibility to reinforcement by certain kinds of consequences and a supply of behavior less specifically committed to eliciting or releasing stimuli. (Most operants are selected from behavior which has little or no relation to such stimuli.)

When the selecting consequences are the same, operant conditioning and natural selection work together redundantly. For example, the behavior of a duckling in following its mother is apparently the product not only of natural selection (ducklings tend to move in the direction of large moving objects) but also of an evolved susceptibility to reinforcement by proximity to such an object, as Peterson has shown (1). The common consequence is that the duckling stays near its mother. (Imprinting is a different process, close to respondent conditioning.)

Since a species which quickly acquires behavior appropriate to a given environment has less need for an innate repertoire, operant conditioning could not only supplement the natural selection of behavior, it could replace it. There were advantages favoring such a change. When members of a species eat a certain food simply because eating it has had survival value, the food does not need to be, and presumably is not, a reinforcer. Similarly, when sexual behavior is simply a product of natural selection, sexual contact does not need to be, and presumably is not, a reinforcer. But when, through the evolution of special susceptibilities, food and sexual contact become reinforcing, new forms of behavior can be set up. New ways of gathering, processing, and ultimately cultivating foods and new ways of behaving sexually or of behaving in ways which lead only eventually to sexual reinforcement can be shaped and maintained. The behavior so conditioned is not necessarily adaptive: foods are eaten which are not healthful and sexual behavior strengthened which is not related to procreation.

Much of the behavior studied by ethologists—courtship, mating, care of the young, intraspecific aggression, defense of territory, and so on—is social. It is within easy range of natural selection because other members of a species are one of the most stable features of the environment of a species. Innate social repertoires are supplemented by imitation. By running when others run, for example, an animal responds to releasing stimuli to which it has not itself been exposed. A different kind of imitation, with a much wider range, results from the fact that contingencies of reinforcement which induce one organism to behave in a given way will often affect another organism when it behaves in the same way. An imitative repertoire which brings the imitator under the control of new contingencies is therefore acquired.

The human species presumably became much more social when its vocal musculature came under operant control. Cries of alarm, mating calls, aggressive threats, and other kinds of vocal behavior can be modified through operant conditioning, but apparently only with respect to the occasions upon which they occur or their rate of occurrence (2). The ability of the human species to acquire new forms through selection by consequences presumably resulted from the evolution of a special innervation of the vocal musculature, together with a supply of vocal behavior not strongly under the control of stimuli or releasers—the babbling of children from which verbal operants are selected. No new susceptibility to reinforcement was needed because the consequences of verbal behavior are distinguished only by the fact that they are mediated by other people (3).

The development of environmental control over the vocal musculature greatly extended the help one person receives from others. By behaving verbally people cooperate more successfully in common ventures. By taking advice, heeding warnings, following instructions, and observing rules, they profit from what others have already learned. Ethical practices are strengthened by codifying them in laws and special techniques of ethical and intellectual self-management are devised and taught. Self-knowledge or awareness emerges when one person asks another such a question as "What are you going to do?" or "Why did you do that?" The invention of the alphabet spread these advantages over great distances and periods of time .They have long been said to give the human species its unique position, although it is possible that what is unique is simply the extension of operant control to the vocal musculature.

A Third Kind of Selection

Verbal behavior greatly increased the importance of a third kind of selection by consequences, the evolution of special environments or cultures. The process presumably begins at the level of the individual. A better way of making a tool, growing food, or teaching a child is reinforced by its consequence—the tool, the food, or a useful helper, respectively. A culture evolves when practices originating in this way contribute to the success of the practicing group in solving its problems. It is the effect on the group, not the reinforcing consequences for individual members, which is responsible for the evolution of the culture.

In summary, then, human behavior is the joint product of (i) the contingencies of survival responsible for the natural selection of the species and (ii) the contingencies of reinforcement responsible for the repertoires acquired by its members, including (iii) the special contingencies maintained by an evolved social environment. (Ultimately, of course, it is all a matter of natural selection, since operant conditioning is an evolved process, of which cultural practices are special applications.)

Similarities and Differences

Each of the three levels of variation and selection has its own discipline—the first, biology; the second, psychology; and the third, anthropology. Only the second, operant conditioning, occurs at a speed at which it can be observed from moment to moment. Biologists and anthropologists study the processes through which variations arise and are selected but they merely reconstruct the evolution of a species or culture. Operant conditioning is selection in progress. It resembles a hundred million years of natural selection or a thousand years of the evolution of a culture compressed into a very short period of time.

The immediacy of operant conditioning has certain practical advantages. For example, when a currently adaptive feature is presumably too complex to have occurred in its present form as a single variation, it is usually explained as the product of a sequence of simpler variations, each with its own survival value. It is standard practice in evolutionary theory to look for such sequences, and anthropologists and historians have reconstructed the stages through which moral and ethical codes, art, music, literature, science, technology, and so on, have presumably evolved. A complex operant, however, can actually be "shaped through successive approximation" by arranging a graded series of contingencies of reinforcement (4).

A current question at level i has parallels at levels ii and iii. If natural selection is a valid principle, why do many species remain unchanged for thousands or even millions of years? Presumably the answer is either that no variations have occurred or that those which occurred were not selected by the prevailing contingencies. Similar questions may be asked at levels ii and iii. Why do people continue to do things in the same way for many years, and why do groups of people continue to observe old practices for centuries? The answers are presumably the same: either new variations (new forms of behavior or new practices) have not appeared or those which have appeared have not been selected by the prevailing contingencies (of reinforcement or of the survival of the group). At all three levels a sudden, possibly extensive, change is explained as due to new variations selected by prevailing contingencies or to new contingencies. Competition with other species, persons, or cultures may or may not be involved. Structural constraints may also play a part at all three levels.

Another issue is the definition or identity of a species, person, or culture. Traits in a species and practices in a culture are transmitted from generation to generation, but reinforced behavior is "transmitted" only in the sense of remaining part of the repertoire of the individual. Where species and cultures are defined by restrictions imposed upon transmission—by genes and chromosomes and, say, geographical isolation respectively—a problem of definition (or identity) arises at level ii only when different contingencies of reinforcement create different repertoires, as selves or persons.

Traditional Explanatory Schemes

As a causal mode, selection by consequences was discovered very late in the history of science—indeed, less than a century and a half ago—and it is still not fully recognized or understood, especially at levels ii and iii. The facts for which it is responsible have been forced into the causal pattern of classical mechanics, and many of the explanatory schemes elaborated in the process must now be discarded. Some of them have great prestige and are strongly defended at all three levels. Here are four examples:

A prior act of creation. (i) Natural selection replaces a very special creator and is still challenged because it does so. (ii) Operant conditioning provides a similarly controversial account of the ("voluntary") behavior traditionally attributed to a creative mind. (iii) The evolution of a social environment replaces the supposed origin of a culture as a social contract or of social practices as commandments.

Purpose or intention. Only past consequences figure in selection. (i) A particular species does not have eyes in order that its members may see better; it has them because certain members, undergoing variation, were able to see better and hence were more likely to transmit the variation. (ii) The consequences of operant behavior are not what the behavior is now for; they are merely similar to the consequences which have shaped and maintained it. (iii) People do not observe particular practices in order that the group will be more likely to survive; they observe them because groups which induced their members to do so survived and transmitted them.

Certain essences. (i) A molecule which could reproduce itself and evolve into cell, organ, and organism was alive as soon as it came into existence without the help of a vital principle called life. (ii) Operant behavior is shaped and brought under the control of the environment without the intervention of a principle of mind. (To suppose that thought appeared as a variation, like a morphological trait is genetic theory, is to invoke an unnecessarily large *saltum*.) (iii) Social environments generate self-knowledge ("consciousness") and self-management ("reason") without help from a group mind or Zeitgeist.

To say this is not to reduce life, mind, and Zeitgeist to physics; it is simply to recognize the expendability of essences. The facts are as they have always been. To say that selection by consequences is a causal mode found only in living things is only to say that selection (or the "replication with error" which made it possible) defines "living." (A computer can be programmed to model natural selection, operant conditioning, or the evolution of a culture but only when constructed and programmed by a living thing.) The physical basis of natural selection is now fairly clear; the corresponding basis of operant conditioning, and hence of the evolution of cultures, has yet to be discovered.

Certain definitions of good and value. (i) What is good for the species is whatever promotes the survival of its members until offspring have been born and, possibly, cared for. Good features are said to have survival value. Among them are susceptibilities to reinforcement by many of the things we say taste good, feel good, and so on. (ii) The behavior of a person is good if it is effective under prevailing contingencies of reinforcement. We value such behavior and, indeed, reinforce it by saying "Good!" Behavior toward others is good if it is good for the others in these senses. (iii) What is good for a culture is whatever promotes its ultimate survival, such as holding a group together or transmitting its practices. These are not, of course, traditional definitions: they do not recognize a world of value distinct from a world of fact and, for other reasons to be noted shortly, they are challenged.

Alternatives to Selection

An example of the attempt to assimilate selection by consequences to the causality of classical mechanics is the term "selection pressure," which appears to convert selection into something that forces a change. A more serious example is the metaphor of storage. Contingencies of selection necessarily lie in the past; they are not acting when their effect is observed. To provide a current cause it has therefore been assumed that they are stored (usually as "information") and later retrieved. Thus, (i) genes and chromosomes are said to "contain the information" needed by the fertilized egg in order to grow into a mature organism. But a cell does not consult a store of information in order to learn how to change; it changes because of features which are the product of history of variation and selection, a product which is not well represented by the metaphor of storage. (ii) People are said to store information about contingencies of reinforcement and retrieve it for use on later occasions. But they do not consult copies of earlier contingencies to discover how to behave; they behave in given ways because they have been changed by those contingencies. The contingencies can perhaps be inferred from the changes they have worked, but they are no longer in existence. (iii) A possibly legitimate use of "storage" in the evolution of cultures may be responsible for these mistakes. Parts of the social environment maintained and transmitted by a group are quite literally stored in documents, artifacts, and other products of that behavior.

Other causal forces serving in lieu of selection have been sought in the structure of a species, person, or culture. Organization is an example. (i) Until recently, most biologists argued that organization distinguished living from nonliving things. (ii) According to Gestalt, psychologists and others, both perceptions and acts occur in certain inevitable ways because of their organization. (iii) Many anthropologists and linguists appeal to the organization of cultural and linguistic practices. It is true that all species, persons, and cultures are highly organized, but no principle of organization explains their being so. Both the organization and the effects attributed to it can be traced to the respective contingencies of selection.

Another example is growth. Developmentalism is structuralism with time or age added as an independent variable. (i) There was evidence before Darwin that species had "developed." (ii) Cognitive psychologists have argued that concepts develop in the child in certain fixed orders, and Freud said the same for the psychosexual functions. (iii) Some anthropologists have contended that cultures must evolve through a prescribed series of stages, and Marx said as much in his insistence upon historical determinism. But at all three levels the changes can be explained by the "development" of contingencies of selection. New contingencies of natural selection come within range as a species evolves, new contingencies of reinforcement begin to operate as behavior becomes more complex, and new contingencies of survival are dealt with by increasingly effective cultures.

Selection Neglected

The causal force attributed to structure as a surrogate of selection causes trouble when a feature at one level is said to explain a similar feature at another, the historical priority of natural selection usually giving it a special place. Sociobiology offers many examples. Behavior described as the defense of territory may be due to (i) contingencies of survival in the evolution of a species, possibly involving food supplies or breeding practices; (ii) contingencies of reinforcement for the individual, possibly involving a share of the reinforcers available in the territory; or (iii) contingencies maintained by the cultural practices of a group promoting behavior which contributes to the survival of the group.

Similarly, altruistic behavior (i) may evolve through, say, kin selection; (ii) may be shaped and maintained by contingencies of reinforcement arranged by those for whom the behavior works an advantage; or (iii) may be generated by cultures which, for example, induce individuals to suffer or die as heroes or martyrs. The contingencies of selection at the three levels are quite different and the structural similarity does not attest to a common generative principle.

When a causal force is assigned to structure, selection tends to be neglected. Many issues which arise in morals and ethics can be resolved by specifying the level of selection. What is good for the individual or culture may have bad consequences for the species, as when sexual reinforcement leads to overpopulation or the reinforcing amenities of civilization to the exhaustion of resources; what is good for the species or culture may be bad for the individual, as when practices designed to control procreation or preserve resources restrict individual freedom; and so on. There is nothing inconsistent or contradictory about these uses of "good" or "bad," or about other value judgments so long as the level of selection is specified.

An Initiating Agent

The role of selection by consequences has been particularly resisted because there is no place for the initiating agent suggested by classical mechanics. We try to identify such an agent when we say (i) that a species adapts to an environment rather than that the environment selects the adaptive traits; (ii) that an individual adjusts to a situation rather than that the situation shapes and maintains adjusted behavior; and (iii) that a group of people solve a problem raised by certain circumstances, rather than that the circumstances select the cultural practices which yield a solution.

The question of an initiating agent is raised in its most acute form by our own place in this history. Darwin and Spencer thought that selection would necessarily lead to perfection but species, people, and cultures all perish when they cannot cope with rapid change and our species now appears to be threatened. Must we wait for selection to solve the problems of overpopulation, exhaustion of resources, pollution of the environment, and a nuclear holocaust, or can we take explicit steps to make our future more secure? In the latter case, must we not in some sense transcend selection?

We could be said to intervene in the process of selection when as geneticists we change the characteristics of a species or create new species, or when as governors, employers, or teachers we change the behavior of persons, or when we design new cultural practices; but in none of these ways do we escape from selection by consequences. In the first place, we can work only through variation and selection. At level i we can change genes and chromosomes or contingencies of survival, as in selective breeding. At level ii we can introduce new forms of behavior—for example, by showing or telling people what to do with respect to relevant contingencies—or construct and maintain new selective contingencies. At level iii we can introduce new cultural practices or, rarely, arrange special contingencies of survival—for example, to preserve a traditional practice. But having done these things, we must wait for selection to occur. (There is a special reason why these limitations are significant. It is often said that the human species is now able to control its own genetics, its own behavior, and its own destiny, but it does not do so in the sense in which the term control is used in classical mechanics. It does not for the very reason that living things are not machines; selection by consequences makes the difference.) In the second place, we must consider the possibility that our behavior in intervening is itself a product of selection. We tend to regard ourselves as initiating agents only because we know or remember so little about our genetic and environmental histories.

Although we can now predict many of the contingencies of selection to which the human species will probably be exposed at all three levels and can specify behavior that will satisfy many of them, we have failed to establish cultural practices under which much of that behavior is selected and maintained. It is possible that our effort to preserve the role of the individual as an originator is at fault and that a wider recognition of the role of selection by consequences will make an important difference.

The present scene is not encouraging. Psychology is the discipline of choice at level ii, but few psychologists pay much attention to selection. The existentialists among them are explicitly concerned with the here and now, rather than the past and future. Structuralists and developmentalists tend to neglect selective contingencies in their search for causal principles such as organization or growth. The conviction that contingencies are stored as information is only one of the reasons why the appeal to cognitive functions is not helpful. The three personae of psychoanalytic theory are in many respects close to our three levels of selection; but the id does not adequately represent the enormous contribution of the natural history of the species; the superego, even with the help of the ego ideal, does not adequately represent the contribution of the social environment to language, self-knowledge, and intellectual and ethical self-management; and the ego is a poor likeness of the personal repertoire acquired under the practical contingencies of daily life. The field known as the experimental analysis of behavior has extensively explored selection by consequences, but its conception of human behavior is resisted, and many of its practical applications rejected, precisely because it has no place for a person as an initiating agent. The behavioral sciences at level iii show similar shortcomings. Anthropology is heavily structural and political scientists and economists usually treat the individual as a free initiating agent. Philosophy and letters offer no promising leads.

A proper recognition of the selective action of the environment means a change in our conception of the origin of behavior which is possibly as extensive as that of the origin of species. So long as we cling to the view that a person is an initiating doer, actor, or causer of behavior, we shall probably continue to neglect the conditions which must be changed if we are to solve our problems (5).

References and Notes

1. N. Peterson, *Science* 132, 1395 (1960).
2. The imitative vocal behavior of certain birds may be an exception but if it has selective consequences comparable with those of cries of alarm or mating calls they are obscure. The vocal behavior of the parrot is shaped, at

best, by a trivial consequence involving the resemblance between sounds produced and sounds heard.

3. B. F. Skinner, *Verbal Behavior* (Appleton, New York. 1957).
4. Patterns of innate behavior too complex to have arisen as single variations may have been shaped by geologic changes due to plate tectonics [B. F. Skinner, *? Neurobiol. Exp.* 35, 409 (1974); reprinted in *Reflections on Behaviorism and Society* (Prentice-Hall, Englewood Cliffs, N.J.. 1978)].
5. .... *Beyond Freedom and Dignity* (Knopf. New York, 1971).

THE SCIENCE OF ANIMAL COGNITION: PAST, PRESENT, AND FUTURE

Edward A. Wasserman (1997). *Journal of the Experimental Psychology: Animal Behavior Processes, 23(2),* 123-135.

One of the things that makes us human is our exceptional ability to remember the past and plan for the future, profiting from our mistakes. Wasserman provides a detailed historical analysis of the interrelationships between psychology and biology revealing the strengths of cross fertilization and the misadventures resulting from egotistical group identity.

The field of animal cognition is strongly rooted in the philosophy of mind and in the theory of evolution. Despite these strong roots, work during the most famous and active period in the history of our science—the 1930s, 1940s, and 1950s—may have diverted us from the very questions that were of greatest initial interest to the comparative analysis of learning and behavior. Subsequently, the field has been in steady decline despite its increasing breadth and sophistication. Renewal of the field of animal cognition may require a return to the original questions of animal communication and intelligence using the most advanced tools of modern psychological science. Reclaiming center stage in contemporary psychology will be difficult; planning that effort with a host of strategies should enhance the chances of success.

Science and public policy make strange bedfellows. Science usually proceeds along distinctly different paths from the goals of the public to provide immediate cures for the woes that plague it. Still, if it were not for the support of numerous federal agencies, then science as we know it would not exist. So, when the Committee on Appropriations of the U.S. Senate requested a report on the status of basic behavioral science research from the National Institute of Mental Health (NIMH) of the National Institutes of Health (NIH), dozens of government staff personnel and research scientists labored over 2 years to respond to this request. The result was a 137-page document, "Basic Behavioral Science Research for Mental Health: A National Investment," issued in 1995 by the National Advisory Mental Health Council (NAMHC) and widely disseminated to governmental and university officials (NIMH Basic Behavioral Science Task Force of the NAMHC, 1995).

Why should scientists care about this report? Quite simply, the report may help to shape funding priorities in behavioral science for the next decade. Just what might be the impact on research that appears in the *Journal of Experimental Psychology: Animal Behavior Processes*? A clue may come from the lines that open the section on Animals in Behavioral Science Research:

> Human beings conceptualize, reason, and have language and conscious mental states; in addition, they create social and cultural structures. These features combine to make humans qualitatively different from other animals, and for this reason the largest part of basic behavioral science research focuses on humans. Nonetheless, studies involving rats, cats, birds, monkeys, and many other nonhuman animals—both in their natural environments and in laboratories—are also important components of research on mental health and illness. Such studies are essential to advance understanding in all behavioral and social domains, including emotion, social behavior, and cognitive function. They permit investigators to control a greater number of genetic, environmental, and experimental variables, and to examine more extensive manipulations of behavioral conditions that may be done with human subjects (p.6).

Readers of the *Journal* may find these lines to be both reassuring and discomforting. On the one hand, they defend basic scientific research in animal behavior processes, arguing that this research affords several advantages to those interested in elucidating the situational and biological determinants of human action. On the other hand, they offer no compelling reason outside of investigative convenience for studying animal behavior, especially in light of the seemingly contradictory claim that human behavior is "qualitatively different" from that of all other animals. (A much less widely disseminated 1993 NIH Program Announcement PA-93-57, "Comparative Approaches to Brain and Behavior," more specifically and satisfactorily justifies the study of animal behavior in terms of "animal models' of human health and disease and "evolutionary perspectives" that seek to determine more general behavioral principles).

The NAMHC report was intended to serve a number of functions, not the least of which was to inform citizens and legislators of the valuable work in behavioral science that is presently supported by the NIMH, and to urge that such work be given continued funding in the future. Those of us who study animal learning and behavior in the United States greatly appreciate the backing that the NIMH provides to our field and we genuinely hope that it is able to sustain that support for the foreseeable future.

Given the NIMH's legislative charge to improve our nation's mental health through research into the etiology, diagnosis, treatment, and prevention of mental disorders, it is understandable and appropriate that the NIMH should view basic research into animal behavior processes from the vantage point of the human condition. Nevertheless, the intellectual quest to comprehend the causes and functions of animal behavior is one of the main reasons that many researchers entered the field of animal learning and cognition in the first place, quite apart from any practical benefits to humanity that this study may yield. The ultimate fate of our field could very well depend on how effectively we communicate the basic scientific significance of that quest to our many audiences: grade school, high school, and college students; colleagues and administrators in higher education; governmental representatives and officials; and the general public. As much as we might like to deny it, we are in the midst of an intense battle for the hearts, minds, and resources of these diverse constituencies, a battle that most observers of the field contend we are losing.

In this essay, I will briefly review the origins of the science of animal cognition, I will assess the current state of the field, and I will look toward the future with a special eye on how we might reclaim center stage in the realm of experimental psychology. Regaining the respect and resources that we have lost over the last quarter century will not be easy. An important part of that process involves a reacquaintance with the excitement and promise of the field. We cannot hope to convince others that our science is important and relevant if we ourselves are either unable or disinclined to articulate the important and relevance of the field. I turn first to that historical overview and then to the current status and future prospects of our science.

Historical Review

Contrary to the claims of our field's harshest critics, the study of animal behavior and learning is no idle or isolated undertaking; it is absolutely central to understanding the nature and origin of humankind. Two monumental moments in the history of human thought place the study of animal behavior and learning squarely at the forefront of philosophical and scientific inquiry: (a) Rene Descartes's distinction between humans and brutes, and (b) Charles Darwin's hypothesization of mental continuity between human beings and nonhuman animals.

Descartes (1637/1994) believed that human beings were fundamentally different from brutes. Animals were mere machines. They had intricate bodily mechanisms that controlled their physiology and behavior, but they lacked what humans alone possessed—a rational soul. The rational soul was specially created by the deity, it was not derived from the potentiality of matter, nor was it even located in the human body. Critically, the operation of the rational soul had two unique behavioral consequences: (a) it allowed us to use words or other overt signs to communicate our private thoughts and feelings to fellow human beings, and (b) it permitted our intelligence to appropriately tailor our bodily reactions to a vast variety of intricate and ever changing environmental situations. Descartes believed that animals were incapable of using words, or other signs to declare their thoughts to others, if indeed they had any such thoughts, and that animals were bound to respond innately, without the intervention of intelligence.

Against this backdrop of Cartesian thinking, Darwin (1871/19220) made the revolutionary proposal that the nature and descent of human beings was not a matter for theology or philosophy, but for biology. Extensive naturalistic and anecdotal studies convinced Darwin that human and animals were not fundamentally different from one another nor did they have different origins; we are each the product of organic evolution. In stark contrast to Descartes, Darwin viewed both communication and intelligence from a natural scientific perspective; rudimentary antecedent or even highly advanced forms of each of these behavioral abilities were to be found throughout the animal kingdom, thus disclosing mental continuity between human and nonhuman animals. As Domjan (1987) observed, Darwin's ideas made the study of animal behavior relevant to, and in fact crucial to the understanding of human behavior. For, if humans evolved from lower animal forms, then the study of animal cognitive functioning is essential to understanding the biological precursors of the human mind.

The most celebrated pioneers in the science of animal learning and cognition—Edward Thorndike and Ivan Pavlov—were keenly aware of the profound issues that were at stake in this fledging field. They saw their new experimental methods as at last allowing the objective and experimental analysis of behavioral processes that permitted both humans and animals to adjust to complex and constantly changing environmental conditions and to retain those behavioral adjustments for appreciable periods of time. Pavlov was primarily interested in an account of conditioning in terms of the activity of the central nervous system. He also gleaned the origins of human language in advanced associative learning processes. Thorndike was primarily interested in the ontogeny and phylogeny of learning, and his studies helped to stimulate a comparative analysis of learning. These various interests were clearly the outgrowth of the Darwinian revolution and were anathema to Cartesian philosophy and theology.

The major figures in the field of animal learning during the 1930s, 1940s, and 1950s—Clark Hull, Kenneth Spence, Edward Tolman, and B. F. Skinner—pursued their increasingly focused and detailed research and theory with generally less regard to the larger scientific and philosophical issues than had Thorndike and Pavlov. That later research and theory represented what might be called the "second phase" of the scientific study of animal learning and cognition. Despite (or because of) its very focus and detail, it came to dominate the field of experimental psychology. This was, after all, the heyday of learning theory. Theory testing and development were the prime scientific objectives then, not the broad study of animal communication or intelligence (Bitterman, 1975). As related by one of Spence's students, the field was "in a Zeitgeist concerned with the Hull/Spence enterprise of developing a 'behavior theory' and the rat was the simple 'preparation' that permitted the empirical manipulation of the variables of importance" (Webb, 1990, quoted in Dewsbury, 1996). Skinner did broaden behaviorism to include communication, problem solving, personal control, and freedom; but, he too limited his experimental analysis to rat and pigeon behavior largely for reasons of economy and convenience.

Perhaps epitomizing the apparent disinterest of learning theorists in many of the larger biological and philosophical implications of animal intelligence was Skinner's Project Pigeon, a wartime effort to use the technology of operant conditioning to train pigeons to guide armed missiles to their military targets (described after its declassification by Skinner in 1960). Just why did Skinner pick pigeons as the subjects for this project in applied behavior analysis? "We have used pigeons, not because the pigeon is an intelligent bird, but because it is a practical one and can be made into a machine, from all practical points of view" (Skinner, 1944, quoted in Capshew, 1993). Rightly or wrongly, the pigeon could be construed as little more than another piece of hardware for Skinner, as much a component of his famous box as the operandum or the reinforcer delivery mechanism.

Against this background of research and theory in acquired animal behavior, the cognitivist revolution of the 1960s, 1970s, and 1980s did not have to look long or hard for a caricature of what it took to be its arch nemesis—animal learning theory. Theorists of this general persuasion could, with some justification, be portrayed as preoccupied with minor disputes of little enduring interest or relevance, unconcerned with evolutionary, developmental, or physiological aspects of learning, and more interested in the technology of conditioning than in its functional or biological significance. Of course, the major figures in the field of animal learning and behavior, especially Skinner, did address these matters; but, the evolution, development, and biology of learning were surely not the field's prime problems of research and theory.

Where We Stand

No less than the behavior of our nonhuman research subjects, the behavior of experimental and comparative psychologists is affected by its consequences. Many of the criticisms of cognitivists and those leveled on related scores by ethologists and ecologists have helped to inspire a far more catholic and liberal view of the field of animal learning (Cook, 1993; Hulse, 1993; Mackintosh, 1994). An increased interest in biological influences on learned behavior was signaled by the influential volumes that were edited by Seligman and Hager (1972) and by Hinde and Stevenson-Hinde (1973). An increased readiness to explore the role of cognitive processes in learned behavior was signaled by the important volumes that were edited by Hulse, Fowler, and Honig (1978) and by Roitblat, Bever, and Terrace (1984). Those who are acquainted with our field no doubt appreciate that the last quarter century has in many ways been the most exciting and innovative in the history of animal learning and behavior, perhaps because of the more eclectic and less doctrinaire view of the field that workers have adopted. In Cook's opinion, "this modern synthesis of animal learning, cognitive science, and behavioral ecology has enormously expanded the breadth, nature, and sophistication of the psychological issues studied in animals" (1993, p. 174).

Unfortunately, those of us who are now active in the field are suffering from the negative reputation that, deserved or not, was precipitated by the research and theory of our predecessors. Deaths and retirements of workers in our field are dutifully acknowledged by their younger colleagues, but replacements more often than not come from the fields of cognitive science and neuroscience. Those same fields are also more likely to produce officers and representatives to professional organizations and boards, as the number of researchers in animal learning and behavior dwindles. Also dismaying the shrinking number of aspiring graduate students who are prepared to work from 4 to 6 years to obtain a Ph.D. in an area where employment possibilities are becoming disappointingly slim. Finally, the legislative efforts of "animals rights" activists have burdened animal researchers with escalating financial costs, and their public relations efforts have subjected us to intense ethical and moral scrutiny (Rollin, 1985).

I have discussed these matters at great length with many of my professional colleagues, and I have tried to develop strategies for revitalizing our field. I fear that we will have to act soon or face the very real prospect of our disappearance as a distinct area of scientific inquiry. What plans might help to put the science of animal learning and cognition back on course?

Planning Our Future

Address the Big Issues

Descartes wrote to the Marquess of Newcastle in 1646:

> The reason why animals do not speak as we do is not that they lack the organs but that they have no thoughts. It cannot be said that they speak to each other and that we cannot understand them; because since dogs and some other animals express their passions to us, they would express their thoughts also if they had any. I know that animals do many things better than we do, but this does not surprise me. It can even be used to prove that they act naturally and mechanically, like a clock which tells the time better than our judgment does. (1970, p. 207)

In this letter and in other writings, Descartes laid down two key challenges to succeeding generations of scholars interested in the comparative analysis of cognition: (a) prove that animals can communicate their thoughts to others and (b) show that they are capable of intelligent, flexible action. Concentrating on these two key challenges should help us to plan and to organize our experimental and theoretical efforts. Providing empirical answers to these compelling questions should also increase the general public's interest in and appreciation of our field.

Perhaps the most widely known research in comparative cognition is that concerned with teaching human language to apes. If that innovative effort had been an unqualified success, then we might profess to having already met Descartes's first challenge. The case for semantic learning in apes has been strong but the case for syntactic learning has not, leading many to conclude that early claims of language acquisition by nonhuman apes were premature (for reviews, see Rumbaugh & Savage-Rumbaugh, 1994; Wasserman, 1993). Further research into the communicative abilities of animals is obviously warranted. Promising lines include vocal (Pepperberg, 1981), gestural (Gardner & Gardner, 1984; Herman, Morrel-Samuels, & Pack, 1990), token-based (Premack & Premack, 1972), and computer-based (Rumbaugh, 1977) language schemes. Also promising are research projects with a number of different animal species that are aimed at elucidating the perceptual and cognitive processes on which human language may be built (Braaten & Hulse, 1993; Terrace, 1993; Weisman, Njegovan, & Ito, 1994). Those precursors of language are of interest, because they reveal the phylogenetic ancestry of human cognition and disclose important differences in the cognitive processes of different species.

Research on Descartes's second challenge may not be as well known to the general public, but investigations into the continuity of human and animal intelligence have actually generated the main empirical foundation of the field of comparative cognition. This research, which uses a variety of conditioning procedures, attests to many common cognitive processes across a broad range of animal species. Critically, that work stands as strong evidence against Descartes's assertion that "the word…is the sole sign and the only mark of thought hidden and wrapped in the body" (1649/1972, pp. 152-153).

Several reviews of past research in the comparative psychology of cognition describe how workers have experimentally addressed both of Descartes's challenges (e.g., Pearce, 1987; Roitblat, 1987; Wasserman, 1993; Weiskrantz, 1985). For Terrace (1993), future research "provides a variety of opportunities to study the phylogeny and ontogeny of cognition. At the very least, it should expose the stale and antiquated doctrine that animals do not think" (p. 168). Here are the kinds of major issues that we should endeavor to keep at the forefront of our science.

Regain a Sense of Focus

Demarest (1980) observed that from 1968 to 1971 at least five articles in the *American Psychologist* eulogized the passing of comparative psychology. Further, Wilson (1975) in his provocative book *Sociobiology* predicted that comparative psychology would soon be cannibalized by several fields of biology, among them sociobiology. Demarest noted additional symptoms of this unhealthy state of affairs, including a loss of professional status in the American Psychological Association and in college curricula and the poorest prospects for academic positions in all of the various subfields of psychology.

What was the reason for these signs of distress? According to Demarest (1980), comparative psychology does suffer from a serious malady, but it is not a lack of theory as Hodos and Campbell (1969) had argued or a lack of truly comparative research as Beach (1950) had proclaimed, but rather a lack of a clear identity.

Just what is the central focus of comparative psychology? Here, Mason (1980) vigorously argued that the evolution of mental processes has been, and is, the central substantive issue for comparative psychology. Or take the similar assessment of Dore and Kirouac (1987) that comparative psychology is about animal mind; this has been the tradition and the foundation of the field. Losing sight of this focus during the "second phase" of research on animal learning may very well have left the field vulnerable and unresponsive when ethologists and cognitivists mounted their assaults on the comparative psychology of learning in the 1960s, 1970s, and 1980s.

The obvious answer to this problem of the identity of comparative psychology is to stay focused on the central issue under study; namely, comparing cognition in all animals species. For Dore and Kirouac (1987), "it still is the basic issue, and the future of the field should be built on this tradition" (p. 246). History is now clear on the consequences of losing this focus: denigration of the field and its possible incorporation by rival schools of thought. Dore and Kirouac (1987) offer the following prescriptions: "Comparative psychology will ensure a stable and consistent progress of its field of investigation by not duplicating the achievements of other animal behavior sciences or by continuously reacting to their criticisms. It will do so by maintaining its long and fruitful tradition and by developing the concepts that are actually lacking and that are required to improve our understanding of animal mind, and therefore of animal behavior" (p. 246).

Play Both Ends Against the Middle

Today, several controversies surrounding the study of mind and behavior have captured the imagination and interest of scholars inside and outside of experimental psychology. Many of these intellectual debates center on private experience and consciousness. Do animals have private experience and consciousness? Is there a physical basis of human experience and consciousness? These and other related questions usually generate much heat, but rather little light.

Discussions about mind in humans and animals invariably repeat ideas and arguments made hundreds of years ago. Adler (1980) has observed that many competing arguments center on the underlying contradiction between the humanization of animals and the dehumanization of humans. According to Adler's (1980) astute historical analysis, the modern conflict may be traced to Descartes, whose dualistic approach forced him to dichotomize between humans and animals. Descartes's countryman, De la Mettrie (1748/1912), carried the argument one step farther by obliterating the distinction between humans and animals and proposing, in 1748, a completely mechanistic view of humans in his *L'Homme Machine*. Finally, Darwin's 1859 theory of evolution effectively turned the tables by humanizing animals.

A comparative analysis of cognition finds itself precariously placed between these extreme views. On the one hand, viewing animal behavior in light of human cognition suggests that many cognitive processes like attention, memory, and conceptualization may be exhibited in the behavior of nonhuman animals, thereby humanizing animals. On the other hand, viewing human cognition in light of animal behavior suggests that many cognitive processes like categorization and causal judgment might be explained by associative learning mechanisms and may not require advanced logical or statistical thinking, thereby dehumanizing humans.

Appreciating and addressing this interesting conflict may actually help us to reach audiences who might otherwise pay us little heed. Especially relevant are cognitive scientists who have thus far failed to incorporate the findings of animal behavior research into their intellectual realm. Rilling and Neiworth (1986) have remarked that "as a consequence of resistance to animal research...cognitive psychology remains a somewhat egocentric discipline with an inevitable bias toward the human mind. Consequently, theories of human cognition have not been integrated with theories of animal learning" (p. 19). Hulse (1993) has observed that "human cognitivists have not availed themselves of the information a comparative approach can provide about the properties of cognition that make humans unique" (p. 154). Church (1993) has noted that "much of modern cognitive psychology is designed to apply to human subjects, and perhaps intelligent machines, but not to lower animals. There is no special virtue in finding principles that apply to only a single species, even our own. Human psychology is enriched, not diminished, by its similarity to animal psychology" (p. 170). More critically, Terrance (1993) has commented that "Darwin's application of the theory of evolution to intelligence has exerted little influence on modern investigators of human cognition. Their attitude toward phylogenetic antecedents of human cognition ranges from benign neglect to outright rejection on the grounds of irrelevance" (p. 162). In light of such strong preconceptions on the part of many cognitive scientists, we must redouble our efforts to convince them that our work is important and relevant to their interests. But, how?

As one example, my laboratory's recent research on conceptualization in pigeons (Wasserman, 1995) has been informed by and has directly addressed central issues in contemporary cognitive psychology, thereby making it difficult for cognitivists to dismiss the work as either isolated or irrelevant to their own program. That research has systematically progressed from studying basic-level concepts (Bhatt, Wasserman, Reynolds, & Knauss, 1988; Wasserman, Kiedinger, & Bhatt, 1988), where stimulus similarity might effectively mediate transfer from training to testing stimuli, to superordinate (Wasserman, DeVolder, & Coppage, 1992) and abstract concepts (Wasserman, Hugart, & Kirkpatrick-Steger, 1995), where stimulus similarity cannot account for transfer of training. These clear cases of conceptualization in pigeons surely challenge cognitivists' common belief that conceptualization is a uniquely human competence that critically depends on linguistic processes.

As a second example of this research strategy, my laboratory has conducted collaborative research with a well-known visual scientist, I. Biederman, into object recognition in both pigeons and humans. We have used similar stimuli and tasks with pigeons and humans to determine the extent to which object recognition might be a general process across organisms with rather different visual and nervous systems. The research that has been completed so far has not only encouraged us that a general process account might hold, but it has also helped to constrain the nature of that process (Kirkpatrick-Steger, Wasserman, & Biederman, 1996; Van Hamme, Wasserman, & Biederman, 1992; Wasserman, Gagliardi, et. al., 1996; Wasserman, Kirkpatrick-Steger, Van Hamme, & Biederman, 1993).

My laboratory's recent research on causal judgment in college students (Wasserman, 1990; Wasserman, Kao, Van Hamme, Katagiri, & Young, 1996) has taken the decidedly different tactic of showing that this advanced cognitive competence can be understood as an illustration of associative learning, a process that has been extremely well investigated and well documented in nonhuman animals (Wasserman & Miller, 1997). Our work on causal judgment has examined both classical and instrumental conditioning contingencies, noncompetitive and competitive interevent relations, and constant and changing interevent relations. The general conclusion of this work is that Rescorla and Wagner's (1972) theory of associative learning does an excellent job in accounting for human's judgements of interevent relations in all of the above circumstances. By incorporating the modification recently suggested by Van Hamme and Wasserman (1994)—that nonpresented cues actually have nonzero salience and undergo changes in associative strength despite their nonpresentation on training trials—Rescorla and Wagner's theory can even account for backward blocking and backward conditioned inhibition, behavioral effects that have proven to be especially difficult for associative learning theories to explain.

Mind and mechanism. Human and animal. Humanizing animals and dehumanizing humans. Where do we come down on these distinctions? Generally, our science prefers mechanistic to mentalistic interpretations. We also hope that our accounts are broadly applicable rather than peculiar only to animals or to humans. We have no vested interest in making humans out of animals or animals out of humans. Rather, we seek parsimonious and falsifiable accounts of behavior and cognition that can be subjected to clear empirical evaluation.

Make Connections

One thing that particularly dismays many comparative psychologists is that they often feel cut off from the rest of psychological science. Adler (1980) has observed that after a promising beginning, comparative psychology has become a secondary field in most universities. Glickman (1980) has suggested that in terms of its representation in psychology departments, comparative psychology has been a "fringe" area of research and teaching for at least four decades. As such, it is particularly vulnerable to disruptive influences of both intellectual and nonintellectual origins. One way to help combat this isolation and its many negative repercussions is to expand our contacts with other disciplines that share common substantive concerns.

An excellent illustration of how basic issues in animal learning and cognition might be expanded into other domains is the question of configural versus elemental control by compound conditioned stimuli. This issue was first raised generations ago by Gestalt psychologists, and it has been continuously and systematically investigated by researchers of animal learning since that time (for a review, see Wasserman & Miller, 1997).

Stemming largely from the work of Rudy and Sutherland (1989), there has been growing interest in compound stimulus control in the neuroscience community. Rudy and Sutherland provocatively proposed that the hippocampal formation is necessary for rats to learn and to remember Thorndikean appetitive configural discriminations, a proposal for which Rudy and his associates have reported supportive experimental evidence (Alvardo & Rudy, 1995; Rudy & Sutherland. 1989). Rudy (1991, 1992) has also suggested that there is a clear developmental trajectory to configural versus elemental stimulus control: Configural control develops after elemental control, perhaps because configural control depends on the functionality of more slowly developing neural systems. Support for configural control developing after elemental control has not only come from the behavior of infant rats, but also from the behavior of human children (Rudy, Keith, & Georgen, 1993), thereby extending comparative questions of compound stimulus control into the realm of developmental psychology. This extension is doubly important because the developmental path in humans might have been explained by the increasing verbal competence of children; however, the parallel development path in rats strongly argues against this interpretation. Finally, increasing attention is now being paid to computer and neural net models that may account for the occurrence and details of configural and conditional discrimination learning (Kehoe, 1988; Schmajuk & DiCarlo, 1992). These models offer interesting new alternatives to comparisons between different species or ages of organisms.

All in all, it is evident that the more connections that we forge with other scholars working on related problems, the less isolated we will be from the rest of the community of psychological scientists—from cognitive and behavioral neuroscientists, to developmental psychologists, to cognitive scientists. Such ties can only enhance the regard in which we are held by individuals in these other fields of scholarship.

Go From the General to the Specific

Church (1993) has recently observed that Darwin's legacy includes evidence for impressive continuity of both body and mind among animal species. The most prevalent approach for research in comparative cognition has been to assiduously study a single species in a single project and to compare the results of that research project with findings reported by other workers under analogous conditions in different species, particularly human beings. Shettleworth (1993a) has suggested that this largely anthropocentric investigative strategy springs directly from Darwin's hypothesis of mental continuity. Darwin thus set the stage for a research program designed to document continuity between nonhuman species and humans in cognitive abilities. Indeed, in some, like Tolman (1987) and Medioni (1987), the main vision of comparative psychology is as a distinctly human psychology whose main purpose is to understand and to specify the rules of human psychological functioning, as well as their degree of zoological generality.

Shettleworth (1993a) suggests that this anthropocentric program is comparative cognition in only a very limited sense. She urges researchers also to study the behavior of more strategically selected species to shed greater light on the natural and evolutionary histories of the chosen animals. Adopting this more ethological and ecological approach means that one may compare either closely related species that face divergent cognitive demands or unrelated species that face similar demands. Such study may not only help to identify the selection pressures for complex behavior and cognition, but it might also help to identify any specialized behavioral or cognitive adaptations (Domjan & Galef, 1983; Shettleworth, 1993b).

There are times in the scientific literature when these two approaches to the study of comparative cognition are portrayed as conflicting with one another, but there really is no inherent conflict on this score because the two programs ask different questions about animal cognition (Shettleworth, 1993a; also see Bitterman, 1975; Wasserman, 1994). Cook (1993) has observed that the generalist approach has concentrated on a few taxonomically distant "focus" animals to understand the general processes shared among species, whereas the ecological approach has concentrated on a variety of more closely related species to elucidate the cognitive mechanisms of specific adaptive behaviors and their ecological determinants. Together, the parallel use of both strategies should make for a powerful and complementary alliance for the future study of animal cognition. Indeed, Galef (1987) has suggested that the availability of alternative perspectives can only enrich our discipline.

One final remark on general processes of cognition is in order. The generalist approach looks across species for cognitive processes of wide representation. Yet another sense of generality is that to be seen within a single species across several different situations. Thus, some cognitive processes may operate in diverse problem settings, suggesting to Riley and Langley (1993) that many cognitive mechanisms central to the field of animal cognition, including perception, attention, and discrimination learning, are not easily assigned specific functions for which they may have been selected as adaptations. Determining these generalities obviously requires a third investigative strategy of studying the same species under a variety of different experimental conditions.

Explore the Limits of Animal Intelligence

Rilling and Neiworth (1986) have identified two main tasks for the field of comparative cognition: (a) to determine the nature of animal cognition, and (b) to compare the cognitive processes of different species. Interest in the limits of animal intelligence appears not to have occupied researchers of an ethological or naturalistic persuasion, but it has been of particular interest to experimental psychologists working on laboratory settings. Experimental psychologists' greater familiarity with the limits of human intelligence in daily life and in educational and laboratory situations may be one reason for this research interest.

Zentall (1993) has recently discussed the interest in exploring the limits of animal intelligence and the problem posed by naturalistic study alone. To him, it is not at all unreasonable to expect that evidence of cognitive behavior will be found in an "unnatural" laboratory setting, in spite of the fact that many animals typically exhibit little sign of cognitive behavior when they are observed in their natural environment. Zentall believes that laboratory experimentation is especially useful because it may be the only way to elicit latent cognitive strategies whose use results in higher levels of, or more efficient, behavior. It may be necessary to expose an animal to artificial procedures both to rule out explanations of behavior in terms of simple learning principles as well as to induce the animal to use advanced cognitive capacities.

Be Daring

> Comparative psychology is about the evolution of mental processes, and the various forms and aspects of minding in different animal species. That has been, and is, the central substantive issue for comparative psychology. This is not a parochial concern. The issue is fundamental. Even if we choose to ignore it and to direct our attention toward more tractable problems, we can be sure that it will be taken up by others. (Mason, 1980, p. 964).

Mason's concern over what some might take to be the timidity of comparative psychology during the "second phase" in the study of animal mind may have been a reaction to Griffin's (1976) inauguration of cognitive ethology, a field whose main professed aim is analysis of the possible conscious thoughts and experiences of nonhuman animals (see Mason, 1976, for his initial reaction to this field, and Blumberg & Wesserman, 1995, for a more recent appraisal). At first blush, cognitive ethology, with its mentalistic vantage point and its reliance on folk psychological theory (Michel, 1991), would appear to be a nonstarter, a veritable throwback to the earliest origins of the science of comparative psychology (for more on those origins, see Wasserman, 1981, 1993). However, cognitive ethology is still with us a full 20 years later. And, based on the growing number of advocates who enthusiastically espouse its mentalistic premises and the increasing coverage that it is receiving in the popular press, cognitive ethology can even be said to be flourishing (see the edited volume by Ristau, 1991, for several cogent analyses of cognitive ethology; see Cheney & Seyfarth, 1990, for a well-known study of monkey social behavior adopting the mentalistic method of cognitive ethology; see Allen & Hauser, 1991, for more on the growing ties between cognitive ethologists and mentalistic philosophers; and see Angier, 1994, for a recent national newspaper piece publicizing the cognitive ethology movement). One of its ardent supporters considers the main accomplishment of cognitive ethology to be that the very ideas of animal thinking and consciousness have gone from being "heretical" to "respectable" (Jolly, 1991). Another supporter (Beck, 1996) believes that an objective, behavioral approach is "politically correct," but "bad science," which may actually encourage the inhumane treatment of animals.

At least part of cognitive ethology's appeal has been its daring to deal with matters of mind that had fallen out of the behaviorist agenda; but behaviorism need not be a conservative school. Indeed, at the outset, Watson (1913) had extremely bold and ambitious aims for this branch of psychological science. He was convinced that all meaningful facets of mental functioning including perception, memory, imagination, judgment, reasoning, and conception would eventually yield to behavioral analysis: "Psychology as behavior will, after all, have to neglect but few of the really essential problems with which psychology as an introspective science now concerns itself. In all probability even this residue of problems may be phrased in such a way that refined methods in behavior (which certainly must come) will lead to their solution" (p. 177).

Recent years have in fact seen some bold and exciting moves to extend behavioristic methods and analyses to problems that have historically been associated with cognitive approaches and theories. Here, I focus on two: imagery and the communication of private states.

Imagery. Rilling and Neiworth (1987) returned to the study of imagery in animals, a problem in animal learning that had attracted little experimental attention for over 100 years (see Williams, 1974, for an earlier study of negative afterimages in pigeons). For Rilling and Neiworth, the challenge for investigating imagery in animals was to retain the methodological rigor of behaviorism, while simultaneously conducting psychologically valid research on processes that were presumed to be uniquely human. Calling on classic human research by Shepard and Cooper (1982), Rilling and Neiworth's experimental response to this challenge was to have a pigeon view a moving clock hand on a computer monitor for a short while, for the clock hand to disappear for a brief period, and for the pigeon to report whether the location of the clock hand when it reappeared at test was in the correct spot given its earlier position and trajectory. According to Rilling and Neiworth's logic:

> The presentation of a sample stimulus followed by a retention interval during which a transformation to the sample occurs provides a powerful paradigm for determining how the process of perception interacts with the process of retention...A reasonable assumption is that the organism transforms representations of a stimulus in the same way that a visible stimulus changes...In this case, the stimulus transformation is visible at first, disappears during a retention interval or imagery component, and terminates with the reappearance of the transformed stimulus at the end of the trajectory...This procedure reduces the problem of imagery in animals to the problem of identifying the type of representation present during a retention interval, a problem which is familiar to students of animal memory...The advantage of this procedure is that the rate and type of stimulus transformation is explicitly manipulated by the experimenter. The percentage of correct responses provides an explicit dependent variable. (1987, pp. 65-66).

Rilling and Neiworth's empirical data provided strong support for the proposal that pigeons can project the trajectory of a moving stimulus, thereby conforming to the definition of imagery as a "transformable representation." Not only in broad brush strokes, but in fine detail, their pigeon data accorded with the results of human beings given similar training and testing procedures. Sadly, Rilling and Neiworth's promising technique for addressing the question of imagery in animals has not yet stimulated subsequent systematic research.

Private experience. No areas of psychology have been so wedded to introspective study as have those of private experience and consciousness. Yet, Lubinski and Thompson (1993) have recently proposed that behavioral procedures are capable of permitting animals to communicate with others based on their own private states. The medium of this form of interindividual communication is completely in the world of public discriminative stimuli, operant responses, and reinforcing and punishing consequences.

Of greatest significance to Lubinski and Thompson's application of behavioral analysis to communication based on private events was their establishing two pigeons' interactive behavioral repertoires based on one bird's receipt of one of three different pharmacological discriminative stimuli: injections of cocaine, pentobarbital, or normal saline. The different stimulus conditions induced by these drugs could only be discriminated internally; no external discriminative stimuli were available because all three drugs were injected hypodermically. By means of differential reinforcement of three different operant responses in the three different pharmacological conditions, the drugged pigeon was taught to provide the undrugged bird with one of three different visual discriminative stimuli that informed the undrugged bird which of the three different operant responses that it could perform would lead to reinforcement; the undrugged bird then responded in accord with the discriminative stimuli given to it by the drugged pigeon. The undrugged bird's behavior also was the product of simple contingencies of reinforcement.

Lubinski and Thompson proposed that their interesting laboratory demonstration had special significance to the problem of private stimuli. However, critics of their provocative paper observed that drugs are not notably different from, say, visual stimuli in the discriminative control of operant behavior; each kind of discriminative stimulus emanates from outside the body and is later processed by internal bodily mechanisms (Thompson, 1993; Zuriff, 1993). The phenomenological consequences of each form of stimulation are directly evident to the perceiving organism, but they are only indirectly knowable by external observers (Laasko, 1993; Zuriff, 1993). Furthermore, Lubinski and Thompson did not effectively simulate the critical problem of interobserver agreement, thereby preventing the pigeons from engaging in any empathic responses that are arguably fundamental to humans' interactions about private states (Garrett, 1993; Hardcastle, 1993; Laasko, 1993; Mitchell, 1993).

These reservations notwithstanding, Lubinski and Thompson expressed confidence that the experimental pursuit of the problem of private events does fall within the purview of behaviorism (Skinner, 1945). They further held that such pursuit will illuminate the problem in a way quite different from cognitive ethology and introspective psychology.

Here, Lubinski and Thompson's distinction between Leibnizian and Skinnerian privacy is relevant to the contrasting philosophies and agendas of cognitive ethology and comparative cognition. On the one hand, Leibnizian privacy is in principle inaccessible to more than one individual; it pertains to subjective experience, as opposed to stimulus events and their behavioral accompaniments. On the other hand, Skinnerian privacy concerns the physical nature of the spatial and temporal properties of the variables controlling behavior; it does not address the experience of the individual who is being acted on by exteroceptive or interoceptive stimuli. From this view, Zuriff (1993) concluded that private events, as conceptualized by Skinner and his successors, are theoretical entities. These hypothesized events, along with their associated processes, are inferred rather than observed; they thus qualify as hypothetical constructs rather than as empirically observed stimuli and responses. Skinner's behavioristic analysis thus converges on the earlier analyses of complex behavior and cognition proffered by Hull and Spence (Zuriff, 1985).

In any event, private events and consciousness may yet yield to behavioral analysis, as predicted by Watson (1913). Pursuit of these matters from a comparative vantage point may be of unique importance as the animals under study need not be human beings nor use human language. Still, as in the case of imagery, no systematic experimental research on the communication of private events between animals has been undertaken since Lubinski and Thompson's project.

Reach Out to the Public

King and Viney (1992) recently analyzed the reported declines of comparative psychology. The reasons for the declines are, in their opinion, complex; but, all go back to an eroding social support base. One way to rectify the situation is to make a much greater effort to communicate directly with the general public than has generally been the case. "The education of the public in such popular sources as cultural magazines and newspapers will help guard against insularity and will serve scientific and social interests. It will also resurrect the pioneering tradition of Haggerty, Jastrow, Thorndike, Watson, and Yerkes" (King & Viney, 1992, p. 194).

Most students of animal learning and behavior are acquainted with the writings of Thorndike, Watson, and Yerkes to which King and Viney (1992) refer. But, who were Jastrow and Haggerty? And, what can we learn from their pioneering efforts that will help us to renew the comparative psychology of learning and cognition? A brief bit of history may prove illuminating.

Joseph Jastrow was the first Professor of Experimental and Comparative Psychology in the United States. He assumed that position at the University of Wisconsin in 1888, after completing his graduate studies at John Hopkins University. This professorial title appears to have been chosen to reflect the latest developments in psychological science in the United States and in Europe. Jastrow, himself, never conducted psychological research in animal behavior, and his academic title was shortened to Professor of Psychology in 1903. But, he did publish two articles on comparative psychology in the widely read magazine *The Popular Science Monthly*.

The first article—which preceded Thorndike's (1898) pioneering monograph by some 6 years—introduced the new science of "animal psychology" to the general public, that field's goals being "to arrange in orderly sequence the various forms of mentality from protozoon to man, to discover in what this advance consists, to establish orderly relations between mental powers and the nervous system, and the like" (Jastrow, 1892-1893), p. 35). The second article exposed the myth behind many famous animals performances, like those of the horses Kluge Hans and Jim Key, Here, Jastrow observed that, when witnessing a highly touted act of animal behavior, "the first attitude is naturally that of wonder, and in lack of any detailed knowledge of what the trick may be, the tendency to credit, at least in part, the explanations that are advanced [by the trainers]. Once this attitude is overcome and the kind of training that prepares for the performance is understood, the whole affair loses its marvelous aspect and becomes a mildly interesting demonstration of animal training" (Jastrow, 1906, p. 146). It is the comparative psychologist's business to cultivate a more critical attitude toward animal behavior and learning in order "to determine by all the various kinds of evidence and reasoning that he can bring to bear upon the data, just what kinds of thinking the favored animal can and can not master" (Jastrow, 1906, p. 139; for more on Jastrow's contributions to psychology, see Cadwallader, 1987).

Mark Haggerty made more notable contributions to the field of comparative cognition. Under Yerkes's supervision, Haggerty earned his Ph.D. in psychology at Harvard University in 1910 (after receiving an M.A. degree there in 1909) and then taught at Indiana University until 1916, rising to the rank of Associate Professor. During his graduate years at Harvard University and his postgraduate years at Indiana University (he was a native Hoosier and received both A.B. and M.A. degrees at Indiana University in 1902 and 1907, respectively), Haggerty published papers on imitation (1909, 1912) and learning theory (1913b). His interests then veered toward human learning and educational measurement, and he moved to the University of Minnesota in 1915, where he remained until his death in 1937. At Minnesota, he was promoted to Professor of Educational Psychology and served as Dean of the College of Education from 1920 to 1937.

Haggerty's most interesting works in the comparative psychology of learning and behavior may have been the two articles that he published in the *Atlantic Monthly* (1911, 1913c; he published another magazine piece on learning in apes in *McClure's Magazine* in 1913a). These two articles, entitled "Animal Intelligence" and "Upon the Threshold of the Mind," respectively, were really remarkable essays on the promise and procedures of a science of animal mind. I believe that many of the points that Haggerty made in those articles are worth repeating here, not only for their historical and substantive significance, but for conveying to us the sense of mission that we need to recapture in today's science of animal mind.

Haggerty observed that the psychologists of his time, stimulated largely by the writings of William James, had shown an increasing desire to know the genesis of the human mind. Two possible avenues of approach presented themselves: (a) the study of the child, and (b) the study of the mind as it appears in the animal world. These two approaches have indeed done much over the ensuring decades to elucidate the origins of the human mind, as Haggerty had anticipated.

To study animal mind, Haggerty advocated a "new science." That new science was needed because of the unreliability and inaccuracy of anecdotal and observational evidence, the primary data with which comparative psychologists since Romanes had to deal (Wasserman, 1984). "If we were to have a phylogenesis of mind that was in the least degree reliable we must have new data collected under conditions that were accurately known" (Haggerty 1911, p. 600). That new science would also need to be experimental, because of the impossibility of observational evidence alone answering the most critical questions about animal intelligence. "However engrossing...observation may be to the naturalist...the science of animal behavior and comparative psychology must be founded on something more analytic and more verifiable" (1911, p. 602). An analytical approach was especially necessary when it come to the daunting complexity of human and animal nature. "It is just because of natural complexities that science is called into being. Confronted with the multitudinous shifting forms and processes in the world about him, man tries to understand and to control. This is far easier when he can simplify and reduce to laws;...the experimental laboratory has come to be the chief instrument of progress" (1913c, p. 250).

Haggerty also observed the frequent and unfortunate use that is made of observational evidence: "The necessarily fragmentary character of such material will always leave the animal mind a region of myth into which the would-be comparative psychologist can project the fanciful conceptions of his own mind; conceptions which serve not nearly so much to illuminate the field as the actual discovery of [for instance] some small power of sense-perception or the exact part imitation plays in animal learning. It is to find an answer to such questions as the naturalist cannot answer that the experimental method has come into being" (1911, p. 603).

Haggerty was no knee-jerk experimentalist. He thoughtfully remarked that "there is no virtue in a fact merely because it has come through a laboratory, nor is a fact any the less because it has been picked up in the woods. Nor should there finally be any opposition between the facts that have been gathered from the two sources. Possibly when we have pushed our work far enough we shall see that the two methods supplement each other" (1913c, p. 253). Haggerty respected both experimental and observational evidence. "Personally, I have always thought that we should get our experimental problems from the observation of animals in their free life. Only by such observation can one really penetrate the strategic problems and invent the adequate experimental methods" (1913c, p. 253). Indeed, failure to appreciate the natural history of animals carries with it considerable methodological and interpretive peril. "Without a doubt we blunder in trying to apply the methods of human psychology directly to the animal mind, or in applying the method that has proved efficient in the case of one animal to an individual of a different species. For the correction of such blunders, and for the suggestion of important problems, we can never know too much of animals in the wild" (1913c, p. 253).

Beyond the previously stated reasons for the new science of animal learning and behavior, Haggerty believed that an experimental approach would counterbalance the often uncritical rush to postulate overly elaborate explanations of animal behavior. He urged us "to proceed with extreme caution, to allow the animal mind no attribution of intelligence, the possession of which has not been demonstrated by rigidly-controlled experimentation" (1911, p. 606). This cautious attitude can also be seen in Haggerty's appraisal of Darwin's thesis of mental continuity. "The impassable gulf between man and the beasts is an illusion, as Darwin thought it was. The confirmation of the doctrine, however, has not come about by demonstrating the presence in animals of clear-cut intellectual processes, but by showing that the sort of learning that does hold in animals is the very root of all that is developed in the mind of man" (1911, p. 606).

At that early period in the history of the field of animal learning and behavior, Haggerty was keenly aware of the need for precise experimental methods and devices of investigation. He noted how important refined methods and instruments had been to the scientific development of other young fields that relied on novel techniques like microscopy and spectroscopy. The same would also be true of the new science of animal behavior and learning. "A decade ago the new interest in the behavior of animals had no...elaborate instruments of research at its command. The technique had to be created outright" (1913c, p. 251). In those few years, some progress was made. Nevertheless, "for very few of our animal problems are there as yet adequate methods of investigation. The immediate concern of every student of animal psychology must be the discovery and the perfection of methods" (1913c, p. 251). (Richelle's 1993 characterization of the Skinner box as "psychology's microscope" is of particular interest in connection with Haggerty's discussion of research techniques and instruments.)

Although more than 80 years have passed since Haggerty wrote his pioneering papers, there appears to be no slaking of the public's thirst for information about psychological science in general and about animal intelligence in particular. Yet, little or no concerted effort to educate the public about the science of comparative cognition has recently been undertaken. Cultivating the interest and support of the general public is essential to the future health and wellbeing of our field. The importance of this effort is all the more significant given the success of animal rights activists in turning the public toward their particular position through expensive media campaigns.

Learn From the Experience of Others

Recently, Dewsbury (1996) polled several researchers who had stopped studying animal behavior after having earlier done so. He uncovered a host of reasons for workers' getting in and getting out of this area of scientific study. It may prove to be helpful to those who are contemplating entry into the field to learn more about those reasons. It may also prove to be useful to those of us who are still active in the field to better understand those reasons, so that we might effectively inform and encourage students to get into the field and to make their professional careers more enduring and productive once they have entered it.

Getting in. According to Dewsbury's survey, one main attraction of research with animals was the theory of evolution, especially the idea of the evolution of mind. Given the possibility of mental evolution, another attraction was the opportunity of working out general behavioral principles and laws that would apply both to animals and to people. Some respondents also believed that a true science of behavior might be more readily achieved through the study of animals than through the study of human beings; this "hard" psychological science would be experimentally based, with animals being best suited to the controlled manipulation of variables of interest, some of which could not easily or ethically be explored in people. All of these attractions are still strong reasons for entry into the field; their espousal in our classes and in our publications should continue to bring budding scientists into our discipline.

Getting out. Many investigators left animal research because of the efforts of animal rights activists. Their departure was rarely the result of direct contact with these activists; rather, it was usually due to the financial and bureaucratic burdens that are now associated with animal research. As well, other workers came to question the value of animal research in terms of its ethical merits and its human relevance, these questions having often been raised in the animal rights debate. Other reasons for leaving the field included the lack of colleagues and collaborators and the failure of the broad psychological community to recognize and to appreciate the importance of research in this area. I genuinely hope that following my earlier suggestions might help to counteract these negative forces and that Mackintosh (1994) is correct in his prediction that "the study of animal learning and cognition will soon be able to claim again an honored and important, even if not central, position in experimental psychology" (p. 11).

Conclusion

When Stewart Hulse (personal communication, November 7, 1995) kindly invited me to prepare this essay, he included few instructions. He did say that he wanted "something that looks to the future and gives your perspective on where the field, broadly defined, is headed." He appreciated that "this may not be any easy task, but it seems to me that the general field of animal cognition has a great many issues facing it these days, some of which threaten its viability in the future."

I (Wasserman, 1993) and other observers (Cook, 1993; Mackintosh, 1994) have previously suggested that the general direction of the field of animal cognition is toward increasing contact with cognitive science, neuroscience, and experimental ethology. To reiterate that point here with more extensive documentation would, I believe, have been a wasted opportunity; forecasting the details of the future means precious little if our field has no future. Instead, I have chosen to look back to the origins of our field, because I believe that those origins provide the key to our future viability as a science (also see Dore & Kirouac, 1987, who cleverly used the phrase "back to the future" to characterize the need for comparative psychologists to return to the original organizing themes of the field). We must build on the particular questions that inspired our science in the first place, we must pursue those questions with the utmost enthusiasm and imagination, and we must try harder than ever to keep our field at the forefront of psychological science and in the public limelight. The issues in which we are interested as a science are simply too important for us to do anything less, however difficult and frustrating the conditions may be at the moment for accomplishing our aims.

Let the final words of wisdom and inspiration about the future of the science of animal cognition be Haggerty's:

> Animal senses, animal memory, animal instincts, animal learning, animal thinking, all have surrendered some of their secrets to the experimental method. What has already been achieved gives us sufficient reason to think that much more can be gained by the extension of the laboratory into this realm of nature; that, in fact, a new science will ultimately replace our at present inadequate ideas of the animal mind. (1913c, p. 253).

References

Adler, H. E. (1980). Historical dialectics. *American Psychologist*, *35*, 956-958.

Allen, C., & Hauser, M. D. (1991). Concept attribution in nonhuman animals: Theoretical and methodological problems in ascribing complex mental processes. *Philosophy of Science*, *58*, 221-240.

Alvarado, M. C., & Rudy, J. W. (1995). Rats with damage to the hippocampal-formation are impaired on the transverse-patterning problem but not on elemental discriminations. *Behavioral Neuroscience*, *109*, 204-211.

Angier, N. (1994, August 9). Flouting tradition, scientists embrace an ancient taboo. *The New York Times*, pp. B5, B8.

Beach, F. A. (1950). The snark was a boojum. *American Psychologist*, *5*, 115-124.

Beck, A. M. (1996, May 17). The common qualities of man and beast. *The Chronicle of Higher Education*, B3.Bhatt, R. S., Wasserman, E. A., Reynolds, W. F., Jr., & Knauss, K. S. (1988). Conceptual behavior in pigeons:

Categorization of both familiar and novel examples from four classes of natural and artificial stimuli. *Journal of Experimental Psychology: Animal Behavior Processes*, *14*, 219-234.

Bitterman, M. E. (1975). The comparative analysis of learning. *Science, 188*, 699-709.

Blumberg, M. S., & Wasserman, E. A. (1995). Animal mind and the argument from design. *American Psychologist, 50,* 133-144.

Braaten, R. F., & Hulse, S. H. (1993). Perceptual organization of auditory temporal patterns in European starlings (*Sturnus vulgaris*). *Perception and Psychophysics*, *54*, 567-578.

Cadwallader, T. C. (1987). Origins and accomplishments of Joseph Jastrow's 1888-founded chair of comparative psychology at the University of Wisconsin. *Journal of Comparative Psychology*, *101*, 231-236.

Capshew, J. H. (1993). Engineering behavior: Project Pigeon, World War II, and the conditioning of B. F. Skinner. *Technology and Culture*, *34*, 835-857.

Cheney, D. L., & Seyfarth, R. M. (1990). *How monkeys see the world: Inside the mind of another species*. Chicago: University of Chicago Press.

Church, R. M. (1993). Human models of animal behavior. *Psychological Science*, *4*, 170-173.

Cook, R. G. (1993). The experimental analysis of cognition in animals. *Psychological Science*, *4*, 174-178.

Darwin, C. (1920). *The descent of man: and selection in relation to sex* (2nd ed.). New York: D. Appleton. (Original work published 1871).

De la Mettrie, J. (1912*). L'homme machine* (M. Calkins, Trans.). Chicago: Open Court. (Original work published 1748).

Demarest, J. (1980). The current status of comparative psychology in the American Psychological Association. *American Psychologist*, *35*, 989-990.

Descartes, R. (1970). *Descartes's philosophical letters* (A. Kenny, Ed. and Trans.). Oxford, United Kingdom: Clarendon. (Original work published 1646)

Descartes, R. (1972). Letter to Henry More. In Z. Vendler, *Res Cogitans*. Ithaca, NY: Cornell University Press. (Original work published 1649).

Descartes, R. (1994). *Discourse on the method* (G. Heffernan, Ed. and Trans.). Notre Dame, IN: University of Notre Dame Press. (Original work published 1637).

Dewsbury, D. A. (1996). Animal research: Getting in and getting out. *The General Psychologist*, *32*, 19-25.

Domjan, M. (1987). Comparative psychology and the study of animal learning. *Journal of Comparative Psychology*, *101*, 237-241.

Domjan, M., & Galef, B. G., Jr. (1983). Biological constraints on instrumental and classical conditioning: Retrospect and prospect. *Animal Learning and Behavior*, *11*, 151-161.

Dore, F. Y., & Kirouac, G. (1987). What comparative psychology is all about: Back to the future. *Journal of Comparative Psychology*, *101*, 242-248.

Galef, B. G., Jr. (1987). Comparative psychology is dead! Long live comparative psychology. *Journal of Comparative Psychology*, *101*-259-261.

Gardner, R. A., & Gardner, B. T. (1984). A vocabulary test for chimpanzees (*Pan troglodytes*). *Journal of Comparative* Psychology, *98*, 381-404.

Garrett, R. (1993). A human model for animal behavior. *Behavioral and Brain Sciences*, *16*, 648-649.

Glickman, S. E. (1980). Notes on survival. *American Psychologist*, *35*, 962-964.

Griffin, D. R. (1976). *The question of animal awareness: Evolutionary continuity of mental experience*. New York: The Rockefeller University Press.

Haggerty, M. E. (1909). Imitation in monkeys. *Journal of Comparative Neurology and Psychology*, *19*, 337-455.

Haggerty, M. E. (1911). Animal intelligence. *Atlantic Monthly*, *107*, 599-607.

Haggerty, M. E. (1912). Imitation and animal behavior. *Journal of Philosophy, Psychology, and Scientific Methods*, *9*, 265-272.

Haggerty, M. E. (1913a). Plumbing the minds of apes. *McClure's Magazine*, *41*, 151-154.

Haggerty, M. E. (1913b). The laws of learning. *Psychological Review*, *20*, 411-422.

Haggerty, M. E. (1913c). Upon the threshold of the mind. *Atlantic Monthly*, *112*, 245-253.

Hardcastle, V. G. (1993). Communication versus discrimination. *Behavioral and Brain Sciences*, *16*, 649-650.

Herman, L. M., Morrel-Samuels, P., & Pack, A. A. (1990). Bottle-nosed dolphin and human recognition of veridical and degraded video displays on an artificial gestural language. *Journal of Experimental Psychology: General*, *119*, 215-230.

Hinde, R. A., & Stevenson-Hinde, J. (Eds.). 1973). *Constraints on learning*. London: Academic Press.

Hodos, W., & Campbell, C. B. G. (1969). Scala naturae: Why there is no theory in comparative psychology. *Psychological Review*, *76*, 337-350.

Hulse, S. H. (1993). The present status of animal cognition: An introduction. *Psychological Science, 4*, 154-155.

Hulse, S. H., Fowler, H., & Honig, W. K. (Eds.). (1978). *Cognitive processes in animal behavior*. Hillsdale, NJ: Erlbaum.

Jastrow, J. (1892-1893). The problems of comparative psychology. *The Popular Science Monthly*, *42*, 35-48.

Jastrow, J. (1906). Fact and fable in animal psychology. *The Popular Science Monthly*, *69*, 138-146.

Jolly, A. (1991). Conscious chimpanzees? A review of recent literature. In C. A. Ristau (Ed.), *Cognitive ethology: The minds of other animals* (pp. 231-252). Hillsdale, NJ: Erlbaum.

Kehoe, E. J. (1988). A layered network model of associative learning: Learning to learn and configuration. *Psychological Review*, *95*, 411-433.

King, D. B., & Viney, W. (1992). Modern history of pragmatic and sentimental attitudes toward animals and the selling of comparative psychology. *Journal of Comparative Psychology*, *106*, 190-195.

Kirkpatrick-Steger, K., Wasserman, E. A., & Biederman, I. (1996). Effects of spatial rearrangement of object components on picture recognition in pigeons. *Journal of the Experimental Analysis of Behavior*, *65*, 465-475.

Laasko, A. (1993). Pigeons and the problem of other minds. *Behavioral and Brain Sciences, 16*, 652-653.

Lubinski, D., & Thompson, T. (1993). Species and individual differences in communication based on private states. *Behavioral and Brain Sciences, 16*, 627-680.

Mackintosh, N. J. (1994). Introduction. In N.J. Mackintosh (Ed.), *Animal learning and cognition* (pp. 1-13). San Diego, CA: Academic Press.

Mason, W. A. (1976). Windows on other minds. *Science, 194*, 930-931.

Mason, W. A. (1980). Minding our business. *American Psychologist, 35*, 964-967.

Medioni, J. (1987). Comparative psychology as a search for invariant rules. *Journal of Comparative Psychology, 101*, 275-276.

Michel, G. F. (1991). Human psychology and the minds of other animals. In C. A. Ristau (Ed.), *Cognitive ethology*: *The minds of other animals* (pp. 253-272). Hillsdale, NJ: Erlbaum.

Mitchell, R. W. (1993). Pigeons as communicators and thinkers: *Mon oncle d'Amerique deux*? *Behavioral and Brain Sciences, 16*, 655-656.

National Institute of Mental Health Basic Behavioral Science Task Force of the National Advisory Mental Health Council (1995). *Basic behavioral science research for mental health: A national investment* (NIH Publication No. 95-3682). Bethesda, MD: National Institutes of Health. National Institutes of Health. (1993*). Comparative approaches to brain and behavior* (PA-93-57) [Program announcement]. Bethesda, MD: Author.

Pearce, J. M. (1987). *Introduction to animal cognition.* Hillsdale, NJ: Erlbaum.

Pepperberg, I. M. (1981). Functional vocalizations by an African grey parrot (*Psittacus erithacus*). *Zeitschrift fur Tierpsychologie*, *55*, 139-160.

Premack, A. J., & Premack, D. (1972). Teaching language to an ape. *Scientific American*, *227*, 92-99.

Rescorla, R. A., & Wagner, A. R. (1972). A theory of Pavlovian conditioning: Variations in the effectiveness of reinforcement and nonreinforcement. In A. H. Black & W. F. Prokasy (Eds.), *Classical conditioning II: Current research and theory* (pp. 64-99). New York: Appleton-Century-Crofts.

Richelle, M. N. (1993). *B. F. Skinner: A reappraisal.* Hillsdale, NJ: Erlbaum.

Riley, D. A., & Langley, C. M. (1993). The logic of species comparisons. *Psychological Science, 4*, 185-189. Rilling, M., & Neiworth, J. J. (1986). Comparative cognition: A general process approach. In D. F. Kendrick, M. Rilling, & M. R. Denny (Eds.), *Animal memory* (pp. 19-33). Hillsdale, NJ: Erlbaum.

Rilling, M., & Neiworth, J. (1987). Theoretical and methodological considerations for the study of imagery in animals. *Learning and Motivation, 18*, 57-79.

Ristau, C. A. (Ed.) (1991). *Cognitive ethology: The minds of other animals*. Hillsdale, NJ: Erlbaum.

Roitblat, H. L. (1987). *Introduction to comparative cognition.* New York: Freeman.

Roitblat, H. L., Bever, T. G., & Terrace, H. S. (Eds.). (1984). *Animal cognition.* Hillsdale, NJ: Erlbuam.,

Rollin, B. E. (1985). The moral status or research animals in psychology. *American Psychologist*, *40*, 920-926.

Rudy, J. W. (1991). Elemental and configural associations, the hippocampus, and development. *Developmental Psychobiology*, *24*, 221-236.

Rudy, J. W. (1992). Development of learning: From elemental to configural associative networks. *Advances in Infancy Research*, *7*, 247-289.

Rudy, J. W., Keith, J. R., Georgen, K. (1993). The effect of age on children's learning of problems that require a configural association solution. *Developmental Psychobiology*, *26*, 171-184.

Rudy, J. W., & Sutherland, R. J. (1989). The hippocampal formation is necessary for rats to learn and remember configural discriminations. *Behavioural Brain Research*, *34*, 97-109.

Rumbaugh, D. M. (1977). *Language learning by a chimpanzee: The Lana project*. New York: Academic Press.

Rumbaugh, D. M., & Savage-Rumbaugh, E. S. (1994). Language in comparative perspective. In N. J. Mackintosh (Ed.*), Animal learning and cognition* (pp. 307-333). San Diego, CA: Academic Press.

Schmajuk, N. A., & DiCarlo, J. J. (1992). Stimulus configuration, classical conditioning, and hippocampal function. *Psychological Review*, *99*, 268-309.

Seligman, M. E. P., & Hager, J. L. (Eds.). (1972*). Biological boundaries of learning*. Englewood Cliffs, NJ: Prentice-Hall.

Shepard, R. N., & Cooper, L. A. (1982). *Mental images and their transformations*. Cambridge, MA: MIT Press.

Shettleworth, S. J. (1993a). Where is the comparison in comparative cognition? Alternative research programs. *Psychological Science*, *4*, 179-184.

Shettleworth, S. J. (1993b). Varieties of learning and memory in animals. *Journal of Experimental Psychology: Animal Behavior Processes*, *19*, 5-14.

Skinner, B. F. (1945). The operational analysis of psychological terms. *Psychological Review*, *52*, 270-271, 291-294.

Skinner, B. F. (1960). Pigeons in a Pelican. *American Psychologist*, *15*, 28-37.

Terrace, H. S. (1993). The phylogeny and ontogeny of serial memory: List learning by pigeons and monkeys. *Psychological Science*, *4*, 162-169.

Thompson, N. S. (1993). Are some mental states public events? *Behavioral and Brain Sciences*, *16*, 662-663.

Thorndike, E. L. (1898). Animal intelligence: An experimental study of the associative processes in animals. *Psychological Monographs*, 2.

Tolman, C. W. (1987). Comparative psychology: Is there any other kind? *Journal of Comparative Psychology*, *101*, 287-291.

Van Hamme, L. J., & Wasserman, E. A. (1994). Cue competition in causality judgments: The role of nonpresentation of compound stimulus elements. *Learning and Motivation*, *25*, 127-151.

Van Hamme, L. J., Wasserman, E. A., & Biederman, L. (1992). Discrimination of contour-deleted images by pigeons. *Journal of Experimental Psychology: Animal Behavior Processes*, *18*, 387-399.

Wasserman, E. A. (1981). Comparative psychology returns: A review of Hulse, Fowler, and Honig's *Cognitive processes in animal behavior. Journal of the Experimental Analysis of Behavior*, *35*, 243-257.

Wasserman, E. A. (1984). Animal intelligence: Understanding the minds of animals through their behavioral "ambassadors." In H. L. Roiblat, T. G. Bever, & H. S. Terrace (Eds.), *Animal cognition* (pp. 45-60). Hillsdale, NJ: Erlbaum.

Wasserman, E. A. (1990). Detecting response-outcome relations: Toward an understanding of the causal texture of the environment. In G. H. Bower (Ed.), *The psychology of learning and motivation* (pp. 27-82). New York: Academic Press.

Wasserman, E. A. (1993). Comparative cognition: Beginning the second century of the study of animal intelligence. *Psychological Bulletin*, *113*, 211-228.

Wasserman, E. A. (1994). Common versus distinctive species: On the logic of behavioral comparison. *The Behavior Analyst*, *17*, 221-223.

Wasserman, E. A. (1995). The conceptual abilities of pigeons. *American Scientist*, *83*, 246-225.

Wasserman, E. A., DeVolder, C. L., & Coppage, D. J. (1992). Nonsimilarity-based conceptualization in pigeons via secondary or mediated generalization. *Psychological Science*, *3*, 374-379.

Wasserman, E. A., Gagliardi, J. L., Cook, B. R., Kirkpatrick-Steger, K., Astley, S. L., & Biederman, I. (1996). The pigeon's recognition of drawings of depth-rotated stimuli. *Journal of Experimental Psychology: Animal Behavior Processes*, *22*, 205-221.

Wasserman, E. A., Hugart, J. A., & Kirkpatrick-Steger, K. (1995). Pigeons show same-different conceptualization after training with complex visual stimuli. *Journal of Experimental Psychology*: *Animal Behavior Processes*, *21*, 248-252.

Wasserman, E. A., Kao, S.-F., Van Hamme, L. J., Katagiri, M., & Young, M. E. (1996). Causation and association. In D. R. Shanks, K. J. Holyoak, & D. L. Medin (Eds.), *The psychology of learning and motivation: Causal learning*. San Diego: Academic Press.

Wasserman, E. A., Kiedinger, R. E., & Bhatt, R. S. (1988). Conceptual behavior in pigeons: Categories, subcategories, and pseudocategories. *Journal of Experimental Psychology: Animal Behavior Processes*, *14*, 235-246.

Wasserman, E. A., Kirkpatrick-Steger, K., Van Hamme, L. J., & Biederman, I. (1993). Pigeons are sensitive to the spatial organization of complex visual stimuli. *Psychological Science*, *4*, 336-341.

Wasserman, E. A., & Miller, R. R .(1997). What's elementary about associative learning? *Annual Review of Psychology*, *48*, 573-607.

Watson, J. B. (1913). Psychology as the behaviorist views it. *Psychological Review*, *20*, 158-177.

Weiskrantz, L. (1985). *Animal intelligence*. New York: Oxford University Press.

Weisman, R. G., Njegovan, M., & Ito, S. (1994). Frequency ratio discrimination by zebra finches (*Taeniopygia guttata*) and humans (*Homo sapiens*). *Journal of Comparative Psychology*, *108*, 363-372.

Williams, J. L. (1974). Evidence of complementary afterimages in the pigeon. *Journal of the Experimental Analysis of Behavior*, *21*, 421-424.

Wilson, E. O. (1975). *Sociobiology*: *The new synthesis*. Cambridge, MA: Harvard University Press.

Zentall, T. R. (1993). Animal cognition: An approach to the study of animal behavior. In T. R. Zentall (Ed.), *Animal cognition: A tribute to Donald A. Riley* (pp. 3-15). Hillsdale, NJ: Erlbaum.

Zuriff, G. E. (1985). *Behaviorism: A conceptual reconstruction*. New York: Columbia University Press.

Zuriff, G. E. (1993). What's the stimulus? *Behavioral and Brain Sciences*, *16*, 664.

FROM EVOLUTION TO BEHAVIOR: EVOLUTIONARY PSYCHOLOGY AS THE MISSING LINK

Leda Cosmides & John Tooby (1987). . In J. Dupre (Ed.), *The latest on the best: Essays on evolution and optimality.*

The seminal articles in this book where not immediately recognized as historically significant, but as evolution teaches us, that which works is preserved. Over the years these articles became classics because they continued to be used and referenced more and more frequently. If indeed ideas are viruses of the mind, these articles were particularly contagious. The article "From Evolution to Behavior" by Cosmides & Tooby is a more contemporary article but it has already achieved the status of a classic in the field largely because it is not a typical article; it is a manifesto for the evolutionary psychology revolution. In it Cosmides & Tooby delineate eleven basic tenants and six procedural guidelines that distinguish and define evolutionary psychology and explicate how it functions in contrast to existing more traditional paradigms. Several of these tenants remain controversial and may not, in fact, stand the test of time. Nevertheless these tenants have become the pillars of evolutionary psychology.

Popular wisdom has it that arguments against new ideas in science typically pass through three characteristic stages, from

1. "It's not true," to
2. "Well, it may be true, but it's not important," to
3. "It's true and it's important, but it's not new —we knew it all along.

If the papers in this volume are any indication, then the application of evolutionary biology to the understanding of human behavior has entered the "It's true but not important" stage.

Yet evolutionary theory is important for understanding human behavior, and not everyone knows it—in fact, those most involved in the scientific investigation of "human nature" are generally the most unaware of its implications. We shall argue that the reluctance of many social scientists to appreciate or take advantage of the richness of the evolutionary approach is a direct consequence of a widespread tendency to overlook a crucial link in the causal chain from evolution to behavior: the level of innate psychological mechanisms, described as information processing systems. This level is pivotal, because it describes the mechanisms that actually link the evolutionary process to manifest behavior. It is these mechanisms that evolve over generations; within any single generation it is these mechanisms that, in interaction with environmental input, generate manifest behavior. The causal link between evolution and behavior is made through the psychological mechanism.

Efforts that skip this step in the evolutionary analysis of behavior, as valuable as they may be in other ways, have contributed to an erroneous caricature of the evolutionary approach to behavior as offering nothing more than post hoc compilations of correspondences between behavior and loosely reinterpreted evolutionary theory. But a rejection of the evolutionary approach based on such an incomplete and misleading characterization of its nature and valid possibilities is mistaken: as we shall discuss, the search for order in human behavior requires the application of the emerging principles of evolutionary psychology. We shall argue that an approach drawn from evolutionary psychology, consistently applied, can repair many of the deficiencies that have hampered progress in the social sciences.

1. Natural Selection Theory Does Not Predict Invariance in the Manifest Behavior of Different Individuals

Sciences prosper when researchers discover the level of analysis appropriate for describing and investigating their particular subject: when researchers discover the level where invariance emerges, the level of underlying order. What is confusion, noise, or random variation at one level resolves itself into systematic patterns upon the discovery of the level of analysis suited to the phenomena under study. The lack of success the behavioral sciences have had since their founding has been explained either by the claim that no such science is possible (e.g., human complexity intrinsically transcends any attempt to discover fundamental patterns) or by the view we share, that progress has been slow because scientific efforts have not yet, for the most part, been framed using concepts and organizing principles suitable to the phenomena under study. Can such an appropriate level of inquiry be found for a science of human behavior? Because humans are the product of the evolutionary process, the explanation for their characteristics must be sought in the evolutionary process: for a science of human behavior, the level of underlying order is to be sought in an evolutionary approach.

However, using evolution as an informing concept is not enough. During the formative period of modern behavioral ecology in the 1970s, many researchers thought that evolutionary biology would revolutionize research in human behavior; this conviction spread after the publication of E. O. Wilson's *Sociobiology* drew widespread attention to the dramatic advances that were taking place in the application of evolution to behavior. Many thought that evolutionary theory would reveal the level of underlying order, that the apparent variation in human behavior would resolve itself into systematic patterns, that invariant relationships would be identified, and that a true social science would emerge. However, after more than a decade, this is a revolution still waiting to happen.

We shall argue that the reason that progress has been slow is that, in the rush to apply evolutionary insights to a science of human behavior, many researchers have made a conceptual "wrong turn," leaving a gap in the evolutionary approach that has limited its effectiveness. This wrong turn has consisted of attempting to apply evolutionary theory directly to the level of manifest behavior, rather than using it as a heuristic guide for the discovery of innate psychological mechanisms.

The attempt to find evolutionary invariants at the level of manifest behavior has created a series of difficulties, from forced typological approaches, to using the "optimality" of manifest behavior (or the lack of it) as the measure of the success of the evolutionary paradigm. The assumption that manifest behavior should be invariant across individuals has invited a brute force, typological approach to variation in, for example, cross-cultural studies and primate behavior. All too often, the researcher would take the observed variation, average it, and typify the species or group by that average (see Tooby and DeVore, 1987, for a more extensive discussion of this problem). The variation itself is considered noise, or an embarrassment to be explained away. Those social scientists skeptical that biology had anything to offer to an understanding of human behavior would dwell on the extraordinary complexity of human behavior, and its enormous and engaging variety, and counterpose this richness to the clear explanatory inadequacy of what they considered to be naïve and simplistic typological characterizations.

Yet natural selection theory itself predicts that the manifest behavior of different individuals will vary enormously. Furthermore, it deductively implies that an individual's behavior will often appear far from "optimal," when optimality is defined without respect to the individual's social environment. The reasons why this is so are summarized by Tooby and DeVore (1987), in their discussion of hominid behavioral evolution. They include the following:

1. The interests of different individuals are often in conflict; in fact, much of modern evolutionary theory analyzes the conflicting fitness interests of different categories of individuals [e.g., self versus kin (Hamilton, 1964), parent versus offspring (Trivers, 1974), male versus female (Trivers, 1972)]. An interaction between individuals whose fitness interests conflict cannot, in principle, produce an outcome that is optimal for both individuals. The outcome will either be optimal for one party but not the other, or it will be nonoptimal for both.
2. Therefore, larger patterns of social behavior are not necessarily optimal for any individual or group of individuals, but rather may be the emergent result of the conflicting interests of interacting individuals, each selected to promote its own inclusive fitness. Frequently, therefore, the behavior of an individual cannot be understood in isolation; its behavior will be the mutual result of its interests and the counterstrategies of those with whom the individual is associated.
3. Individuals are selected to be adapted to their individual situation, not simply to their local habitat. For example, an individual's best behavioral strategy may depend on its size, its health, its aggressive formidability, its facility at accruing resources, or the number of sibs it can rely on for support. This means that organisms may be selected to be facultative strategists (where appropriate) rather than inflexibly committed to the same behavior or morphology. Consequently, individuals with the same psychological programming may manifest different behaviors in response to the different information they derive from assessing their own abilities and resources.
4. For certain social and reproductive behaviors, the favored strategy will depend on the distribution of other behaviors in the population [the prevailing analytic tool for dealing with this is game theory and evolutionarily stable strategies (Maynard Smith and Price, 1973)]. In such situations, selection can produce facultative psychological mechanisms that are sensitive to information indicating the distribution of relevant behaviors in the local population.
5. To be selected for, a trait need not be advantageous under every conceivable circumstance. It need only be of benefit *on balance*. This means it must be advantageous more often than not, or that the frequency with which it is advantageous, times the magnitude of the advantage, outweighs the frequency of disadvantage times the cost. Thus, selection for a trait is always against a background probability distribution of ancestral environmental conditions, and cannot be understood when abstracted from this background.
6. Therefore, natural selection cannot be expected to produce behavioral responses that maximize fitness under every imaginable circumstance. The situational specificity of adaptation depends on the selective history of similar situations. The degree of situational adaptation manifested by individuals will be a matter of (a) how common in the species' evolutionary history that situation has been, (b) how long (in phylogenetic terms) it has been recurring, and (c) how large its fitness consequences are. Organisms will be well adapted to common, important situations, reasonably adapted to common less important situations and uncommon highly important situations, but not adapted to uncommon, unimportant situations.
7. The recognition that adaptive specializations have been shaped by the statistical features of ancestral environments is especially important in the study of human behavior. Our species spent over 99% of its evolutionary history as hunter-gatherers in Pleistocene environments. Human psychological mechanisms should be adapted to those environments, not necessarily to the twentieth-century industrialized world. The rapid technological and cultural changes o the last several thousand years have created many situations, both important

and unimportant, that would have been uncommon (or nonexistent) in Pleistocene conditions. Evolutionary theorists ought not to be surprised when evolutionarily unprecedented environmental inputs yield maladaptive behavior. Our ability to walk fails us hopelessly when we are chased off a cliff.

Consequently, behavioral variation is not an embarrassment to evolutionary theory, it is a prediction of evolutionary theory. Equally, the assumption that individuals pursue strategies that will tend to promote their inclusive fitness deductively entails that (1) an individual's theoretically "optimal" behavioral strategy will vary, depending on the composition of its social group, and (2) an interaction between individuals whose fitness interests conflict cannot, in principle, produce an outcome that is optimal for both individuals. Typological approaches to manifest human behavior, involving attempts to interpret such behavior in terms of evolutionary optimality, violate these deductive implications of natural selection theory. For these and other reasons, the search for invariance on the level of manifest behavior will have very limited success.

When the appropriate level of analysis is found, variation becomes fuel in the search for order: instead of averaging out variation, one looks for systematic relations among the different varying elements. What is variable at one level manifests order—that is, invariance—at another. Instead of lamenting the complex variations in human behavior, researchers can use patterns in behavioral variation positively, as clues to the nature of the psychological mechanisms that produce behavior.

2. Evolution→Psychological Mechanism→Behavior

To speak of natural selection as selecting for "behaviors" is a convenient shorthand, but it is misleading usage. The error is worth belaboring, because the failure to appreciate it has delayed the fruitful application of evolutionary theory to human behavior by years. When used too casually, this shorthand misleads because it obscures the most important level of proximate causation: the psychological mechanism.

Natural selection cannot select for behavior per se; it can only select for mechanisms that produce behavior. There is nothing special about behavior in this regard; the same can be said, for example, of digestion. Natural selection can only rearrange patterns in tissues and molecules; these rearrangements have *effects*, and it is because they have these effects that they are selected for or not. Natural selection gives us teeth, salivary amylase, a peristaltic esophagus, an acid-filled stomach, an absorptive colon: mechanisms that produce digestion. The operation of these mechanisms causes certain molecules to be extracted from plant and animal tissues and incorporated into our own tissues: an effect that we call digestion. Natural selection gives us food processing machinery, and the operation of this machinery results in digestion, which is an effect of the functioning of mechanisms.

Behavior, like digestion, is an effect of the functioning of mechanisms. Natural selection can give you a reflex arc, and the functioning of this arc causes an effect: your leg swings when your knee is tapped. But this effect cannot occur in the absence of a mechanism for producing it. Behavior cannot occur sui generis; behavior is an effect produced by a causal system: proximately, by psychological mechanisms. Although researchers would acknowledge these points as patently obvious, in practice, many simply methodologically leapfrog this level, with unfortunate consequences such as those discussed. Their desire to do this stems, in many cases, from the belief that the exploration of mechanisms means the exploration of the neurophysiological bases of behavior, a difficult endeavor, and one that, at the present state of knowledge, is limited to addressing only very simple kinds of behaviors. However, there exists an alternative approach to the study of psychological mechanisms that does not involve neurophysiology, with its present limitations. This is the characterization of psychological mechanisms in terms of their information processing structure. This approach dovetails smoothly with evolution, because in the adaptive regulation of behavior, information is key.

Behavior is not randomly emitted; it is elicited by information, which is gleaned from the organism's external environment, and, proprioceptively, from its internal states. Natural selection gave us information processing machinery to produce behavior, just as it gave us food processing machinery to produce digestion. This machinery selects—and frequently seeks—particular information from the environment; it manipulates it, extracts inferences from it, stores some of it in memory in altered form, the machinery's output is used to make mental models, to inform other parts of the system, and to instruct the motor neurons responsible for behavior. *The evolutionary function of the human brain is to process information in ways that lead to adaptive behavior*; the mind is a description of the operation of a brain that maps informational input onto behavioral output.

Thus, behavior is one output of our information processing machinery. Behavioral output differs with informational input; the information processing machinery that maps informational input onto behavioral output is a psychological mechanism.

The psychology of an organism consists of the total set of proximate mechanisms that cause behavior. Natural selection, acting over evolutionary time, shapes these mechanisms so that the behavior of the organism correlates to some degree with its fitness. However, in the lifetime of any particular animal, it is the proximate mechanisms that actually cause behavior—not natural selection. If these proximate mechanisms can be understood, behavior can be predicted more exactly; understanding the fitness-promoting strategies studied by evolutionary theorists allows only approximate prediction. Behavior correlates exactly with proximate mechanisms, but only approximately with the fitness-promoting strategies that shaped those mechanisms.

Evolutionary psychology (Tooby, 1985) relates explanations in terms of adaptive strategy to explanations in terms of proximate mechanisms. Correct characterization of adaptive strategies gives precise meaning to the concept of function for proximate mechanisms. Reciprocally, a detailed analysis of the proximate mechanisms of a species gives rich insight into the present and past selective pressures that have acted on it. Psychological mechanisms constitute the missing causal link between evolutionary theory and behavior. Evolutionary theory frequently appears to lack predictive value because most researchers skip this crucial predictive and explanatory level. Yet it is the proximate mechanisms that cause behavior that promise to reveal the level of underlying order for a science of human behavior.

3. *The Cognitive Level of Explanation*

Psychological mechanisms can be studied on different descriptive and explanatory levels. Most biologically informed studies of proximate mechanisms have described psychological mechanisms in terms of their physiological underpinnings, finding, for example, that birth spacing is mediated by lactation, which suppresses ovulation, that testosterone levels change with shifts in dominance, thereby affecting agonistic behavior, or that one part of the brain controls language while another part controls sexual behavior.

But natural selection theory, so far, has made only limited contributions to the investigation of physiology. Just as different kinds of hardware can run the same computer program, different physiological mechanisms can accomplish the same adaptive function. Both humans and pitcher plants digest animal tissues, but the physiological mechanisms by which humans and pitcher plants accomplish this function are different. And there is another, pragmatic problem: unless you know that a particular information processing system exists and what its function is, it is very difficult to discover its physiological underpinnings. Who would look for the physiological mechanisms responsible for the contraction of the heart unless they first knew that the heart exists and that its function is to pump blood?

Although valuable, physiological studies do not address a crucial *functional* level of explanation, a level that describes what a mechanism does, rather than how it does it. Evolutionary oriented students of human behavior have neglected what may prove to be the most important level of proximate causation: the cognitive level. *Adaptive behavior* is *predicated on adaptive thought*: an animal must process information from its environment in ways that lead to fit behavior while excluding unfit behaviors. The cognitive level of explanation describes psychological mechanisms in functional terms, as programs that process information.[1]

Traditionally, ethologists have studied very simple cognitive programs: a newborn herring gull has a cognitive program that defines a red dot on the end of a beak as salient information from the environment, and that causes the newborn to peck at the red dot upon perceiving it. Its mother has a cognitive program that defines pecking at her red dot as salient information from her environment, and that causes her to regurgitate food into the newborn's mouth when she perceives its pecks.

Note that the descriptions of these simple programs are entirely in terms of the functional relationships among different pieces of information; they describe two simple information processing systems. Naturally, these programs are instantiated in some kind of neurological "hardware." However, knowledge of this hardware would add little to our understanding of these programs as information processing systems—presumably, one could build a silicon-based robot that would produce the same behavioral output in response to the same informational input. The robot's cognitive programs would maintain the same functional relationships among pieces of information, and therefore be identical to the cognitive programs of the herring gull. However, the robot's "neural" hardware would be totally different. The specification of a cognitive program constitutes a complete description of an important level of proximate causation, independent of any knowledge of the physiological mechanisms by which the program is instantiated.

We assume that the cognitive programs of different individuals[2] of a species are essentially the same—that cognitive programs are species-typical traits. However, the parameters fed into them can be expected to differ with individual circumstance. Insofar as individual variation in personal qualities (such as aggressive formidability or sexual attractiveness), in opportunities to engage in particular behaviors (to mate, to threaten, to help), and in the social and physical environment, are all parameters that feed into the same cognitive programs, variations in these parameters will produce variations in manifest behavior across individuals. Therefore, although the cognitive programs of different individuals should be essentially the same, the manifest behavior of different individuals may be different.[3] Cognitive programs constitute the level of invariance for a science of human behavior, not behavior itself.

When applied to behavior, natural selection theory is more closely allied with the cognitive level of explanation than with any other level of proximate causation. This is because the cognitive level seeks to specify a psychological mechanism's function, and natural selection theory is a theory of function. Natural selection theory specifies how an organism should respond to different kinds of information from its environment. It defines adaptive information processing problems that the organism must have some means of solving. Cognitive programs are solutions to information processing problems.

An evolutionary approach to understanding the cognitive level of proximate causation asks, What kind of programming must an organism have if it is to extract and process information about its environment in a way that will lead to adaptive behavior? How does the organism use information from its environment to compute what constitutes the "right" behavior at the right place and the right time (Staddon, this volume)?

4. *Evolution and the Cognitive Level*

It is nearly impossible to discover how a psychological mechanism processes information unless one knows what its function is, what it was "designed" or selected to do. Trying to map out a cognitive program without knowing what its function is, is like attempting to understand a computer program by examining it in machine language, without knowing whether it is for editing text, accounting, or launching the Space Shuttle. It is possible that a gifted programmer may finally figure it out, but not probable. If, on the other hand, the programmer knows that the program she is trying to map out is a text editor, she can begin by looking for a way of loading text, or for a command that will delete a word, or for a procedure that will move a whole paragraph. It is far easier to understand the architecture of a "black box" if one knows what it was designed to do.

Recognizing this, a number of cognitive scientists, such as Chomsky, Shepard, Fodor, and Marr, recently have argued that the best way to understand any mechanism, either mental or physical, is first to ask what its purpose is, what problem was it designed to solve (e.g., Chomsky, 1975; Shepard, 1981; Fodor, 1983; Marr and Nishihara, 1978).

This is exactly the question that evolutionary theory allows one to address—it allows one to pinpoint the kinds of problems the human mind was "designed" to solve, and consequently should be very good at solving. And although it cannot tell one the exact structure of the cognitive programs that solve these problems, it can suggest what design features they are likely to have. It allows one to develop a "computational theory" for that problem domain: a theory specifying what functional characteristics a mechanism capable of solving that problem must have (Marr, 1982; Marr and Nishihara, 1978).

Many cognitive psychologists assume that the human mind is a general-purpose computer with domain-general, content-independent processes. We shall argue that from an evolutionary point of view, this is a highly implausible and unparsimonious assumption, and logically impossible to sustain. There are domains of human activity for which the evolutionarily appropriate information processing strategy is complex, and deviations from this strategy result in large fitness costs. An organism that relied on the vagaries of trial-and-error learning for such domains would be at a selective disadvantage (see also Shepard, 1981).

Instead, for such domains, humans should have evolved "Darwinian algorithms"—specialized learning mechanisms that organize experience into adaptively meaningful schemas or frames (Cosmides, 1985). When activated by appropriate environmental or proprioceptive information, these innately specified "frame-builders" should focus attention, organize perception and memory, and call up specialized procedural knowledge that will lead to domain-appropriate inferences, judgments, and choices. Like Chomsky's language acquisition device, these inference procedures allow you to "go beyond the information given"—to reason adaptively even in the face of incomplete or degraded information (Bruner, 1973).

There are may domains of human activity that should have Darwinian algorithms associated with them. Aggressive threat, mate choice, sexual behavior, pair-bonding, parenting, parent-offspring conflict, friendship, kinship, resource accrual, resource distribution, disease avoidance, predator avoidance, and social exchange are but a few. The dynamics of natural selection rigidly constrain the patterns of behavior that can evolve in such domains, and therefore provide insights into the structure of the cognitive programs that produce these patterns.

In the remainder of this article we present arguments supporting this perspective.

5. Complex Adaptive Problems Should Be Defined in Computational Theories

The signal lesson lurking beneath the surface of modern evolutionary theory is that adaptive behavior requires the solution of many information processing problems that are highly complex—far more complex than commonly supposed. The cognitive programs that allow the newborn herring gull to gain sustenance from its mother are relatively simple: they directly connect the perception of an environmental cue with an adaptively appropriate behavioral response. But not all adaptive problems are so easily solved, and many complex adaptive problems can be solved only by complex cognitive programs.

Discovering the structure of complex cognitive programs requires a great deal of theoretical guidance. A series of hunt-and-peck experiments may uncover a few simple cognitive programs, but it is unlikely that a research program that is blind to function will ever uncover the structure of a complex information processing system—such as the human mind.

What form should this theoretical guidance take? In his pioneering studies of visual perception, David Marr argues that "computational theories" of each information processing problem must be developed before progress can be made in experimentally investigating the cognitive programs that solve them (e.g., Marr, 1982; Marr and Nishihara, 1978). A computational theory specifies the nature of an information processing problem. It does this by incorporating "constraints on the way the world is structured—constraints that provide sufficient information to allow the processing to succeed" (Marr and Nishihara, 1978, p. 41). A computational theory is an answer to the question, What must happen if a particular function is to be accomplished?

For example, the information processing problem that Marr wanted to understand was how an organism reconstructs three-dimensional objects in the world from a two-dimensional retinal display. As you walk around a table with a square top, for example, light reflected from the tabletop hits your retina, projecting upon it a two-dimensional trapezoid of changing dimensions. Yet you do not perceive an ever-deforming, two-dimensional trapezoid. Instead, your cognitive programs use these data to construct a "percept" of a stable, three-dimensional, square tabletop.

To understand how we compute solid objects from data like this, Marr and his colleagues first examined relevant constraints and relationships that exist in the world, like the reflectant properties of surfaces. They consider the discovery of such constraints the "critical act" in formulating a theory of this computation, because these constraints must somehow be used by and embodied in any cognitive mechanism capable of solving this problem (Marr, 1982; Marr and Nishihara, 1978). Marr calls the specification of such constraints, together with their deductive implications, a "computational theory" of an information processing problem.

Natural selection, in a particular ecological situation, defines and constitutes "valid constraints on the way the world is structured," and therefore can be used to create computational theories of adaptive information processing problems. For example, the cognitive programs of an organism that confers benefits on kin cannot violate the [cost to self < (benefit to kin member) x (coefficient to relatedness to kin member)] constraint of kin selection theory. Cognitive programs that violate this constraint cannot be selected for. Cognitive programs that instantiate this constraint can be selected for. This is inherent in the dynamics of natural selection, true of any species on any planet at any time. A species may lack the ability to confer benefit on kin, but if it has such an ability, then it has it by virtue of cognitive programs that produce behavior that respects this constraint.

The production of behavior that respects constraints imposed by the evolutionary process is a cognitive program's *adaptive function*: the reason it was selected for, the reason it could outcompete other cognitive programs and spread through the population to become a species-typical trait.

The specification of constraints imposed by the evolutionary process—the specification of an adaptive function—does not, in itself, constitute a complete computational theory. These constraints merely define what counts as adaptive behavior. Cognitive programs are the means by which behavior—adaptive or otherwise—is produced. The important question for a computational theory to address is, What kind of cognitive programs must an organism have if it is to behave adaptively?

Natural selection theorists do not usually think of their theories as defining information processing problems, yet this is precisely what they do. For example, kin selection theory raises—and answers—questions such as, How should the information that X is your brother affect your decision to help him? How should your assessment of the cost to you of helping your brother, versus the benefit to your brother of receiving your help, affect your decision? Will the information that Y is your cousin have a different effect on your decision that if you thought Y were your brother? In general, how should information about your relatedness to X, the costs and benefits to you of what X wants you to do for him, and the costs and benefits to X of your coming to his aid, affect your decision to help X?

As these questions show, an organism's behavior cannot fall within the bounds of the constraints imposed by the evolutionary process unless it is guided by cognitive programs that can solve certain information processing problems that are very specific. To confer benefits on kin in accordance with the constraints of kin selection theory, the organism must have cognitive programs that allow it to extract certain specific information from its environment: who are its relatives? which kin are close and which distant? what are the costs and benefits of an action to itself? to its kin? The organism's behavior will be random with respect to the constraints of kin selection theory unless (1) it has some means of extracting information relevant to these questions from its environment , and (2) it has well-defined decision rules that use this information in ways that instantiate the theory's constraints. A cognitive system can generate adaptive behavior only if it can perform specific information processing tasks such as these.

The fact that any organism capable of conferring benefits on its kin must have cognitive programs capable of solving these information processing problems does not imply that different species will solve each problem via the same cognitive program. There are many reasons why such programs may differ. For example, different environmental cues may have different reliabilities and accessibilities for different species. Moreover, each species occupies a different ecological niche, and hence the value of particular actions will differ across species: the cognitive programs of a baboon will assign a different value to social grooming than will the cognitive programs of a whale. But cognitive programs that perform the same function in different species may differ in more profound ways: the cognitive programs for recognizing kin might operate through phenotype matching in one species, but through early imprinting in another species. Both programs will accomplish the same important adaptive function. Yet they will embody radically different information processing procedures, and they will process different information from the environment.

Natural selection theory can be used to develop computational theories of adaptive information processing problems. As we shall show below, such computational theories are valuable as heuristic guides for psychological research, despite the fact that evolutionary theory does not uniquely specify which cognitive programs will be used to accomplish a given function.

6. The Importance of Computational Theories

The most essential part of a computational theory is a catalog of the specific information processing problems entailed by the constraints of natural selection theory. They should be made explicit, for they are the building blocks of psychological theories. There are two reasons why this is so.

The first is obvious. Knowing, for example, that an organism must have some means of distinguishing kin from nonkin may not uniquely determine the structure of a cognitive program, but it does help narrow hypotheses. The cognitive program responsible must be sensitive to environmental cues that correlate with kin, but do not correlate with non-kin. In most cases, very few cues from the species environment of evolutionary adaptedness will be sufficiently reliable or accessible, and the researcher can very quickly discover which are used by the organism's cognitive programs. Discovering which cues are used will illuminate other of the program's information processing procedures: early exposure suggests an imprinting process, whereas facial similarity suggests phenotype matching procedures. Step by step, deduction by deduction, the cognitive programs responsible for kin recognition can be mapped. In the meantime, the researcher who is blind to function will not even be looking for a program that guides kin recognition, let alone figure out which environmental stimuli it monitors, and how it processes them.

The second reason why a fully elaborated computational theory is essential is less obvious, but far more important. The computational theory allows a test of adequacy that any proposed psychological theory must be able to pass. The test is this: *Is the hypothesized system of cognitive programs powerful enough to realize the computational theory? That is, is the proposed mechanism capable of solving the adaptive problem?*

Any proposed cognitive system must be powerful enough to produce adaptive behavior while *not* simultaneously producing maladaptive behavior. Not just any cognitive program will do: our cognitive programs must be constructed in such a way that they somehow lead to the adaptive results specified by evolutionary theory on the basis of the information available. This crucial test of adequacy may allow researchers to eliminate whole categories of hypotheses, for current research in cognitive psychology and artificial intelligence suggests that many of the general-purpose learning theories that were popular in psychology's past are not powerful enough to solve even simple computational problems, let alone the complex problems posed by natural selection theory.

7. The Computational Theory Test

Thirty years ago, the study of the psychology of language took a major stride forward when Noam Chomsky developed a computational theory that allowed him to test whether certain hypothesized learning mechanisms were powerful enough to account for how humans acquire the ability to produce grammatical sentences. By this method, he was able to falsify the hypothesis that humans learn language through operant conditioning. Subsequently, others have used this method as a primary tool in constructing alternative psychological theories of language that are more powerful, and therefore more promising (for review, see Wanner and Gleitman, 1982). This incident shows that the "computational theory test" can provide an enormously effective tool for psychological theory.

Chomsky's (1957, 1959) computational theory was the grammar of the English language: a set of rules that can generate all the grammatical sentences of English, but no ungrammatical sentences. The information processing problem to be solved was, How do we learn this grammar? Can it be learned via the simple, stimulus-response (S-R) information processing mechanisms proposed by the behaviorists of the time, or does the acquisition of a natural language grammar require cognitive programming that is more specialized and complex?

Chomsky demonstrated that the general-purpose, S-R learning mechanisms proposed by the behaviorists were not powerful enough to allow one to acquire English grammar: they were not powerful enough to permit the speaker to produce many grammatical sentences, nor could they prevent the speaker from producing many ungrammatical sentences.

Native speakers of English have internalized its grammar; Chomsky showed that the behaviorists' learning mechanisms could not, in principle, account for this fact. He thereby falsified the hypothesis that we acquire grammar via such mechanisms. In fact, this computational theory test allowed him to eliminate a whole class of hypotheses: those invoking learning mechanisms that embody a "finite state grammar" (Chomsky, 1957).

This demonstration was an important turning point in the development of modern psychology. Up until that point, psychology has been dominated by behaviorism's general-purpose learning theories. These theories were *domain general*: the same process was supposed to account for learning in all domains of human activity, from suckling at the beast to the most esoteric feat of modern technology. Yet by specifying what actually needed to be accomplished in order to produce grammatical utterances, Chomsky showed that a task routinely mastered by two-year-old children was too complexly structured to be accounted for by behaviorist learning theory.

Chomsky' specification of a computational theory convinced many psychologists that no general-purpose learning mechanism would be powerful enough to permit the acquisition of the grammar of a natural language under natural conditions. But what kind of learning mechanism *would* have the requisite power? Chomsky (1980) argued that just as the body has many different organs, each of which is specialized for performing a different function—a heart for pumping blood, a liver for detoxifying poisons—the mind can be expected to include many different "mental organs." A mental organ is an information processing system that is specialized for performing a specific cognitive function. A mental organ instantiates learning theories that are *domain specific*: its procedures are specialized for quick and efficient learning about an evolutionarily important domain of human activity. Chomsky argued that the acquisition of a grammar could be accomplished only through a highly structured and complex "language acquisition device": a functionally distinct mental organ that is specialized for learning a language.

The controversy between Chomsky and the behaviorists has broad applicability. Many psychologists think of it as a controversy about innateness, but, as we shall see below, it was not. "Innate" is not the "opposite" of "learned." Every coherent learning theory—even Hume's associationism—assumes the existence of innate cognitive mechanisms that structure experience.[4] A "blank slate" will stay forever blank: Without innate cognitive mechanisms, learning is impossible (e.g., Hume, 1977/1748; Kant, 1966/1781: Quine, 1969; Popper, 1972). Rather, the controversy in psycholinguistics is important because it highlights the ambiguity of the most central concept in the history of psychology: learning.

8. "Learning" Is Not an "Alternative Hypothesis"

Many common concepts in the social sciences are used as if they are hypotheses and explanations, but in fact are not. "Learning" is a concept that many people believe is fully freighted with meaning; analytically, however, the only meaning to the word "learned" is environmentally influenced." As a hypothesis to account for mental or behavioral phenomena, it is nearly devoid of meaning. Processes categorized as "learning" are accomplished through information processing mechanisms. Such mechanisms may be simple or complex, domain general, or domain specific. An organism may have many different learning mechanisms, or just a few. The belief that the human mind contains only one, simple, domain general cognitive process that results in "learning"—be it "induction" or "hypothesis testing" or "conditioning"—is nothing but conjecture. It has no basis in fact, and can only be explained as a metatheoretical holdover from the heyday of behaviorism.

In reality, the controversy in psycholinguistics was over whether the innate learning mechanisms that allow humans to acquire a grammar are simple and domain general or complex and domain specific (e.g., Atherton and Schwartz, 1974; Chomsky, 1975; Katz, 1975; Marshall, 1981; Putnam, 1967). The behaviorists thought that the simple, domain general processes of classical and operant conditioning could account for language; Chomsky showed that they could not, and proposed the existence of learning mechanisms that were complex and domain specific. Both camps agreed that language is "learned"; they disagreed about *how* it is learned.

The failure to grasp this point leads to enormous conceptual confusion in the behavioral sciences. The common belief that "learning" is an alternative hypothesis to an evolutionary theory of adaptive function is a category error. Learning is a cognitive process. An adaptive function is not a cognitive process; it is a problem that is solved by a cognitive process. Learning is accomplished through psychological mechanisms (whose nature is not yet understood), and these were created through the evolutionary process, which includes natural selection. Consequently, the issue is not whether a behavior is the result of natural selection "or" learning. The issue is, What kind of learning mechanisms would natural selection have produced?

When models of cognitive programs become sufficiently well specified actually to account for empirical results, they often turn out to be complex and domain specific. When researchers present such well-specified models together with the empirical results that support them, they are often met with the counter-claim that "people might learn to think that way." Yet, the invocation of an unspecified learning process does not constitute a valid alternative hypothesis. Suggesting that "learning" is an alternative hypothesis is comparable to claiming that an alternative hypothesis to a well-specified theory of vision, such as Marr's (1982), is, "Light hits the retina and this causes the organism, to see three-dimensional objects. This is not an explanation; it is a description of the phenomenon to be explained. All the intervening steps are missing: it does not count as an "alternative hypothesis" because no one has bothered to specify the nature of the cognitive programs that cause it to happen.

"Learning" designates the phenomenon to be explained. A complex, domain specific cognitive program is a learning mechanism; how, then, can "learning" be construed as an "alternative hypothesis"?

The claim that a behavior is the product of "culture" is not an "alternative hypothesis" either. It entails nothing more than the claim that surrounding or preceding individuals are an environmental factor that have influenced the behavior under discussion in some way. It leaves the learning mechanisms that allow humans to acquire and generate culture completely unspecified (Tooby and Cosmides, 1987).

In speaking with evolutionary biologists and evolutionarily oriented anthropologists, we find that many operate from the implicit premise that an organism can "decide" which course of action, however complex, will maximize its inclusive fitness simply be inspecting the environment. These researchers interpret the fact that humans were produced by the evolutionary process to mean that humans must be maximizing their inclusive fitness in all situations—even in evolutionarily unprecedented modern environments. This view makes sense only if one believes that the organism has a "simple" cognitive program that says, "Do that which maximizes your inclusive fitness." Yet this is merely a veiled way of claiming that the organism "learns" what to do to maximize its fitness. It is not a hypothesis. It leaves "learning" a mysterious, omniscient, and utterly unspecified process.

It is improper to invoke an undefined process as an explanation. "Learning" should not be invoked to explain other phenomena at this point in the history of science, because it is itself a phenomenon that requires explanation. The nature of the cognitive processes that allow learning to occur are far from understood.

The tendency to assume that learning is accomplished only through a few simple domain general mechanisms lingers in cognitive psychology. We believe this metatheoretical stance is seriously flawed, and persists only because psychologists and evolutionary biologists have not joined forces to create computational theories that catalog the specific and detailed information processing problems entailed by the need to track fitness under Pleistocene conditions. Below, we join Rozin (1976, Shepard (1981), and Symons (1987) in arguing that a consideration of such problems suggests that natural selection has produced a great many cognitive programs that are complex and highly domain specific.

In this article, cognitive programs that evolved to accomplish important adaptive functions are called "Darwinian algorithms" (Cosmides, 1985).[5] We now turn to the question, Does natural selection theory suggest that most Darwinian algorithms will be domain general, or domain specific?

9. Why Should Darwinian Algorithms Be Specialized and Domain Specific?

Nature has kept us at a great distance from all her secrets, and has afforded us only the knowledge of a few superficial qualities of objects; while she conceals from us those powers and principles, on which the influence of these objects entirely depends. Our senses inform us of the color, weight, and consistence of bread; but neither sense nor reason can ever inform us of those qualities, which fit it for the nourishment and support of a human body. (David Hume, 1977/1748, p. 21)

Genes coding for psychological mechanisms that promote the inclusive fitness of their bearers will outcompete those that do not, and tend to become fixed in the population. The promotion of inclusive fitness is an evolutionary "end"; a psychological mechanism is a means by which that end is achieved. Can the human mind be comprised primarily of domain general and content-independent psychological mechanisms, and yet realize this evolutionary end? We shall argue that natural selection could not have produced such a psyche, nor could such a hypothetical psyche successfully promote fitness, that is, regulate behavior adaptively.

Consider how Jesus explains the derivation of the Mosaic code to his disciples:

> Jesus said unto him, "Thou shalt love the Lord, they God, will all thy heart, and with all thy soul, and with all thy mind. This is the first and great commandment. And the second is like it, Thou shalt love they neighbor as theyself. *On these two commandments hang all the law and the prophets.*" (Matthew 22:37-40, emphasis added)

Jesus has given his disciples a domain general, content-independent decision rule to be used in guiding their behavior. But what does it mean *in practice*? Real life consists of concrete, specific situations. How, from this rule, do I infer what counts as "loving my neighbor as myself" when, to pick a standard biblical example, my neighbor's ox falls into my pit? Should I recompense him, or him me? By how much? How should I behave when I find my neighbor sleeping with my spouse? Should I fast on holy days? Should I work on the Sabbath? What counts as fulfilling these commandments? How do I know when I have fulfilled them?

In what sense does all the law "hang" from these two commandments?

These derivations are not obvious or straightforward. That is why the Talmud was written. The Talmud is a "domain specific" document: an interpretation of the "law" that tells you what actions fulfill the injunctions to "love God" and "love your neighbor" in the concrete, specific situations you are likely to encounter in real life. The Talmud solves the "frame problem" (e.g., Boden, 1977; Fodor, 1983) posed by a "domain general" rule like Jesus'.

A domain general decision rule such as "Do that which maximizes your inclusive fitness" cannot guide behavior in ways that actually do maximize fitness, because what counts as fit behavior differs from domain to domain. Therefore, like the Talmud, psychological mechanisms governing evolutionarily important domains of human activity must be domain specific.

The easiest way to see that Darwinian algorithms must be domain specific is to ask whether the opposite is possible: In theory, could one construct a domain general, content-independent decision rule, that, for any two courses of action, would evaluate which better serves the end of maximizing inclusive fitness?

Such a rule must include a criterion for assessing inclusive fitness: there must be some observable environmental variable against which courses of action from any domain of human activity can be measured. As the maximization of inclusive fitness means differential representation of genes in subsequent generations, the time at which the consequence of an action can be assessed is remote from the time the action is taken. For simplicity's sake, let us assume that number of grandoffspring produced by the end of one's life is an adequate assessment of inclusive fitness. Using this criterion, the decision rule can be rephrased more precisely as, "Choose the course of action that will result in more grandoffspring produced by the end of one's life.

But how could one possibly evaluate alternative actions using this criterion? Consider a simple, but graphic example: Should one eat feces or fruit?

Clearly, no individual has two parallel lives to lead for purposes of comparison, identical except that he or she eats feces in one life and fruit in the other. Will trial and error work? The individual who eats feces is far more likely to contract parasites or infectious diseases, thereby incurring a large fitness cost. And if this individual instead eats fruit and leaves a certain number of grandoffspring, he or she still does not know whether eating feces would have been better: for all that individual knows, feces could be a rich food source that would greatly increase fecundity.

Does learning from others constitute a solution to the problem? Imitation is useless unless those imitated have themselves solved the problem of the adaptive regulation of behavior. If the blind lead the blind, there is no advantage in imitation. However, if others are monitored not as role models for imitation but instead as natural experiments, such monitoring does allow the comparison of alternative courses of action. However, each individual life is subject to innumerable uncontrolled and random influences that the observer would have to keep track of to make valid inferences. If the observer watches some people eat fruit, and others eat feces, and waits to see which have a larger number of grandoffspring, how would the observer know whether these individuals' differential fitness was caused by their diet or by one of the may other things they experienced in the course of their lives? Of course, perhaps the major problem is that of time delay between action and the cue used to evaluate the action: grandoffspring produced. It is fundamentally impractical to have to wait two generations to determine the value of choices that must be made today.

Moreover, why would others choose to learn through trial and error while the observer does not? The population of self-experimenters would be selecting themselves out, compared to the observers who parasitize their risky experiments.

Can the use of perceptual cues solve the problem? The individual could decide to eat what smells good and avoid what smells bad. However, this method violates the assumption that the information processing system is domain general, and side-steps the "grandoffspring produced" criterion entirely. Nothing smells intrinsically bad or good; the smell of feces if attractive to dung flies. Moreover, what establishes the knowledge that foul-smelling entities should not be eaten? Admitting smell or taste preferences is admitting domain specific innate knowledge. Admitting the inference that foul-smelling or foul-tasting entities should not be ingested is admitting a domain specific innate inference.

Without domain specific knowledge such as this, what kind of mechanism could result in learning to avoid feces and ingest fruit? Even if it were possible, an individual with appropriate domain specific knowledge would enjoy a selective advantage over one who relied on "trial and possibly fatal error" (Shepard, this volume). The tendency to rely on trial and error in this domain would be selected out; domain specific Darwinian algorithms governing food choice would be selected for, and become a species-typical trait.

There is also the problem of deciding which courses of action to evaluate. The possibilities for action are infinite, and the best a truly domain general mechanism could do is generate random possibilities to be run through the inclusive fitness decision rule. When a tiger bounds toward you, what should your response be? Should you file your toenails? Do a cartwheel? Sing a song? Is this the moment to run an uncountable number of randomly generated response possibilities through the decision rule? And again, how could you compute which possibility would result in more grandchildren? The alternative: Darwinian algorithms specialized for predator avoidance, that err on the side of false positives in predator detection, and, upon detecting a potential predator, constrain your responses to flight, fight, or hiding.

The domain general "grandchildren produced" criterion fails even in these simple situations. How, then, could it work in more complicated learning situations—for example, when an action that increases your inclusive fitness in one domain decreases it in another? Suppose the hypothetical domain general learning mechanism somehow reached the inference that sexual intercourse is a necessary condition for producing offspring. Should the individual, then, have sex at every opportunity?

According to evolutionary theory, no. There are large fitness costs associated with, for example, incest (e.g., Shepher, 1983). Given a potential partner with a physique, personality, or resources that would normally elicit sexual desire, the information that the potential partner is close kin must inhibit sexual impulses.

How could this be learned? Again, if a female engages in incest, then loses her baby after a few months, how would she know what caused the miscarriage? Each life is a series of many events (perhaps including sex near the time of conception with nonkin as well as kin), any one of which is a potential cause. Why conclude that sex with one individual, who physically and psychologically resembles other members of his sex in many respects, caused the loss of the baby?

The need to avoid incest implies the ability spontaneously and automatically to acquire the category "kin versus nonkin" by merely observing the world—even if it were possible to learn it by engaging in incest, the fitness costs would be too high. But the "number of grandoffspring produced" decision rule cannot be used to acquire evolutionarily crucial categories through mere observation: unless a categorization scheme is used to guide behavior, it has no consequences on fitness.

Kin recognition requires Darwinian algorithms tuned to environmental cues that are correlated with kin but not with nonkin. These cues must be used in a particular way: either they must be used to match self to other, as in facial or olfactory phenotype matching, or they must categorize others directly, as when one imprints during a critical period on those with whom one was raised. There are an infinite number of dimensions that could be used to carve the environment into categories; there is no assurance that a general-purpose information processing system would ever isolate those useful for creating the kin/nonkin categorization scheme, and the "grandchildren produced" criterion cannot guide such a system toward the appropriate dimensions.

Additionally, there is the problem of generalization. Suppose the psyche somehow had correctly inferred that avoiding sex with kin had positive fitness consequences. How could one generalize this knowledge about the kin/nonkin categorization scheme to other domains of human activity? Would one, for example, avoid any interaction with kin? This would be a mistake; selectively avoiding sex with kin has positive fitness consequences, but selectively avoiding helping kin has negative fitness consequences (given a certain envelope of circumstances—Hamilton, 1964).

Thus, not only must the acquisition of the kin/nonkin categorization scheme be guided by domain specific Darwinian algorithms, but its adaptive use for guiding behavior is also domain specific. In the sexual domain, kin must be avoided; in the helping domain, they must be helped; when one needs help, kin should be among the first to be asked (Hamilton, 1964); when one is contagiously ill, kin should be selectively avoided (Tooby, 1982). The procedural knowledge governing how one behaves toward kin must differ markedly from domain to domain. Only Darwinian algorithms with procedural knowledge specific to each of these domains can assure that one responds to kin in evolutionarily appropriate ways. Simply put, *there is no domain general criterion of fitness that could guide an equipotential learning process toward the correct set of fit responses.*

Trial-and-error learning is inadequate, not only because it is slow and unreliable, but because there is no domain-independent variable for signaling error. In the sexual domain, error = sex with kin. In the helping domain, error = not helping kin given the appropriate envelope of conditions. In the disease domain, error = infecting kin.

Consequently, there are only two ways the human mind can be built. Either

1. All innate psychological mechanisms are domain general, and therefore do not track fitness at all.

or

2. Some innate psychological mechanisms are domain specific Darwinian algorithms with procedural knowledge specialized for tracking fitness in the concrete situations hominids would have encountered as Pleistocene hunter-gatherers.

Clearly, the first alternative is no alternative at all. Unguided plasticity is evolutionarily fatal there are an infinite number of unfit courses of action, and only a narrow envelope of fit behaviors. A psyche without Darwinian algorithms is incapable of keeping the organism within this narrow envelope. The idea that humans evolved from cognitively constrained ancestors into general problem solvers, now nearly devoid of adaptive specializations but equipped instead with generalized learning mechanisms, cannot be sustained. No one has yet been able to specify a general learning mechanism or general cognitive problem solver that has the power to solve the complex array of adaptive problems faced by humans, either in principle or in practice. Moreover, not only are more general sets of decision procedures less likely to provide correct guidance, but also they tend to be slower than sets of procedures designed to take advantage of the recurrent features of defined adaptive problems. In sum, advocates of the idea that the human mind is comprised predominantly of a set of domain general learning procedures has to explain how genes that code for such a maladaptive system could outcompete genes that code for existing successful adaptive specializations.

10. Darwinian Algorithms Solve the "Frame Problem"

Darwinian algorithms can be seen as scheme- or frame-*builders*: as learning mechanisms that structure experience along adaptive dimensions in a given domain. Positing them solves the "frame problem"—which is the name artificial intelligence researchers gave to the family of problems with domain general mechanisms that emerged in their own work, and that parallel those raised in the discussion above.

Researches in artificial intelligence have found that trial and error is a good procedure for learning only when a system already has a well-specified model of what is likely to be true of a domain, a model that includes a definition of what counts as error. Programmers call this finding the "frame problem" (e.g., Boden, 1977; Fodor, 1983). To move an object, make the simplest induction, or solve a straightforward problem, the computer must already have a sophisticated model of the domain in question: what counts as an object or stimulus, what counts as a cause, how classes of entities and properties are related, how various actions change the situation, what goal is to be achieved. Unless the learning domain is severely circumscribed and the procedure highly specialized and content-dependent—unless the programmer has given the computer what amounts to vast quantities of "innate knowledge"—the computer can move nothing, learn nothing, solve nothing. The frame problem is a concrete, empirical demonstration of the philosophical objections to the *tabula rasa*. It is also a cautionary tale for advocates of domain general, content-independent learning mechanisms.

Unfortunately, the lesson has been lost on many. Although most cognitive psychologists realize that their theories must posit some innate cognitive architecture, a quick perusal of textbooks in the field will show that these still tend to be restricted to content-independent operation system characteristics: short-term stores, domain general retrieval and storage processes, imager buffers. Researchers who do insist on the necessity of positing content-dependent schemas or frames (e.g., Minsky, 1977; Schank and Abelson, 1977) seldom ask how these frames are built. Their approach implicitly presumes that frames are the product of experience structured only by domain general learning mechanisms[7]—yet the building of frames must also be subject to the frame problem. Even Fodor (1983), a prominent exponent of the view that the mind's innate architecture includes specialized, content-dependent modules, restricts these to what he calls "input systems": perceptual or quasi-perceptual domains like vision, hearing, and language. He doubts the existence of modules governing "central" processes like reasoning and problem solving. Yet one wonders: Without domain specific inference processes, how can all these perceptual data be expected to guide our behavior in adaptive directions?

Restricting the mind's innate architecture to perceptual systems, a content-independent operating system, a domain general concept learning mechanism, a content-independent hypothesis testing procedure, and a small ragbag of dimensions for construing similarity might be sufficient if it did not matter what a person learned—if, for example, learning that E is the most frequently used letter in the English language were as critical to one's inclusive fitness as learning that a hungry tiger can leave a sizable hole in one's life plan. But what a person learns does matter; and not only what, but when, how reliably, and how quickly. Even more important is what a person *does* with that knowledge. The purpose of learning is, presumably, to guide behavior. Should one eat gravel? Should one engage in incest? How willing should a person be to give up the last remaining food available for feeding one's own children? Natural selection theory provides definite answers to questions like these, because the wrong decision can be shown to result in large fitness costs. How can an equipotential learning system that simply looks for relations in the world provide information about the relative value, in inclusive fitness terms, of alternative courses of action? It cannot; it has no standard for assessing it.

Cognitive psychologists can persist in advocating such systems only because they are not asking what problems the mind was designed, by natural selection, to solve. The Darwinian view is that humans have innately specified cognitive programs that allow them to pursue goals that are (or once were) correlated with their inclusive fitness. These innately specified programs cannot all be domain general. Behavior is a transaction between organism and environment; to be adaptive, specific behaviors must be elicited by evolutionarily appropriate environmental cues. Only specialized, domain specific Darwinian algorithms can ensure that this will happen.[8]

11. The Frame Problem and So-Called "Constraints" on Learning

Biologists and psychologists have an unfortunate tendency to refer to the properties of domain specific (but no domain general) mechanisms as "constraints." For example, the one-trial learning mechanism, discovered by Garcia and Koelling (1966), that permits a blue jay to associate a food taste with vomiting several hours later is frequently referred to as a "biological constraint on learning." Books reporting the existence of domain specific learning mechanisms frequently have titles like *Biological Boundaries of Learning* (Seligman and Hager, 1972) or *The Tangled Wing: Biological Constraints on the Human Spirit* (Konner, 1982). This terminology is seriously misleading, because it incorrectly implies that "unconstrained" learning mechanisms are a theoretical possibility; it implicitly denies the existence of the frame problem.

All constraints are properties, but not all properties are constraints. Calling a property a "constraint" implies that the organism would have a wider range of abilities if the constraint were to be removed.

Are a bird's wings a "constraint on locomotion"? Birds can locomote by flying or hopping. Wings are a property of birds that enables them to locomote by flying, but wings are not a "constraint on locomotion." On the contrary. Wings expand the bird's capacity to locomote—with wings the bird can fly *and* hop. Removing a bird's wings reduces its capacity to locomote—without wings, it can hop, but not fly. Wings cannot be a constraint, because removing them does not give the bird a wider range of locomoting abilities. If anything, wings should be called "enablers," because they enable an additional form of locomotion. Having them expands the bird's capacity to locomote.

A thick rubber band placed in such a way that it pins a bird's wings to its body is a constraint on the bird's ability to locomote: With the rubber band the bird can only hop; without it the bird can both fly and hop.

Similarly, there is no evidence that the domain specific mechanisms that permit one-trial learning of an association between taste and vomiting are "constraints on learning." Removing the specific properties that allow the efficient learning of this particular association would not expand the bird's capacity to learn; it would reduce it. Not only would the blue jay be unable to associate a food taste with an electric shock; it would also be unable to associate a food taste with vomiting.

The tendency to refer to such innate knowledge as "constraints on learning" is perhaps the result of the mistaken notion that a *tabula rasa* is possible, that learning is possible in the absence of a great deal of domain specific innate knowledge. If true, then a property that "prepares" an organism to associate a taste with vomiting might preclude it from associating a taste with an electric shock. However, if an organism with this prepared association also had a domain general associative mechanism, there is no a priori reason why that mechanism should not work to pair taste with electric shocks. In order to call the prepared association a "constraint" on the learning caused by the general purpose mechanism, one would have to demonstrate empirically that the activation of the prepared association by the presence of food somehow causes the general-purpose mechanism to shut down.

Rozin and Schull (1987) have pointed out another way in which the terminology of constraint is misleading: it implies that the human mind was "built down" from a more general-purpose cognitive system present in our ancestors. Yet such a phylogenetic history seems far from likely: it presumes that our primate ancestors had a capacity to learn that was broader and more powerful than our own.

12. Conclusions

Many evolutionary biologists seem to think that once they have identified an adaptive function, their job is done: specifying how the organism accomplishes the function is a trivial matter. This is comparable to thinking that once Einstein had shown that $E = mc^2$, designing a nuclear power plant was a trivial matter. Understanding what properties a cognitive program must have if it is to accomplish an adaptive function is far from trivial—it is one of the most difficult and challenging problems of this century.

There is emerging a new method, here called evolutionary psychology, which is made possible by the simultaneous maturation of evolutionary biology, paleoanthropology, and cognitive psychology. Together, these disciplines allow the discovery and principled investigation of the human psyche's innate cognitive programs. We propose that they be combined according to the following guidelines:

1. Use evolutionary theory as a starting point to develop models of adaptive problems that the human psyche had to solve.
2. Attempt to determine how these adaptive problems would have manifested themselves in Pleistocene conditions, insofar as this is possible. Recurrent environmental features relevant to the adaptive problem, including constraints and relationships that existed in the social, ecological, genetic, and physical situation of early hominids, should be specified; these constitute the conditions in which the adaptive problem arose, and further define the nature of the adaptive problem. Such features and relationships constitute the only environmental information available to whatever cognitive program evolved to solve the adaptive problem. The structure of the cognitive program must be such that it can guide behavior along adaptive paths given only the information available to it in these Pleistocene conditions.
3. Integrate the model of the adaptive problem with available knowledge of the relevant Pleistocene conditions, drawing whatever valid and useful implications can be derived from this set of constraints. Catalog the specific information processing problems that must be solved if the adaptive function is to be accomplished.

This constitutes a computational theory of the adaptive information processing problem. The computational theory is then used as a heuristic for generating testable hypotheses about the structure of the cognitive programs that solve the adaptive problem in question.

4. Use the computational theory to (a) determine whether there are design features that *any* cognitive program capable of solving the adaptive problem must have and (b) develop candidate models of the structure of the cognitive programs that humans might have evolved to solve the adaptive problem. Be sure the model proposed is, in principle, powerful enough to realize the computational theory.
5. Eliminate alternative candidate models with experiments and field observation. Cognitive psychologists have already developed an impressive array of concepts and experimental methods for tracking complex information processing systems—these should be used to full advantage. The end result is a validated model of the cognitive programs in question, together with a model of what environmental information, and other factors, these programs take as input.
6. Finally, compare the model against the patterns of manifest behavior that are produced by modern conditions. Informational inputs from modern environments should produce the patterns of manifest behavior predicted by the model of the cognitive programs already developed.

As previously discussed, some who adopt the evolutionary perspective attempt to leap directly from step one to step six, neglecting the intermediate steps, searching only for correspondences between evolutionary theory and modern manifest behavior.

Attempts to finesse a precise characterization of the cognitive programs that cause human behavior have led to a series of roadblocks in the application of evolutionary biology to the behavioral sciences. Because they leave the causal chain by which evolution influenced behavior vague and unspecified, such attempts have sown the widespread confusion that hypotheses about economics, culture, consciousness, learning, rationality, social forces, etc., constitute distinct alternative hypotheses to evolutionary or "biological" explanations. Instead, such hypotheses are more properly viewed as proposals about the structure of evolved cognitive programs and the kinds of information they take as input.

Cognitive psychology and evolutionary biology are sister disciplines. The goal of evolutionary theory is to define the adaptive problems that organisms must be able to solve. The goal of cognitive psychology is to discover the information processing mechanisms that have evolved to solve them. Alone, each is incomplete for the understanding of human behavior. Together, applied as a unified research program, they offer the promise that by using their organizing principles, the level of analysis appropriate for describing and investigating human behavior has, at last, been found.

Notes

1. See, for example, Block (1980) or Fodor (1981) for more discussion of the nature of cognitive explanations.
2. At least of the same sex and age.
3. Of course there can be individual variation in cognitive programs, just as there is individual variation in the size and shape of stomachs: this can be true of any structure or process in a sexually recombining species, and such genetic variation constitutes the basis for "inherited" or "constitutional" psychological differences. However, because even simple cognitive programs or "mental organs" must contain a large number of processing steps, and so must have complex polygenic bases, they necessarily evolve slowly, leading to variation being mostly "superficial." There is a large amount of variation among humans concerning single or quantitative characteristics of specific organ systems, but there is almost no variation among humans in what organs exist, or the basic design of each organ system. Everyone has a heart, and a liver, and so on, and everyone's heart and liver function in much the same way. We expect that this pattern holds for "mental organs" as well. Such variation, whether it is of "physical" or "mental" organ systems, can modify the functioning of these systems between individuals—sometimes

drastically. Phenylketonuria is the result of a single gene modification. Nevertheless, such variation must be recognized as modifications of a design whose integrity is largely intact, and is not likely to consist of a wholly different design, differing "from the ground up." We find implausible, on the basis of population genetics considerations, the notion that different humans have fundamentally different and competing cognitive programs, resting on wholly different genetic bases.

For these and other reasons, we believe such variation can be better detected and understood if behavioral scientists devote most of their early research effort to elucidating the most commonly shared and basic design features of human cognitive programs.

A more likely kind of phenomenon is one in which wholly different cognitive programs become activated in different individuals, but exist latently in all individuals, based on a species-typical genetic basis. Such facultative programs can be differentially activated early in the life cycle (setting individuals along different developmental tracks), by short-term situational elicitation, or even as the result of superficial (in the sense discussed above) genetic differences in other parts of the genome (e.g., constitutional differences or gender). Gender is the most dramatic example of this facultative latency: although the profound differences between male and female have a large genetic basis, each gender has the full genetic specification for both genders. Which set of simultaneously coexisting genes becomes activated in any particular individual depends on the presence or absence of a single gene, the H-Y antigen, on the Y chromosome.

4. Herrnstein (1977) points out that Skinnerian learning theorists were able to avoid discussion of the cognitive mechanisms governing generalization and discrimination only by ignoring the problem. Available in the environment are an *infinite* number of dimensions that could be used for generalization and discrimination—but which does the organism actually use?

5. They have been called "adaptive specializations" by Rozin (1976), "modules" by Fodor (1983), and "cognitive competences" by Chomsky (1975). In our view, such mechanisms have two defining characteristics: (1) they are most usefully described on the cognitive level of proximate causation and (2) they are adaptations. We prefer "Darwinian algorithms" to the other terms because it emphasizes both characteristics.

6. The argument holds whether you characterize the process as trial and error, induction, or hypothesis testing.

7. Recently, this belief was stated explicitly by Cheng and Holyoak (1985), who cite "induction" as the process that builds their content-dependent "pragmatic reasoning schemas."

8. We would like to direct the reader to Rozin (1976), Herrnstein (1977), Staddon (1987), and Symons (1987) for similar arguments from slightly different perspectives.

Bibliography

Atherton, M., and R. Schwartz (1974). Linguistic Innateness and Its Evidence. *The Journal of Philosophy* LXXI:6.

Block, N. (1980). What Is Functionalism? In N. Block (ed.), *Readings in Philosophy of Psychology*, Cambridge, MA: Harvard University Press.

Boden, M. (1977). *Artificial Intelligence and Natural Man.* New York: Basic Books.

Bruner, J. S. (1973). *Beyond the Information Given* (J. M. Anglin, ed.). New York: Norton.

Cheng, P. W. and K. J. Holyoak (1985). Pragmatic Reasoning Schemas. *Cognitive Psychology* 17:391-416.

Chomsky, N. (1957). *Syntactic Structures*. The Hague: Mouton.

Chomsky, N. (1959). Review of Skinner's "Verbal Behavior." Language 35:26-58.

Chomsky, N. (1975). *Reflections on Language*. New York: Random House.

Chomsky, N. (1980). *Rules and Respresentations*. New York: Columbia University Press.

Cosmides, L. (1985). Deduction or Darwinian Algorithms?: An Explanation of the "Elusive" Content Effect on the Wason Selection Task. Doctoral dissertation, Department of Psychology and Social Relations, Harvard University.

Fodor, J. A. (1981). The Mind-Body Problem. *Scientific American* 244(1): 124-133.

Fodor, J. A. (1983). *The Modularity of Mind.* Cambridge, MA: MIT Press.

Garcia, J., and R. A. Koelling (1966). Relations of Cue to Consequence in Avoidance Learning. *Psychonomic Science* 4:123-124.

Hamilton, W. D. (1964). The Genetical Evolution of Social Behavior. *Journal of Theoretical Biology* 7:1-52.

Herrnstein, R. J. (1977). The Revolution of Behaviorism. *American Psychologist* 32:593-603.

Hume, D. (1977/1748). *An Enquiry Concerning Human Understanding* (E. Steinberg, ed.). Indianapolis: Hackett.

Kant, I. (1966/1781). *Critique of Pure Reason*. new York: Anchor Books.

Katz, J. J. (1975). Innate Ideas. In S. P. Stich (ed.), *Innate Ideas*, Berkeley: University of California Press.

Konner, M. (1982). *The Tangled Wing: Biological Constraints on the Human Spirit*. New York: Holt, Rinehart, & Winston.

Marr, D. (1982). *Vision: A Computational Investigation into the Human Representation and Processing of Visual Information*. San Francisco: Freeman.

Marr, D., and H. K. Nishihara (1978). Visual Information Processing: Artificial Intelligence and the Sensorium of Sight. *Technology Review* October: 28-49.

Marshall, J. C. (1981). Cognition at the Crossroads. *Nature* 289:613-614.

Maynard.Smith, J., and G. R. Price (1973). The Logic of Animal Conflict. *Nature* (London) 246:15-18.

Minsky, M. (1977). Frame-System Theory. In P. N. Johnson-Laird and P. C. Wason (eds.). *Thinking: Readings in Cognitive Science.*, Cambridge: Cambridge University Press.

Popper, K. R. (1972). *Objective Knowledge: An Evolutionary Approach.* London: Oxford University Press.

Putnam, H. (1967). The "Innateness Hypothesis" and Explanatory Models in Linguistics. *Synthese* 17:12-22.

Quine, W. V. O. (1969). *Ontological Relativity and Other Essays*. New York: Columbia University Press.

Rozin, P. (1976). The Evolution of Intelligence and Access to the Cognitive Unconscious In J. M. Sprague and A. N. Epstein (eds.). *Progress in Psychobiology and Physiological Psychology*, New York: Academic Press.

Rozin, P., and J. Schull (1987). The Adaptive-Evolutionary Point of View in Experimental Psychology. In R. C. Atkinson, R. J. Herrnstein, G. Lindsey, and R. D. Luce (eds). *Handbook of Experimental Psychology*.

Schank, R., and R. P. Abelson (1977). *Scripts, Plans, Goals, and Understanding*. Hillsdale, NJ: Lawrence Erlbaum Associates.

Seligman, M. E. P. and J. L. Hager (1972). *Biological boundaries of Learning*. New York: Meredith.

Shepard, R. N. (1981). Psychophysical Complementarity. In M. Kubovy and J. R. Pomerantz. *Perceptual Organization*, Hillsdale, NJ: Erlbaum.

Shepard, R. N. (1984). Ecological Constraints on Internal Representation. Resonant Kinematics of Perceiving, Imagining, Thinking, and Dreaming. *Psychological Review* 91:417-447.

Shepard, R. N. (this volume). Evolution of a Mesh between Principles of the Mind and Regularities of the World. In J. Dupré (ed.), *The Latest on the Best*, Cambridge, MA: MIT press.

Shepher, J. (1983). *Incest: A Biosocial View*. New York: Academic Press.

Staddon, J. E. R. (1987). Learning as Inference. In R. C. Bolles and M. D. Beecher (eds.). *Evolution and Learning*, Hillsdale, NJ: Erlbaum.

Staddon, J. E. R. (this volume). Optimality Theory and Behavior. In J. Dupré (ed.). The Latest on the Best, Cambridge, MA: MIT Press.

Symons, D. (1987). If We're All Darwinians, What's the Fuss About? In C. Crawford, D. Krebs, and M. Smith (eds.), *Sociobiology and Psychology*, Hillsdale, NJ: Erlbaum

Tooby, J. (1982). Pathogens, Polymorphism and the Evolution of Sex. *Journal of Theoretical Biology* 97:557-576.

Tooby, J. (1985). The Emergence of Evolutionary Psychology. In D. Pines (ed.), *Emerging Syntheses in Science*, Santa Fe: Santa Fe Institute.

Tooby, J. and L. Cosmides (1987). Evolutionary Psychology and the Generation of Culture Part I: Theoretical Considerations. *Ethology and Sociobiology*.

Tooby, J. and I. DeVore (1987). The Reconstruction of Hominid Behavioral Evolution through Strategic Modeling. In W. G. Kinzey (ed.), *Primate Models for the Origin of Human Behavior*, New York: SUNY Press.

Trivers, R. L. (1972). Parental Investment and Sexual Selection. In B. Campbell (ed.), *Sexual Selection and the Descent of Man* 1871-1971. Chicago: Aldine.

Trivers, R. L. (1974). Parent-Offspring Conflict. *American Zoologist* 14:249-264.

Wanner, E., and L. R. Gleitman (1982). *Language Acquisition: The State of the Art*. Cambridge: Cambridge University Press.

Wilson, E. O. (1975). *Sociobiology: The New Synthesis*. Cambridge, MA: Harvard University Press.

EXAPTATION: A CRUCIAL TOOL FOR AN EVOLUTIONARY PSYCHOLOGY

Stephen Jay Gould (1991). *Journal of Social Issues,(47) 3,* 43 - 65.

Building on an article written in biology with Elizabeth Vbra, Stephen Jay Gould extends his reasoning about "how things got to be the way they are" emphasizing one of the basic themes infusing the articles chosen for this book, ***the absolute importance of understanding your organism****. Gould and Vbra recognized the error of inferring a trait's evolutionary cause based solely upon its current function. This paper sheds light on the confusion regarding the concept of adaptation. In an attempt to ameliorate the situation they coined the term exaptation which describes a trait that may not have originally evolved for its present function. The most common example of adaptation and exaptation can be seen in the flight of birds. How did birds develop the ability to fly when their wings were originally used for thermo insulation? The bird's wing became an exaptation for catching insects. Over time natural selection exaggerated the bird's feathers and the wings function was co-opted into something new. The large feathers became exaptations for flight. Exaptation use to be called pre-adaptation but this is misleading because it implies that evolution can foresee what is going to occur in the future and that there has been previous preparatory planning. This is exactly what Darwin was arguing against and why he did not use the word evolution in the Origin. At the time the word evolution meant development, something like a species growing up the way a child grows up, passing through predetermined stages of development. Gould argues that evolutionary psychology should focus on exaptations instead of adaptation. This article discusses in detail how exaptations apply to psychological reasoning.*

Evolutionary theory lacks a term for a crucial concept—a feature, now useful to an organism, that did not arise as an adaptation for its present role, but was subsequently coopted for its current function. I call such features "exaptations" and show that they are neither rare nor arcane, but dominant features of evolution—though previously unappreciated in the context of the overly adaptationist neo-Darwinian theory. This article argues that exaptation overcomes the fallacy of human sociobiology, helps us to understand the major patterns of flexibility and contingency in life's history, revises the roles of structure and function in evolutionary theory, serves as a centerpiece for grasping the origin and meaning of brain size in human evolution, and thereby cries out for recognition as a key to evolutionary psychology. Historical origin and current utility are distinct concepts and must never be conflated.

A Terminological Odyssey

In his classis treatise, "On the Nature of Limbs," published in 1849, Richard Owen presented a conundrum for biologists committed to the principle of adaptation—a word and concept of ancient pedigree, long antedating Darwin's later explanation in terms of evolution by natural selection. Mammals, and humans especially, must begin life with a tight squeeze—the passage of the relatively large fetal head through the narrow birth canal. The bones of the skull are not yet fully ossified or sutured together. Consequently, the nonrigid head can be "molded" as the bones alter their positions to allow this first essential adjustment to extrauterine life. If this molding could not occur, birth with such a large head would be impossible. Thus, we seem to have a *prima facie* case for a *vitally important adaptation* in this delayed ossification of skull bones. After all, big heads are a key to human success, and delayed ossification permits big heads. (With limited brain growth after birth, small neonatal heads and later expansion may not represent an option for an alternative pathway.)

Yet Owen, Britain's greatest vertebrate anatomist and first director of the independent natural history branch of the British Museum, denied that delayed ossification could rank as a mammalian adaptation—for the excellent reason that "lower" vertebrates (and mammalian ancestors), which need only to break free from an egg, share this feature with us. Owen wrote, linking the case to a general critique of adaptationism by way of Sir Francis Bacon's famous simile about the barrenness of teleology in general:

> Such a final purpose is indeed readily perceived and admitted in regard to the multiplied points of ossification of the skull of the human fetus, and their

> relation to safe parturition. But when we find that the same ossific centers are established, and in similar order, in the skull of the embryo kangaroo, which is born when an inch in length, and in that of the callow bird that breaks the brittle egg, we feel the truth of Bacon's comparison of "final causes" to the Vestal Virgins, and perceive that they would be barren and unproductive of the fruits we are laboring to attain. (1849, p. 40)

Charles Darwin, whose strongly adaptationist theory set the problem (by imposing limits of thought) that this paper addresses, took Owen's point and example to heart, and repeated the case in a cautionary note on overindulgence in adaptationist explanation (Darwin, 1859, p. 197):

> The sutures in the skull of young mammals have been advanced as a beautiful adaptation for aiding parturition, and no doubt they facilitate, or may be indispensable for this act; but as sutures occur in the skulls of young birds and reptiles, which have only to escape from a broken egg, we may infer that this structure has arisen from the laws of growth, and has been taken advantage of in the parturition of the higher animals.

This case raises some of the deepest issues in evolutionary theory but, for now, let me pose a question almost laughably trivial in comparison (yet deceptively profound as an opening to the generalities): If the term "adaptation" be inappropriate for reasons given by Owen and Darwin, what shall we call this eminently useful delay of ossification in the human embryo? We cannot maintain a clear concept if we have no name for the primary phenomenon so illustrated.

We might honor the fact that delayed ossification did not arise "for" its current role in parturition by calling it a "nonadaptation" or a "nonaptation" (and such cumbersome terms are in frequent use, by yours truly among others—see Gould, 1984). But such a resolution would be unsatisfactory for at least two reasons beyond infelicity: (a) active concepts should not be defined negatively by what they are not, and (b) "nonaptation" would not get at the heart of the evolutionary meaning of the phenomenon—that a useful structure may arise for other reasons and then be coopted for its present role.

I can imagine two solutions to this terminological problem:

1. We might extend "adaptation"—the great warhorse term of Darwinian evolution—to cover this phenomenon. Delayed ossification is useful in parturition, and "adaptation" is about use—so why not extend a term for a *process of building utility* into a general description for the *state of utility*, whatever its origin? (Insofar as evolutionary biologists have considered the issue at all, they have favored this extension. Nonetheless, most extensions of "adaptation" from process to state do not represent an active decision, consciously devised and defended, but rather a passive oozing forth of a favored term beyond a logical border into a defenseless territory. Many biologists have not even considered the crucial difference between historical origin and current utility. In a thoughtless analog of the contemporary motto "if it feels good, do it," they have simply taken the line, "if it works, call it adaptation.") But this extension should be rejected for two reasons:

(a) *Historical.* Adaptation, throughout the history of English usage in biology, has been a "process term," not a "state term." This definition inheres in etymology, for an adaptation is, literally, something fit (*aptus*) by active construction for (*ad*) its usage. The process meaning conforms with vernacular use; we can adapt a bicycle for a young beginner by installing training wheels, but no one would call a credit card an adaptation for opening certain kinds of locked doors, even though the card works as well for this purpose as does the altered bike for a stable ride. Moreover, and most importantly, the process definition affirms a long tradition of professional usage within evolutionary biology. The previous quotation from Darwin himself clearly supports the "process" definition—for Darwin states that some colleagues have called delayed ossification an adaptation, but they are wrong because this eminently useful feature has been coopted, rather than built for, successful parturition. This usage enjoys an unbroken pedigree, and is explicitly defended in the most important modern work on adaptation—for Williams (1966, p. 6) argues that we should speak of adaptation only if we can "attribute the origin and perfection of this design to a long period of selection for effectiveness in this particular role."

(b) *Conceptual and utilitarian.* For a historical scientist, no conceptual tool can be more important than the clear separation of *historical origin* and *current utility*. The false conceptual passage from present function to initial construction ranks with the post hoc fallacy and the confusion of correlation with cause as primary errors of reasoning about temporal sequences. We all understand this principle in the case of human artifacts: No one would claim that the U.S. Mint made dimes thin so that all Americans could carry surrogate screwdrivers in their change purses. And we all laugh at Voltaire's Dr. Pangloss when he exclaims: "Everything is made for the best purpose. Our noses were made to carry spectacles, so we have spectacles. Legs were clearly intended for breeches, and we wear them."

2. We might recognize a lacuna (favorite fancy word of scholars, though the vernacular "gap" will do nicely) in current terminology and coin a new term for the important phenomenon illustrated by the case of delayed ossification—i.e., vital current utility based on cooptation of structures evolved in other contexts and for other purposes (or perhaps for no purpose at all). We who dwell in the jargon-polluted groves of academe should propose new words only with the greatest caution, in the direst of circumstances, and in the absence of any other reasonable solution to a problem. The most compelling justification for a new term resides in conceptual gaps and persistent errors in thought reasonably connected with the absence of a category in the taxonomy of ideas. For a concept without a name often lies hidden from identification and use.

Elisabeth Vrba and I struggled with this issue in our attempts to formulate theories of large-scale evolutionary change. We finally decided that the absence of a term for "useful structures not evolved for their current function, but coopted from other contexts" had produced a sufficiently long-standing and serious muddle to warrant a new term by the criteria suggested above. We therefore proposed the term

Table 1. A Taxonomy of Fitness

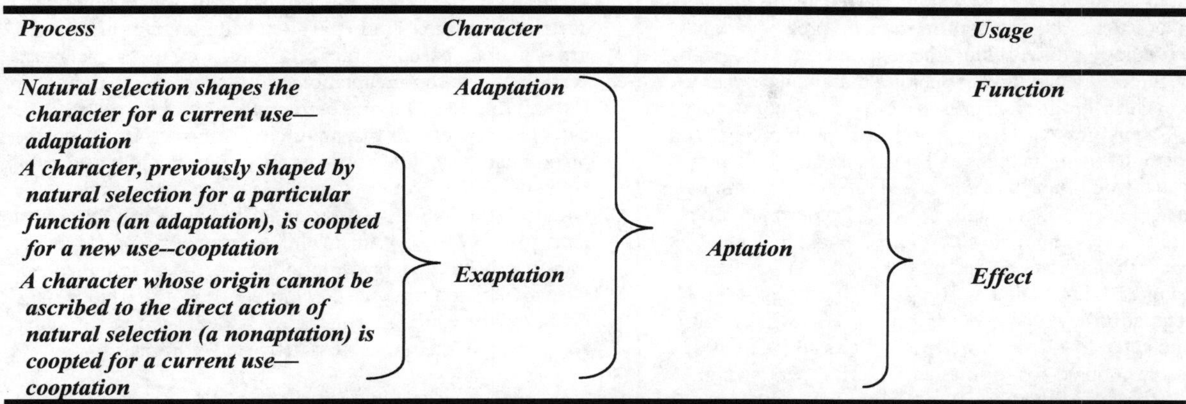

Process	*Character*		*Usage*
Natural selection shapes the character for a current use—adaptation	***Adaptation***		***Function***
A character, previously shaped by natural selection for a particular function (an adaptation), is coopted for a new use--cooptation		***Aptation***	
A character whose origin cannot be ascribed to the direct action of natural selection (a nonaptation) is coopted for a current use—cooptation	***Exaptation***		***Effect***

"exaptation" for "features that now enhance fitness, but were not built by natural selection for their current role" (Gould & Vrba, 1982, p. 4). The extent of immediate commentary (Lewin, 1982) and later usage and debate (Endler & McLellan, 1988; Gans, 1988; Pierce, 1988; Chatterton & Speyer, 1989; and many others) convinces us process, traditional adaptation (Darwin's usage) occurs when natural selection shapes a feature for its current use. If characters are built for other reasons, and then "seized" for an altered utility, we speak (using a vernacular term) of "cooptation." Coopted characters may have been built by natural selection for a different function (e.g., the proto-wing, initially evolved as an adaptation for thermoregulation and later coopted for flight, according to the standard, classic conjecture), or may have risen for no adaptive purpose at all (e.g., as a sequel or consequence of another adaptation, in what Darwin called "correlation of growth"). In either case, coopted structures will probably undergo some secondary modification—counting as superimposed, true adaptation—for the newly seized function. (The feather, for example, will need some redesign for efficient flight—as we can scarcely imagine that a structure evolved for thermoregulation would be accidentally and optimally suited for something so different as aerial locomotion.) But such secondary tinkering does not alter the primary status of such a structure as coopted rather than adapted.

For current state, we reluctantly permit *stare decisis* in retaining "adaptation" for characters built by selection of their current use. (We assume, for example, that the elaborate plumages and behavioral displays of male birds of paradise are true adaptation for mating success.) We do regret the retention of the same word—adaptation—for both a process and a utility arising by the process, but we bow to entrenched convention here. We then fill the previous gap by coining *exaptation* for useful structures coopted from other contexts—for such structures are fit (*aptus*) not by explicit molding for (*ad*) current use, but as a consequence of (*ex*) properties built for other reasons.

that, at the very least, we identified a conceptual weakness not sufficiently appreciated by evolutionary biologists in the past.

In our "taxonomy of fitness" (see Table 1), process, state (character), and usage must be distinguished. In the realm of

We recognize, of course, that distinction of adaptation from exaptation requires knowledge of historical sequences—and that such evidence is often, probably usually, unavailable. In such cases, we may only know that a structure is currently useful—and we may be unable to identify the source of utility. In such cases, we urge that the neutral term "aptation" (encompassing both ad- and ex-aptation) be used in place of the conventional and falsely inclusive "adaptation." (Vrba and I are delighted that since publication of our revised taxonomy in 1982, this recommendation has been followed by many biologists—see Vermeij, 1987, and Allmon, in press—whatever their feeling about our term "exaptation.")

In the final category of usage, adaptations have functions, but "function" cannot describe the utility of an exaptation. To cite Williams' (1966) amusing but profound example, flying fishes fall back into the water by virtue of gravity, and this descent is essential to their continued existence. But weight, as an inevitable property of matter in Newton's world, is an exaptation for falling back, clearly not an adaptation. In ordinary English usage, we would not call falling back a function of weight. We therefore, following Williams, designate the utility of an exaptation as an "effect" (again choosing vernacular English—falling back is an effect of weight).

One final point on terminology: Evolutionists have always recognized that some currently useful structures must be coopted rather than adapted—if only because cooptation provides the classical solution to the famous "problem of the incipient stages of useful structures." In plain English and concrete form, how can wings evolve for flight it 5% of a wing confers no conceivable aerodynamic benefit? The classical solution argues that wings evolved for something else (thermoregulation, in the most common scenario) and were then coopted.

In standard terminology, the proto-wing is called a "preadaptation" for flight. I doubt that any other evolutionary term has been so widely viewed as misleading and problematical. All teachers introduce "preadaptation" with an apology, disavowing the explicit etymological claim for foreordination, and explaining that the term really does not mean what it plainly says. But we did not decide to coin "exaptation" as a mere etymological nicety. If "preadaptation" had included all that "exaptation" now supplies, we would not have suggested our revision. As its major inadequacy, "preadaptation" covers only one of the two styles of cooptation, and therefore cannot subsume all exaptations. Preadaptations are built for one purpose, and then coopted for another (e.g., wings built for thermoregulation are coopted for flight). But what about the second category?—structures not built as adaptations at all, but later coopted for utilities just as vital (e.g., weight existing by virtue of the physics of matter, is then coopted for falling back into the water). Preadaptation does not cover the large domain of nonaptations later coopted for utility – and "exaptation" is therefore needed to fill a substantial lacuna. I argue in the next section that the concept of coopted nonaptation is the key to a proper evolutionary psychology for the human brain – and exaptation is therefore especially vital in human affairs.

I need hardly mention—for it forms the underlying theme of this paper—that the conceptual incubus of this entire tale is the overreliance on adaptation so characteristic of English evolutionary thought, and the insufficiently critical acceptance of this bias in cognate fields that, however properly, have borrowed evolutionary concepts for their own explanations.

The Cardinal Dilemma of an Evolutionary Psychology

As bodies, humans are a poor (or at best an average) work among mammals. Our insecure status between ape and angel arises from the state of our brains as "continuous with yet somehow transcending" (or at least awfully special—and I do mean "awful" in the old sense of inspiring awe). The truth of continuationism leads us to apply evolutionary concepts as keys to elucidating our own mental functioning—for should not the cardinal theory of biology unlock the secrets of a structure that attained its unique power by evolving large size and attendant complexity? But the appearance of transcendence inspires us to seek something special to resolve something unique.

My own reaction to this dilemma (old-fashioned rationalist and materialist that I am) leads me toward the continuationist pole for two basic reasons. First, new qualities can arise from accretion and diversification of quantity—and human mental uniqueness might therefore emerge from a brain altered and enlarged under natural selection. Second, I recognize that affirmations of unbridgeable uniqueness represent the lingering solace of Western philosophical traditions more than any empirical claim upon our attention. But as I veer toward continuationism and evolutionary reductionism, I am stopped by the equally biased ills of that pole—particularly by the rationales for dubious social behaviors (from the colonial expansionism and industrial exploitation of Darwin's day, to modern sexism) that have been sought in evolutionary arguments. And if the 19th-century themes found their rationalization primarily in the evolutionary doctrine of progress (and the attendant notion of higher and lower people, based on race, class, or sex), the 20th-century version relies on adaptationism ("never say higher or lower," to quote Darwin, but empirical differences may be evolved solutions to disparate circumstances based on the preeminent calculus of individual reproductive success). And so—choose your metaphor—we are stuck between the horns of a dilemma, Scylla and Charybdis, a rock and a hard place. We want an evolutionary psychology, but the traditional offerings of evolutionists seem so wrongheaded. Do we abandon the quest, or do we seek a more adequate evolutionary version? This paper is dedicated to the latter solution—an attempt to steer between the horns.

The Horn of Scylla (Who is Indeed a Rock)

We sense a basic fallacy (or at least an unconscious ideological embeddedness) in a proposed evolutionary psychology, but we are told that its proposals are deduced and necessary consequences of something worth our ultimate respect, and usually called "Darwinism," or simply "evolutionary theory"—so we must either take it, or leave the whole (and abstractly sensible) enterprise.

The latest widely bruited proposal for such an evolutionary psychology has been issued by the self-proclaimed discipline of sociobiology. (If "sociobiology" is used generically and loosely to refer to any evolutionary account of organismal behavior, then its status is unexceptionable and deniable only by creationists. Do any of us wish to assert that behavior does not evolve? The "sociobiology debate" has occurred because this term did not arise (and has not been used) generically, but quite specifically to label the particular style of theorizing advocated by E.O. Wilson (1975).

Wilson is a strict Darwinian (an ultra-Darwinist in the terminology of Blanc, 1990). I have great respect for this powerful and coherent intellectual position, though I regard it as deeply wrong in the most interesting way (Gould, 1982; Gould & Lewontin, 1979; Vrba & Gould, 1986). Strict Darwinism is a monistic, one-level theory of evolutionary causation. It holds that, with exceptions of trivial relative frequency, all evolution occurs by natural selection acting upon individual organisms that are struggling (metaphorically to be sure) for personal reproductive success. Since such success must be measured in transmission of genes to the next generation, any behavior that maximizes the passage will be favored. In particular, an organism need not prevail by its own copulations; helping relatives who share enough genes may do just as well—hence Haldane's famous dictum as an evolutionary calculus: "I am prepared to lay down my life for more than 2 brothers or more than 8 first cousins" (reported in Hamilton, 1964/1971, p. 42). For this reason, kin selection, the central concept of modern sociobiology, is a buttress to ultra-Darwinism (not a statement about group selection—i.e., aid to unrelated others at a cost to oneself—as it is sometimes misinterpreted in popular accounts; for it takes behaviors (like altruism) that seem contrary to the key Darwinian belief in personal struggle and renders them adaptive in the service of individual reproductive success.

In my view, this Darwinian apparatus is true and powerful at its own level, but limited in scope both in its own domain (because constraints of many kinds, both positive and negative, have as much influence as natural selection in determining evolutionary pathways—see Gould, 1989) and in its power to explain evolution at infra- and supra-organismal levels (for selection and other evolutionary processes also occur at levels below and above individuals—on genes and species, for example—and a hierarchical account of causation is therefore required).

Adaptation is the key concept of ultra-Darwinism—for natural selection on individuals, in this view, holds almost exclusive sway, and natural selection produces adaptation (defined as genetically based forms and behaviors that foster individual reproductive success). Selection is difficult to ascertain directly, but its product—adaptation—is always present and palpable. Thus, the actual research program of ultra-Darwinism relies upon the identification of adaptations and the inference to their genetic basis and production by natural selection.

We now come to the crux of the fatal flaw in human sociobiology. As an ultra-Darwinian account of human behavior, the theory is committed to explanation in terms of adaptation. It must use the following general research strategy: break up the behavioral repertoire into items, posit an advantage for each item in terms of individual reproductive success, assume an genetic basis for the behavior (not necessarily direct), and then infer that natural selection built the item for its implied advantages in the great calculus of reproductive struggle.

The political debate on sociobiology has focused on the politically conservative implications of arguing that group differences in behavior (particularly between the sexes) are naturally sanctioned as adaptations, and hard or impossible to alter as a consequence of their genetic basis. But it would be wrong to argue, as some have, that a political agenda motivated the theory. Rather, these consequences flow from ultra-Darwinian commitment to the hegemony of adaptation; they are logical entailments of a biological theory, not overt political programs masquerading as science.

Human sociobiology is fundamentally wrong because (for reasons elaborated in the next section) ultra-Darwinism, especially in its commitment to adaptationism, is fallacious (or at least vastly overextended)—not because many of us do not like its political implications. If any overt politics motivated the origin of human sociobiology, blame the academic jockeying of disciplinary extension, prestige, and imperialism (e.g., reduction of the social sciences to biology), not the larger social constructs of conservatism and laissez-faire. (And if you, as social scientists, wish to take a compassionate view of our efforts in biological imperialism—in a sermon-on-the-mount manner of loving one's adversaries—then do understand that we have often been subject to the same denigration by physicists and chemists. It is a sad fact that the oppressed often take up the tools of oppression.)

The Horn of Charybdis (Who, as a Whirlpool, Is Indeed a Hard Place)

Wilson did argue, and even illustrate pictorially (1975, p. 5), that the behavioral sciences as now constituted would be cannibalized to nothingness by absorption into cellular biology (on the one side) and into evolutionary biology (on the other). In the context of such a battlecry, I can hardly blame social scientists for rallying about their own flag, and digging deeper into their own trenches for defense of territorial integrity. And thus we understand the temptations of Charybdis; for if Scylla be the acceptance of thralldom, then Charybdis is the whirlpool of self-reference and exclusion of all external influence. But surely this will not do—and will ultimately prove as harmful as Scylla—for an obvious reason: Humans are animals, products, like every other twig on the tree of life, of billions of years of evolutionary history. It would be the most extraordinary happening in all intellectual history if the cardinal theory for understanding the biological origin and construction of our brains and bodies had no insights to offer to disciplines that study the social organizations arising from such evolved mental power. We may reject blinkered or inadequate accounts of human behavior (i.e., the part-by-part adaptationism of ultra-Darwinian sociobiology), and we should certainly combat proposed "partnership" by destruction and incorporation (the reduction of social sciences to evolutionary biology). But, surely, the struggle in social science must be to find and use a more adequate evolutionary biology, not to reject proffered aid and genuine partnership because certain previous proposals have been poisoned apples of temptation rather than pipes of peace and shared feasts. This paper is really dedicated to a simple proposition in this vein—that such a partnership of mutual respect and enlightenment can be forged, and that the key intellectual instrument can be found in the concept of exaptation.

The Human Brain as a Prima Facie Case for Dominant Exaptation in the Radical Mode

The strict, or ultra-Darwinian, style of evolutionary argument grew in popularity during the 1940s and 1950s, and peaked in the international orgy of celebrations attending the centenary of the *Origin of Species* (and the sesquicentenary of Darwin's birth, for he published his greatest work conveniently at age 50 in 1859). As a main feature of this "hardening of the evolutionary synthesis" (as I have called this historical trend—see Gould, 1983, and affirmation of my thesis in Provine, 1986), reliance upon adaptationist explanations, to the near exclusion of everything else, became a watchword of evolutionary argument. This tendency culminated in sociobiology, and reached its caricatured hypertrophy (for all theories engender a dark side among uncritical acolytes) in speculative excesses of pop human sociobiology in the adaptationist mode (see Kitcher, 1985, for a critique).

But, since the 1970s, the main focus of evolutionary theory has begun to move in the opposite direction toward a critique of ultra-Darwinian narrowness and an expansion of concepts (with a retained Darwinian core). The two major themes of this expansion have a common thrust in revoking the hegemony of adaptationism and substituting a plurality of reasons for evolved forms and behaviors.

1. ***Levels and hierarchy***. If natural selection works simultaneously on several levels of an ascending genealogical hierarchy, and if events at one level have effects at other levels by upward and downward causation (see Vrba & Gould, 1986), then phenomena at the organismic level need not be interpreted as Darwinian adaptations (the only available reading under ultra-Darwinism), for effects of other levels may also influence organismal phenotypes. Any feature promoting species selection by enhancing speciation rate will appear in more and more species of a clade (a branch of an evolutionary tree), but not for any advantage in the reproductive struggle among individuals. Any genetic element that can promote its own replication may provide several copies to the entire set of genes, with marked potential effects on evolution of the phenotype but without selection at the conventional Darwinian level of organismic struggle.

2. ***Constraints and channels***. In the purest form of Darwinism, variation is raw material only—copious in amount, small in extent, and randomly distributed in all directions about a modal form. Thus, all directional change occurs by natural selection, and all evolved forms may be interpreted as adaptations. Of course, no biologist has ever advocated total purity. Organisms are not congeries of atomized parts, each independent of all others. Adaptive change in one part entails correlated alteration of others, often for structural and developmental reasons unrelated to immediate adaptation. (Darwin took a great interest in this subject, which he called "correlation of growth.") The architecture of genetic and embryological system sets channels of possible change. Selection may be required to push an organism down a channel, but the channel itself, though not an adaptation, acts as a major determinant of evolutionary direction. Above all, constraints of genealogy strictly limit the realm of conceivable adaptation (e.g., wheels might work well for locomotion, but organisms, built of physically connected parts, cannot fashion them).

No Darwinian has ever rejected the existence of constraints and channels. Rather, the conventional Darwinian argument denies them any important relative frequency in the production of phenotypes. Correlations exist, but can be broken by selection. Constraints occur, but powerful selection always finds a way (for example, even if a thumb must be built from a wrist bone, as when the panda's carnivoran heritage irretrievably altered its first digit to preclude opposability—Gould, 1980). The proper refutation of this argument must also invoke relative frequency—that is, by claiming high and irrevocable importance for the nonaptations of channels and constraints. Exaptation provides a rationale for such an argument.

If we allow that revocation of adaptationist hegemony is a major reform of modern evolutionary theory, how does exaptation contribute—and how can this reform provide a more adequate evolutionary psychology? Of the two categories of exaptation, the second goes further in questioning adaptationist orthodoxy. In the first category, features evolved by natural selection for one purpose are coopted for another. This mode of exaptation breaks the false link of current utility with historical origin and, in doing so, refutes a great deal of muddled thinking that often passes for science in evolutionary reasoning about human origins. Thus, hands may be very good for throwing rocks, shooting arrows, and pressing triggers, but we may not infer that manipulability therefore arose as an adaptation for success in aggression. But this first mode of exaptation is not an argument against adaptationist hegemony because a feature's origin still resides in adaptation, and this mode speaks only of a shift in utility.

But in the second category—illustrated by delayed skull ossification and flying fish falling into water—presently useful characters did not arise as adaptations of all, but owe their origin to side consequences of other features (inevitable physical properties of mass for flying fish, an unknown reason for developmental delay of the cranium for ossification). In other words, the presently useful character (an aptation in our revised terminology) arose for nonadaptive reasons—and the conventional Darwinian style of adaptationist argument cannot, in principle, resolve its origin. If exaptations of this second type are common, then classical Darwinism encounters a serious limit.

Spandrels

Gould and Lewontin (1979) have referred to these coopted nonaptations as "spandrel," borrowing an architectural term for spaces left over between structural elements of a building (e.g., the triangular space between the outer curve of an arch and the straight-sided walls and ceiling that bound the arch). Spandrels are not adaptations, but spaces left over following an architectural decision (which we may view as an analog of adaptation) to build with arches. But the bare spandrels are often ornamented later, and the chosen designs may fit the space with uncanny genius and beauty (e.g., four evangelists and four Biblical rivers in the four spandrels of the central dome in Venice's Cathedral of San Marco in our "type" example—Gould & Lewontin, 1979). No one would argue that the spandrels exist to house the evangelists, no matter how good the fit. Yet lesser biological fits of form to function are often viewed as adequate evidence of adaptation.

Many Darwinian biologists had never considered the spandrels argument at all, and our choice of a clear (and ideologically neutral) architectural example did serve as a guide to comprehension and acceptance. But again, as with constraints and channels (see above), no cogent adaptationist rebuttal has ever denied the possibility or actuality of spandrels (which manifestly, after all, do exist). The sciences of natural history (and the social sciences as well) are domains of relative frequency, not (at least usually) of crucial experiments and single-case refutations based on laws of nature. The issue is not whether spandrels exist, but whether we encounter them frequently and whether they matter in the broad sweep of evolution. The adaptationist acknowledges their intelligibility, but constructs an argument to relegate them to a periphery of unimportance. (Nearly all arguments in evolutionary science proceed in this manner. Even for the most fundamental phenomenon of natural selection itself, no one has ever claimed exclusivity, but only predominant relative frequency. The main alternative, genetic drift, is inescapable in theory and undeniable in nature. The adaptationist ploy must argue for unimportance, not nonexistence—as in the classic claim that drift only occurs in tiny populations on the brink of extinction anyway.)

The adaptationist attack on spandrels therefore adopts the two classic strategies for winning an argument about relative frequency—what I call the "sequelae" and the "nooks and crannies" themes. The sequelae argument claims that spandrels only occur later and secondarily—as correlated consequences of a primary adaptation, never as active phenomena in themselves. To this I reply: (1) The claim is not always true (the weight of a flying fish just is; weight is not secondary to or subordinately correlated with any adaptation). (2) The importance issue is not status at origin, but later evolutionary meaning; the last shall be first, and the correlated consequence may emerge as the directing feature. To say it one more time: Historical origin and current utility are different concepts.

The nooks and crannies argument holds that spandrels are just funny little spaces left over after adaptation sketches the major features of form and behavior. Again, I offer a twofold response: (1) Spandrels can be spatially extensive whatever their temporal status (the pendentive supports of a dome mounted on arches may cover more area than the dome itself). (2) The design and secondary utilization of spandrels may then feed back and determine major features of the entire structure. San Marco is a good example because mosaic decorations on the radially symmetrical central domes are designed in four-part symmetry, in clear harmony with the four pendentives below—so the form and number of spandrels determines the design of the "main" structure in this case.

The pro-spandrel arguments are clear enough in concept, but can we cash them out in practice? Can we locate important cases in which spandrels become more numerous and more important than the primary forms that generate them? If so, then the radical category of explanation—current utility based on original nonaptation ("spandrels," for an easier tag)—assumes great importance in evolution (and becomes much more than an interesting theoretical wrinkle in an abstract taxonomy of evolutionary possibilities).

The Human Brain

As the primary point of this paper, I wish to present an argument for regarding the human brain as, *prima facie*, the best available case for predominant exaptation—in other words, for a near certainty that exaptations must greatly exceed adaptations in number and importance (the proper criterion of relative frequency). Based on this argument, exaptation becomes a crucial concept for an evolutionary psychology. Much of our cultural tradition has been devoted to defining human uniqueness, particularly in terms of brain power and action. We may epitomize the evolutionary version of this massive interdisciplinary effort by stating that the human brain is, *par excellence*, the chief exemplar of exaptation.

The case can be best developed by recalling a famous episode from the history of evolutionary theory. Charles Darwin drew no boundaries in applying his theory of natural selection to organic nature. He specifically included the human brain—the structure that he had called "the citadel itself" in an early notebook—and he wrote two books (Darwin, 1871, 1872) on the evolution of human bodies, brains, and emotional expressions.

Alfred Russel Wallace, codiscoverer of natural selection, applied the theory (far more rigidly than Darwin, as we shall see) to everything else, but stopped short at the human brain. Our intellect and morality, Wallace argued, could not be the result of natural evolution. Some higher power must have intervened to construct this latest and greatest of evolutionary innovations—natural selection for absolutely everything else; God for the human brain.

Darwin was aghast at his colleague's *volte face* right at the finish line itself. He wrote to Wallace in 1869: "I hope you have not murdered too completely your own and my child" (Marchant, 1916, g. 197). A month later, he added ruefully: "If you had not told me, I should have thought that [your remarks on the brain] had been added by some one else. As you expected, I differ grievously from you, and I am very sorry for it" (Marchant, 1916, p. 199). Wallace, sensitive to the rebuke, thereafter referred to his theory of the human brain as "my special heresy."

The outlines of this tale are well known, but the usual interpretation of Wallace's motives is not only wrong, but backwards. Sources cite Wallace's interest in spiritualism, or simply suggest intellectual cowardice in failing to extend an argument to its most threatening limit. I do not claim to have any insight into Wallace's psyche (where such factors may be relevant), but I can at least report that his explicit logical argument for cerebral uniqueness flowed not from reticence or active theological belief, but (ironically) from a fierce and opposite commitment to the exclusive power of natural selection as an evolutionary agent.

Darwin viewed natural selection as a dominant but not exclusive force. Wallace, ironically, was the hyper-Darwinian of his age. He held that all forms and behaviors, including the most trivial, must be directly built by natural selection for utility. He wrote in 1867 (reprinted in Wallace, 1890):

> No special organ, no characteristic form or marking, no peculiarities of instinct or of habit, no relations between species or between groups of species, can exist but which must now be, or once have been, useful to the individuals or races which possess them.

Wallace would not admit the existence of spandrels, or of any nonaptations correlated with features built by natural selection:

> The assertion of "inutility" in the case of any organ is not, and can never be, the statement of a fact, but merely an expression of our ignorance of its purpose or origin.

Paradoxically, this very hyperadaptationism led Wallace to deny that natural selection could have built the human brain—for the following interesting and idiosyncratic reason. Wallace, almost uniquely among 19th-century Western natural scientists, was a genuine nonracist who believed in at least the near intellectual equality of all peoples. Yet he was a cultural chauvinist, who asserted a massive superiority of Western ways over "savage" practices. Consequently, under his hyperadaptationism, an insoluble paradox arises: natural selection can only build for immediate use; savages (surrogates for ancestors) have brains as good as ours but do not employ them to nearly their full capacity in devising complex culture. Hence, natural selection did not construct the human brain.

To cite just one example, Wallace argued that the human ability to sing beautifully must have arisen long before any call upon this capacity, and cannot therefore be a product of natural selection. He wrote:

> The habits of savages give no indication of how this faculty could have been developed by natural selection, because it is never required or used by them. The singing of savages is a more or less monotonous howling... This wonderful power... only comes into play among civilized people. It seems as if the organ had been prepared in anticipation of the future progress in man, since it contains latent capacities which are useless to him in his earlier condition. (Wallace, 1895, p. 198)

Darwin was dumfounded, primarily because he did understand the concept of spandrels (and also because he had more appreciation for the complexities of "savage" cultures). Wallace's illogic can be illustrated by the following anachronistic metaphor: If I put a computer in the business office of my small company, its capacities are not limited by the purposes of my installation. My computer, by virtue of its structural complexity and flexibility, maintains latent and unused capacities that must vastly outnumber the explicit reasons for my design or purchase. And the more complex the computing device, the greater the disparity between its field of potential and my explicit purposes (e.g., the calculator attached to my Casio watch may not perform much beyond my needs; but a Cray supercomputer can do more than I could ever even imagine).

Similarly for the evolution of the human brain. For the sake of argument, I will accept the most orthodox of Darwinian positions—that the human brain achieved its enlarged size and capacity by natural selection for some set of purposes in our ancestral state. Large size is therefore an adaptation. Does this mean that everything the enlarged brain can do must be a direct product of the natural selection that built the structure? Wallace certainly thought so, in arguing that "latent capacities" must imply preparation in "anticipation of future progress"—and therefore indicated intelligent design by God. But the principle of exaptation and the concept of spandrels expose Wallace's dilemma as a non-problem. Natural selection built the brain; yet, by virtue of structural complexities so engendered, the same brain can perform a plethora of tasks that may later become central to culture, but that are spandrels rather than targets of the original natural selection—singing Wagner (to cite Wallace's example, though some, even today, regard the *Ring* as monotonous howling), not to mention reading and writing.

Surely, for something so complex and so replete with latent capacity as the human brain, spandrels must vastly outnumber original reasons, and exaptations of the brain must greatly exceed adaptations by orders of magnitude. (The adaptations, moreover, are probably unidentifiable, given the limits of historical evidence about the ecological circumstances of human origins.) Surely, the central traits of human culture, and the essences that define our concept of human nature, must arise more often as exaptations than as adaptations.

The concept of exaptation provides a one-line refutation of human sociobiology—and I do not regard such a statement as flippant or facetious. Sociobiology is an ultra-Darwinian theory based on adaptation. If, in principle, most culturally useful features of the brain are exaptations rather than adaptations, then they cannot be explained within the sociobiological research program without fatal revisions in its basic intent. A centrally functional feature of human culture or psychology, if it arises as a consequence of structural complexity and enters our explicit repertoire later by cooptation, cannot have a sociobiological explanation, whatever its current importance. At the very most, secondary adaptation might explain some aspects of current maintenance for the feature; but adaptation cannot, in principle, constitute the historical origin of a spandrel—and evolutionary studies are, preeminently, inquiries into origins. The human brain, as nature's most complex and flexible organ, throws up spandrels by the thousands for each conceivable adaptation in its initial evolutionary restructuring. What, then, by the criterion of relative frequency, is the best strategy for a useful evolutionary psychology—the sociobiology of strict Darwinism (which can only access the tiny proportion of adaptive traits), or a structural and correlational analysis that tries to map the spandrels of the brain's evolved capacity?

The Example of Religion

To choose just one overly broad and oversimplified example, must sociobiological effort has been expended in devising adaptive scenarios for the origin of religion (most center on the importance of tribal order and cohesion). But consider Freud's alternative, an argument based on spandrels. The origin of consciousness in our enlarged brain forced us to deal explicitly with the most frightening of all conceivable facts—the certainty of our personal mortality. To assuage this fear, we devised a great cultural variety of concepts with a central theme of mitigation—from metempsychosis (transmigration of souls), to resurrection of the body, to eternal realms for immaterial souls. These concepts form the core of religion as a cultural institution.

I am not so naïve as to imagine that anything so complex and so multi-faceted as religion could be fully rendered by either of these monistic propositions, but they do provide alternative approaches to a basis. The recognition of personal mortality is clearly a spandrel of our large brains, for surely no one would seek the adaptive advantage of increased brain size in achievement of this knowledge! If Freud is right, this focal and organizing concept of religion is a spandrel of a brain enlarged for other reasons; the religion did not arise as an adaptation (whatever its current function, and despite the cogency of a claim that all societies need institutions to promote and maintain group cohesions—for religion need not supply this function).

Go down the list of what you regard as human universals and cultural predictabilities. How many would you putatively assign to adaptation, and therefore view as amenable to sociobiological explanation? Incest avoidance? Such universal gestures as eyebrow flashing? Fine—but how long is your list and how much of our human essence, how much of what really makes culture, will you find? On the other side of the scale place the basis of religion as exaptation; add anything that relies on reading, writing, or any form of mental expression not in the initial repertoire of large-brained populations; add most of the fine and practical arts, the norms of commerce, the practices of war. Exaptation may be historically subsequent to adaptation, and may only coopt the structures and capacities built by adaptation. (But do not be so sure that the brain necessarily became large as an adaptation for more complex conceptualization; other alternatives exist, and consciousness itself may be exaptive.) No matter, the list of exaptations is a mountain to the adaptive molehill. Structural consequences have outstripped original bases. Human uniqueness, human power, human nature itself, lies in the consequences.

The Importance of Exaptation

Adaptation has been the canonical concept of English evolutionary thought, and of Darwinian traditions. The concept is easy to grasp, and it strikes a deep cultural resonance with a cardinal source of our solace—a cherished belief in the world's essential rightness. John Ray, in the late 17th century, and William Paley, in the early 19th, used the word to describe the exquisite natural design that implied both God's existence and benevolence; Darwin, in a sense, only changed the causal framework.

Adaptations also became canonical for their ease and lack of ambiguity in illustration—and iconography is a powerful source of bias. All textbooks present lovely photos of adaptations for their primary illustrations of evolution—for who can fail to grasp the meaning of a butterfly that looks like a dead leaf, or the streamlined form of a dolphin? This popularity of the concept leads to the false impression that adaptations dominate both in frequency and importance for evolutionary change.

In fact, most classical adaptations are small, immediate adjustments or dead-end specializations—e.g., peacocks' trails or elaborate antlers. Adaptations tend to be restrictive, at least with respect to evolutionary innovation. Vrba and I (1986) argued that the key to long-term macroevolutionary success lies in the concept of an "exaptive pool"—a range of cooptable potentials inherent in structures built for other reasons. Quirky and presently unemployed potential is often the key to evolutionary breakthroughs.

Consider some major events that made the evolution of complex human consciousness possible; all are exaptive. Chromosomes and their precise division in the process of meiosis gave us requisite variability through sexual recombination, but the provision of variation for evolutionary futures cannot have been the initial adaptive value of sex (Maynard Smith, 1978). Gene duplication, as argued previously, made complexity of organisms possible by freeing copies for change, but the multiple copies may have arisen by selection at the gene level, with no initial relationship to phenotypes at all. And, to jump to the most recent point and crux of this article, the major features of human mentality may be exaptive as nonselected structural products of a brain grown large for a small set of adaptive reasons.

The same principle applies when we consider the specific history of any lineage, including our own. Most major transitions are exaptations, not adaptations. Recent discoveries (Coates & Clack, 1990) on streamlined shapes and supernumerary digits indicate that the tetrapod limb originally evolved for locomotion in water, and was fortuitously cooptable for later life on land (Edwards, 1989). The retention of five digits by our quadrupedal mammalian ancestors (rather than specialized adaptive reduction to hoofs or pads) permitted a later and crucial flexibility in manipulation of tools by our hands (Jarvik, 1980). Stereoscopic vision probably arose for precision of locomotion in the three-dimensional world of trees (Jerison, 1973), not for the purposes so central to modern human life. For that matter, since primates always exceeded other mammals in relative brain size, initial enlargement of the brain could not have occurred in the service of what we now call consciousness.

The same argument reinforces my claim that evolutionary psychology should seek its basis in a concept of exaptation, not adaptation. Consider just a few random jottings in conclusion (this paper has been egotistical enough; I have preached to my colleagues in cognate fields, but I dare not claim a handle on the good examples. I only suggest to you who know the examples that their evolutionary meaning is likely to lie in exaptation).

Fundamental Institutions

Freud's exaptive argument for religion could be applied to most institutions equally distant from biological immediacy and equally rich in conceptual structure. (I would be more open to adaptive explanations for more explicitly biological traits shared with other related species lacking our cultural richness—e.g., facial gestures, behaviors of sexual and parent—child bonding. Yet, even here, a crucial role for exaptation must be considered. The genetic argument for adaptation in avoidance of incest is strong and plausibly supported by high relative frequencies of incest taboos in human cultures. But what learning rule do we follow in deciding whom to avoid in sexual relations? Experiments on quail and other animals hint that an abstract rule of "prefer close but not too close" may function a general aesthetic principle in tetrapods. If so, avoidance of incest may be but one specific manifestation of the rule—with forms of xenophobia as another example at the other pole. In this case, the rule itself may have some ancient adaptive basis, and incest avoidance may simply be a highly useful exaptive instantiation.)

Whatever one decides on the generality of religion itself, the exaptive basis of many specific religious practices seems clear. When I wrote my original paper on spandrels, I was struck by Harner's (1977) postulate that massive human sacrifice among the Aztecs arose as an adaptation to beef up the meat supply (as limbs of victims were consumed). E. O. Wilson (1978) then welcomed this example as a primary illustration of an adaptive and genetic predisposition for carnivory in humans. Harner's argument fails on several specific grounds (Ortiz de Montellano, 1978)—from the inefficiency of the human butchery (only three limbs per torso), to the availability of sufficient protein from other sources, to the key observation that only people of high status, who needed supplementary protein least, were allowed to eat sacrificial victims. But I was most intrigued by Harner's failure to consider the obvious exaptive alternative—that cultural practices arising for other reasons (and greatly extended as positive feedback raised the numbers of victims, almost surely to the point of cultural maladaptation) generated lots of bodies that were then available for consequent use. Why invert the explanatory chain and see a consequence (cannibalism) as the hidden source of the entire complex phenomenon? Yet this story almost became an early classic of sociobiology.

Fundamental Attributes

Those characteristics that we share with other closely related species are most likely to be conventional adaptations. (For example, I accept my colleague Steve Pinker's (1985) argument for the basic mechanics of the visual system, while rejecting his extensions to special properties of human consciousness.) But attributes unique to our species, and constituting the essence of what we call *human* consciousness, are likely to be exaptations by the arguments of the last section.

As an obvious candidate, consider the greatest and most contentious of all subjects embodying claims for our uniqueness: human language. The adaptationist and Darwinian tradition has long advocated a gradualistic continuationism—constructing scenarios that language "grew" from gestural and calling systems of other species; trying to teach chimpanzees the rudiments of human linguistic structure, etc. Noam Chomsky, on the other hand, has long advocated a position corresponding to the claim that language is an exaptation of brain structure. (Chomsky, who has rarely written anything about evolution, has not so framed his theory, but he does accept my argument as a proper translation of his views into the language of my field—Chomsky, personal communication.) Many adaptationists have so misunderstood Chomsky that they actually suspect him of being an odd sort of closet creationist. For them, evolution means adaptive continuity, and they just cannot grasp the alternative of exaptive seizure of latent capacity that is present for other reasons.

The spectacular collapse of the chimp language experiments, and their exposure as some combination of wishful thinking and the Clever Hans effect, have made Chomsky's alternative all the more plausible. Cross-species continuity must exist, of course, in the growth of conceptual powers, but why should our idiosyncratic capacity for embodying much of this richness in the unique and highly peculiar mental structure called language be seen as an expression of this continuity? The traits that Chomsky (1986) attributes to language—universality of the generative grammar, lack of ontogeny (for language "grows" more like a programmed organ than like memorizing the kings of England), highly peculiar and decidedly nonoptimal structure, formal analogy to other attributes, including our unique numerical faculty with its concept of discrete infinity—fit far more easily with an exaptive, rather than an adaptive, explanation. The brain, in becoming large for whatever adaptive reasons, acquired a plethora of cooptable features. Why shouldn't the capacity for language be among them? Why not seize this possibility as something discrete at some later point in evolution, grafting upon it a range of conceptual capacities that achieve different expression in other species (and in our ancestry)?

Evolutionary Scenarios

Consider everyone's favorite game in evolutionary reconstruction—the spinning of behavioral and ecological scenarios for human origins. We usually consider these efforts as exercises in adaptationism. But, given the cardinal property of adaptation as usually limiting and restricting, and given the need to posit structures that permit flexibility and opportunity in conceptualizing human origins, these scenarios almost always make a claim for *exaptation* at crucial junctions (not, perhaps, in the radical mode of spandrels, but at least in the more conventional style of quirky functional shifts from an original reason to a very different consequence).

As just one example, recently subject to much discussion and debate, consider Falk's (1990) "radiator theory" (so close to Aristotle's old idea that the brain cools the blood). In her theory, gracile (slender) and robust (heavy-boned) australopithecines evolved different adaptations for adequate cranial blood flow in bipedal creatures—robusts via a greatly enlarged occipital/marginal sinus system, graciles via a widespread network of veins becoming more elaborate with time. This network system, an efficient cooling device, may have arisen as an adaptive response to the more intense solar radiation of savanna habitats favored by graciles. But this "radiator" then released a thermal constraint on brain size—allowing a larger brain to cool adequately. The graciles could evolve into the large brained *Homo* lineage; the robusts were stuck. Thus, the radiator system, arising as an ecological adaptation in initially small-brained graciles, became an exaptation for cooling the enlarged brain of their descendants. If Falk is right, we would not be here today but for this crucial exaptation.

Current Utility

If you doubt all the other arguments for exaptation, just make a list of the most important current uses of consciousness. Start with reading, writing, and arithmetic. How many can even be plausibly rendered as adaptations?

Even so committed a hereditarian (and adaptationist) as Bouchard (of the Minnesota twin study) has seen the point, at least for the variability underlying human cognitive differences. Bouchard et al. (1990) write:

> Whatever the ancient origins and functions of genetic variability, its repercussions in contemporary society are pervasive and important. A human species whose members did not vary genetically with respect to significant cognitive and motivational attributes...would have created a very different society than the one we know. (p. 228)

They even recognize that most of this variability, in ancestral contexts, might have been "evolutionary debris, unimportant to fitness and perhaps not expressed in prehistoric environments" (p. 228). Bravo, for this is a radical exaptive hypothesis with a vengeance (and almost surely correct)—describing a trait now vital to our social constitution, but so nonaptive at its origin that it achieved no phenotypic expression.

Yet just as these erstwhile adaptationists see the light, they retrogress with a knee-jerk assertion of the orthodox position that they denied in their primary specific interpretation!

> Evolutionary psychologists or sociobiologists attempt to delineate species-typical proclivities or instincts and to understand the relevant evolutionary developments that took place in the Pleistocene epoch and were adaptive in the lives of tribal hunter-gatherers. The genes sing a prehistoric song that today should sometimes be resisted but which it would be foolish to ignore. (1990, p. 228)

And yet, the authors just told us that these particular genes probably were not singing at all back then, despite their crucial role in framing human society today. I interpret this inconsistency as a lovely example of working through the logic of a specific argument correctly (the claim for exaptation of a spandrel), but then missing the implication and spouting a contradictory orthodoxy. Clearly, we need to make the notion of exaptation explicit and available.

An evolutionary psychology properly grounded in the centrality of exaptation would be a very different, and less threatening, construct (for those feeling the breath of biological imperialism) than the conventional Darwinian account of continuity in adaptation, with its implications of gradualism, predictability, and simple transfer from overt cultural expression to underlying biological basis. Exaptation, with its quirky and unpredictable functional shifts (e.g., thermoregulation to flight) and its recruitment of nonadaptive, even invisible structures (e.g., repeated copies of genes providing for future flexibility; the "debris" of unexpressed genetic variability leading to later cultural diversity), produces a cultural history with unanticipated changes in direction, potentially abrupt transitions, and no simply derived status of cultural expressions (for the path from biological substrate to overt manifestation passes through the switches of exaptive shift). The concept of exaptation honors the contingency of history, the unpredictable discontinuity of change in complex systems, and the plurality of legitimate sources of insight from biological substrate through quirky shift to social expression. We can therefore recall Haldane's dictum that "the universe is not only queerer than we suppose, but queerer than we *can* suppose." And lest we be tempted to read this (as Haldane most surely did not) as nihilism or pessimism (rather than as joy for being in such a fascinating place), we should also remember Einstein's equally famous remark that the Lord God is subtle, but not malicious (*Raffiniert ist de Herr Gott, aber boshaft ist er nicht*).

References

Allmon, W.D. (in press). On the role of aptation in speciation. *Journal of Paleontology*.

Blanc, M. (1990). *Les heritiers de Darwin*. Paris: Seuil.Bouchard, T. J., Lykken, D.T., McGue, M., Segal, N.L., Jr., & Tellegen, A. (1990). Sources of human psychological differences: The Minnesota study of twins reared apart. *Science*, *250*, 223-228.

Chatterton, B.D.E., & Speyer, S.E. (1989). Larval ecology, life history strategies, and patterns of extinction and survivorship among Ordovician trilobites. *Paleobiology*, *15*, 118-132.

Chomsky, N. (1986). Knowledge of language: *Its nature, origins, and use*. New York: Praeger.

Coates, M.I., & Clack, J.A. (1990). Polydactyly in the earliest known tetrapod limbs. *Nature, 347*, 66-69.

Darwin, C. (1859). *On the origin of species*. London: John Murray.

Darwin, C. (1871). *The descent of man and selection in relation to sex*. London: John Murray.

Darwin, C. (1872). *On the expression of the emotions in man and animals*. London: John Murray.

Edwards, J.L. (1989). Two perspectives on the evolution of the tetrapod limb. *American Zoologist, 29*, 235-254.

Endler, J.A., & McLellan, T. (1988). The processes of evolution: Toward a newer synthesis. *Annual Review of Ecological Systems, 19*, 395-421.

Falk, D. (1990). Brain evolution in *Homo*: The "radiator" theory: *Behavioral and Brain Sciences*, *13*, 333-381.

Gans, C. (1988). Adaptation and the form-function relation. *American Zoologist, 28*, 681-697.

Gould, S. J. (1980). *The panda's thumb*. New York: Norton.

Gould, S. J. (1982). Darwinism and the expansion of evolutionary theory. *Science, 216*, 380-387.

Gould, S. J. (1983). The hardening of the modern synthesis. In M. Greene (Ed.), *Dimensions of Darwinism* (pp. 71-93). Cambridge, U.K.: Cambridge University Press.

Gould, S. J. (1989). A developmental constraint in *Cerion*, with comments on the definition and interpretation of constraint in evolution. *Evolution, 43*, 516-539.

Gould, S. J., & Lewontin, R.C. (1979). The spandrels of San Marco and the Panglossian paradign: A critique of the adaptationist programme. *Proceedings of the Royal Society of London, B, 205*, 581-598.

Gould, S. J., & Vrba, E.S. (1982). Exaptation—a missing term in the science of form. *Paleobiology, 8*, 4-15.

Hamilton, W.D. (1971). The genetical evolution of social behavior, I. In G..C. Williams (Ed.), *Group selection* (pp. 23-43). Chicago: Aldine. (Reprinted from *Journal of Theoretical Biology*, 1964, *7*, 1-16)

Harner, M. (1977). The ecological basis for Aztec sacrifice. *American Ethnologist, 4*, 117-135.

Jarvik, E. (1980). *Basic structure and evolution of vertebrates*. New York: Academic Press.

Jerison, H.J. (1973). *The evolution of the brain and intelligence*. New York: Academic Press.

Kitcher, P. (1985). *Vaulting ambition*: *Sociobiology and the quest for human nature*. Cambridge, MA: MIT Press.

Lewin, R. (1982). Adaptation can be a problem for evolutionists. *Science, 216*, 212-213.

Marchant, J. (1916). Alfred Russel Wallace: *Letters and reminiscences*. New York: Harper.

Maynard Smith, J. (1978). *The evolution of sex*. Cambridge, U.K.: Cambridge University Press.

Ortiz de Montellano, B.R. (1978). Aztec cannibalism: An ecological necessity? *Science, 200*, 611-617.

Owen, R. (1849). *On the nature of limbs*. London: Van Voorst.Pierce, C.L. (1988). Predation avoidance, microhabitat shift, and risk-sensitive foraging in larval dragonflies. *Oecologia, 77*, 81-90.

Pinker, S. (1985). *Visual cognition*. Cambridge, MA: MIT Press.

Provine, W.B. (1986). *Sewall Wright and evolutionary biology*. Chicago: University of Chicago Press. Vermeij, G.J. (1987). *Evolution and escalation*. Princeton, NJ: Princeton University Press.

Vrba, E.S., & Gould, S.J. (1986). The hierarchical expansion of sorting and selection: Sorting and selection cannot be equated. *Paleobiology, 12*, 217-228.

Wallace, A.R. (1890). *Darwinism*. London: Macmillan.

Wallace, A.R. (1895). *Natural selection and tropical nature*. London: Macmillan.

Williams, G.C. (1966). *Adaptation and natural selection*. Princeton, NJ: Princeton University Press.

Wilson, E.O. (1975). *Sociobiology. The new synthesis*. Cambridge, MA: Harvard University Press.

Wilson, E.O. (1978). *On human nature*. Cambridge, MA: Harvard University Press.

THE ORIGINS OF COGNITIVE THOUGHT

B. F. Skinner (1989). *American Psychologist, 44,* 13-18.

One of the most revealing things about the career of B. F. Skinner is how he was continually re-inventing himself. His autobiography should be required reading for anyone aspiring to be a scientist. In the article "On the Origins of Cognitive Thought" Skinner argues that we need to re-invent the conceptual labels we use to describe the functioning organism emphasizing the use of verbs rather than nouns. Billy Yellow, a Navajo shaman once said, "You have thousands of being words, we have thousands of doing words". This is a functional perspective and one that is imminently compatible with the cognitive functionalism outlined by Skinner.

ASTRACT: Words referring to feelings and states of mind were first used to describe behavior or the situations in which behavior occurred. When concurrent bodily states began to be noticed and talked about, the same words were used to describe them. They became the vocabulary of philosophy and then of mentalistic or cognitive psychology. The evidence is to be found in etymology. In this article, examples are given of words that have come to describe the feelings or states of mind that accompany doing, sensing, wanting, waiting, thinking, and several other attributes of mind. The bodily states felt or introspectively observed and described in these ways are the subject of physiology, especially brain science

What is felt when one has a feeling is a condition of one's body, and the word used to describe it almost always comes from the word for a cause of the condition felt. The evidence is to be found in the history of the language—in the etymology of the words that refer to feelings (Skinner, 1987). Etymology is the archaeology of thought. The great authority in English is the *Oxford English Dictionary* (1928), but a smaller work such as Skeat's (1956) *Etymological Dictionary of the English Language* will usually suffice. We do not have all the facts we should like to have, because the earliest meanings of many words have been lost, but we have enough to make a plausible general case. To describe great pain, for example, we say *agony*. The word first meant struggling or wrestling, a familiar cause of great pain. When other things felt the same way, the same word was used.

A similar case is made here for the words we use to refer to states of mind or cognitive processes. They almost always began as references either to some aspect of behavior or to the setting in which the behavior occurred. Only very slowly have they become the vocabulary of something called mind. *Experience* is a good example. As Raymond Williams (1976) has pointed out, the word was not used to refer to anything felt or introspectively observed until the 19th century. Before that time, it meant, quite literally, something a person had "gone through" (from the Latin *expiriri*), or what we would now call an exposure to contingencies of reinforcement. In this article, I review about 80 other words for states of mind or cognitive processes. They are grouped according to the bodily conditions that prevail when individuals are doing things, sensing things, changing the way they do or sense things (learning), staying changed (remembering), wanting, waiting, thinking, and "using their minds."

Doing

The word *behave* is a latecomer. The older word was *do*. As the very long entry in the *Oxford English Dictionary* shows, the word *do* has always emphasized consequence—the effect one has on the world. We describe much of what we ourselves do with the words we use to describe what others do. When we are asked, "What did you do?", "What are you doing?", or "What are you going to do?" we say, for example, "I wrote a letter," "I am reading a good book," or "I shall watch television." But how can we describe what we feel or introspectively observe at the time?

There is often very little to observe. Behavior often seems spontaneous; it simply happens. We say it "occurs" as in "It occurred to me to go for a walk." We often replace "it" with "thought" or "idea" ("The thought—or idea—occurred to me to go for a walk"), but what, if anything, occurs is the walk. We also say that behavior comes into our possession. We announce the happy appearance of the solution to a problem by saying "I have it!"

We report an early stage of behaving when we say "I feel like going for a walk." That may mean "I feel as I have felt in the past when I have set out for a walk." What is felt may also include something of the present occasion, as if to say "Under these conditions I often go for a walk," or it may include some state of deprivation or aversive stimulation, as if to say "I need a breath of fresh air."

The bodily condition associated with a high probability that we shall do something is harder to pin down, and we resort to metaphor. Because things often fall in the direction in which they lean, we say we are *inclined* to do something, or have an *inclination* to do it. If we are strongly inclined, we may even say we are *bent* on doing it. Because things also often move in the direction in which they are pulled, we say that we *tend* to do things (from the Latin *tendere*, to stretch or extend) or that our behavior expresses an *intention*, a cognitive process widely favored by philosophers at the present time.

We also use *attitude* to refer to probability. An attitude is the *position*, *posture*, or *pose* we take when we are about to do something. The pose of an actress suggests something of what she is engaged in doing or is likely to do in a moment. The same sense of pose is found in *dispose* and *propose* ("I am disposed to go for a walk," "I propose to go for a walk"). Originally a synonym of propose, the word *purpose* has caused a great deal of trouble. Like other words suggesting probable action, it seems to point to the future. The future cannot be acting now, however, and elsewhere in science purpose has given way to words referring to *past* consequences. When philosophers speak of intention, for example, they are almost always speaking of operant behavior.

As the experimental analysis has shown, behavior is shaped and maintained by its consequences, but only by consequences that lie in the past. We do what we do because of what *has* happened, not what *will* happen. Unfortunately, what has happened leaves few observable traces, and why we do what we do and how likely we are to do it are therefore largely beyond the reach of introspection. Perhaps that is why, as I will show later, behavior has so often been attributed to an initiating, originating, or creative act of will.

Sensing

In order to respond effectively to the world around us, we must see, hear, smell, taste, or feel it. The ways in which behavior is brought under control of stimuli can be analyzed without too much trouble, but what we observe when we see ourselves seeing something is the source of great misunderstanding. We say we *perceive* the world in the literal sense of taking it in (from the Latin *per* and *capere*, to take). (*Comprehend* is a close synonym, part of which comes from *prehendere*, to seize or grasp.) We say "I take your meaning." Because we cannot take in the world itself, it has been assumed that we must make a copy. Making a copy cannot be all there is to seeing, however, because we still have to see the copy. Copy theory involves an infinite regress. Some cognitive psychologists have tried to avoid it by saying that what is taken in is a representation—perhaps a digital rather than an analog copy. When we recall ("call up an image of") what we have seen, however, we see something that looks much like what we saw in the first place, and that would be an analog copy. Another way to avoid regress is to say that at some point we "interpret" the copy or representation. The origins of *interpret* are obscure, but the word seems to have had some connection with price; an interpreter was once a broker. Interpret seems to have meant evaluate. It can best be understood as something we do.

The metaphor of copy theory has obvious sources. When things reinforce our looking at them, we continue to look. We keep a few such things near us so that we can look at them whenever we like. If we cannot keep the things themselves, we make copies of them, such as paintings or photographs. *Image*, a word for an internal copy, comes from the Latin *imago*. It first meant a colored bust, rather like a wax-work museum effigy. Later it meant ghost. *Effigy*, by the way, is well chosen as a word for a copy, because it first meant something constructed (from the Latin *fingere*). There is no evidence, however, that we construct anything when we see the world around us or when we see that we are seeing it.

A behavioral account of sensing is simpler. Seeing is behaving and, like all behaving, is to be explained either by natural selection (many animals respond visually shortly after birth) or operant conditioning. We do not see the world by taking it in and processing it. The world takes control of behavior when either survival or reinforcement has been contingent on it. That can occur only when something is done about what is seen. Seeing is only part of behaving; it is behaving up to the point of action. Because behavior analysts deal only with complete instances of behavior, the sensing part is out of reach of their instruments and methods and must, as I will show later, be left to physiologists.

Changing and Staying Changed

Learning is not doing; it is changing what we do. We may see that behavior has changed, but we do not see the changing. We see reinforcing consequences but not how they effect a change. Because the observable effects of reinforcement are usually not immediate, we often overlook the connection. Behavior is then often said to *grow* or *develop*. Develop originally meant to unfold, as one unfolds a letter. We assume that what we see was there from the start. Like pre-Darwinian evolution (where to evolve meant to unroll as one unrolled a scroll), developmentalism is a form of creationism.

Copies or representations play an important part in cognitive theories of learning and memory, where they raise problems that do not arise in a behavioral analysis. When we must describe something that is no longer present, the traditional view is that we recall the copy we have stored. In a behavioral analysis, contingencies of reinforcement change the way we respond to stimuli. It is a changed person, not a memory, that has been "stored."

Storage and retrieval become much more complicated when we learn and recall how something is done. It is easy to make copies of things we see, but how can we make copies of the things we do? We can model behavior for someone to imitate, but a model cannot be stored. The traditional solution is to go digital. We say the organism learns and stores rules. When, for example, a hungry rat presses a lever and receives food and the rate of pressing immediately increases, cognitive psychologists want to say that the rat has learned a rule. It now knows and can remember that "pressing the lever produces food." But "pressing the lever produces food" is a description of the contingencies we have built into the apparatus. We have no reason to suppose that the rat formulates and stores such a description. The contingencies change the rat, which then survives as a changed rat. As members of a verbal species, we can describe contingencies of reinforcement, and we often do so because the descriptions have many practical uses (for example, we can memorize them and say them again whenever circumstances demand it), but there is no introspective or other evidence that we verbally describe every contingency that affects our behavior; indeed, there is much evidence to the contrary.

Some of the words we use to describe subsequent occurrences of behavior suggest storage. *Recall*—call back—is obviously one of them; *recollect* suggests "bringing together" stored pieces. Under the influence of the computer, cognitive psychologists have turned to *retrieve*—literally "to find again" (cf. the French *trouver*), presumably after a search. The etymology of *remember*, however, does not imply storage. From the Latin *memor*, it means to be "mindful of again," and that usually means to do again what we did before. To remember what something looks like is to do what we did when we saw it. We needed no copy then, and we need none now. (We *recognize* things in the sense of re-cognizing them—responding to them now as we did in the past.) As a thing, a memory must be something stored, but as an action "memorizing" simply means doing what we must do to ensure that we can behave again as we are behaving now.

Wanting

Many cognitive terms describe bodily states that arise when strong behavior cannot be executed because a necessary condition is lacking. The source of a general word for states of that kind is obvious: When something is wanting, we say we want it. In dictionary terms, to want is to "suffer from the want of." *Suffer* originally meant to undergo, but now it means to be in pain, and strong wanting can indeed be painful. We escape from it by doing anything that has been reinforced by the thing that is now wanting and wanted.

A near synonym of want is *need*. It, too, was first closely tied to suffering; to be in need was to be under restraint or duress. (Words tend to come into use when the conditions they describe are conspicuous.) *Felt* is often added: One has a *felt need*. We sometimes distinguish between want and need on the basis of the immediacy of the consequence. Thus, we *want* something to eat, but we *need* a taxi in order to do something that will have later consequences.

Wishing and *hoping* are also states of being unable to do something we are strongly inclined to do. The putted golf ball rolls across the green, but we can only *wish* or *will* it into the hole. (Wish is close to will. The Anglo-Saxon *willan* meant wish, and the *would* in "would that is were so" is almost the same as the past tense of will.)

When something we need is missing, we say we *miss* it. When we want something for a long time, we say we *long* for it. We long to see someone we love who has long been absent.

When past consequences have been aversive, we do not hope, wish, or long for them. Instead, we *worry* or feel *anxious* about them. Worry first meant choke (a dog worries the rat it has caught), and anxious comes from another word for choke. We cannot do anything about things that have already happened, though we are still affected by them. We say we are *sorry* for a mistake we have made. Sorry is a weak form of *sore*. As the slang expression has it, we may be "sore about something." We *resent* mistreatment, quite literally, by "feeling it again" (*resent* and *sentiment* share a root).

Sometimes we cannot act appropriately because we do not have the appropriate behavior. When we have lost our way, for example, we say we feel lost. To be *bewildered* is like being in a wilderness. In such a case, we *wander* (wend our way aimlessly) or *wonder* what to do. The wonders of the world were so unusual that no one responded to them in normal ways. We stand in *awe* of such things, and awe comes from a Greek word that meant *anguish* or *terror*. Anguish, like anxiety, once meant choked, and terror was a violent trembling. A *miracle*, from the Latin *admirare*, is something to be wondered at—or about.

Sometimes we cannot respond because we are taken unawares; we are *surprised* (the second syllable of which comes from the Latin *prehendere*, to seize or grasp). The story of Samuel Johnson's wife is a useful example. Finding Johnson kissing the maid, she is said to have exclaimed "I am surprised!"

"No," said the doctor, "I am surprised; you are astonished!" *Astonished*, like *astounded*, first meant to be alarmed by thunder. Compare the French *étonner* and *tonnere*.

When we cannot easily do something because our behavior has been mildly punished, we are *embarrassed* or barred. Conflicting responses find us *perplexed*: They are "interwoven" or "entangled." When a response has been inconsistently reinforced, we are *diffident*, in the sense of not trusting. Trust comes from a Teutonic root suggesting consolation, which in turn has a distant Greek relative meaning whole. Trust is bed by consistency.

Waiting

Wanting, wishing, worrying, resenting, and the like are often called "feelings." More likely to be called "states of mind" are the bodily conditions that result from certain special temporal arrangements of stimuli, responses, and reinforcers. The temporal arrangements are much easier to analyze than the states of mind that are said to result.

Watch is an example. It first meant "to be awake." The night watch was someone who stayed awake. The word *alert* comes from the Italian for a military watch. We watch television until we fall asleep.

Those who are awake may be aware of what they are doing; aware is close to *wary* or *cautious*. (Cautious comes from a word familiar to us in *caveat emptor*.) Psychologists have been especially interested in awareness, although they have generally used a synonym, *consciousness*.

One who watches may be waiting for something to happen, but *waiting* is more than watching. It is something we all do but may not think of as a state of mind. Consider waiting for a bus. Nothing we have ever done has made the bus arrive, but its arrival has reinforced many of the things we do while waiting. For example, we stand where we have most often stood and look in the direction in which we have most often looked when buses appeared. Seeing a bus has also been strongly reinforced, and we may see one while we are waiting, either in the sense of "thinking what one would look like" or by mistaking a truck for the bus.

Waiting for something to happen is also called *expecting*, a more prestigious cognitive term. To *expect* is to look forward to (from the Latin *expectare*). To anticipate is to do other things beforehand, such as getting the bus fare ready. Part of the word comes from the Latin *capere*—to take. Both expecting and anticipating are forms of behavior that have been adventitiously reinforced by the appearance of something. (Much of what we do when we are waiting is public. Others can see us standing at a bus stop and looking in the direction from which buses come. An observant person may even see us take a step forward when a truck comes into view or reach for a coin as the bus appears. We ourselves "see" something more, of course. The contingencies have worked private changes in us, to some of which we alone can respond.)

Thinking

It is widely believed that behavior analysts cannot deal with the cognitive processes called thinking. We often use *think* to refer to weak behavior. If we are not quite ready to say "He is wrong," we say "I think he is wrong." Think is often a weaker word for know; we say "I think this is the way to do it" when we are not quite ready to say "I know this is the way" or "This *is* the way." We also say *think* when stronger behavior is not feasible. Thus, we think of what something looks like when it is not there to see, and we think of doing something that we cannot at the moment do.

Many thought processes, however, have nothing to do with the distinction between weak and strong behavior or between private and public, overt and covert. To think is to do something that makes other behavior possible. Solving a problem is an example. A problem is a situation that does not evoke an effective response; we solve it by changing the situation until a response occurs. Telephoning a friend is a problem if we do not know the number, and we solve it by looking up the number. Etymologically, to *solve* is to loosen or set free, as sugar is *dissolved* in coffee. This is the sense in which thinking is responsible for doing. "It is how men think that determines how they act." Hence, the hegemony of mind. Again, however, the terms we use began as references to behavior. Here are a few examples.

1. When no effective stimulus is available, we sometime *expose* one. We *discover* things by uncovering them. To *detect* a signal does not mean to respond to it; it means to remove something (the *legmen*) that covers it.

2. When we cannot uncover a stimulus, we sometimes keep an accessible one in view until a response occurs. *Observe* and *regard* both come from words that meant to hold or keep in view, the latter from the French *garder*. *Consider* once meant to look steadily at the stars until something could be made of them (*consider* and *sidereal* have a common root). *Contemplate*, another word for think, once meant looking at a template or plan of the stars. (In those days all one could do to make sense of the stars was to look at them.)

3. We not only look at things in order to see them better, but we also *look* for them. We *search* or *explore*. To look for a pen is to do what one has done in the past when a pen came into view. (A pigeon that pecks a spot because doing so has been occasionally reinforced will "look for it" after it has been taken away by doing precisely what it did when the spot was there—moving its head in ways that brought the spot into view.) We search in order to find, and we do not avoid searching by *contriving* something to be seen, because contrive, like retrieve, is from the French *trouver*, to find.

4. We bring different things together to make a single response feasible when we *concentrate*, from an older word *concentre*, to join in a center.

5. We do the reverse when we separate things so that we can more easily deal with them in different ways. We *sift* them, as if we were putting them through a sieve. The *cern* in *discern* (Latin *cernere*) means to separate or set apart.

6. We *mark* things so that we will be more likely to notice them again. *Distinguish*, a good cognitive term, once meant to mark by pricking. Mark is strongly associated with boundaries; animals mark the edges of their territories.

7. To *define* is literally to mark the bounds or end (*finis*) of something. We also *determine* what a word means by indicating where the referent terminates.

8. We *compare* things, literally, by putting them side by side so that we can more easily see whether they match. The *par* in compare means equal. Par value is equal value. In golf, par is a score to be matched.

9. We *speculate* about things in the sense of looking at them from different angles, as in a *specula* or mirror.

10. *Cogitate*, an old word for think, first meant to "shake up." A *conjecture* is something "thrown out" for consideration. We *accept* or *reject* things that occur to us in the sense of taking or throwing them back, as if we were fishing.

11. Sometimes it helps to change one mode of stimulation into another. We do so when we convert the "heft" of an object into its weight, read on a scale. By weighing things we react more precisely to their weight. *Ponder*, *deliberate*, and *examine*, good cognitive processes, all once meant weigh. (*Ponder* is part of ponderous; the *liber* in deliberate is the Latin *libra*, a scales; and *examine* meant the tongue of a balance.)

12. We react more precisely to the number of things in a group by *counting*. One way to count is to recite *one*, *two*, *three*, and so on, while ticking off (touching) each item. Before people learned to count, they recorded the number of things in a group by letting a pebble stand for each thing. The pebbles were called *calculi* and their use *calculation*. There is a long, but unbroken, road from pebbles to silicon chips.

13. After we have thought for some time, we may reach a decision. To *decide* once meant simply to cut off or bring to an end.

14. A better word for decide is *conclude*, to close a discussion. What we conclude about something is our last word.

It is certainly no accident that so many of the terms we now use to refer to cognitive processes once referred either to behavior or to the occasions when behavior occurs. It could be objected, of course, that what a word once meant is not what it means now. Surely there is a difference between weighing a sack of potatoes and weighing the evidence in a court of law. When we speak of weighing evidence, we are using a metaphor. But a metaphor is a word that is "carried over" from one referent to another on the basis of a common property. The common property in weighing is the conversion of one kind of thing (potatoes or evidence) into another (a number on a scale or a verdict). Once we have seen that done with potatoes, it is easier to see it done with evidence. Over the centuries human behavior has grown steadily more complex as it has come under the control of more complex environments. The number and complexity of the bodily conditions felt or introspectively observed have grown accordingly, and with them has grown the vocabulary of cognitive thinking.

We could also say that weight becomes abstract when we move from potatoes to evidence. The word is indeed abstracted in the sense of being drawn away from its original referent, but it continues to refer to a common property, and as in the case of metaphor, in a possibly more decisive way. The testimony in a trial is much more complex than a sack of potatoes, and "guilty" probably implies more than "10 pounds." But abstraction is not a matter of complexity. Quite the contrary. Weight is only one aspect of a potato, and guilt is only one aspect of a person. Weight is as abstract as guilt. It is only under verbal contingencies of reinforcement that we respond to single properties of a thing or person. In doing so, we abstract the property from the thing or person.

One may still argue that at some point the term is abstracted and carried over, not to a slightly more complex case, but to something of a very different kind. Potatoes are weighed in the physical world; evidence is weighed in the *mind*, or with the *help* of the mind, or *by* the mind. And that brings us to the heart of the matter.

Mind

The battle cry of the cognitive revolution is "Mind is back!" A "great new science of mind" is born. Behaviorism nearly destroyed our concern for it, but behaviorism has been overthrown, and we can take up again where the philosophers and early psychologists left off.

Extraordinary things have certainly been said about the mind. The finest achievements of the species have been attributed to it; it is said to work at miraculous speeds in miraculous ways. But what it is and what it does are still far from clear. We all speak of the mind with little or no hesitation, but we pause when asked for a definition. The dictionaries are of no help. To understand what "mind" means, we must first look up *perception*, *idea*, *feeling*, *intention*, and many of the other words we have just examined. We will find that each of them is defined with the help of the others. Perhaps it is of the very essence of mind that it cannot be defined. Nevertheless, we can see how the word is used and what people seem to be saying when they use it.

Mind is often spoken of as if it were a place. When it occurs to use to do something, we say that "it comes to mind." If we go on doing it, it is because we "keep it in mind." We miss an appointment when it "slips our mind." Mind is also spoken of as an organ. People "use their minds" to solve problems. It may be significant that we are more likely to say "Use your head" or "Use your brains" than "Use your mind," as if we felt the need for something more substantial. Mind also sometimes means "made more likely to act." An early use ("I was minded to go") still survives in the word *remind*. An appointment book reminds us of an appointment, and someone we meet reminds us of a friend if we respond to some extent as we respond to the friend.

Often, however, "mind" means little more than "do." "I have a mind to tell you" means "I am inclined to tell you." Those who "speak their mind" say what they have to say. We are cautioned to avoid falling by "minding the step" in the sense of noticing it. Students "mind their teachers" in the sense of obeying them, and teachers "mind their students" in the sense of watching them. "Do you mind my smoking?" means "Do you object?" In reply to "Will you have a drink?", "I don't mind if I do" means "I won't refuse if you offer me one."

The mind that the cognitive revolution has restored to prominence is also the doer of things. It is the executor of cognitive processes. It perceives the world, organizes sense data into meaningful wholes, and processes information. It is the double of the person whose mind it is, a replica, a surrogate, a *Doppelgänger*. Take any sentence in which the mind does something and see if the meaning is substantially changed if person is substituted. It is said, for example, that "the mind cannot comprehend infinity." Does that mean anything more than that no person can comprehend infinity? Cognitive processes are behavioral processes; they are things people do.

The crucial age-old mistake is the belief that they are something more, that what we feel as we behave is the cause of our behaving. From the time of the early Greeks, the search has been on for internal determiners. The heart, lungs, liver, kidneys, spleen, not to mention the humours, and at last the brain have all been promising candidates. As organs, they have had the advantage that they could be observed in a possibly more reliable way in dead bodies, but philosophers were soon contending that perceptions, feelings, intentions, and the like had an independent existence. Unfortunately, we cannot report any internal event, physical or metaphysical, accurately. The words we use we learned from people who did not know precisely what we were talking about, and we have no sensory nerves going to the parts of the brain in which the most important events presumably occur. Many cognitive psychologists recognize these limitations and dismiss the words we have been examining as the language of "common sense psychology." The mind that has made its comeback is therefore not the mind of Locke or Berkeley or Wundt or William James. We do not observe it; we infer it. We do not see ourselves processing information, for example. We see the materials that we process and the product, but not the producing. We now treat mental processes, such as intelligence, personality, or character traits, as things no one ever claims to see through introspection. Whether or not the cognitive revolution has restored mind as the proper subject matter of psychology, it has not restored introspection as the proper way of looking at it. The behaviorists' attack on introspection has been devastating.

Cognitive psychologists have therefore turned to brain science and computer science for confirmation of their theories. Brain science, they say, will eventually tell us what cognitive processes really are. They will answer, once and for all, the old questions about monism, dualism, and interactionism. By building machines that do what people do, computer science will demonstrate how the mind works.

What is wrong with all of this is not what philosophers, psychologists, brain scientists, and computer scientists have found or will find; it is the direction in which they are looking. No account of what is happening inside the human body, no matter how complete, will explain the origins of human behavior. What happens inside the body is not a beginning. By looking at how a clock is built, we can explain why it keeps good time, but not why keeping time is important, or how the clock came to be built that way. We must ask the same questions about a person. Why do people do what they do, and why do the bodies that do it have the structures they have? We can trace a small part of human behavior, and a much larger part of the behavior of other species, to natural selection and the evolution of the species, but the greater part of human behavior must be traced to contingencies of reinforcement, especially to the very complex social contingencies we call cultures. Only when we take those histories into account can we explain why people behave as they do.

That position is sometimes characterized as treating a person as a black box and ignoring the contents. Behavior analysts would study the invention and uses of clocks without asking how clocks are built. But nothing is being ignored. Behavior analysts leave what is inside the black box to those who have the instruments and methods needed to study it properly. There are two unavoidable gaps in any behavioral account: one between the stimulating action of the environment and the response of the organism, and one between consequences and the resulting change in behavior. Only brain science can fill those gaps. In doing so it completes the account; it does not give a different account of the same thing. Human behavior will eventually be explained (as it can only be explained) by the cooperative action of ethology, brain science, and behavior analysis.

The analysis of behavior need not wait until brain scientists have done their part. The behavioral facts will not be changed, and they suffice for both a science and a technology. Brain scientists may discover other kinds of variables affecting behavior, but they will turn to a behavioral analysis for the clearest account of the effects of these variables.

Conclusion

Verbal contingencies of reinforcement explain why we report what we feel or introspectively observe. The verbal culture that arranges such contingencies would not have evolved if it had not been useful. Bodily conditions are not the causes of behavior, but they are collateral effects of the causes. People's answers to questions about how they feel or what they are thinking often tell us something about what has happened to them or what they have done. We can understand them better and are more likely to anticipate what they will do. The words they use are part of a living language that can be used without embarrassment by cognitive psychologists and behavior analysts alike in their daily lives.

But these words cannot be used in their science! A few traditional terms may survive in the technical language of a science, but they are carefully defined and stripped by usage of their old connotations. Science requires a language. We seem to be giving up the effort to explain our behavior by reporting what we feel or introspectively observe in our bodies, but we have only begun to construct a science needed to analyze the complex interactions between the environment and the body and the behavior to which it gives rise.

References

Oxford English Dictionary: (1928). Oxford University Press.

Skeat, W.W. (1956). *An etymological dictionary of the English language*. Oxford: Clarendon Press.

Skinner, B.F. (1987, May 8). Outlining a science of feeling. *The Times Literary Supplement*, p. 490.

Williams, R. (1976). *Keywords: A vocabulary of culture and society*. New York: Oxford University Press

EUCLIDIAN PSYCHOLOGY:
A Review of "The Evolution and Function of Cognition" By Felix Goodson

Mike Knight & Christina Almstrom (in press). *Contemporary Psychology.*

In the preface to the previous article we used the phrase cognitive functionalism deliberately as a segue to this article, which is a review of Felix Goodson's book "The Evolution and Function of Cognition". You have no doubt heard of the, "the modern synthesis" that successfully integrates the theory of natural selection and genetics. In like manner Felix Goodson set himself the task of bringing psychology into this synthesis. This review explains how this remarkable feat was accomplished.

In the forward to *The Evolution and Function of Cognition*, Figueredo writes, "Prediction is risky, but I suspect that this volume might become to evolutionary psychology what Euclid was to geometry", (p. xv); which leads one to wonder what would prompt such a lofty comparison. What was Euclid's contribution to geometry and how was it accomplished?

Euclid was the architect of a way of thinking about the natural world. He lived in Alexandria on the shores of the Mediterranean Sea around 300 B.C. and his *Elements* has influenced mathematics ever since. Even beyond mathematics, no single work has had a more profound effect on science and scientific reasoning. What was most revolutionary about Euclid's *Elements* was the parsimonious logic of its method and its precision and rigor in eliminating ambiguity in order to facilitate mutual understanding. All of this Euclid achieved through his reliance on three guiding principles: Be explicit in defining terms to avoid ambiguity, use postulates to make concepts unequivocal thus avoiding unstated assumptions, and use rules of logic to deduce logical consequences from these postulates and previously proven theorems (Mlodinow, 2001).

Euclid's theorems were not original, but his systemization of existing knowledge was. In this regard Goodson is indeed his heir. This slim volume elegantly encapsules the historical continuity of contemporary ideation; interrelating the many facets of mainstream psychology using evolution as the binding force of amalgamation.

Inclusive Fitness

The organizing theme for a recent series of evolutionary psychology book reviews, Knight (1999, 2003a, 2003b) and more recently Knight & Almstrom (in press) has been psychology's pursuit of a *Weltanschauung,* an interdisciplinary worldview unifying the natural and social sciences; an "... ideation of reality that informs theory building" (Knight, 1999). In Knight & Almstrom (in press) we formulated the idea that this is evolutionary psychology's missing link, an explicit interdisciplinary articulation of the Darwinian worldview. Essential to this review is an examination of whether Goodson's Euclidian approach to theory construction achieves this potential for unification or simply muddies the waters.

Over the past decade evolutionary psychology has become evermore contentious behaving, "as if a Kuhnian revolution mandates an opponent and the dismantling of existing doctrine" (Knight & Almstrom, in press). At times even appearing elitist and discriminatory, prompting Andy Lock (2003) to comment,

> In the past decade or so, an evolutionary perspective has re-emerged in psychology as a programme that terms itself 'Evolutionary Psychology', associated with names such as Buss, Cosmides, Pinker, and Tooby. This is, I suggest, an unfortunate appropriation to a relatively narrow set of concerns and claims about the nature of the 'human mind' of what should be a generic term for the application of evolutionary thinking in psychology. One can be an evolutionary psychologist without being an Evolutionary Psychologist. (p. 104)

"Evolutionary Psychology", with its emphasis on domain-specific modularity, has storied as "unclean" any account, historical or contemporary, which is of a domain-general nature. Unfortunately this excludes a majority of psychological phenomenon; for example, the words learning and memory are rarely found in evolutionary psychology textbooks. In contrast Goodson, far from being oppositional, follows the lead of Darwin in emphasizing historical continuity and unabashedly embraces all of mainstream psychology, examining traditional topics like perception, psychophysics, classical and operant conditioning, observational learning, memory, and cognition, all from an evolutionary perspective.

In particular, learning and memory in the associationist tradition are integral to Goodson's description of progressive steps in evolution (progressive in a non-directional, hierarchical sense where higher or lower are merely a matter of perspective), a description which is not dissimilar to emergent complexity. Goodson quite effectively shows how domain-general functioning not only can emerge from domain-specific computational operations (the modularity hypothesis) but is necessitated by the demand characteristics of increased complexity. His functional depiction of learning and memory as mutually exclusive, interdependent, complementary processes is particularly effective and reminiscent of object oriented computer analysis and design where, "A complex system that works is invariably found to have evolved from a simple system that worked", (Booch, 1993 p. 13). What this shows is not only an elegance in reformulating our understanding of phenomena within the evolutionary milieu, but, to borrow a phrase, an inclusive fitness; in praise of diversity.

Diversity, whether genetic, behavioral, or ideational is the essential ingredient for adaptation. In their article, *Unified Psychology,* Sternberg and Grigorenko (2001) champion the position of unity through diversity, arguing that a unified psychology must, of necessity be a "...multiparadigmatic, multidisciplinary, and integrated study of psychological phenomena through converging operations" (p. 1069). They point to the "bad habits" of reliance on a single methodology, identification with subdisciplines rather than phenomena, and paradigmatic exclusivity as the proximate cause for disunity; with homogeny as a consequence.

It is at exactly this juncture that Goodson is most distinguishable. As with Euclid, his theoretical formulations are few and parsimonious, his deductive reasoning rigorous and precise, avoiding ambiguity and unstated assumptions, and as a consequence facilitating mutual understanding and inclusivity.

Goodson's stated purpose is to provide a comprehensive theory of how living organisms function as lawful energy systems reflecting the demand characteristics of their physical, biological, and social environments. Beginning with an understanding of how energy systems function dynamically, in accord with the ubiquitous expression of the inverse square law, Goodson deduces two fundamental postulates: The Postulate of Process, "All overt or covert activity serves the immediate function of impelling the organism toward equilibrium" (p. 46), and The Postulate of Inference, "Every attribute that has remained characteristic of a species for an enduring period contributes (or once contributed) to the survival of genetic material" (p. 51). There is also a fundamental corollary to the Postulate of Process which is integral to the theory: The Negative Feedback Corollary: "Within the limits imposed by structure and available expendable energy, the more an organism deviates from equilibrium, the greater its compensatory activity will be" (p. 48), which is derived from the inverse square law. Using just these postulates, every bit as parsimonious and precise as Euclid's theorems, Goodson follows where they lead through the progressive steps of evolution, from organisms restricted to responding within a single energy dimension to more complex environmental interactions involving inherited associations, learning, memory, language and most importantly observational learning. Goodson places particular emphasis on observational learning because it, "... involves a capacity to encode replicas of sensory input", and, "accounts for most of the learning that takes place in human beings", (p. 65). This is a theory of cognitive functioning and how it got to be that way,

> Combining evolutionary and cognitive perspectives provide a conceptual framework for integrating much seemingly disparate information. This, after all, is the function of theory: to render complexity into simplicity, to subsume the seemingly incompatible and disconnected into an integrative structure that will allow understanding and insight where previously there was a clutter of particulars (p. 33).

Along with Hillix, Marx, and others, Goodson has long been a student of the nature and function of theory in science (see Goodson & Morgan, 1976, for an excellent review of the criteria for evaluating the worth of a theory). In that sense this volume is the culmination of a life's endeavor.

Cognitive Functionalism

Many psychologists, chief among them Edward L. Thorndike and William James (Metwan, 2002), were students of Darwin's intoxicating worldview and as do all students of this "dangerous idea" (Dennett, 19xx) they quickly discovered the importance of questioning function; recognizing that what may appear to be a simplistic design, is upon closer examination, a parsimonious expression of complex order. Nature operates as a dynamic functioning system and failure to acknowledge this is to deny the significance of not only the individual organism but the structure coupled relationship among organisms which is of equal importance (Maturana, 1975). This is the essence of Darwin's theory and recognizes that all life evolves not only structurally, but functionally and systemically through time. It is also the essence of Goodson's exposition of how cognitive functioning came to be what it is.

Goodson's theory is functionalism with a difference. With its emphasis on observational learning and the necessity for any organism to refine the techniques for realigning the precarious imbalances that characterize vulnerable life, this theory of cognitive functioning stresses the fact that all living things are functional analogues of the natural forces of selection that have shaped them. In this worldview living organisms are understood as functioning organisms where cognitive life is a functional not a literal analogue of reality; "colors, sounds, and odors exist only in our heads, but they are functional translations of energy shifts in the external environment" (p. 79).

The human mind did not evolve to understand the world but to apprehend it, to represent sensory input well enough to survive from moment to moment with increasing selective pressure to adjust the misalignments of cognitive functioning. This is Goodson's worldview of "progressive" evolution. Interestingly, E. O. Wilson suggests that this is the ultimate goal of science, to diagnose and correct the misalignments between objective reality and it internal representation (Knight & Almstrom, in press; Wilson, 1998).

Evolutionary psychology textbooks and evolutionary psychologists have provided us with the "whys", the reasons for a unified psychology. Like Euclid, Goodson has shown us the "hows", quietly as Darwin did. Moreover, Goodson set himself the formidable task of bringing psychology into the evolutionary synthesis; and he does so gracefully, with an enviable richness of scholarship.

References

Booch, G. (1993). *Object-oriented analysis and design with applications.* Boston, MA: Addison-Wesley.

Dennett, D. (1995). *Darwin's dangerous idea: Evolution and the meaning of life.* New York: Simon & Schuster.

Euclid, (2002). *Euclid's elements.* Santa Fe, NM: Green Lion Press.

Figueredo, A. J. (2003). Forward to the evolution and function of cognition. In F. E. Goodson, *The evolution and function of cognition.* Mahwah, NJ: Erlbaum.

Goodson, F. E. & Morgan, G. A. (1976). Evaluation of theory. In M. H. Marx & F. E. Goodson (Eds), *Theories in contemporary psychology.* New York: Macmillan.

Knight, M. (1999). The Darwinian algorithm and scientific enquiry. [Review of the book *Handbook of evolutionary psychology: Ideas, issues, and applications].* *Contemporary Psychology, 44 (2),* 150-152.

Knight, M. (in press). Teaching evolutionary psychology. [Review of the book *Evolution and human behavior*]. *Contemporary Psychology.*

Knight, M. (in press). Of paradigms and paradiddles. [Review of the book *Human evolutionary psychology*]. *Contemporary Psychology.*

Knight, M. & Almstrom, C. M. (in press). The worldviews of evolutionary psychology. [Review of the book *Evolutionary psychology: The ultimate origins of human behavior*]. *Contemporary Psychology.*

Lock, A. (2003). Review of the evolution and function of cognition. *Human Nature Review, 3,* 104-107.

Maturana, H. R. (1975). The organization of the living, A theory of the living organization. *International Journal of Man-Machine Studies, 7,* 313-332.

Menand, L. (2002). *The metaphysical club: A story of ideas in America.* New York: Farrar Straus & Giroux;

Mlodinow, (2001). *Euclid's window.* New York: The Free Press.

Sternberg, R. J. & Grigorenko, E. L. (2001). Unified psychology. *American Psychologist, 56,* 1069-1079.

Wilson, E. O. (1998). *Consilence*: *The unity of knowledge.* New York: Alfred A. Knopf, Inc.